Teaching German in America

Prolegomena to a History

Edited by

David P. Benseler
Walter F. W. Lohnes
Valters Nollendorfs

Published for *Monatshefte*
The University of Wisconsin Press

The University of Wisconsin Press
114 North Murray Street
Madison, Wisconsin 53715

The University of Wisconsin Press, Ltd.
1 Gower Street
London WC1E 6HA, England

5 4 3 2 1

Printed in the United States of America

Library of Congress Cataloging-in-Publication Data

Teaching German in America: prolegomena to a history / edited by
  David P. Benseler, Walter F. W. Lohnes, Valters Nollendorfs.
    320 p.   cm.—(Monatshefte occasional volumes; no. 7)
    Papers from a conference sponsored by the Dept. of German and the
  Max Kade Institute for German-American Studies of the University of
  Wisconsin—Madison, held at the University Apr. 1983.
    Includes index.
    ISBN 0-299-97022-1   ISBN 0-299-970923-X (pbk.)
    1. German philology—Study and teaching—United States–
-Congresses. 2. Germanists—United States—Biography—Congresses.
I. Benseler, David P. II. Lohnes, Walter F. W. III. Nollendorfs,
Valters. IV. University of Wisconsin—Madison. Dept. of German.
V. Max Kade Institute for German–American Studies (University of
Wisconsin—Madison)   VI. Series.
PF3068.U6T4   1988   88-2957
438'.007'073—dc19   CIP

Contents

Acknowledgments

The editors gratefully thank the following for their assistance and support:

The Anonymous Fund of the University of Wisconsin–Madison for its financial support of the conference "Teaching German in America: The Historical Perspective," 21–23 April 1983.

The Department of German and the Max Kade Institute for German-American Studies of the University of Wisconsin–Madison for their sponsorship of the 1983 conference and for subsidizing the publication of this volume.

The Modern Language Association and the University of Pennsylvania Press for permission to reprint previously published material.

Suzanne S. Moore for help with the proofs.

Introduction

During the past decade, numerous anniversaries have stimulated interest in the history of the United States. The American Bicentennial commemorated the founding and development of the country; the 300th anniversary of the first German settlement in North America focused on the contributions of Germans in the United States; and the centennial of the Modern Language Association called attention to the history of teaching and research in modern languages and literatures. The present volume is, in many ways, an outgrowth of this interest in our past. We hope that the contributions presented here will stimulate further research into the history of the profession and lead to additional publications along similar lines. Such activities should help us arrive at an understanding of what is specifically American in our discipline, as compared to German *Germanistik,* which has often been accused of forcing its scholarly and ideological imprint upon German studies in America.[1] The historical self-analysis begun in this volume shows trends and countertrends since the late nineteenth century. We hope it puts some focus on the evolution of the teaching of German in America.

We should note here that the university reform movement in the sixties and seventies in the Federal Republic of Germany produced a similar interest in historical self-evaluation. Jürgen Kolbe's two volumes, *Ansichten einer künftigen Germanistik* and *Neue Ansichten einer künftigen Germanistik,* appeared at the height of the movement and were meant more as a radical criticism of the old *Germanistik* than as an historical assessment.[2] A recent major project headed by Wilhelm Voßkamp at the University of Bielefeld is attempting to provide such an assessment on a broad interdisciplinary basis.

Our volume derives directly from a conference held at the University of Wisconsin–Madison in April of 1983, where many of the present articles were read and discussed. Most of them have been refined and reshaped since then, and several contributions have been added. The idea to produce this volume was conceived during the many discussions among a group of colleagues that led to the publication of the first volume in the *Monatshefte* series (see Note 1). The topic was first publicly discussed at the 1982 MLA Convention in Los Angeles. The panel, consisting of Victor Lange (Princeton), Walter F. W. Lohnes (Stanford), Valters Nollendorfs (Wisconsin–Madison), Henry J. Schmidt (Ohio State), and Egon Schwarz (Washington

University, St. Louis), dealt with the rationale and the need for the project, with methodological and practical approaches, and with the problem of locating sources. Also, considerable discussion focused on the urgent need to produce oral histories.[3] Another panel, consisting of David Benseler (Ohio State), Ruth Bottigheimer (Princeton), Valters Nollendorfs, and Helga Slessarev (Cincinnati), dealt at the 1983 MLA Convention in New York City with the topic of oral history and the importance of obtaining source materials.

The articles in the present volume cover a wide range of topics, from the general to the very specific. Essays are essentially arranged in a loose chronological order, from some of the earliest evidence of the teaching of German in the United States to the mid-twentieth century. The period since World War II was left largely untouched but should definitely be the topic of a future undertaking.

We include histories of the teaching of German at two specific institutions, West Point and Princeton; several contributions deal with the teaching of German language in the second half of the nineteenth century, a period when the study of German was preeminent and when much German teaching took place in monolingual German schools. A few articles discuss the crucial period after the United States entered World War I— when German teaching all but vanished in the American educational establishment. The Nazi period, another critical time in the development of the profession, is the topic of two authors. The volume ends with an interview with Hermann Weigand, conducted in 1980 by Henry J. Schmidt, a splendid example of the kind of interview envisaged for an eventual oral history project. Weigand's death as this book was being edited indicates again the urgency of such a project.

We also include two "historical" documents. Edwin H. Zeydel's "The Teaching of German in the United States from Colonial Times to the Present" first appeared in the massive *Reports of Surveys and Studies in the Teaching of Modern Foreign Languages,* commissioned by the MLA in 1959–61, and was reprinted in *The German Quarterly* (37 [1964]: 315–92). It is printed here in abbreviated form, ending with the World War I period. Alexander R. Hohlfeld's 1918 "Address to the Graduating Class of the National Teachers Seminary at Milwaukee" was given at a time when the very survival of German in the United States was at stake. It has never been published, and we consider it significant enough to be included here.

Even a cursory look at the table of contents reveals many lacunae; the essays included here are indeed merely prolegomena to a history. Much research needs to be done to shed light on our past. The following remarks suggest some aspects of what could complete the investigation of our history.

The task of documentation has become much easier with the advent of the computer, but it will take considerable concentrated effort on the part of many colleagues to assemble the material now located in numerous institutions and private holdings across the land.

It should now be possible to produce and keep up-to-date complete bibliographical files on the history of the teaching of German in America. What is urgently needed is a complete textbook bibliography, which should include the earliest known German texts published in America and to which new titles should be added as they appear. The University of Wisconsin–Madison has assembled an extensive collection of textbooks, numbering some 1000 volumes. The collection is named after the late Indiana University professor, Frances H. Ellis, whose holdings provided its basis. Preparation of a catalog and provision of access have been delayed until a planned addition to the library at the University of Wisconsin is completed. This repository should become as complete as possible and could serve as a major research tool in the history of methodology. Ideally, there should be two additional such collections, one in the East, and one in the West.

It should now also be possible to produce a computerized listing of the holdings of relevant archives, which would show the status of local cataloguing. Such materials are found not only in departmental archives, but also in those of college and university administrations, in budget records, and so forth. The problem with archival material, invariably, is that too much is simply thrown out. We are fascinated when we find a department head's correspondence from the early part of this century, but we tend to tell departmental secretaries to discard everything that is more than five years old. Thus, the records of many distinguished members of the profession have vanished, and in some cases it is almost impossible to find the barest biographical data. Departments should ensure that at least their most important papers are turned over to archives to be catalogued. Regrettably, many colleagues move their papers to their homes upon retirement; unless these papers are presented to archives or other central repositories, they will eventually be lost.

We urge the establishment of several documentation centers, ideally in the same locations as the textbook collections (East, Midwest, West), to serve as repositories of information and materials gathered throughout the country. These centers would also become the collecting points for documents related to the proposed oral history project. This project should have top priority and be initiated as soon as possible. A number of emeriti who are still living began their careers in the early decades of this century. Their recollections will be invaluable, not only concerning their own experiences, but also because of what they will be able to tell us about members of the previous generation, under whom they worked and who themselves may have started to teach as early as 1880. A major oral history project is both time-consuming and costly, especially if the interviews are to be transcribed. Furthermore, techniques for oral history interviews that will serve our particular needs must be developed, and a number of volunteers will be required to conduct these interviews. Interviewees should be not only the movers and shakers of the profession in colleges and universities, but those in less visible spots as well, including high school teachers, who undoubtedly can contribute different and fascinating views of local and regional scenes, and who can also comment on national developments from their own point of view. Interviewees should come not only from the ranks of the retired; there should also be interviews with members now in their forties and fifties who have been active in the profession during the past two or three decades.

We have no systematic and reliable data for many aspects of the profession. These data, to be collected by the documentation centers, can be gathered only with the cooperation of German departments and of colleagues willing to dig through archives. It would be invaluable, for example, to have as complete a bio-bibliographical listing as possible of professors of German from the earliest days of the profession to the present. Such a listing would show the ratio of native born Americans to German immigrants and allow us to determine how large a percentage of Germanists in the nineteenth and early twentieth centuries studied abroad and received their degrees from German universities. Such a listing would also document the waves of German immigrants, those who came as emigrés in the 1930s, those who came after World War II, especially in the 1950s, and those who arrived just recently, in many cases to avoid the overcrowded German universities. It could be supplemented by lists of department heads, officers of professional organizations, and editors of learned journals in the discipline. A comprehensive listing of all German courses offered in American institutions of higher education as gleaned from catalogues and course bulletins is also an essential desideratum. All of this information together would enable us to gain clear insights into the evolution of elements of intellectual history and teaching practices that have dominated in our profession.

It would be more difficult to obtain a roster of Central Europeanists in related disciplines, such as history and political science, but such a listing would indicate the extent of research and teaching in the broader area of German Studies as we now conceive it. It would at the same time provide the statistical data for a history of the German Studies movement, which began in the early 1970s, but whose roots undoubtedly go back much further.

The development of a comprehensive data base could yield other results as well, such as the number, rank, and status of women and other minority members at all levels of the profession at any given time, and of Germanists who have served in university and college administrations, who thus may have had a strong influence on the development of German and German Studies in their own institutions and beyond.

In addition to the gathering of statistical data, an urgent need exists for the writing of detailed histories of various aspects of the profession. Biographies and autobiographies could shed much light on developments in the profession which otherwise simply would not be recorded. Many innovations and many controversies have rather obscure origins not documented in writing which might be reconstructed by those who participated in the decision making.

Histories of individual German departments can further provide detailed accounts of the ups and downs of the study of German during the past century, including the almost total collapse after 1917 and the slow resurgence of German which culminated in the late fifties in the National Defense Education Act (NDEA). Histories of graduate departments would be particularly valuable because they have always played an important part in shaping the profession at large.

The role and impact of study overseas needs to be investigated. Individual students have, of course, always gone to the German-speaking countries to study, but we know relatively little about organized overseas study programs, especially during the period between the two World Wars. We have no reliable statistics on the number of American high schools, colleges, and universities which at one time or another had their own programs, sent students to other institutions' programs, or affiliated with European institutions or programs. We also do not know how many graduate departments have or have had regular exchange arrangements with universities in German-speaking countries.

Some major developments of the last few decades are slowly slipping into the past and should be described and evaluated while those who played an active role are still around. One major example might be the National Defense Education Act, which provided a cornucopia of funds for foreign language teaching and research. Large numbers of NDEA graduate fellowships were awarded, but we do not know what percentage of those students who received them remained in the profession. Also in connection with the NDEA, the history of summer institutes for secondary school teachers, held from 1959 to 1969, should be written. Thousands of teachers participated in these institutes at government expense, but to our knowledge no thorough and reliable follow-up study shows the qualitative or quantitative impact these institutes had on the teaching of German in American secondary schools.

Critical histories and assessments of our professional organizations and journals ought also to be written. These, too, would depend on access to archival materials, which in some cases, and for certain periods of time, simply may no longer exist, since, we suspect, the records of organizations and journals have frequently tended to stay with a president or editor at the end of his or her term, especially in cases where there were no national offices or permanent editorial headquarters.

Finally, we want to suggest the writing of a number of introspective critical investigations dealing with the profession as a whole and with its relationships to certain other bodies. Topics for such histories might include: (1) a critical study of curricular development on all levels, including the teaching of language in secondary schools and colleges, undergraduate major programs, and graduate curricula; (2) critical studies of textbooks as reflections of prevalent language curricula and teaching methods at any given time, and, in the case of literature and culture readers, their role in shaping attitudes and ideological biases; (3) the relationship or, in many cases, the absence of a relationship between introductory language courses and upper division literature courses (to be done both diachronically and synchronically); (4) the impact of extramural funding, especially federal funding, of which the most significant example is the NDEA; (5) the relationship of German studies to other foreign language studies, showing frequent divergence during the period before World War II and, in recent years, an increasing interdependence because of shrinking enrollments and cutbacks of funds; (6) the relationship of German to other related disciplines, such as history, political science, and more recently, international relations, which has greatly contributed to the current concept of German Studies in a nontraditional and very broad sense.

This outline covers a large agenda, but we have reason to believe that this agenda will be turned into action, because large numbers of our colleagues are aware of its history and of the value of such an undertaking. We are confident that in the not too distant future we will be able to look into our past with a much sharper focus and with greater understanding than has previously been possible.

Ohio State University   DAVID P. BENSELER
Stanford University   WALTER F. W. LOHNES
University of Wisconsin–Madison   VALTERS NOLLENDORFS

Notes

1 See, for example, Jeffrey Sammons, "Some Considerations of our Invisibility," *German Studies in the United States: Assessment and Outlook,* ed. Walter F. W. Lohnes and Valters Nollendorfs, *Monatshefte* Occasional Volume 1 (Madison: University of Wisconsin Press, 1976) 17–23.
2 Jürgen Kolbe, ed., *Ansichten einer künftigen Germanistik* (München: Hanser, 1969) and *Neue Ansichten einer künftigen Germanistik* (München: Hanser, 1973).
3 *Monatshefte* 75 (1983): 242–70.

Teaching German in America

The History of German Studies in America: Ends and Means

VICTOR LANGE
Princeton University

It is in troubled times like ours, at moments of doubt in the efficacy of our social and intellectual assumptions, under the pressure of changes that challenge and unsettle our self-confidence, that we turn to the consolations of history. In better times we, as Americans, may have been inclined to doubt the usefulness of shaping our present and future upon the models of the past; we have always tended to think of history as a picturesque spectacle to be cultivated in periodic displays of old buildings or colorful costumes, nostalgically evoking times safely enshrined in images of myth or proud sentiment; or we have taken history as something to be put behind us as we move into a future of promise and novelty.

Yet, retrospection is an important dimension of our vision, and retrospection is merely the complement of introspection. We are here tonight and in subsequent days to test some aspects of the general proposition which I have just touched upon. Having for more than a century and a half operated as American transmitters of a foreign language and a foreign culture, we are invited to ask ourselves if we have learned from the history of our profession, if at any given time the degree and kind of introspection has been adequate, and whether we should not now take a fresh and critical look at our goals and the assumptions of our practices.

What can the history of the field of study teach us, that has moved, at times irrationally, from near the center of American cultural convictions to a place on the periphery of our educational enterprise; it is an area of interest that was defined at one time by the conviction that the German tradition and its living energy offered exemplary material for an understanding of our own social potential, but that today appears to many teachers of German in schools and colleges no longer sustained by vigorous interest or strong faith.

What is the justification, this should be the first question to be raised, for an historical, retrospective view of German studies in the American educational system? Let me confine myself to this specific academic perspective. It will soon become clear that the question, however much we may pretend to confine it to a pragmatic survey of the teaching of the

3

German language, is embedded in a whole tangle of far-reaching premises that have to do with the image which German life offers at a given time, the view which we, as Americans, appear to hold of the Germans, and, ultimately, the image we have of our own social aspirations and convictions within which it may be fascinating or even productive to take seriously, to interpret, and to urge upon our students and through them, upon society, the usefulness of acquiring and of transmitting an awareness of another culture, of a society as different from ours as the German.

If we take the pursuit of "German studies" in America as our aim it may, first of all, be desirable to create an awareness of the German contribution to American life, of the German ingredient in the fabric of American society. This has, indeed, for long been a rich field of inquiry, preeminently cultivated by American and German historians, some motivated by pride in the German heritage, some by the conviction that a pluralistic society requires an accounting of its parts. The history of American-German relations is the history of the influence of German immigrants between 1683 and today, the shaping of facets of American life during important periods of our self-definition by religious, philosophical, academic, artistic, and, important beyond measure, economic energies and practices, by German printers, journalists, merchants, brewers, actors, painters, musicians—the list is too long to be completed.

To record these contributions and the circumstances that created them is a noble and rewarding academic task. It may well be useful from time to time to take a fresh look at the perspectives from which that history of German-American relations is being written. For history, even so well-defined a history as that of the German element in America, is not an immutable given, but a topic that comes alive as successive points of view are brought to bear upon it. We must have the greatest respect for men like A. B. Faust, and shall for long be indebted to scholars like Henry Pochmann and Harold Jantz: their work should be recognized as indispensable, and the intellectual convictions prompting their historical studies will be a model for future scholars.

The Institute for German-American Studies, which has been established here at Wisconsin will contribute to this historical canon in as critical a spirit as possible, free of positivistic or ideological bias, transcending local pride, the preoccupation with factual minutiae, with vague notions of elusive influences.

German departments have in only a few rare instances included this German-American give-and-take as a central area of their work. They have, rather, concentrated on the teaching of the German language as a means of approach—sometimes thought to be the most rewarding form of access—to German social and intellectual life, with an emphasis, not surprisingly, upon the superior instrumentality of literature. All facets of this pattern of conventional American German studies require definition and a careful and detailed inquiry into their premises and the convictions that have sustained and justified their methods, their role, and their goals.

I have touched upon the fact that the history of German studies in America has had its fluctuations—its shifts in scope or the manner of practicing the teaching of German, its prevailing ambition, its moments of high pride and near-fatal depressions. But the teaching of German has, undeniably, been a continuous and respected ingredient in the American educational system. Its role has been a remarkably active one since the subject matter was first admitted, in slowly conceded competition with classical languages, early in the nineteenth century, at Harvard and Virginia, Columbia, Yale, Brown, and, much later but with new conviction, at Johns Hopkins. It has, throughout, been a language-teaching enterprise, and must therefore be studied and assessed in constant awareness of comparable studies in American colleges, with French, Russian, Chinese—not, that is to say, primarily in its relationship to native and foreign language studies in Germany, in an entirely different institutional and social context.

To recognize the particular character of American studies in German is, it seems to me, the first requirement of a descriptive history of German studies in America and indeed, of any evaluation of the achievements and failures of those studies. I will not at this point enter into a discussion of the history of the shifting methods of language teaching. This is certainly a telling facet of our enquiry, especially since this is not merely a matter of technical procedures. Methods reflect the convictions of their practitioners; they imply far-reaching questions as to the preparation of German teachers, their equipment, ranging from a purely philosophical, historical, even political training (such as Follen's) to the employment of more or less cultivated but not specifically trained German men and women, or the educated but unprepared and in essential pedagogical respects uninformed refugees from Hitler.

If we assume that German departments exist almost exclusively by the grace of the numbers of language learners, this topic, the history of the nature and the uses of language teaching, seems to me of the utmost importance.

Part of that inquiry would concern itself with the effect of German "philological" assumptions in the teaching of the German language. The philological ingredient has, well into our century, been a key element in German higher education. The learning of classical languages was an instrument of character building, and the means of access to the canon of classical and elevating literature. We (and the Germans) have during the past half-century seen the shift from "philological" convictions to modern linguistics, from an historical view of language and language teaching to a presumption that language is a pragmatic vehicle for the communication of information.

This is a change of considerable methodological consequence for us as teachers: for language learning and language teaching remain the basis of our work; it provides the chief motivation as well for those in schools and colleges who elect to make use of our services. We are only too familiar with the loss of active student interest in German once the first one or two years of voluntary or enforced language learning are past. What the material that sustains the technical instruction has been, may be or should be, yes, must be an important topic of our historical survey. What textbooks, what materials are used?—Are they literary, historical or topically social?—Are they, if literary, anthologized or "easy" standard masterpieces? Do they betray a bias, however faint, of social or even patriotic sentimentality? A descriptive history of our textbooks is as yet lacking and needs to be compiled.

We shall certainly find ourselves compelled to ask if these materials are determined by what I would summarily characterize as American presuppositions. Are they sensibly aimed at a comparative view, and do they offer subject matter for reflection rather than titillation? Or do these texts abound in adulatory, picturesque selections of tourist views of Neuschwanstein, the Lüneburger Heide, Rothenburg dream shots and bland, homogenized (that is, "easy") bits of literature, whether Schiller, Heine, Storm, Böll, or Kafka?

A history of language teaching in America, its methods and materials, will compel us to define our assets and defects, our motives and prejudices, our goals and the strength or weakness of our role among the teachers of other languages.

Let me move from language teaching, this by no means merely preliminary but central ingredient in a history of German studies, to the far more complex aspect of our work as interpreters of German literature in its most comprehensive sense.

That literature should be the most rewarding vehicle of German studies has, from the beginning, been a nearly axiomatic assumption. Where, after all, if not in literary achievements is the power and the glory of a language more palpably realized? Poets, novelists, philosophers, theologians are, it is said, the master craftsmen of language, more telling, more persuasive by their "style" than social scientists, political pamphleteers, theoreticians of architecture or music.

If this centrality of literature is granted, if in its documents the continuity of a vital tradition of German self-consciousness seems to become graspable, our history of German studies will find its most challenging and perhaps most controversial topic in the assessment of the assumptions upon which the presentation and interpretation of German literature within an American educational system, and for the benefit of American students, has in the past depended and relied.

The assumption that literature, and literature of a high and demanding sort, should be the target of German studies has produced that firm network of convictions to which any historical appraisal of the profession must turn its critical attention. Let me grant, for a moment, that literature is ultimately the most rewarding efflorescence of a language, and that we should not, perhaps, be unduly troubled by the proposition of anthropologists that literature may well play a relatively distinct role in various societies, that it may well "function" differently in America and Germany. For our immediate purpose of historical enquiry we can assume, until quite recently, the centrality of literature in German studies, an assumption that yet raises a number of questions.

Literature, literary texts of whatever nature, form a body of intellectual achievement, a body of information and reflection which we as teachers must approach and weigh selectively. Is there a pattern of choice, of emphasis, of assent recognizable in the selection, throughout our history, of conspicuous German literary texts? Is there perhaps a canon or type, consciously or subconsciously accepted, of titles which has remained fairly constant from Follen to Francke, Fife, Hohlfeld, Morgan, and Feise to our own day? The answer is that, indeed, throughout the history of our subject, three sorts of German literature seem to have been given preference by teachers and students: certain classics, from Lessing to Hebbel, certain specimens of current German literature, whether realistic, naturalistic, expressionist, Neue Sachlichkeit, post-World War II, or writing in the GDR and, thirdly, specifically "easy" texts, such as *Immensee, Emil,* or even a Kafka parable.

Let us enquire which texts in each of these three categories have been chosen at various times, which texts have been persistently present, and which have proved ephemeral, but, for that reason, no less indicative. Indeed, the history of our reading material should be the enveloping concern of our survey. It will be difficult to establish the reasons for their adoption, chiefly because that choice almost invariably has to do with the troublesome dependence of our criteria upon those prevailing in German schools and universities or literary and scholarly journals. But before I discuss this pivotal issue, let me stay with the adopted texts.

How have these texts (always, and as a matter of deep conviction, in the German original and never in translation!) been read, discussed, interpreted and evaluated? An account of successive approaches (not in loose generalities but in concrete detail, such as Richard Spuler's study of the American reception of German classicism between 1870 and 1905)[1] is bound to be one of the most rewarding chapters in our retrospective survey. If properly undertaken, critically but without condescension, it should lay bare the entire neurological system of our profession, its mode of operation as well as the range and limits of its effectiveness within the American education system.

The first pervasive principle of judgment and organization which we can trace back to the early nineteenth century is the broadly historical approach, an historical approach in general terms, valuable and perhaps indispensable. But it is itself an approach that is historically delimited and that, as a method of interpretation is neither sacrosanct nor without deficiencies. There is no reason why we should not be conscious of the difference between diachronic and synchronic historical perspectives. We cannot, at any rate, fail to recognize that the historical mode has been determined and advanced by German nineteenth-century thought and may well prove to be fundamentally in conflict with a certain American scepticism towards history as the compelling premise of judgment or understanding.

In saying this—more bluntly perhaps than sensible discourse would concede—I touch upon the long-standing, stubborn and seemingly self-evident reliance, from the earliest teaching of German to this day, upon German categories of description, understanding and interpretation. Upon the recognition and evaluation of this interlocking relationship between American German studies and their presumed German counterpart, German *Germanistik,* will hinge much of the critical thrust of our history.

Is this, our dependence upon *Germanistik* (in the German sense) so obvious that it need only be observed and stated in its successive forms? Are we, as *teachers* of German in American colleges, naturally a branch, however different in its bark, of *Germanistik?* Has the identity, the affinity, or the difference ever been felt or clearly stated? It requires little persuasion to agree that the role of German studies in America, its premises, practices and purposes, is fundamentally different from that of *Germanistik* in Germany.

In its broadest definition, the teaching of German literature in Germany, in schools and universities, is a vast and diffuse educational undertaking, only incidentally related to individual research in German language, literature, and folklore. To compare the two within a single pedagogical context is impossible and perhaps irrelevant. While the history of the German discipline as an educational instrument shows, until recently, a close dependence upon scholarship in the universities, the history of German studies in America will, I suspect, suggest that the *teaching* of German and of German literature is, broadly speaking, carried out with little dependence on American scholarship in German literature. This, I hasten to add, is not true in the area of linguistics, where the effect of academic studies upon the teaching of foreign languages has in the past forty years been profound.

We must recognize an area of scholarship, whether editorial or critical, in which no national distinctions can or should be made. Kurrelmayer's *Wieland* edition, Bruford's (to take an eminent Englishman) work on the social features of the Goethe-period, Calvin Thomas's *Faust* edition, James Lyon's work on *Brecht in America*—these are contributions to the comprehensive investigation of German literary history in which national sensibilities, even ideological perspectives, play a relatively small part. That sort of *Germanistik* in America must be judged by the quality of its contribution to an overriding enterprise of scholarship and in that sense, American scholarship in German literature must not be inferior to German *Germanistik*. But—and this we must focus upon—should the American study and *teaching* of German literature (an eminently conviction-bound enterprise!) see itself as largely in step with German *Germanistik?* An historical survey will reveal that that dependence has amounted to an axiom if not to a quasi-religious article of faith; it will show a deep-seated and persistent admiration on the part of American teachers and learners of German, of a superiority not only in German ways and beliefs in general, but in the critical tenets of native German *Germanistik* in particular.

Our survey must address itself urgently to the difference between the function of *Germanistik* in the German academic context, and that of German studies in an American pedagogical framework. It is true that much salutary attention has been paid recently to the obtuseness of American German teachers, who fail to respond to the radical modifications of the role and self-definition of *Germanistik* in Germany: this is entirely appropriate and useful, but it is merely the obverse of the problem of dependence with which I am here concerned.

To what extent this present attention to what some believe to be a fresh and superior kind of critical attitude in the German establishment is merely a differently colored variant of the admiration with which in former generations American German teachers looked up to the nationalistic ethos and pathos of nineteenth-century German philology, is a matter for careful historical enquiry. If American scholars of German, not necessarily trained in Germany, presented German literature in the spirit or methodology of Scherer or Roethe, of Dilthey, Korff, Petersen, Strich, or Adorno, they cannot have faced the question of the suitability or relevance of these approaches to the receptivity of American students. We need not be surprised or scandalized that these critical procedures, at a given time eagerly embraced by American teachers and scholars, may seem ludicrous or unacceptable in our present detached perspective. Those approaches were offered to American students who were thought to be exceptionally lucky to be confronted by materials and methods that were startling in their strangeness but indifferent to the students' basic equipment. If that native equipment was meant to be enlarged or modified by the radiant offerings of German literature and historical criticism, the result, we must admit, was more often blind romantic enthusiasm than an enhanced perception.

Unless I am mistaken, this close relationship between American scholarship in German and German *Germanistik* is as obvious in the earlier history of our field as it is in its most recent. What has, in the last twenty years, been attempted and achieved by the "critical" stance of the Wisconsin department is, I would think, in principle no less an effort at mobilizing German academic convictions for the enlivening of American German studies. I am aware of the differences in the underlying motivation between previous patriotic or metaphysical impulses and the entirely plausible critical intentions of the present, but the American dependence upon German scholarly models and theories seems to have remained constant.

American scholarship in German seems largely directed, not at the American student, but at an audience of German *Germanistik*. This, as a survey of American and German learned journals will show, has been true throughout the history of American German studies. An obvious confirmation is the series of American histories of German literature (Bayard Taylor, George Madison Priest, Werner Friedrich) which, you may be willing to agree, offer more often than not, merely American versions of German models, foreshortened, summarizing and frequently dependent in perspective and evaluation upon standard German histories. Kuno Francke's celebrated *Social Forces in German Literature* (1896) has had its deserved and uncommon effect upon the American teaching of German literature; yet, it is not a work written with unmistakable American intellectual presuppositions, but on the contrary, with the intention of celebrating the spiritual and artistic foundations of a recently united Germany.

Is this dependence inherent in our subject matter? We are, admittedly, reporters and interpreters of German life and institutions—but from the history of German studies in America must we not increasingly derive the conclusion that the manner of our interpreting Germany and German literature will be the more effective if it draws upon American experiences and sensibilities? When we look, in analogy, at German studies of English literature or French studies in American letters, their grounding in the German or French literary experience is unmistakable. It would be well for our historical survey to look into this complex matter: it is the vital premise of the resonance of our work and should be explicated and discussed in all its consequences.

Not the least reason for the dependence I have characterized is, as we must recognize throughout the history of German studies in America, the overwhelming share in the teaching of German, whether language or literature and on whatever level, of German natives whose instinctive linguistic equipment has often concealed their ignorance of, or indifference to, or even their not always silent condescension towards, the convictions and mores of American society, its history, its literary masterpieces and traditions. Have they had more than a cursory training in meeting the legitimate expectations of American students? As a native-born German who has taught German literature in America for half a century, I may be forgiven for touching upon this issue.

Here, then, is another profoundly influential factor in the history of American studies of German life, perhaps another reason why German departments have sometimes found themselves in relative isolation: the German native provenance of their members appears to have been valued more highly than their capacity to relate German cultural materials not as superior, slightly arcane abstractions but as comparable social achievements to be understood and judged by Americans.

Let me turn to another, less controversial topic: the historian of our discipline should consider the readiness (or the capacity) of professors of German to look seriously at what their neighboring English or French departments offer as literary criticism. As long as, in the nineteenth century, societies competed with one another for the recognition of their superiority, the spirit of antagonism and competition may well have provided an appealing strategy. Certainly today and in the recent past any kind of pedagogical offering that proceeds from an assumption of the superiority of German or French or Spanish culture is arrogant and without any hope of a lasting and genuine effect upon the students. What, the historian of German studies must ask, was at any time, the critical scaffolding, cultural or aesthetic, of work in the English or French departments, and to what extent did German departments take cognizance of it?

I leave it to you—and to our historians—to reflect on the traditionally more instinctive appeal of French as against German culture and literature, for American students, or, making another point, to look into the vastly important matter of support which modern language studies have received from native German cultural agencies—as a not illegitimate extension of diplomacy—into the effect of visiting professors (at one time "Kaiser-Wilhelm-Professoren"!) of the Goethe Institute or Humboldt Foundation, of the German suppliers of cultural information, of books, posters, and travel brochures.

All this will turn out to have been of considerable impact upon a history of the teaching of German in America: it reinforces the conviction, held for 150 years, that the German department dispenses German language competence and a view of German literature in its original language. There is significance of historical moment in the fact that a shift in student interests has persuaded many departments to widen the fixed focus of their offerings from "literature" to the broader (and as yet methodologically uncertain) "German Studies," with an increasing tolerance for reading in translation.

There is, in the history of the American appreciation of German culture, an important element, the offering of translations by individuals not always involved in teaching—translations of German masterpieces in poetry and prose, fiction or theater. To name a few—C. T. Brooks, H. Longfellow, G. Bancroft, F. H. Hedge, Margaret Fuller, C. Hodges, and, more recently, James Huneker, H. L. Mencken or Ludwig Lewisohn—is merely to point to the power and radiance drawn, even in translation, from German literature. That tradition must be described as to its impulses, its motives, its linguistic character, its promoters, and its intended audience. Since we are primarily concerned with the *history* of our profession, I shall not elaborate on my own strong conviction that we must in one context or another increase our willingness to make use of translations in our teaching, whatever its scope. Fortunately, German departments have— after long and stubborn resistance—included courses dealing in translation with masterpieces of German literature. We must be grateful for the solicitude with which in the past English departments introduced translations of *Faust,* Kafka, or Mann to eager students. Yet, should that interest not self-evidently be met by the teachers and interpreters of German literature?

The historian may well ask if the traditional service function of German studies with its exclusive offerings of German, German language, German texts, German lectures—can you imagine a *German* Slavist lecturing to his German students in Russian, A. W. Schlegel in Spanish, Rückert in Arabic or even my own teacher Levin Schücking in English?— has not isolated and alienated our subject, our departments, our teachers? Indeed, more than is normal in pedagogical traffic, it has been personalities rather than the substance of our field that have provided the magnetism of German departments. Has this isolation—or merely peripheral effectiveness—historically been a constant feature? Has that certain shy and distant admiration for us as purveyors of a difficult, somewhat mysterious German world brought us closer to our colleagues in other fields? Or has it relegated us to areas in a remote corner of the campus?

Whatever guidance for present or future a well-documented and well-conceived history of our subject may provide, it must, by inference, and more explicitly than in the past, remind us that we are apt to fumble and remain dependent upon German models if we do not come to grips with the questions of purpose, of motivation, of interdependence. As long as German studies contributed, as they did in the nineteenth century, to a universal, ultimately homogeneous, only historically differentiated conception of culture and of literature, the function of a national literature was relatively easy to define in terms of pride or aspiration, of glory, or of special fascination.

As this all-inclusive view has given way to a spectrum of interrelated, not nationally justified and competing but comparative and interdependent literatures, we can use national literatures only as examples and illustrations of common, transnational literary and cultural efforts. In our enthusiasm for the singular German achievement, we have tended to relate the texts we have offered to the German terrain rather than to issues and problems, whether social or aesthetic, that properly engage the interest of our American students for which, indeed, the German documents should and will supply significant material.

This is, of course, not to deny strong and characteristic indigenous impulses in a given literature and in each of our societies; and insofar as we wish to deal with German studies by offering our students a distinctive set of convictions, we would do well to learn from the history of our profession that to offer these differences in terms of national characteristics, of notions of what the Germans "are like" rather than how they cope with fundamental common social concerns, leads to myth-making, to sentimental effusion, to a blurring of critical faculties.

I have argued for a history of the changing function of German studies within American educational presuppositions, of the targets which German studies in America have customarily set for themselves, of the relationship between the learning of language and the appreciation of literature, and ultimately, of the interpretation of one culture to another. I have touched upon the tools, the texts, the materials, and the forms of persuasion, the rhetoric, which has, under shifting political conditions, attempted to justify our enterprise.

I have not concealed the weaknesses that have often been the obverse of our strength, the risk of isolation and irrelevance of German studies within the academic community; I have suggested that the seemingly self-evident magisterial or preceptorial role of German *Germanistik* has (in the context of American presuppositions) possibly been harmful rather than productive. And I have suggested that a history of our discipline must recognize the close relationship in playing our role and widening our resonance, between ends and means.

The means towards our effectiveness have changed under the pressures of political events as well as the often parochial educational notions held by our society. To define these pressures and their impact and to enquire into the motives that have, from one generation to another, shaped the spirit and the rhetoric of German studies in this country, will be the comprehensive task of a projected history.

Self-scrutiny has not often been a pressing concern of the American teachers of German. May the proposed history articulate for the present and the future a well-defined view of what German studies can and should contribute not only towards a knowledge of another society but towards an American critical self-awareness.

Notes

This paper, originally delivered as the introductory address at the conference on Teaching German in America: The Historical Perspective (University of Wisconsin–Madison, 21 April 1983), was previously published in *Monatshefte* 75 (1983): 245–56.

1 Richard Spuler, *"Germanistik" in America: The Reception of German Classicism, 1870–1905* (Stuttgart: Heinz, 1982).

The Teaching of German in the United States from Colonial Times through World War I

EDWIN H. ZEYDEL
University of Cincinnati

Introduction

This attempt to write a fairly comprehensive historical account of the teaching of German in the United States from early Colonial days down to our own time must depend to a not inconsiderable degree upon the researches of numerous predecessors, at least so far as developments before the outbreak of the Second World War are concerned. Chief among these are the 150-page pioneer tract of Charles Hart Handschin, *The Teaching of Modern Languages in the United States* (1913), representing a prodigious amount of original research, and E. W. Bagster-Collins' "History of Modern Language Teaching in the United States" (1930).[1] The work of Bagster-Collins leans somewhat upon Handschin, as does the present monograph, but he carries the investigation through the twenties of the present century, the principal event of the period after Handschin being the Modern Foreign Language Study of which Bagster-Collins' tract forms a part.

Neither of these studies, of course, deals exclusively with German. This more limited subject is treated in some detail for the eighteenth and nineteenth centuries by Louis Viereck in *German Instruction in American Schools* (1900–1901).[2] Bagster-Collins does not seem to have made direct use of this work, perhaps because of Viereck's strong German bias. There is reference to the book in Handschin (31 and 116). Our general subject is also touched upon, in some cases with details, in the seventy-page monograph of John A. Walz, *German Influence in American Education and Culture*.[3]

Additional information and help were culled from a variety of sources, such as the studies of Robert Francis Seybolt, among them his "Source Studies in American Colonial Education, The Private School"[4] and *Private Schools of Colonial Boston*,[5] also C. E. Castañeda's *Modern Language Instruction in American Colleges, 1770–1800*,[6] and the Annual Reports of the Boards of Education of various major cities, the Reports of the United States Commissioner of Education, the histories of various universities, and numerous other reports and fugitive articles, some very difficult to come by.[7] The typed Cincinnati Master's thesis of Sister M. Clarissa Riebenthaler is also valuable for its historical data, statistics, and bibliography, as is the recent University of Massachusetts booklet *Language Development in Action*.[8] All these sources and many more have been used so far as opportunity and time have permitted, but the writer makes only the hopeful claim that his data will prove representative, nothing more. One of the principal problems in any such undertaking as this is one of selection based on judgment of comparative significance.

Another source of information was furnished by the German textbooks of the various eras, insofar as they were available. They were able to throw much light not only upon what was taught but also upon the prevailing methods of teaching, choice and presentation of material, and many other imponderables.

What has been said thus far applies particularly to the earlier periods of the teaching of German in this country, the Colonial era, the late eighteenth century (a particularly difficult period to treat because of the separate and disparate cultural centers of Boston, New York, Philadelphia, Jamestown, and the Carolinas), and the first half of the nineteenth. Our information becomes fuller after 1850, and ever more overwhelming as time goes on. The sources for these later periods will be indicated as they are used. My own experience with the learning and teaching of German goes back to the time I entered a public high school in Brooklyn, N.Y., in 1907. It is marked from 1916 on by over forty years of teaching; from the twenties on by authorship of numerous articles and reviews, over a dozen textbooks, by service on the staff of *Monatshefte,* by many years as Assistant Managing Editor in charge of German book reviews, and five as Managing Editor of *The Modern Language Journal* (and incidentally as delegate to the National Federation of Modern Language Teachers' Associations), and seven years as Managing Editor of *The German Quarterly*. That experience has of course been drawn upon, too.

It is pleasant to record that the most recent period—since the Second World War with its ASTP-FALSC (Army Specialized Training Program, Foreign Area and Language Study Curriculum)—may by and large be called the most fruitful and healthiest in the entire history of the teaching of German in the United States. It can be treated on the basis of the events themselves, still fresh in the memory of all who have played a part in them. To be sure, German has ceased to be the leading language in the curriculum of most public or private secondary schools and, for that matter, of most colleges or universities, as it had been until the First World War almost put an end to German instruction in this country. But once again it occupies a respectable place, especially in the colleges and universities, and it seems to be gaining in the secondary field because of the international political situation and thanks to the dynamic efforts of the Modern Language Association of America, under the leadership of William Riley Parker, Kenneth Mildenberger, Donald D. Walsh, and George Winchester Stone, Jr., and to the reports of Dr. James Bryant Conant, which are opening many eyes to the need for language study. In some important centers, too, it has penetrated to the elementary school field with the backing, or at least the sanction, of local Boards of Education.

If the work on this report has brought some lessons home to me more clearly than ever, their chief import is that in spite of the basically unstable position of the modern languages in the American curriculum, of which Bagster-Collins had already complained, their prestige now stands higher than ever; that if one language is damaged, as German was from 1917 to 1920, all the rest will suffer as well; and that a teacher of French, German, Italian, Modern Hebrew, Russian, Spanish, or whatever other language one may name, is first and foremost a modern language teacher with a strong collegial bond attaching him to all other modern foreign language teachers. If some of what is said, especially in the last section, duplicates matter to be found in the historical accounts of the teaching of French and Spanish, this is due to the fact that these closer ties now bind the languages together and that all of them have been equally affected by recent happenings.

In closing this Introduction, I should emphasize that like Handschin and Bagster-Collins, I will stress the field covered by the teaching of German to the English-speaking school and college population, although not neglecting entirely the exceptional schools that taught exclusively in the German tongue as late as the nineteenth century, to accommodate recently immigrated German and Austrian families that had not yet heard of Americanization or of "one hundred per cent Americans."

Section VI [not reproduced in this volume] has enjoyed the immeasurable benefit of Professor Parker's suggestions. The whole history has profited from the criticisms of Emma Birkmaier, Bayard Quincy Morgan, and Donald D. Walsh. Others who supplied valuable information are mentioned in the appropriate places. To all these I express my deep gratitude.

I. The Colonial Era

The notion has long persisted that the earliest German impact upon the literature and culture of the American Colonies dates from the period just before the Revolutionary War, but that this influence did not become really significant until after the Colonies had secured their independence. The date often given is 1814, when George Ticknor developed an interest in German thought through the book of Mme de Staël on Germany and the

work of Charles Villers on the German universities. Ticknor says in his
Life, Letters and Journals (1876), dictated from memory over fifty years
later, that at that time he found it most difficult to procure books in New
England from which to learn German.[9] However, the researches of Harold
S. Jantz during the past twenty years have exploded these claims most
convincingly.[10] He has shown that the intellectual leaders in New England,
even before the middle of the seventeenth century, among them Robert
Child, Governor John Winthrop the Younger, his son Wait, and later his
grandson John, and Increase, Cotton, and Samuel Mather, followed intellectual pursuits which reveal a striking interest in and acquaintance with
German learning. Further evidence of this is furnished by preserved libraries and book lists of seventeenth-century New England scholars, such
as Samuel Fuller, Governor William Bradford, Captain Miles Standish,
and particularly, William Brewster. They all owned English works on
German subjects and German scholarly books, mostly written in Latin, to
be sure. The official library of the Massachusetts Bay Colony possessed
a number of German theological books, and in John Harvard's collection
German works ranked second only to the English.

After the younger Winthrop came to America to live in 1631 he
continued to receive book catalogs from Frankfurt and to correspond with
over a dozen German scholars. Nor was he the only New England contemporary who knew German. Nathaniel Ward and Robert Child were
both acquainted with the language. There were also in the Harvard College
Library of those days many textbooks from Germany in the fields of
chemistry, physics, theology, and almost every other branch of learning.

It follows that although the German influence in New England from
1620 to the end of the century was chiefly one of books and of correspondence, this served as a good climate for the learning of the language. As
for emigrants from Germany, Jantz has found records of a few in New
England at this time, particularly of four physicians. The most important
of these was a Dr. Christian Lodowick (Ludwig) of Rhode Island, who
later returned to Germany. Jantz compares him in importance with his
contemporary Franz Daniel Pastorius of Germantown. No record of any
German teachers, however, has emerged from the research into the role
played by Germany in colonial New England, although some private instruction in German was given, as later in the case of Ticknor, who was
tutored by an Alsatian mathematician in Jamaica Plain.

Bearing in mind that culture in the seventeenth-century colonies was
by no means homogeneous, we turn to other centers such as New York,
Philadelphia, Jamestown, and Charleston, South Carolina. While French
was doubtless the first foreign language to be taught—even before the
middle of the century, especially in Charleston and New York, not to
mention Louisiana—and while instruction in Italian, Spanish, and Portuguese followed soon after, German did not trail far behind.

The New Englanders Winthrop, Ward, Child, and later William Bentley undoubtedly acquired their knowledge of German either by themselves or in England, or possibly with the help of private tutors who were native Germans. The same is probably true of seventeenth-century scholars in New York, Philadelphia, and Charleston. But the earliest records we have of the actual teaching of German to groups point to Germantown and Philadelphia. There German is recorded as having been taught in 1702 to the children of immigrants who had come over, some with Pastorius in August 1683, the next group following in October, a year after the arrival of William Penn. Indeed, although proof is lacking, we are probably safe in assuming that such instruction had already begun in Germantown, at least informally, as early as the eighties, soon after the arrival of Pastorius and his little band. These were followed presently by additional immigrants from German-speaking Europe. The school of Pastorius was not directly supported by the church but by fees and special private contributions. It was coeducational and also held evening classes for adults.

At first the textbooks employed in Germantown were those brought along from Germany, but by 1702 the new all-German primer of Pastorius himself was in general use. Pastorius, a German lawyer, was an exceptionally skilled teacher. His early desultory activity as such was followed by two years of formal teaching (1698–1700) at the English Quaker School in Philadelphia before he assumed his duties as a teacher of German in Germantown in 1702. Nor was Pastorius, who had studied at the universities of Strassburg, Basel, and Jena, a teacher only, but a most versatile man and a polymath, like Benjamin Franklin and many other distinguished men of his time. He served in Germantown as burgomaster and judge, and he wrote over forty books on a wide variety of subjects, including a comprehensive encyclopedia.

Born in 1651 near Würzburg, he visited Frankfurt in 1682 after extensive travels and became acquainted there with the Pietist group of Spencer, who had connections with the English Quakers, heard about the royal charter granting Penn a huge tract of land, and read the printed account of "the Province of Pennsylvania" (1681), which had already been translated into German. The Frankfurt Company was then founded. It purchased some land in Pennsylvania and appointed Pastorius its field agent. Pastorius became a close friend of Penn. He was an enthusiastic propagator of the best in German cultural life, but at the same time a firm believer in the importance of English as the "country language" of America, as he called it, although he knew very little English when he arrived and at first conversed in Latin with those who knew no German. He was also convinced that practical training in such fields as printing and engineering was of more importance for the time and place in which he lived than the abstract philosophy and metaphysics in which he had been trained. He died in Germantown in 1719.

Much but (as we shall see) not all of the early instruction in German offered in Pennsylvania, as well as in New York, Virginia, and the Carolinas, was given in conjunction with the various churches which were established as soon as the new immigrants had a chance to settle on their land. They represented numerous sects—Lutherans, Dunkers, Moravians, Quakers, Reformed Lutherans—or they were dissenters, but all agreed in fostering religion and, closely bound up with it, education. The catechism and the religious tenets of their creed were taught assiduously, and pains were taken to make it possible for the younger generation to follow the German sermons of the preacher, who usually served also as the teacher. Little English was introduced in church or school. In fact these early preachers were scarcely familiar enough with the new language to teach it. It cannot be said that the quality of this instruction was good, for the general intellectual level of these clergymen was low. Discipline, however, was stern.

The value and the influence of these early schools have been debated. Viereck was favorably impressed:

> . . . the first parochial schools sometimes attained the level of passably good public schools, such as at that time were hardly to be found outside of New England, if anywhere. These schools were particularly important for the progress of culture in Pennsylvania, in which state the English Quakers did not possess the same deep appreciation for the necessity of public schools as did the Pilgrim Fathers, who established Harvard University at a time when the whole of Massachusetts contained not much over 5,000 inhabitants (1638). (539)

One of his critics, however, P. H. Grummann, considers him prejudiced.[11] The German schoolman, Dr. A. Douai, years before had also judged these schools unfavorably, in a *Special Report of the Commissioner of Education on the Schools of the District of Columbia* (1868, 582):

> During the last two or three decades, it is true, a sufficient number of able German teachers came over from the mother country, so that the character of these denominational schools might have been extensively improved. But there being little intelligence among these congregations and their clergy, they could not understand the requirements of a good school, and that able teachers cannot be expected to thrive on so low salaries as from $200 to $400 a year, and to perform into the bargain the menial work of sextons and attendants to their ministers. Thus it is that hardly half a dozen of the several hundred schools of this kind have been worthy of the name of schools. . . .

Handschin seems to agree with him (31–32).

Usually, then, it was not only German-language instruction as such, but rather general schooling, with German as the language of instruction, a practice which persisted at least in part throughout the eighteenth and nineteenth centuries, and into the twentieth, in certain communities with a sizeable first- or second-generation German population.

A German Mennonite school was founded in Montgomery County, Pennsylvania, in 1706. The teacher, probably from 1714 for a period of ten years, Christopher Dock, is second only to Pastorius in importance for the early years of German instruction in America. He was born in Germany, but neither the date nor the place is known. After his ten years of teaching in Montgomery County he engaged in farming for a while, then in 1738 he took charge of two schools in Skippack and Sallford, between which he divided his time as a teacher until his death in 1771.[12]

His "Schulordnung" (1750) bears the following descriptive and expansive title: "A simple and thoroughly prepared school order in which is clearly defined in what way children are not only best trained in the studies usually taught in schools, but how they may be well instructed in godliness; written out of love for humanity by Christopher Dock, an experienced teacher of long practice, and published by several friends of the common weal." This work of about sixty pages, printed by Christopher Sauer in Germantown, is the first book on educational theories and policy to be published in America. A second edition came out in 1770, shortly before Dock's death. Richard G. Boone pays Dock the tribute of calling him the Pestalozzi of his day.[13]

The first German Moravian boarding school for girls was opened in Germantown in 1742. Not long after, a Moravian girls' school was established in Bethlehem (1749), and German was taught there from the start. It still exists as the Moravian Seminary and College for Women. These and schools like them later took in pupils outside their denomination, and other schools were patterned after them.

There is other abundant evidence that the various Protestant sects, including the members of the Reformed Church, had established church-affiliated German schools in Pennsylvania at an early date. Many probably existed as early as 1720. Marion Dexter Learned names the following teachers and locations of schools during the generation of 1720–40: John Philip Brehm of Whitpain, Montgomery County; George Michael Weiss, who had studied at Heidelberg; George Stiefel of Tulpehocken, Berks County; John Jacob Hock and Kaspar Leutbecker, also of Tulpehocken. Henry Mühlenberg and Michael Schlatter, who had studied in the Halle; Paedagogium of Francke, the correspondent and friend of Cotton Mather, came later in the forties. They all worked for the further advancement of education among people of religious bodies with German connections.[14]

But lay teaching of German to non-Germans also prevailed in Pennsylvania. As early as 1743 there existed a private school in Philadelphia in which English-speaking students were taught German, and in the same year Joseph Crellius and John Schuppy gave evening instruction with a similar objective. Another evening school of this kind was founded in Philadelphia in 1756 by Jacob Ehrenzeller, whose reputation was very good.[15] He was still teaching in 1770. Another popular lay teacher of German in Philadelphia around 1750 was John Mathias Kramer, who also taught Italian. Later he opened a school for the instruction of French, Italian, and German for gentlemen and ladies. Other German teachers in Philadelphia between 1750 and 1780 were Adalbert Ebert, Philip Keryl, Charles Cist, and Jacob Lawn.

As for lay teaching in other colonies, it is interesting to note that for a layman to teach in Dutch New York City, which probably had a population of less than 20,000 at the beginning of the eighteenth century, with some Germans among them, one had to be licensed. And so, on September 13, 1703, Andrew Foucautt (Foucault?) was officially authorized to "teach an English and French school within the City of New York," and on August 29, 1705, the same privilege was accorded Prudent de la Fayole.[16] No license of this kind seems to have been required in Pennsylvania; at least we have found no reference to it. But these "schools" in New York, whether they offered French or German, were probably not much more than private classes held in the dwelling of the teacher or of a student's family, or in rooms leased for the purpose. Sometimes the classes met in the evenings and consisted of adults. That there was a lively and steady demand for foreign language teachers is proved by the fact that the newspapers and gazettes from Boston down to Charleston often ran advertisements seeking such teachers. The motivation for studying a foreign language was in some cases purely cultural, and in other cases quite practical.

The economic situation of the lay teachers thus employed was as a rule precarious. It was noted above that, even later, $200 to $400 a year was no unusual salary. The teachers often followed some vocation on the side. One is reported keeping a general store, another selling orange oil and lemon and orange peel!

A concomitant of instruction in German was the publication of German books, the oldest being a 96-page duodecimo volume of *Divine Hymns of Love and Praise* . . . printed in Philadelphia by Benjamin Franklin in 1730 and commissioned by the monastery of Ephrata. The first Bible to be printed in America was also in German, and the work of Franklin. Until 1738 Franklin enjoyed a monopoly in this field and published numerous German hymnals, breviaries, textbooks, and catechisms; but in that year Christopher Sauer, mentioned above, opened a printing shop in Germantown which offered competition. Sauer got out the first newspaper in America, *Hochdeutscher pennsylvanischer Geschichtsschreiber,* later called *Germantowner Zeitung.* It has been claimed, but not proved, that Franklin had planned (and even issued) a German newspaper, the *Philadelphia-Zeitung,* as early as 1732.

Of greater importance for our purposes are the following two works, for sale by Franklin in 1746: Benedictus Beiler, *A New German Grammar, to which are added some Useful and Familiar Dialogues,* which had first appeared in London in 1731, and Christian Ludwig's *Dictionary of High Dutch and English,* which came out with the German title *Teutsch-Englisches Lexicon* about 1745 in Leipzig. Very popular too was Bachmair's *A Complete German Grammar,* which seems to have been issued originally in England about 1750,[17] with American editions following in 1765, 1772 (also 1774?) and 1788.[18] Seybolt describes it as containing in the first part clear, simple helps in speaking and writing German, while the second part offers familiar words, phrases, expressions, proverbs, and dialogues, pieces of prose (news items, letters), poetry, and adequate vocabulary. There is besides an index of German words similar in sound to English words but of different spelling and meaning, names of occupations, materials, and tools, as well as "explication of a German proverb."[19] One is particularly impressed by the practical nature of this work, a first step toward functionalism. Textbooks will receive more attention below.

The estimate of Charles Lee Smith, author of *A History of Education in North Carolina,* issued by the Bureau of Education in Washington as a Circular of Information (1888), that during the first half of the eighteenth century only 30,000 Germans immigrated to the Colonies, and that three-fifths settled in North Carolina, is almost surely incorrect. Assuming that five thousand had come over before 1700, that would aggregate only 35,000 by 1750. If, as Smith claims, 18,000 of these settled in North Carolina, that would have left only 17,000 Germans in all the rest of the Colonies. However, between 1709 and 1740 thousands of Germans emigrated to the Colonies every year, in 1749 alone over 7,000 (Viereck 542). They settled in Maine (at Broad Bay), New York (not only in Manhattan, but also in Newburgh), Philadelphia-Germantown, and all the way down the coast as far as the Carolinas. A trustworthy authority in such statistical matters, surprisingly enough, was the noted German scholar Christoph Daniel Ebeling, who enjoyed close literary and personal contacts with America, among his correspondents being Thomas Jefferson and Noah Webster. He assures us that in Pennsylvania alone there were one hundred thousand Germans by 1755.[20] My guess, then, would be that by 1750 there were one hundred fifty thousand Germans, all told, in the Colonies. Another authority, Governor Thomas of Pennsylvania, writing to the Bishop of Exeter in 1748, ventured an even higher estimate: "The Germans of that province are, I believe, three-fifths of the whole people, and by their industry and frugality have been the principal instruments of raising it to its present flourishing condition."[21] German churches and schools may be posited wherever Germans lived.

Thomas, it seems, was in favor of immigration, particularly from

Germany, and successfully opposed the efforts of the nativists to arrest
it. His predecessor, Patrick Gordon, had sponsored legislation in the
Colonial Assembly that would assess an entrance duty of 40 shillings on
each immigrant, but this was repealed in 1730 because of the protest of
Franklin and other leaders.

It was through Franklin's influence, too, that the literary and philosophical "Junto Club" was founded in Philadelphia about 1727, and in
1743 the American Philosophical Society. Through the efforts of Franklin
and this Society a school called the Public Academy and College (1749)
and another, the Charity School of the City of Philadelphia, were established. In the constitution of the former, Franklin, who believed in the
practical advantages of learning foreign languages, introduced a provision
that "the trustees shall with all convenient speed endeavor to engage
Persons capable of teaching the French, Spanish and German languages."
Franklin recommended the modern languages particularly for "merchants," but did not wish to exclude any interested student. In December
of 1753 a Mr. Creamer (Krämer), a "gentleman from Germany," was
found who was "very capable of teaching the French and German languages." He actually taught both for a while at a salary of 100 pounds a
year. In 1755 the Academy became a degree-granting college, and in July
of that year relations with him were severed.[22] He is described as also
"qualified" to teach Italian, music, and painting. The Academy and College was the first American school in which German was taught, and the
University of Pennsylvania is an outgrowth of it. But the modern languages
were recommended only "to be studied at leisure hours" (Montgomery
238).

In yet another way Franklin influenced the development of American
education. On his journey to Europe in 1766 he paid a visit to the University
of Göttingen and was invited to a session of the Academy of Sciences
there. B. A. Hinsdale writes as follows about this visit: "It is rather
surprising to find that the man who is the best embodiment of the practical
spirit of American philosophy should have been the first American to show
an interest in the higher education of the land of abstract thought and
sciences. It is surprising also to find that nearly all the facts which we
possess relating to the visit are found in German authorities."[23]

It was therefore not the group of young Americans represented by
Ticknor, Everett, and Bancroft in the early nineteenth century who "discovered" Göttingen, but Benjamin Franklin sixty years before. Viereck
ventures the conjecture (543) that the College was turned into the University of Pennsylvania in 1779 as a result of the impressions which Franklin
brought home.

For a while the Academy and College maintained a so-called German
Institute. In 1780 a professor of "philosophy" was engaged whose duty it

was to teach "Latin and Greek by means of the German language." This clearly indicates that the knowledge of German and the influence of Germans must have been rather strong in the environs of Philadelphia. A prominent Philadelphia clergyman, John Christopher Kunze, who enjoyed an excellent reputation as a teacher, was the German instructor. Kunze also planned a seminary for teachers. In 1773 he had engaged a young emigrant, a student of law from the University of Halle by the name of Leps, as an assistant. This seems to have been the first school of academic rank for the benefit of Germans in America and was modelled on the Paedagogium of Francke in Halle. But it was short-lived. The Revolutionary War put an end to it, as it did to other similar ventures.

With only brief interruptions the University of Pennsylvania has maintained a fine tradition in the teaching of German. After Creamer and Kunze came Helmuth, Varin, and Bokum, later Schaefer, Seidensticker, and Learned. Moreover, in William and Mary College Jefferson had introduced modern languages as early as 1779, while King's College (Columbia University) also offered these languages at an early date, before 1768.[24] But details are lacking. Castañeda reports that Salem College in North Carolina introduced German, probably on a tutorial basis, in 1771.

In Nazareth, Pennsylvania, an all-German Moravian academy was started in 1756, later (1785) reorganized as a boys' boarding school. It lasted through half of the nineteenth century and later accepted also non-Germans and Indians. And in Germantown English and German residents cooperated to found an academy in 1760 with English and German de-partments. In both schools German was on a par with English, and in Nazareth the pupils were "required to express themselves exclusively in one or the other language on alternate days in their intercourse with each other and their preceptors."[25] In New England, however, where academies also developed (Phillips Andover was started in 1778 and Phillips Exeter in 1781), modern languages were taught at an early date but do not seem to have become a regular part of the curriculum until the later nineteenth century (Bagster-Collins 13). A notable exception, the Round Hill School, will be discussed in the next section.

II. From the Revolutionary War to 1825

With the German Institute of the College and the German Seminary, both in Philadelphia, mentioned in the previous section, we have already entered the period of the American Revolution. The war affected education unfavorably and, because of the presence of Hessian and Hanoverian mercenaries, even though they were impressed against their will into the British Colonial Army, German and the Germans soon became unpopular. Moreover, since some of the colonial ports were blockaded part of the time, few ships with emigrants could come through, with the result that scarcely more than 6,000 arrived from anywhere each year during this period. Crude efforts at forced Americanization also militated against newcomers from Germany and Switzerland.

As we have seen, the Seminary became a victim of the war. The Institute, however, did not come to an end until 1787. In spite of the enthusiasm of Justus Helmuth, who succeeded Kunze, a gold medal promised annually by the German Society for the best essay on a theme relating to the Germans in Pennsylvania,[26] and of an article in the *Philadelphia-Correspondenz* in 1783 advocating public schools in which German would be taught, the Institute was forced to close its doors because its enrollment had dropped from sixty to six. This step had to be taken in spite of the expert teaching which had made it possible for the students to read and appreciate so difficult a recent work as Lessing's *Nathan der Weise,* published in 1779.

There was yet another reason for this: dissension and competitive efforts on the part of the Germans of Pennsylvania themselves. Shortly after the installation of a teacher of German, John Daniel Gross, S.T.D., at Columbia College in New York in 1784 (a position which he held for eleven years), and the founding of the Methodist Cokesbury College in 1785 in Maryland, where French and German were to be taught "when the finances of the college will permit" (Handschin 32), a group of Pennsylvania Germans founded Franklin College in 1787 in Lancaster as a rival of the Institute. They had succeeded in interesting the now aged Benjamin Franklin in the plan, naming the college in his honor and appointing Henry Mühlenberg president. The teacher of German was Rev. Frederick Melsheimer, a native of Braunschweig (Castañeda). Franklin's part in the founding of the college was described by Provost Pepper of what is now Franklin and Marshall College in an address in 1891.[27]

For a long time he had taken great interest in the welfare of the Germans, who formed the bulk of the population in some parts of Pennsylvania. He aided in the establishment of schools for them, and served as a trustee of a society for the benefit of the poor among them, and in 1787, although in his eighty-first year, he was active in the promotion of the long-cherished scheme of founding a college for the education of young Germans. On March 10 of that year— 1787—an act was passed by the assembly incorporating and endowing the German College and Charity School in the borough and county of Lancaster, in which act it is recited that "the college is established for the instruction of youth in the German, English, Latin, Greek, and other learned languages, in theology, and in the useful arts, sciences, and literature." The same act of incorporation refers to "a profound respect for the talents, virtues, and services to mankind in general, but more especially to this country, of his excellency Benjamin Franklin, esq., president of the supreme executive council."

Franklin was the largest contributor to its funds, giving of his moderate fortune the sum of $1,000, which may be considered large for those days; and still more when, in the spring of 1787 the corner stone was to be laid in Lancaster, he underwent the pain and fatigue of a journey thither in order to perform that ceremony.

However, the time was not yet ripe for a college of this kind: German had lost some of its appeal, Lancaster was situated too far west, and the Germans of Pennsylvania had been divided by a schism. The result was bad for all concerned. The College had lost its German instruction in the Institute, although Helmuth was permitted to stay on, and "Franklin College also cast off its German tegument" soon, to use Handschin's phrase (32). On the credit side, it is to be borne in mind that Franklin College did not quite go under and later could reinstate its German instruction, and that if it had not been founded, one of America's earliest great scientists might not have attained such prominence. He is Benjamin Smith Barton.

To Barton seems to go the distinction of having been the first American to secure a degree at a German university. Born in Lancaster in 1766, he studied at the College in Philadelphia. In 1787 he journeyed home to witness the laying of the cornerstone of Franklin College by Franklin himself. This so impressed him that he decided to pursue his studies in medicine and science abroad. He first attended the University of Edinburgh, then continued his studies in London, and finally secured his medical degree in Göttingen. Back in Philadelphia he enjoyed a very distinguished career as a physician, a scientific investigator, and a writer. His early study of German at home helped shape this notable career.

A plan for a national university, advocated by Jefferson and worked out in some detail by Dr. Benjamin Rush in 1788, provided for instruction in French and German. But it came to naught.

Turning for a moment to the South, we find that in Chapel Hill, North Carolina, a certain W. A. Richards taught modern languages as early as 1795 or 1796. The university had been founded in the former year. On the first diploma, dated September 22, 1796, his name appears as a teacher of French and English, but according to Kemp P. Battle, Richards taught German, too.[28] But it is not clear whether this was in the university or in the preparatory school attached to it. More likely, though, it was in both. During the same period, Transylvania College in Kentucky introduced the modern languages in 1794 and Williams College in Massachusetts in 1795 (Castañeda 8).

Among the private academies foreign language instruction was by no means common in the earlier periods. Washington Academy in Virginia, to be sure, offered it as early as 1799. New England had almost 150 academies by 1825, and there is some evidence of French instruction in

Phillips Exeter, for instance, but not of German. But in the Round Hill School in Northampton, Mass., founded in 1823 by the historian Bancroft and the bibliographer Cogswell, who had studied in Germany, and modeled on German educational patterns, all the students learned German. It existed for fifteen years. Late in 1824 Charles Follen and Charles Beck, two political refugees just arrived from Germany, were invited to teach at Round Hill. Follen, with a recommendation from Lafayette, had been there less than a year when he was invited to Harvard. His father had called himself Follenius, but the son, born near Giessen in 1769, dropped the Latin ending in America.[29]

In New York State, which had about 650 pupils in such academies by 1805, no evidence of German instruction appears before 1825, but in the South, particularly in North Carolina, it seems to have been more frequent, though second to French. In Illinois and other parts of the Middle West, academies did not begin appearing until after 1815, and foreign languages did not enter the curriculum until some twenty-five years later (Bagster-Collins 13ff.). German instruction in centers like Cincinnati began regularly in the elementary school. It will receive attention in the next section. The case of the Salem (Pennsylvania) Female Academy, founded in 1804, is unusual; it introduced German at its very inception.

The revived interest in Germany and German literature from about 1815 on, when a new generation had grown up to whom the War of Independence was not a personal experience, can probably be explained also by the work of Mme de Staël, already referred to, by Carlyle's writings, and by the activities of men like George Ticknor and Edward Everett. French had been taught at Harvard in desultory fashion as early as 1733. The first licensed German teacher there was Meno Poehls in 1816. But he taught at Harvard only one year, more or less as a tutor, and his subject was not a part of the regular inflexible curriculum.[30] In the next year, though, Ticknor was appointed professor of French and Spanish. He assumed his post in 1819. Although he did not teach German, his influence in introducing European ideas of academic freedom for both faculty and students, his great administrative ability, and his broad vision and interest in German, as well as the literatures which he professed, had a profound and lasting effect upon the whole academic life at Cambridge.

But the status of the foreign languages was only that of an elective subject. In the *Fourth Annual Report of the President of Harvard University* for 1828–29 (xxiiiff.) we read: "The principles which regulate the study of the modern languages are these: No Student is compelled to study any of them. A student, choosing to study either, is compelled to persevere. He is not permitted to quit the study until he has learned the language" (Bagster-Collins 56). Nevertheless, Ticknor had no trouble recruiting a modest number of students.

Before continuing our consideration of Harvard, it is necessary to turn to two other New England colleges, Amherst and Bowdoin, and to the University of Virginia.

At Amherst thoroughgoing German instruction was started in 1824, but not as a subject in the regular course of study. It was, however, recognized as a legitimate subject if taken extramurally. In Bowdoin College instruction was offered in the modern languages as early as 1820. But a professorship in that subject was not established until 1826, when a bequest of one thousand dollars was received for this purpose. A certain J. H. Abbott was engaged to teach them. Then in 1829 Henry Wadsworth Longfellow was elected professor in this field. He took up his duties the next year, after his return from a protracted sojourn abroad. According to one of the College catalogs of the time "the student may at his option study the Ancient, or one of the Modern Languages, Spanish, German, or Italian, instead of the calculus" (Bagster-Collins 52). It was an option of which those weak in mathematics availed themselves freely.

In 1819 Thomas Jefferson's plan for a University of Virginia was approved by the state legislature. The course of study allowed the student full liberty of attending any lectures in any subject, and the curriculum of general studies was built around the study of German, no doubt the result of Jefferson's close personal contacts with Alexander von Humboldt. In 1818, a year before the charter was granted, Jefferson had reported to the legislature: "The German now stands in a line with that of the most learned nations in richness of condition and advance in the sciences. It is, too, of common descent with the language of our own country, a branch of the same original Gothic stock, and furnishes valuable illustrations for us" (Viereck 552). Jefferson's plan was to have Ticknor accept the chair of modern languages at a salary of $2,500 (which today would probably be the equivalent of $25,000), but Ticknor, though approving heartily of the idea, preferred to remain in Massachusetts. Instead, a German linguist, Dr. George Blaettermann, was given the position, which he assumed in 1825 and held for fifteen years. Compared with an ancient language enrollment of 57 in the first year, 73 were enrolled in the general studies division of modern languages.

In 1825, too, as we have seen, Harvard resumed instruction in German with the appointment of Follen. His class in German was at first experimental. Concerning it a member of his first class, Andrew P. Peabody, writes:

> German had never been taught in college before, and it was with no little difficulty that a volunteer class of eight was formed. I was one of that class. We were looked upon with very much the amazement with which a class in some obscure tribal dialect of the remotest Orient would be now regarded. We knew of but two or three persons in New England who could read German,

though there were probably many more of whom we did not know. There were no German books in the bookstores. A friend gave me a copy of Schiller's *Wallenstein,* which I read as soon as I was able to do so, and then passed it from hand to hand among those who could obtain nothing to read. There was no attainable class book that could be used as "reader." A few copies of Nöhden's Grammar were imported, and a few copies of I forgot whose "pocket dictionary," fortunately [sic] too copious for an Anglo-Saxon pocket, and suggesting the generous amplitude of the Low Dutch costume, as described in Irving's mythical "History of New York." The German Reader for Beginners, compiled by our teacher, was furnished to the class in single sheets as it was needed, and was printed in Roman type, there being no German type within easy reach. There could not have been a happier introduction to German literature than this little volume. It contained choice extracts in prose, all from writers that still hold an unchallenged place in the hierarchy of Genius, and poems from Schiller, Goethe, Herder, and several other poets of kindred, if inferior, fame. But in the entire volume Dr. Follen rejoiced especially in several battle poems from Körner, the soldier and martyr of liberty. I have never heard recitations which impressed me so strongly as the reading of those pieces by Dr. Follen, who would put into them all of the heart and soul that made him too much a lover of his country to be suffered to dwell in it. He appended to the other poems in the first edition of the reader, anonymously, a death song in memory of Körner, which we all knew to be his own, and which we read so often and so feelingly that it sank indelibly into permanent memory, and I find that, after an interval of sixty years, it is as fresh in my recollection as the hymns that I learned in my childhood.[31] (Quoted also by Viereck 553.)

It is likely that the gift of a set of Goethe's works by Goethe himself to the Harvard Library in 1819 served also as a fillip to German studies.

By and large, however, the quality of teaching was low in the field of modern languages, and continued so for several generations. Many of the teachers enjoyed only the advantage of being native to the language taught, but had little ability as teachers. Their teaching load was usually quite heavy, as many as seven or eight hours a day, and their salaries were lower than those paid in other fields. Furthermore the courses sometimes did not even carry credit, or at best half-credit (Bagster-Collins 58). Consequently the enrollment in German was low as a rule. As noted above, Peabody spoke of a class of eight at Harvard in 1825–26. Bagster-Collins' figures (57) are a trifle higher. Follen also taught a larger class in Boston.

As for textbooks, it was also noted by Peabody that Follen compiled his own reader as the class progressed. Nöhden, also mentioned by Peabody, was the author of a German grammar as well as a reader, the former based upon the old German work of Adelung. Both of Nöhden's books were commonly used in England. Besides Schiller's *Wallenstein, Maria Stuart* and the *History of the Thirty Years' War* were read a few years later, by the time the class was farther advanced, also Goethe's *Faust,* Part 1 (Bagster-Collins 59). The subject of early textbooks will be continued in the next section.

III. An Uphill Struggle: 1826–76

The fifty years to be considered here will take us from the time of Follen's tenure at Harvard to the founding of the Johns Hopkins University in Baltimore, where the scientific study of the German language and literature—called "Germanistik" in German—was stressed in this country. We shall open the present section with a look at some of the early textbooks.

As noted in Section II, Follen was seriously handicapped by the lack of suitable textbooks when he came to Cambridge in December of 1825 and early the next year took up the teaching of German on an experimental basis. So he set to work immediately and wrote his *Deutsches Lesebuch für Anfänger* (Cambridge, 1826), a book of 250 pages. As the preface states, the author's purpose was to furnish reading matter from recognized German masterpieces, in illustration of the rules and genius of the language, and to give the students a foretaste and first impression of the classical literature. There follows an introduction which offers a brief history of German literature, divided into three periods: Medieval, Reformation, and Modern (the earliest sketch of German literature, perhaps, to appear in America). The selections themselves cover 150 pages of prose and twenty of poetry ranging from Lessing to Theodor Körner. Among the works represented by selections are: Lessing's fables, Herder's *Paramythien,* Schiller's *Geisterseher* and *Abfall der Niederlande,* Novalis' *Heinrich von Ofterdingen,* Wackenroder's *Herzensergießungen,* Goethe's *Italienische Reise* and *Wilhelm Meister,* Wieland's *Abderiten,* Jean Paul's novels, and A. W. Schlegel's lecture on *Macbeth.* There is no end vocabulary, but considerable other help, including superior numbers to clarify word order, e.g., "Es ist nicht angemessen, die Götter in Wände ein zu schliessen." As in most of the textbooks of that time, the printing is crowded and unattractive. How an average modern college freshman with no knowledge of German would be baffled by the difficulty of the language and thought! How he would rebel at the fare which his ancestor, five or six generations removed, was expected to digest!

Nevertheless this book, warmly received by the reviewers, is a landmark in the early college curriculum, as Spindler aptly says.[32] It was still used at Harvard as late as the sixties (the twenty-first edition appeared in 1859) and instilled in generations of Americans an enthusiasm for German literature. In 1833 Follen anonymously published a sequel for more advanced study. It contained Schiller's *Maria Stuart* and Goethe's *Egmont* as well as *Torquato Tasso,* without any critical matter. Much of the textual material was furnished Follen by his colleague Ticknor, who possessed an excellent German library. Five years before, Follen had got out his *Practical Grammar of the German Language* (Boston, 1828), another landmark, and an improvement over the British works of Nöhden and Rowbotham. A preface gives an historical account of the development of the German language and observations on German grammars from Gottsched to Grimm. The main body of the book is in three parts: Elements, Syntax, and Prosody. Spindler comments as follows (102):

> The Elements are divided into orthography and parts of speech. In his classification of consonants Follen deviated from general usage by ranking d, t, l and n with the palatals and r with the linguals. In dealing with the parts of speech he begins with the article and treats successively nouns, adjectives, numerals, pronouns, verbs, adverbs, prepositions and conjunctions. Similar to Heinsius' scheme of declension, he groups the nouns into three classes: all feminines; all masculines having the genitive singular in n or en; and all masculines and neuters whose genitive singular ends in s (s, es, us, eus). In dealing with the verb, the primary tenses, then the secondary are treated; but instead of adopting the new terms 'weak' and 'strong,' as introduced by Grimm, those of 'regular' and 'irregular' are retained. The treatise on prosody, based for the most part on the opinions of Voss and Schlegel, was introduced "in order to contribute to the pleasure of those lovers of poetry," who were becoming interested more and more in the polite literature of Germany.

Judged by modern standards, the work is quite heavy, overly literary and dull. Such trite sentences as this are assigned for translation: "The hen sees the kite in the air and gathers the chickens under her wings."

Finally, Follen's edition of the Gospel of St. John for beginners in German, with a literal English interlinear translation, deserves mention.

With a look at two other widely used textbooks of the same period, issued in Philadelphia in 1832, we will close our study of early German primers. Both are by Hermann Bokum, who was then instructor in the German language and literature at the University of Pennsylvania.

The first, a second edition of which appeared soon, is *An Introduction to the Study of the German Language* "comprising extracts from the best German prose writers with an English interlinear translation, explanatory notes, and a treatise on pronunciation affording the means of a ready and accurate comparison of the idioms of the two languages." It contains about 200 pages. The preface notes that since German is learned in this country "generally only for a practical purpose," this book too pursues a practical end. It pays a tribute to Follen (though he is not named): Bokum hopes his book will become a stimulus to "a careful study of the excellent productions which, emanating from Cambridge, have been greatly conducive to a more general cultivation of German literature." Independently of Follen he offers twenty-three selections, among them passages from Jean Paul, Wieland (*Die Abderiten*), Goethe (*Egmont, Wilhelm Meister*), Schiller (*Geschichte des dreißigjährigen Krieges*), Fichte, Lichtenberg, Lessing, Geßner, Wackenroder, and Tieck, all in prose. In presenting them he goes Follen one better. The first 140 pages give these selections in English word order, e.g.: "Vielleicht Wolken werden bedecken ihn zuweilen . . . ," with the English equivalents underneath. In the case of such an expression as "vor vielen Jahren," the explanation reads: "before many years (ago)." Then on the last sixty pages the same texts are unscrambled and given in idiomatic German.

The second book of Bokum is a slightly revised edition of a grammar by Adolphus Bernays (London, 1830) and bears the title *Bernays' Compendious German Grammar* "with a dictionary of prefixes and affixes, and with alterations, additions and references to an introduction to the study of the German language." It is anything but compendious, consisting of only sixty pages. After the alphabet and sounds (for "lingual ch" the only "help" given is: "like Spanish x in *xifero;*" for guttural ch: "like j in Spanish *oveja* or ch in Scotch *loch*"), the substantives are treated, followed by the pronouns, articles, adjectives, numerals, verbs (*sein* still spelled *seyn*), adverbs, prepositions, syntax, word order, and miscellaneous addenda such as the pleonastic use of *nicht* then still in vogue: "es ist mehr als ein Monat, seitdem er nicht geschrieben hat." Word formation is briefly treated, and an eight-page "dictionary of prefixes and suffixes" concludes the book.

As in all the books considered thus far, the presswork is abominable. In the tiny volume under discussion, with the page measuring only 7½ by 4¼ inches, there are eighty ems to the line and 53 lines normally to the page. In the list of verbs, the font is so minute that about 65 verbs are crowded into a one-page column, so small that one may need a glass to decipher them. There are no exercises whatever, as the book is meant to be a reference grammar.

We return for a moment to Follen. Realizing almost from the start that his position in Cambridge was precarious and still hoping to get into the more congenial field of ethics and morality, he became a Unitarian minister in 1828, but continued teaching German at Harvard. Two years later he acquired American citizenship. Learning in 1830 that he was not to become professor of ethics at Harvard, as he had been led to believe, he accepted the new professorship of German literature, a post which he held from 1831 to 1836. But although he proved very popular with his students, his appointment was not renewed for another term, probably because of his anti-slavery agitation and championship of free speech. In the autumn of 1836 he took the post as minister of the First Unitarian Church in New York.

Hardly had Follen left Harvard when Longfellow returned from Europe to take up the position of Ticknor at Harvard. He served as professor of modern languages there from 1836 to 1854. Although German literature was not his sole specific field, the lectures on Goethe which he began in 1838 were particularly noteworthy. But generally speaking, the teaching of modern languages and literatures remained what it had been, a sort of tutorial sideline or extracurricular activity (see Handschin 37). The remark made by Follen in 1831: "There are now German teachers and German books in all important cities in this country" was to a degree true enough. But as far as language teaching was concerned, Latin and Greek still remained in the saddle, and the ability to use a few phrases of French and to puzzle out a few pages of it was considered a polite accomplishment.

With Follen and, soon after, Longfellow, Harvard undoubtedly snatched away any hegemony that the University of Pennsylvania may have enjoyed up to then, so far as the teaching of German is concerned. We have noted that his new prestige impressed even Herr Bokum in Philadelphia. Institutions of collegiate rank directly north of Pennsylvania seem also to have been impressed. After an interregnum from the time of Gross's retirement in 1795, Columbia appointed Frederick C. Shafer, S.T.D., to teach German in 1830, and in 1844 J. L. Gellkampf, J.U.D., became the first Gebhard professor there in that subject. Theologians, lawyers, and men of many other professions could become Germanists overnight in those days. At Princeton, where there is some evidence that German was taught late in the eighteenth century, the newly formed alumni association provided for a "professorship of living languages" in 1830 and Benedict Jaeger became professor of German and Italian. As in almost all cases, however, the subject was purely voluntary and extracurricular.[33] Yale appointed a teacher of German in 1831 (for one year); the position became more stable in 1834. But German did not gain real distinction at Yale until 1856, when William D. Whitney added German to Sanskrit and enriched the teaching possibilities with his excellent grammar, reader, and dictionary. His daughter Marian became equally famous later at Vassar.

The Sheffield Scientific School at Yale had a modern language requirement in 1846, while Brown gave its first modern language instruction in 1844, and Amherst in 1846. At least two collegiate institutions in the Middle West began teaching German even earlier, Miami of Ohio around 1830, and Woodward College in Cincinnati in 1837 under Dr. Wilhelm Nast, the founder of German Methodism, who had already taught German at Gettysburg Seminary in Pennsylvania.[34]

The most popular college textbooks during the era of the fifties were, besides those of Follen and Bokum, the *Grammar and Exercises* as well as the *Reader* of Ollendorff, the *Reader* of Rölker, Otto's *Conversational Grammar,* and Ahn's grammar. With Ollendorff, Otto, and Ahn, we note a more natural approach to the language, more conversational in tone and down-to-earth, with greater stress on everyday speech. But the grammar-translation method still prevailed. Popular for reading were selections from Jean Paul, Schiller's *Maria Stuart* and *Die Jungfrau von Orleans,* as well as his historical writings, Goethe's *Egmont* and *Dichtung und Wahrheit,* and selections from *Faust,* Part 1. Then in the sixties the books of Whitney and Woodbury were widely adopted. Contemporaneous German writers hardly took root until Heine, Gerstäcker (who, by the way, was in America in the forties and applied for a position as a teacher of German in Cincinnati), Heyse, Storm, and others became better known.

But we must leave the collegiate field for the time being and turn to the teaching of German in the private and public elementary and high schools. Three types of German private schools can be distinguished in the United States at the beginning of the nineteenth century: those of a denominational nature that wanted to perpetuate the German language for family reasons, non-denominational schools based upon the conviction that knowledge of a second language (in particular that of one's forebears) has educational value, and finally those that aimed to transplant to America the system of education which prevailed in Germany and which the better educated German emigrants (especially from 1848 on) deemed superior to that to be had in the American public schools of the time. Often the two latter types were blended in a single school.

The first type has been considered, but the other two, some examples of which endured until the twentieth century, must now be taken up. One of the best illustrations of the strong influence of German upon the educational system of an American city is furnished by Cincinnati. Since 1835 German schools existed there, such as the German Protestant "Emigrant School" (1836), attached to the Lane Seminary, and parochial schools. The teaching of German was introduced in the elementary public schools of the city in 1840 and, though strongly opposed at first, it attracted many children of German families. There was a special reason for this move. In 1836 the Ohio legislature had sent the theologian Professor Calvin E. Stowe of Cincinnati to Europe to study the school systems of various countries. In that same year Stowe had married Harriet Beecher, who was to achieve wide fame as the author of *Uncle Tom's Cabin.* He returned with a very favorable estimate of the Prussian schools, and many of his recommendations were adopted, not only in Ohio, but in Pennsylvania as well.[35] Consequently the quality of the schools in these states was improved and German instruction introduced. Indeed, an Ohio statute of 1842 provided that "a German youth may, if German is not taught in his school district, attend in another district . . ." (Handschin 70).

The German instruction in Cincinnati was optional, and during the early period (but not later) it was restricted to children of German parentage, a form of segregation which, some years later, was sharply attacked in other places, for instance in St. Louis.[36] Like Baltimore, Buffalo, Chicago, Cleveland, Dayton, Denver, Indianapolis, Milwaukee, New York, San Francisco, St. Paul, and Toledo, St. Louis also came around to offering German in its elementary public schools.[37] Even as late as 1914 one-third of the entire Cincinnati elementary school population was learning German throughout the entire eight years. The same situation prevailed in Cleveland, Dayton, and Milwaukee, with others mentioned above not far behind. Until 1917 the Cincinnati school administration had a special staff in charge of German.

The types of class organization, from the point of view of teaching in the German-English schools, were threefold. In Cincinnati, for instance, there was one class teacher in the German schools, and he gave instruction in both languages, sometimes to the prejudice of English. But the German-English schools either had special teachers of German or developed the so-called "parallel-class system," whereby all the pupils who elected German were taught a half day alternately by an English and by a German teacher up to and including the fourth grade. Officially stated, the plan in vogue in Cincinnati in 1914 was as follows: "In the lower grades of the larger schools two teachers were assigned to two classes, one teaching German and the other English to both classes alternately, the German teacher in addition taking charge of such branches as drawing, music, and primary occupation work. The upper grades were generally taught by a German supervising assistant."[38] When the school was small, a few special teachers took charge of all the German, and as such they were regularly employed staff members. By and large this system prevailed in Cincinnati from 1840 to 1917, employing three teachers in 1840 and over 175 by 1914. In other cities very similar arrangements were in vogue, at least for a while, until teacher shortages, budgetary demands, or better counsel dictated otherwise.

As for the quality of teaching and the amount of time devoted to it, Handschin, writing a year before the outbreak of World War I, has the following to say (72): "This instruction in Cincinnati, perhaps the best and most thorough-going of its kind now in the United States, deserves special notice. . . . The time given to German instruction in such classes (i.e., the "parallel classes") does not exceed nine hours a week (in the first four grades). . . . From the fourth to the eighth grades 45 minutes to one hour a day are devoted to German. The instruction, as the writer knows from personal inspection, is very good. The pupils who elect the German keep up their other work very satisfactorily, and no change seems to be desired."

In other cities even more time was devoted to German. As Bagster-

Collins remarks (20): "The equal division of time between English and German, such as we found in the Cleveland schools of 1869–70, represents the high-water mark in the development of German instruction in this country." In general this bilingual nature of many of the schools caused administrators in many cities no end of trouble and some expense.

In New York City German was introduced on an optional basis in the highest grade of the grammar school in 1854, and in 1870 the course was lengthened to the entire eight years. By the mid-seventies there were about 20,000 children enrolled in German. There existed also purely German schools of a private nature in New York as late as the eighties, in which not even the teachers had an adequate command of English.

As late as 1857 the school reports in Pennsylvania and Indiana were published in German translation; in New Jersey this practice persisted until 1888. And in 1870 the U. S. Commissioner of Education reported (55) that "the German language has actually become the second language of our Republic, and a knowledge of German is now considered essential to a finished education."

In a similar vein U. T. Curran, president of the Ohio Teachers' Association in 1873, told the body at its twenty-fifth annual meeting:

> Without doubt, the English will be the language of this country. But the law authorizes the teaching of German in our schools, and it is highly proper that it should be taught. The memories of fatherland are sweet, and the sound of the mother tongue on the lips of the child makes the father feel that his child is not separated from him. The vast storehouse of the German needs but this key to place its riches at the command of him who can use it. There are difficulties presented in the management of our schools where two languages are taught at once. The best experience has taught us that the lines of instruction should be parallel.
>
> The power of thinking in two languages will counterbalance any supposed deficiency in either, and the two languages will give, in their reciprocal influence upon each other, linguistic culture, and will render pupils better trained than those who have drawled through the abstract formulae of so-called English grammar. (Handschin 53ff.)

Perhaps even more enthusiastic about the benefits of the study of German in the elementary schools, specifically those in Cincinnati, was John B. Peaslee, superintendent of schools there from 1874 to 1887, who addressed the *Nationaler Deutsch-Amerikanischer Lehrerbund* at Chicago July 19, 1889, on "Instruction of German and its helpful influence on common school education as experienced in the public schools of Cincinnati."[39]

And yet, even in its heyday between 1852 and 1854, when a total of over 500,000 persons of German tongue arrived, and again between 1866 and 1873, when close to 150,000 poured into the United States every year,

German instruction did not go unchallenged.[40] Many voices were raised against what was termed its exaggerated emphasis, and crimination was followed by recrimination, with the bad feelings that naturally attended.

If the teaching of German during the greater part of the nineteenth century to thousands of young Americans in hundreds of elementary public and private schools represents one of the most singular phenomena in the history of education in this country, and well illustrates what democracy can lead to in the classroom, the situation in the high school field was quite different. Here it was largely a question of teaching a foreign language as such, not of according a special privilege to a huge segment of the population.

The first public high school of which we have any record was opened in Boston in 1821, but German does not seem to have been taught there until thirty years later. In the Free Academy in New York City, however, out of which later grew the College of the City of New York, German was found in the curriculum as early as 1838; in a Philadelphia high school, probably in 1839; in Hartford, Connecticut, in 1847, at the parents' expense. But the first strong impetus to the teaching of the language on the high-school level was given by the immigration of the political refugees from 1848 on. In 1849 Massilon, Ohio, introduced German in its high school, around 1850 Boston, then in 1853 Cincinnati (a three-year course optional with French), followed by Dorchester, Mass. (1854), Newburyport (1855), Lancaster, Ohio, and Cleveland (1856). In the sixties it could also be found in Newark, N. J., Toledo, Ohio, Terre Haute, St. Louis, New Haven, and Louisville.[41]

In 1850 there were thirty-six academies in New York State teaching German, as compared with 148 teaching French, but by 1870 German had all but caught up (140 to 147). In Baltimore, however, where German had been introduced in the public high school as early as the forties, 173 pupils were learning German in 1852, as against 52 in French and 39 in Spanish. And for twenty years from 1867 on German was the only modern foreign language taught in the Central High School of Philadelphia, according to Bagster-Collins (29). From 1860 to 1875 the high schools of the Middle West that we know of had more pupils in German than in French, the ratio being five to two (Bagster-Collins 30).

By the sixties the modern languages had won a recognized though modest place in the curriculum of the better American high schools and academies. The teaching, however, was greatly in need of improvement in more than half of the schools. One of its chief weaknesses was that it came too much under the influence of collegiate instruction. The texts used (e.g., those of Follen, Ollendorff, Otto, Ahn, and Whitney) and the works read (of Lessing, Goethe, and Schiller) were more suitable for use in college, and many indeed were edited by college professors. And the teachers were either trained by the same class of instructors, or they were ill prepared, often enlisted from other subjects to help out simply because they had studied German for two or three years at college. What Handschin said about this deficiency almost fifty years ago (56ff.) is still true today, at least in part.

Realizing these shortcomings, some of the leaders in the profession decided to organize the teachers of German both in the elementary and secondary schools, with a view to bringing about much needed improvements. And so in 1870 the *Nationaler Deutsch-Amerikanischer Lehrerbund* was organized in Louisville. Its organ, first called *Die amerikanische Schulzeitung* (1870), was replaced by *Erziehungsblätter für Schule und Haus* (1874), then by *Die pädagogischen Monatshefte* (1899), later by *Monatshefte für deutsche Sprache und Pädagogik* (1906), then *Monatshefte für deutschen Unterricht,* finally abbreviated to *Monatshefte* (now published by the Department of German of the University of Wisconsin). A teachers' seminary was established in Milwaukee which served as a model of its kind for several generations; it was finally merged with the aforementioned department of the University of Wisconsin.

We close this section with a brief reference to a few major developments in the field of university instruction and research. In 1870 Harvard launched its Graduate School modestly but auspiciously. The University of Michigan inaugurated seminar training (first in the field of history) in 1871, but it had been offering beginners' French since 1847 and began German (a course taking two-thirds of a year) in 1849. In a scientific course begun in 1852, a year of German was required. Michigan advertised a regular M.A. for residence work in 1858.[42]

Harvard granted its first doctorate of philosophy in 1873, Michigan its first in 1876, though neither was in German linguistics or literature.[43] But the most important step of all was the founding of the Johns Hopkins University at Baltimore in 1876. Here graduate work in the humanities as in other fields could be undertaken in earnest. Here, where German was called "the court language of the university," original research in Germanics found a home in the New World.

IV. An Era of Self-Examination: 1876–99

It seems to be axiomatic that when a profession has grown mature enough to organize, as the teachers of German did in 1870 with the establishment of the *Nationaler Deutsch-Amerikanischer Lehrerbund,* it soon begins to grow introspective. This is undoubtedly the tendency manifested, especially in the eighties and nineties, by the American teachers of the modern foreign languages and the teachers of German in particular. In the present case maturity also brought with it a higher degree of self-assertion. And so we find that estimable pioneer in the field of German studies, Professor E. S. Joynes, co-author of the much-used Joynes-Meisnest grammar and editor of the Holt edition of Schiller's *Maria Stuart,* pleading before the National Education Association in 1876 "that the modern languages be elevated from the merely tutorial position which they have so often occupied, to a rank and dignity in our higher institutions of learning commensurate with their disciplinary value, with their literary importance, and with their intimate relations to our own language, history and nation" (Handschin 40). The address of Professor Joynes was widely distributed and exercised a lasting influence. As a matter of fact, the tenor of his plea was already "in the air" before he had uttered it, for in 1875 Harvard had introduced its entrance requirement of French or German, destined soon to be widely copied. And seven years after Joynes's plea came an eloquent protest of Charles Francis Adams against the fetish of Greek in our schools.

The Modern Language Association of America was founded in December 1883, an important landmark not only in research in the literary and linguistic problems of this field, but also in the promotion of the study of the various foreign languages coming within its purview. As we shall see, the latter phase of the Association's interest, very strong during its earlier years, then dropped almost completely for a while, is now once more in the foreground.

Very soon after its establishment the Association commissioned two reports on "the present condition of instruction in modern languages in American colleges" (1884), one for the North, the other for the "late Confederate States." In the report for the North we read that the entrance requirement, if any, is too meager (only elementary grammar); the writers urge beginning the foreign language at an early age and state that in about one-half of the colleges canvassed the language is not begun until the sophomore or junior year. Over one-third of the colleges have no foreign language requirement at all, and German, the report goes on to say, is at a disadvantage compared to French. Finally, the so-called Latin-scientific or philosophy course is called preferable to the arts course because it leaves more opportunity for study of foreign language. The report on the southern states reveals conditions inferior to those in the North but lays the blame chiefly upon the dearth of preparatory schools (Handschin 41ff.).

The next report of some consequence was that of a commission appointed in 1886 by fifteen New England colleges, one purpose of which was to achieve more uniformity in entrance requirements. This report, so far as it dealt with French and German, established fairly uniform entrance requirements throughout the New England area. In some respects the report foreshadowed and anticipated the much more famous report of the Committee of Ten and that of the Committee of Twelve, both on high school language teaching, to be discussed next.

In 1893 the National Education Association Committee of Ten made sweeping recommendations through its subcommittee in the field of secondary school French and German. As Bagster-Collins (43) says, it wished "to determine the position of the modern languages in the course of study below the college level, and to a certain extent the college requirements for admission." Ideally it wanted modern language study begun in the elementary school and for this purpose it stipulated a course of four years there. Wherever this was impossible, the study of the language was recommended for the first year of high school. Still concerned with preserving the hegemony of Latin and Greek wherever they were firmly ensconced, the report advocated a two- or three-year course in a modern language for the classical (then often called "Latin-scientific") high-school course, four years of one modern language and three of another for the "modern language course," and four years of any foreign language (Latin included) for the "English course."

If extensive reading is an ideal which long prevailed, the report of the Committee of Ten was one of the first widespread manifestoes to advocate it formally. It places strong emphasis on reading and includes a recommendation in favor of sight reading, to be begun at the earliest opportunity. The stress was upon reading and more reading, even at the expense of thoroughness, if need be. The more difficult passages were to be glossed over or explained rapidly by the instructor. As for grammar, it was never to be an end in itself and was to be taken up only after a good beginning had been made with several months of reading. The use of the language on an oral basis in conversation, and the cultivation of a good pronunciation, while described as important and highly desirable, are not dwelt upon at length, and a correlation between them and the reading objective is hardly attempted. Not much is said, either, about the type of reading to be done, but suggestions are made concerning the amount to be covered. For the elementary course in German, that is, during the first two years, two hundred duodecimo pages are suggested (for the corresponding French course, twice as much!), while for the third and fourth years a total of at least seven hundred pages is recommended (in French correspondingly more, i.e., about one thousand pages). It is stated, however, that nineteenth-century prose is to be read before the study of the classics is begun.

Unfortunately the report had certain marked weaknesses. It provided no bridge by which the elementary-school pupil could cross the gap to the secondary school in continuing the study of German. Besides, the report was brief and sketchy and too hastily written. Worst of all, in order not to interfere unduly with the courses in Latin and Greek, it provided for the notorious two-year modern foreign language course, which has been the bane of foreign-language teachers ever since. As the number of subjects and courses offered in the American high school increased by leaps and bounds in the next few generations, soon mounting to well over four hundred, and with the expansion of the high school into areas never dreamed of in the nineteenth century, less and less room remained in the curriculum for so "academic" a subject as modern languages. Hence the schedule makers, overlooking the fact that the two-year course was only an expedient suggested for exceptional cases, in order not to interfere unduly with the vested interests of Latin and Greek, treated the two-year course as the norm, which it was never meant to be. The final step, then, was to discredit the teachers of the languages because they could not accomplish in two years what requires at least four (in England, France, Germany, and almost any other country six or more). This has brought about the unhappy situation that the United States is still almost the only civilized country in which men think they can lay claim to education and culture without any knowledge, or with the merest smattering, of a second language. It has also given the United States a place far behind Russia in this field.

An equally important, perhaps even more important, report was that of the Committee of Twelve appointed by the Modern Language Association in 1896 at the suggestion of the National Education Association. It was more comprehensive than that of the Committee of Ten, more lengthy, more maturely thought out, and more helpfully detailed, at least as far as the first two years of language study in high school are concerned. It did not appear until 1899.

The method of teaching advocated was the same as that proposed by the Committee of Ten: extensive reading (i.e., translation) of graded texts buttressed by the study of grammatical principles and accompanied by some small amount of oral drill. Much emphasis was placed upon the first two years of language study, followed by only a sketchy account of what should be done in the third and fourth years. Unfortunately this served only to fortify the erroneous notion outside the profession that two years of language study were to be regarded as the norm in the typical American secondary school. As for foreign-language study in the elementary school, the report stated that it should be optional and was worthwhile only if the child intended to continue it through the secondary school and if the teacher was really competent in the language.

This report, endorsed by the National Education Association, exercised a tremendous influence upon the teaching of the modern foreign languages in America. Its proposals were widely discussed and adopted, and even the less well prepared teachers did their best to modify their soul-deadening translation procedures in accordance with it. For it also proved to be, and was used as, a handbook of method. As Bagster-Collins says (46): "When it appeared there was little material readily accessible in this country dealing with the teaching of modern languages. In brief compass, the report contains well put statements of values, although many may think them in need of revision; and brief but admirable analyses of various language methods then employed, the grammar, natural, psychological, phonetic and reading methods.''

Most of the universities and colleges soon adopted the recommendations of the Committee, especially that of the establishment of three national grades of preparatory instruction, and in 1901, when the College Entrance Examination Board was set up, they were put into effect. But so far as the pernicious overemphasis of the two-year course and its gradual acceptance as the standard are concerned, this report was no better than its predecessor. Indeed, the effect of the two-year recommendation can be observed from the statistics. While in 1894 a canvass of eighty high schools throughout the land showed that one-third of them offered two years of modern language, another third three years, and another third four years (Handschin 55), by 1900 the average time devoted to German or French was less than three years (Bagster-Collins 31).

The founding of three professional journals, all important for the scholar in the field of German language and literature, also falls into this era. They are *Modern Language Notes,* established at the Johns Hopkins University in 1885 and still in existence, *Americana Germanica,* begun at the University of Pennsylvania in 1897 and now extinct, and *The Journal of English and Germanic Philology* (at first *Journal of Germanic Philology*) started in the same year at Indiana University but soon after transferred to the University of Illinois, and still in existence.

We turn once more to the elementary schools. The heyday of German in the public elementary schools of Toledo, Ohio, occurred between 1887 and 1891, when some schools were actually called German-English schools, with a supervising principal of the German Department. Of a total enrollment of 6373 pupils in 1882, twenty-seven percent were taking German. Proportionally the German enrollment declined in the last years of the nineteenth century, although as late as 1911 there were still 2029 pupils enrolled in German.[44]

We also find that in 1885 the New York City grade schools had over 9000 pupils studying German, while fewer than 2000 were learning French. As noted in Section III, at least a dozen larger cities from New York to San Francisco had German classes in their elementary grades, a practice which persisted as late as the nineties. And between 1886 and 1888 we hear complaints from the Dakotas, Minnesota, and Missouri that an articulate German population is instrumental in keeping German as the language of instruction in many schools (Handschin 67).

The budgetary burden of an entire staff of additional teachers of German, however, proved to be quite irksome to many a school board.

As early as 1879 St. Louis adopted the so-called German-English plan, which for better or for worse placed the German instruction in the hands of members of the regular staff. In this way $20,000 could be saved each year. But the plan was never entirely put into effect, and at a city election in 1887 a new policy was approved, providing "that no language but the English should be taught at public expense in the primary and district schools."[45] For identical reasons San Francisco began curtailing German instruction in its public grade schools in the eighties, so that by 1892 such instruction could be characterized by the superintendent in his report as one of the "educational hobbies" of bygone days (Bagster-Collins 24). Boston did not get around to experimenting with German and French in its elementary schools until 1895 but dropped them after two years. Neither a competent staff nor a workable policy had been provided, it seems.

However, German instruction in the public high schools, private academies, and denominational schools increased by leaps and bounds during those years. By 1886–87 over sixty per cent of such schools, as reported by Handschin (55), were offering either French or German, or both. During this period, too, German enjoyed a tremendous boom in many places. Between 1879 and 1895, for instance, the number of high schools and academies in New York State offering German rose from 162 to 537. During the same period the number of these schools introducing French increased only from 125 to 294 (Bagster-Collins 29). And in 1898, Handschin reports (79), German Catholic parochial schools numbered 130,000 pupils, while the corresponding Lutheran schools had 117,000.

Gradually, too, reading texts offering works of contemporary authors became more plentiful, giving teachers wider opportunity to select more modern materials. Many of these works were also better edited than those of earlier days. The editions of Wilhelm Bernhardt from about 1885 on furnish good examples. But prudishness still reigned in the classroom, and such contemporaneous works as the dramas and novels of the early Naturalists were unthinkable in the schoolroom, which no writer, old or recent, could enter unless he was as pure as the driven snow.[46] What is perhaps even worse, the usual reading fare gave no inkling of the Germany of that day, and offered mostly innocuous, romantic tales with little or no local color.

Turning briefly once more to the universities and colleges, and studying their foreign-language requirements for graduation, we find here too that considerable strides were made during this period. While in 1884 only a scattering of these institutions required any modern foreign language for an undergraduate degree (more German for the B.S. than for any other), by 1896 over one-half of the thirty-five institutions canvassed required at least one such language (Bagster-Collins 41, 70).[47]

In the previous section we noted that the Master's degree was offered in this country as early as the fifties. In 1879 Waterman T. Hewett received a Ph.D. from Cornell with a thesis on the Frisian language and literature.[48] It seems that the first woman to earn an American Ph.D. in German was Anne B. Irish in 1882 at what was then the University (now College) of Wooster in Ohio, but neither the subject of her thesis nor the name of the professor in charge is known. We do learn, however, that Miss Irish taught at Wooster from 1880 to 1886. Columbia College granted its first Ph.D. in German to Hugo J. Walther in 1886. Under the direction of H. H. Boyesen, who held the Gebhard professorship, he submitted a thesis on "The Syntax of the Cases in Walther von der Vogelweide."[49] The Johns Hopkins University awarded the Ph.D. degree in 1887 to Marion Dexter Learned for his study of Pennsylvania German (written, it seems, under the direction of Professor Henry Wood), in 1889, to George A. Hench for his study of the Monsee fragments, and in 1892, to Starr W. Cutting for "Der Conjunktiv bei Hartmann von Aue." New York University granted the doctorate to William J. Eckoff in 1891 for a thesis on the educational views of Goethe.

The first University of Chicago Ph.D. in Germanics was awarded to Francis A. Wood in 1895. Under Professors H. Schmidt-Wartenberg and Carl D. Buck he wrote on "Verner's Law in Gothic and the Reduplicating Verbs in Germanic" (almost simultaneously with Brugmann's noted article).[50]

At the present time the larger universities grant, on the average, two or more doctorates each year in Germanics, not enough to satisfy the demand without recourse to Europe. The University of Michigan, for instance, granted 47 between 1937 and 1960, under the chairmanship of Professor H. W. Nordmeyer.

V. From Riches to Rags: The First Decades of the Twentieth Century

In 1900 the languages, and particularly German, occupied a very favorable position in the high-school curriculum. We find that thirty-eight percent of the accredited high schools in California taught two years of German in that year, furthermore that by 1908 the percentage had risen to a phenomenal ninety-eight, with many schools having lengthened their optional German course to three or even four years.[51] In 1913 Handschin could report in this connection that about 72% of *all* high schools in California were teaching German.

As compared with French, German had a tremendous lead in many other states, too. In New York, as we saw in Section IV, there were 537 high schools and academies offering German in 1895, as against 294 that offered French.[52] In the Middle West, of forty schools canvassed, twenty-three offered German in 1900 compared with four for French. Until 1915 modern language enrollment held its own, with German, to be sure, still far in the lead. In that year over 40% of the *public and private* high schools throughout the country were offering French (11%), German (28%) and Spanish (2%). It was in the North Central and West Central areas (e.g., Wisconsin and Kansas) that German was the strongest. Undoubtedly the high schools, public and private, with their German offerings, constituted the backbone of German instruction in the United States during the first fifteen years of the new century. But the competition of the new commercial and social subjects, first introduced in the late nineteenth century and steadily growing, was making itself felt more and more.

The situation in the universities and colleges during this period was less favorable. Yet in 1910, of 340 such institutions, 101 required French or German or both anywhere from one to four years, for entrance. Two-thirds of the 340 required some French or German for graduation, and where no requirement prevailed, the choice of the languages was on an elective basis. Again, of the 340 institutions, all but three taught German, and of these 337 all but four offered more than a single year of it (Handschin 50).

However, statistics like these give us a somewhat *too* rosy picture of the real situation. Even during the first half of the second decade of the twentieth century signs could be detected that the position of the modern foreign languages in the universities and colleges of the land was not as secure as might be thought. A study undertaken by Harry C. McKown in 1924 shows that as early as 1913, in 306 institutions considered, 62, or eleven percent of the total degrees (552), required no foreign language for entrance, and that this percentage increased markedly in the course of the next few years.[53] And as for the foreign-language requirements for the B.A. degree in thirty-five representative universities and colleges in 1916, one required Greek and Latin plus one modern language; two, Latin and two other languages; two, Latin and one other language; four, two foreign languages, thirteen, one foreign language; three, no foreign language at all. Taking into account the opportunity of using Greek as the second language in all these possible options, we find that in twenty-two of these institutions one could "get by" without any modern foreign language at all. And in practically all of them—twenty-nine to be specific—only one or two years in the language was required (Bagster-Collins 70f.).

It is clear, then, that most of the instruction given on the university and college level in the languages, including German, was of an elementary nature even as early as 1916. In some universities, however, such as Wisconsin and Columbia, it was booming on all levels. Many names of outstanding American Germanists during the first decades of the century come to mind: Francke, von Jagemann, and Bierwirth at Harvard; Gruener and Palmer at Yale; von Klenze at Brown; Thomas at Columbia; Faust at Cornell; Priest and Thayer at Princeton; Learned and Shumway at Pennsylvania; Henry Wood, Collitz, and Kurrelmeyer at Johns Hopkins; Hatfield and Curme at Northwestern; Hohlfeld, Voss, and Roedder at Wisconsin; Boucke at Michigan; Goebel and Lessing at Illinois; Cutting, F. A. Wood, and Schütze at Chicago; and the itinerant Prokosch, who left the imprint of his personality on a number of schools.

As for the teaching of German in the elementary schools, it continued unabated in Cincinnati and Milwaukee. Bagster-Collins describes the course given in the latter city in 1911 (22):

> In Milwaukee it was practically identical [in 1911], except as to the textbooks used, with the outline of study published for the year 1892. There were two courses, one chiefly for children whose parents spoke German, the other for children of non-German-speaking parents. The general plan pursued was the same for both courses, the chief difference being in the amount of ground covered. Doubtless also greater use was made of English in those classes containing children from English-speaking homes. The center of instruction was the reader, comprising a "Fibel," and later four graded readers. The selections were taught by the question and answer method and afterward reproduced orally or in writing. Oral work and the vocabulary were also developed, in the earlier stages at least, by means of object and pictures. Some of the selections were assigned for cursory reading. Special attention was given to exercises and dictation and memory work. Beginning with the third grade, supplementary material either read by the teacher or by the pupils was included in the work.

In smaller German communities too, like Westphalia, Missouri, the teaching of the language was still predominant about 1900, as W. A. Willibrand has shown.[54]

A survey of the Buffalo schools, on the other hand, undertaken in 1914–15, shows less favorable results. There the German instruction in the elementary schools was poorly administered and badly given. It consisted mainly of reading a given pensum, without regard to control or teaching of vocabulary. Drill in pronunciation and speaking were haphazard, and a syllabus nonexistent. After six years of this type of hit-or-miss instruction, the children took a uniform examination covering as much as might be achieved in an ordinary one-year high-school course. In 1912–13 about seven percent (740) of the 10,000 enrolled in German took this test, and fewer than 400 took an examination for advanced credit. As the report points out: "Measured by these results, nearly ten thousand pupils are taught by 67 teachers in 43 schools in order that approximately 400 may get what they would have been able to obtain under two or three teachers in one year of the high school course."[55]

It is no libel of modern foreign-language teachers to state that as a group they are conservative in their attitude toward innovations. Since this is so, it is not surprising that the average textbooks used during the first decade of the century still followed the pattern of the old grammar-translation method. One of the most popular, no doubt, was *Essentials of German* by B. J. Vos, first of the Johns Hopkins University, later of Indiana. It originally appeared in 1903 and during the next three decades went through numerous large revised editions. Perhaps the best touchstone for measuring the conservatism of this carefully executed and highly successful book is the fact that it postpones the treatment of the modal auxiliaries, indispensable for the mechanics of everyday speech, to one of the last lessons, normally not reached until the end of a full year.

This does not mean, however, that experiments and progress in the field of teaching the languages were not made. Although such experiments were begun as early as the sixties of the nineteenth century, through the introduction by Heness, a German, and Sauveur, a Belgian, of the so-called Natural Method at several points in New England, and then developed as an inchoate Direct Method by Gouin in the eighties, they did not reveal their full influence on a large scale until the advent of the twentieth century.[56] These methods require a native teacher with great energy, enthusiasm, and skill, almost exclusive use of the foreign language by teacher and pupil, much repetition, and an approach to the written word not by means of grammar but through oral-aural means. The method had many opponents from the start; they claimed that it is too time-consuming, that it encourages glibness rather than depth, and treats adolescent and adult as though they were children.

In spite of the drawbacks of the system, it left its mark upon modern-language teaching in the United States once it had been developed into the Direct Method. Insofar as they stress the spoken word and the oral-aural approach and represent a reaction to the grammar-translation method of the Ollendorff-Otto type of instruction, the Natural and the Direct Method are similar. But the latter is less radical. It exploits the methodology of its predecessors eclectically, does not throw grammar overboard yet never teaches it for its own sake, and follows a well constructed plan of presentation. One of the better textbooks exemplifying the Direct Method is the beginners' book by Max Walter (of the *Musterschule* in Frankfurt, Germany) and Carl A. Krause.[57] But wherever the method was used in high schools, colleges, and universities (e.g., Cornell, Minnesota), it was colored by the personality of those who taught it with varying degrees of success. Bagster-Collins makes the following general remarks about it (90): "Even if reading the foreign language is held to be the legitimate aim of teaching, the need was felt by progressive teachers for a more active control of the vocabulary and grammar than could ever be won through the mere learning of rules, paradigms and translation. The

Direct method suggested that this could be accomplished by developing language material, usually a connected passage, by means of questions and answers. This procedure had long been utilized in the elementary schools, but now began to grow important in high school classes.''

This, then, was the situation as regards the teaching of German in the spring of 1917. In spite of the lukewarm and in some cases cold attitude toward the language on the part of many school administrators, and the several weak spots and danger points that have been signalized above, German was flourishing in the public and private high schools in many parts of the country, and holding its own in the elementary schools of cities where it was firmly entrenched. The war in Europe which had been raging for over two and one-half years had had some repercussions upon German instruction, to be sure, but not of an alarming nature.

But in the spring of that year, when the United States declared war upon Germany, all hell broke loose. The propaganda, which had concentrated upon the German emperor, his army and submarines, with many allegations of atrocities, turned immediately, now that we were at war, against the language, its literature as a whole, and in some cases even against its teachers, who were confronted with the sweeping accusation of being "pro-German." Groups of vigilantes visited the libraries and removed German books; others came to the departmental offices in the universities and confiscated textbooks containing pictures of Emperor William II or equally "subversive" material. The readers of Paul Bacon, for instance, who perhaps had gone too far in "selling" Germany to us, were the objects of special vigilance and drastic condemnation.

State legislatures (twenty-two in number, according to *Language Development in Action,* University of Massachusetts, 1960) and a score of cities vied with one another in forbidding the teaching of German in the public elementary and high schools, or even in prohibiting the speaking of German when more than a given number of persons were present in the gathering. Other bodies politic campaigned against it. Laws were passed, over the protest of the Commissioner of Education, of which no tyrant ancient or medieval had ever dreamed. All of these laws were later held to be unconstitutional. The attorney who argued the case before the United States Supreme Court said: "There can be no liberty in a state where its laws make it a crime for a citizen of the United States to teach or to be taught a foreign language." This argument prevailed before the High Court.

In some cases the pent-up hatred against German emigrants and the feeling that they had pushed too hard in Germanizing the schools in numerous cities as described above, along with the fact that German had enjoyed too sheltered a place in the curriculum, may account for part of this mania. An effective propaganda against Germany which had been going on in the newspapers and magazines for three years can also be cited as a reason, as well as the fear that Americans of German background were in a conspiracy with the enemy. But the best explanation for such madness is undoubtedly the youthful buoyancy and cocksureness of a nation which had not yet become mature. Few were sober enough to stop to think that German is no more the exclusive property of Germany than English is of the United States. In short, it was an ugly period in the history of an America which had become known for its tolerance.

As a result of this hysteria the study of German was either propagandized or actually legislated out of existence. All this came suddenly, like a revolution, and necessitated lightning-like adjustments on the part of school administrators. German, still enjoying riches in 1916–17, was speedily reduced to rags.

A few statistics must suffice to underscore the cataclysm. Between 1917 and 1919 the teaching of German became practically nonexistent in the public and private high schools, 315,884 (28%) of whose students had still been studying it in 1915. By 1922, four years after the end of the war, the high schools had less than 14,000 students of German, or little more than one-half of one percent of the high-school enrollment of 2,500,000. This compares with about 387,000 (15.5%) in French and 250,000 (10%) in Spanish. In 1925 only five high schools in the state of Ohio were offering German.

It should be noted by teachers of all modern foreign languages that although French and Spanish, as well as other languages, profited to a degree by the decline of German, the standing of the languages as a whole suffered markedly thereby. To bring this out drastically, we shall anticipate by looking at registration figures over the next thirty years. During this period proportionate modern foreign language enrollment dropped steadily. By 1949, when the high-school population had risen (from 2,500,000 in 1922) to 5,400,000, French attracted only 4.7 percent of the total enrollment and Spanish 8.2 percent, with German trailing at 0.8 percent. In 1915 German alone had about twenty-eight percent of the total high-school enrollment in its classes (the highest percentage ever achieved in the United States by a modern foreign language), but in 1949 all three languages together could muster only fourteen percent. To be sure, this is partly due to the growing popularity of commercial and social studies, to the host of other more "modern" subjects, and to the hordes of new pupils with vastly different interests and equipment. For we must admit that in comparing the American high school of 1915 with that of 1949 we are comparing two quite different institutions.[58]

But these factors, important as they are, hardly contain the full explanation for so tremendous a loss *in so short a period*. I am convinced that, through the peremptory obliteration of German, all language study suffered. Not even the language needs of the Second World War and the jet age, which have shrunk the earth to ever smaller proportions, not even the F(oreign) L(anguage) and the FLE(lementary) S(chool) Programs of the Modern Language Association of America, not even the far greater emphasis placed on languages by the competitive new and formidable world power which a menacing Russia represents, have up to now fully restored the study of languages to their rightful place in the curriculum, especially in the secondary schools. It is to be hoped that the language teachers will take this lesson to heart and never lose sight of the fact that they are first and foremost teachers of the modern foreign languages, and not of French, German, Italian, Russian, Spanish, or any other single language or group of them.

Notes

This is an abbreviated reprint of the author's monograph "The Teaching of German in the United States from Colonial Times to the Present," which originally appeared in *Reports of Surveys and Studies in the Teaching of Modern Foreign Languages* published by the Modern Language Association of America in November 1961. It was based upon research performed pursuant to a contract with the United States Office of Education, Department of Health, Education, and Welfare. It was republished in the *German Quarterly* 37 (1964): 315–92. The first four sections and most of the fifth, constituting the major portion of the monograph, are reprinted here with the permission of the Modern Language Association. The present version was adopted and edited for this volume by David P. Benseler, Ohio State University.

1 Handschin, *The Teaching of the Modern Languages in the United States,* U. S. Bureau of Education Bulletin No. 3 (1913); E. W. Bagster-Collins, "History of Modern Language Teaching in the United States," *Studies in Modern Language Teaching, Reports Prepared for the Modern Foreign Language Study and the Canadian Committee on Modern Languages,* Publications of the American and Canadian Committees on Modern Languages 17 (New York: Macmillan, 1930). Bagster-Collins' "History" is a 90-page treatise published as the first study in a volume with fourteen authors. The general editor of the series and *spiritus rector* was Robert Herndon Fife.

2 Louis Viereck, "German Instruction in American Schools," *U. S. Bureau of Education: Report of the Commissioner of Education for the Year 1900–01:* 531–708 (with a bibliography; 532–38); the same in German: *Zwei Jahrhunderte deutschen Unterrichts in den Vereinigten Staaten* (Braunschweig, 1903).

3 John A. Walz, *German Influence in American Education and Culture* (Philadelphia: Carl Schurz Memorial Foundation, 1936). This is a revision of a paper read at a Round Table on American-German Relations held in connection with the Institute of Public Affairs at the University of Virginia, July 1935.

4 Robert F. Seybolt, "Source Studies in American Colonial Education, The Private School," *University of Illinois Bulletin* 28 (1925).

5 Robert F. Seybolt, *Private Schools of Colonial Boston* (Cambridge, MA, 1935).

6 C. E. Castañeda, "Modern Language Instruction in American Colleges, 1770–1800," *Catholic Educational Review* (Jan. & Feb. 1925); also published as a pamphlet (Washington, 1925): 22 pp.

7 Like Viereck, Handschin gives extensive bibliographies.

8 M. Clarissa Riebenthaler, "Trends in the Teaching of German in the Secondary Schools of the United States" (1941). *Language Development in Action*, ed. S.C. Goding (U. of Mass., 1960) is a report on current foreign language developments.

9 George Ticknor, *Life, Letters and Journals* (Boston, 1876) 1: 11ff.

10 See particularly his article "German Thought and Literature in New England, 1620–1820, A Preliminary Survey," *Journal of English and Germanic Philology* 41 (1942): 1–45.

11 *Educational Review* 26 (1903): 194ff.

12 Martin G. Brumbaugh, *The Life and Works of Christopher Dock, America's Pioneer Writer on Education, with a Translation of his Works into the English Language* (Philadelphia & London, 1908).

13 *Education in the United States* (New York, 1890) 56.

14 *Americana Germanica* 2. 2: 73.

15 Seybolt, *Journal of English and Germanic Philology* 23 (1924): 418–21. Abbreviated below as Seybolt, *JEGP*. Also noted in Bagster-Collins 9.

16 Seybolt, *Source Studies* 10. Also quoted in Bagster-Collins 8.

17 The second edition, dated London 1752, is listed in the new *General Catalogue of Printed Books* of the British Museum 8 (1934) col. 720. See also C. R. Hildeburn, *A Century of Printing: The Issues of the Press in Pennsylvania, 1685–1784* (Philadelphia, 1886) 2: 33.

18 The edition of 1788 bears the title *A German Grammar containing the theory of the language through all parts of speech*. It contains only the first part of the earlier editions (100 pages as compared with over 300).

19 Seybolt, *JEGP* 23 (1924): 420–21. See also Bagster-Collins 10.

20 *History and Geography of North America* 4: 203.

21 Viereck 542. This would give Pennsylvania 120,000 Germans in 1748.

22 See Thomas H. Montgomery, *A History of the University of Pennsylvania, 1749–1770* (Philadelphia, 1900) 175ff.; see also *Pennsylvania University Biographical Catalogue, 1747–1893* (Philadelphia, 1894).

23 "Notes on the History of Foreign Influence on Education," *Report of Commissioner of Education for 1898* 1: 604. Quoted in Viereck 543. On Franklin and Germany, see the University of Pennsylvania dissertation by B. M. Victory (*Americana-Germanica* 21, 1915); see also D. V. Hegeman in *German Quarterly* 26 (1953): 187f.

24 See Note 6 above. The teacher was Carlo Bellini, who taught French, Italian, Spanish, and possibly German.

25 W. C. Reichel, *Historical Sketch of Nazareth Hall* (Bethlehem, 1876) 11. Quoted in Bagster-Collins 13.

26 The first subject was: "How can the preservation and extension of German in Pennsylvania be best effected?" See Viereck 545.

27 Marshall College of Mercersburg had been merged with Franklin College in 1850. Viereck quotes from Pepper's address on 545ff.

28 *History of The University of North Carolina* (Raleigh, 1907) 115. See Bagster-Collins 54ff. Richards, a Londoner, came to America as a sailor, skipped ship, was an actor for a while, and then became a tutor.

29 A rich mine of information on Follen is George W. Spindler's *The Life of Karl Follen, A Study in German-American Cultural Relations*, Historical Monograph publ. under the auspices of the German-American Hist. Soc. of Ill. 1 (Chicago, 1917).

30 Bagster-Collins 50. The often bitter contest between the ancient and the modern languages continued through three-fourths of the nineteenth century. Ticknor delighted in breaking

a lance for the modern tongues (e.g., in his *Remarks,* 1825, and in his *Lecture on the Best Methods of Teaching the Living Languages,* Boston, 1833). Yale usually supported the classics, while Harvard was a bit more friendly toward the modern languages, as were the younger universities such as Michigan and Cornell. Bold advocacy of French and German by F. A. P. Barnard in 1866 was also a strong factor in their favor.

31 *Harvard Reminiscences* (Boston, 1888) 117.

32 Spindler 100. See also the reviews of Follen's reader in Spindler's monograph.

33 Handschin (37) quotes from the report of a Princeton alumnus (class of 1853) on the failure of the university to provide adequate training in the modern foreign languages as late as the middle of the nineteenth century. However, it is noteworthy that the famous classical philologist Basil L. Gildersleeve laid the groundwork for his excellent knowledge of German at Princeton as early as 1847.

34 The last two paragraphs are based chiefly on Handschin and Bagster-Collins.

35 The Pennsylvania school of law 1837, a direct outgrowth of the Stowe report, placed German public schools on a par with English schools and established some purely German schools. In Ohio the State Legislature passed an Act in 1840 requiring all Boards of Education to introduce German when demanded by seventy-five "freeholders" representing forty or more pupils. I have written a more detailed account of German teaching in Cincinnati for the Ohio Historical Society (20. 1: 29ff.). Much early material on the subject is to be found in John B. Shotwell, *A History of the Schools of Cincinnati* (Cincinnati, 1902) esp. 289–310.

36 I recall meeting Cincinnatians who were not of German extraction—Irish and Negroes among them—but who had learned German in school and could converse in it.

37 St. Louis introduced German in its elementary schools in 1864, Chicago in 1865, Cleveland before 1870, Baltimore in 1874. Others are noted in Handschin 72ff; see especially his chronology on pp. 73f.

38 *Cincinnati Public Schools, 85th Annual Report* (1914): 68.

39 Published as a pamphlet.

40 It is estimated that between 1820 and 1910 about six million Germans immigrated to the United States.

41 See Handschin's table 54; see also Bagster-Collins 28ff.

42 See *The University of Michigan—an Encyclopedic Survey,* Part 3: "The Department of Germanic Languages and Literatures" by Norman L. Willey, and a typed manuscript of 31pp. by Willey in the files of the Michigan German Dept.

43 On this subject see the last paragraphs in Section IV.

44 Statistics kindly furnished by Dr. Richard Pheatt, Director of General Research, Toledo Board of Education.

45 *Annual Report of the President and Board of Directors of the St. Louis Public Schools* (1881): 10. See Bagster-Collins 19.

46 Even Walther von der Vogelweide had to "come clean," which explains why his most famous and delightful poem, "Under der linden," is omitted from Calvin Thomas' *Anthology,* published in 1906.

47 See the two reports of 1884 to the Modern Language Association discussed at the beginning of the present section.

48 Ralph P. Rosenberg, "American Doctoral Studies in Germanic Culture," *Yearbook of Comparative and General Literature* 4 (1955): 30–44. Hewett taught at Cornell for many years.

49 For Miss Irish and Walther, see Rosenberg in *Germanic Review* 29 (1954): 224–29, and in *American German Review* 21.3: 34 and 23.5: 35.

50 The information on Learned was kindly supplied by Prof. Harold Jantz of Johns Hopkins, that on the Univ. of Chicago by Prof. G. J. Metcalf of that institution. Prof. R.-M. S.

Heffner reports that the first M.A. in German was granted by Wisconsin "in 1893–94," and the first Ph.D. earned by C. H. Handschin in 1902 with a German dissertation (under Prof. Ernst Voss) on the proverbs of Hans Sachs.

51 Handschin 56. Over one-third of the high schools of that state had a three-year course by 1908.

52 In 1890, 10.5% of all *public* high schools in the U.S. studied German (5.8% French); in 1900, 14.3% (7.8% French); in 1910, about 24% (10% French).

53 *The Trend of College Entrance Requirements, 1913–1922*. Bureau of Education Bulletin 35 (1924). Quoted by Bagster-Collins 40.

54 *German Quarterly,* 30 (1957): 254ff.

55 *Examination of the Public School System of the City of Buffalo* (Albany, 1916) 105ff. Quoted by Bagster-Collins 21.

56 Reference should also be made to Maximilian Delphinus Berlitz (1852–1921), a watchmaker from Breslau, Germany, the founder of the worldwide Berlitz Schools, which use a special type of "natural" method. These schools still thrive. In 1953 they attracted 25,000 learners in the United States: 37% in Spanish, 26% in French, and 8% in German. They are said to gross $8,000,000 a year now (1961).

57 The method, as successfully used in Frankfurt in English classes and applied in this country for German, is described by Walter in *Englisch nach dem Frankfurter Lehrplan* (Marburg, 1900). On a visit to America he converted Krause to his method.

58 On this subject see James Bryant Conant, *The Revolutionary Transformation of the American High School* (Cambridge, 1959); also the same author's *The American High School Today* (New York, 1959).

Methods of Teaching German in the United States: A Historical Perspective

RENATE A. SCHULZ
University of Arizona

> Auf keinem Gebiete des Unterrichts hat sich eine so große Zahl von Methoden entwickelt als auf dem des Sprachunterrichts; Methoden für Kinder und für Erwachsene—für Einzel- und Klassenunterricht—für die Muttersprache und für die fremde, für alte und moderne, für Selbstunterricht und für die Unterweisung anderer—Sprechmethoden, Lesemethoden, Übersetzungs- und grammatikalische—synthetische und analytische—rezeptive und produktive—mit einem Wort, die Wahl derselben ist Legion. Sie alle zu charakterisieren, eine geschichtliche Entwicklung derselben zu geben, würde Material genug bieten, um ein dickes Buch zu füllen.[1]

The above statement could come from any recent professional publication. It dates, however, back to 1899. To my knowledge, no other discipline has undergone as much methodological upheaval as foreign/second language teaching. Kelly's *25 Centuries of Language Teaching,* which purports to be "an inquiry into the science, art, and development of language teaching methodology" from 500 B.C. to 1969, lists 1,397 published sources dealing with methodological questions.[2] And the search for a "best method" continues.[3]

Several studies have attempted to chronicle German teaching in the United States,[4] yet I find only two publications that focus on German language teaching methodologies in particular: a 1977 dissertation by Janet E. Hildebrand and a 1982 survey article by Richard Helt and David J. Woloshin.[5] The history of methodology for teaching German as a foreign or second language is, of course, closely intertwined with the history of foreign language teaching methodologies in general. While no statistics document the extent to which German teachers in the United States accepted methodological innovations, the publications cited indicate at least an awareness of methodological developments.[6]

Some current textbooks on foreign language teaching methods lead one to believe that before World War II the only methodology used in the United States was Grammar-Translation. Hildebrand emphatically disproves this assumption in her chronicle of college German teaching from 1753–1903.[7] While the Grammar-Translation Method dominated—at least in college German instruction—until well into this century, a number of methodological debates started to have a slow but definite impact on teachers, texts, and the foreign language curriculum in general long before 1900.

Latin and Greek were the mainstays of foreign language instruction during the seventeenth and eighteenth centuries. Modern foreign languages were thought to be "unacademic frills," clearly inferior to the classical languages. In the first half of the eighteenth century Benjamin Franklin questioned the sequence of foreign language study which led students from the classical (dead) languages to the modern ones, stating as translated by Grebner (1906): "Ich glaube daher, daß etwas faul ist in unserer Methode des Fremdsprachen-Unterrichts, in dem wir mit Latein anfangen, um auf seiner Grundlage später die ihm entstammten modernen Sprachen desto leichter erlernen zu können. Das Resultat ist aber in den meisten Fällen ein total negatives: Wir lernen nichts."[8] The belief in the superiority of Latin over the teaching of modern languages lasted, however, well into the twentieth century.

The earliest record of German instruction goes back to 1702, when Franz Daniel Pastorius, a member of the Pietist circle in Frankfurt, started the first German school in Germantown, Pennsylvania, only nineteen years after the first Germans (thirteen Mennonite families from Krefeld) had landed on American soil. The Public Academy and College (later to become the University of Pennsylvania), founded in Philadelphia in 1749 through the efforts of Benjamin Franklin and the American Philosophical Society, was the first American post-secondary institution to offer German as a subject for study.[9] But as with its classical counterparts, the goal and method of German instruction at that time focused on translation rather than face-to-face communication.

Faculty psychology offered a theoretical foundation for the Grammar-Translation Method and supported the study of foreign languages for the purpose of developing mental discipline. The brain was believed to consist of higher and lower learning centers or faculties. These faculties, like muscles of the body, could be developed through practice and exercise and the benefits derived in terms of mental discipline, memorization, and logical reasoning ability would be transferred to other learning tasks.

Initially, the classical languages (particularly their grammar) and algebra and geometry were believed to be the subjects *par excellence* for teaching mental discipline. As late as 1893 foreign language educators found it necessary to justify the use of modern languages for that purpose. Babbitt, for instance, declared that "a certain amount of work properly done by a certain faculty of the mind will give about the same increase of strength and readiness, whether the work be done in ancient or modern languages."[10]

In 1933 Pressey concludes, however, from reviewing a number of psychological studies dealing with the transfer of training theory: "As regards the modern foreign languages the situation seems fairly clear. As they are taught at present, such [transfer of training] values are too slight to give these languages any education vindication; they must find their justification in their own intrinsic worth."[11]

In essence, the "classic" Grammar-Translation Method consisted of memorizing vocabulary lists and grammatical rules (including, of course, their exceptions), and applying those rules to translate German literary works into English. Exercises demanded interlinear translation—often word by word.

The Ollendorff Method (dating to 1846) is a good example of the Grammar-Translation Method, although it was perceived as modern and revolutionary in the mid-nineteenth century because it differed from earlier approaches in that language examples "are not derived from the German Classics; they are neither the ideal language of Poetry, nor the rigorous language of Science, but of *life,*—short sentences, such as one would be most likely to use in conversing in a circle of friends, or in writing a letter."[12]

Ollendorff also paid lip service to the principles of inductive learning, though grammar rules were still prevalent. The method's major goal was the development of reading fluency. The editor writes that the Ollendorff book "possesses every desirable condition of a complete introduction to the reading of the German" and adds with admirable (or despicable?) ethnocentric arrogance: "May it contribute to the spread of study of a language, which in richness and flexibility is the acknowledged superior of all its modern sisters—which in creations of Art and in works of Science yields precedence to none . . ." (viii).

The Ollendorff text is essentially a grammar with exercises and an introduction to pronunciation which claims optimistically that reading, i.e., sound–symbol correspondence, may be acquired in one lesson. The exercises consist exclusively of translation of predominantly disconnected sentences which illustrate a grammatical principle. The 510 pages of the book are filled with such apparently "authentic conversational" utterances as "Have you my bad hat? . . . Have you the bad salt? . . . Have you my ugly paper? (8) . . . I have the golden candlestick of my good baker (11). . . . Which hay has the foreigner? (19) . . . The good education which is given to children is the crown of monarchs (245)".

A description of a 1904 German high school class indicates that even the traditional form of the Grammar-Translation Method (deciphering the writings of great authors) was still being practiced.

After the student had read perhaps ten lines of the German text with no expression, and small regard for natural pauses, he was stopped and asked to translate. After the translation, which was kept as close to the original as possible, the instructor asked questions on syntax, derivation, and other grammatical points. . . . Then perhaps, after the section had been picked to pieces, the teacher would remark that that was one of the most admired parts of Schiller.[13]

In 1903 Altschul classifies the disadvantages of the Grammatical Method as follows:

Erstens: Die strenge Verstandestätigkeit, die sie vom Schüler beständig verlangt, ist ungebührlich anstrengend. Zweitens: Die abstrakte Grammatik ist trocken und für die meisten Schüler interesselos. Drittens: Da, soweit wie möglich, keine andern Sprachformen verwendet werden als solche, die der Schüler grammatisch zu beherrschen gelernt hat, so ist der Lesestoff an einen beschränkten Wortschatz gebunden und besteht meistens aus isolierten Sätzen, die, selbst wenn sie nicht von dem Hund des Bruders, des Spaniers und dem Tintenfaß der Tante, des Gärtners handeln, doch ohne wirklichen Inhalt und ohne alles Interesse sind. Viertens: Der dem Schüler in abstrakter Form gebotene grammatische Stoff wird von ihm oft nur äußerlich angeeignet, geht ihm nicht in Fleisch und Blut über und ist daher eine nur sehr ungenügende Hülfe zum wirklichen Erfassen und Beherrschen der fremden Sprache.[14]

Hepp attributes the "discovery" of the so-called Natural Method to Gottlieb Heness.[15] But as early as 1804 Dufief, building on theories and practices in European language teaching, had published a Spanish textbook which emphasized a "natural method" and advocated that foreign language learning did not necessitate the formal study of grammar.[16] Ticknor referred to a "natural method" in 1832 and recommended that "Persons. . . . who have the opportunity, should learn the living language they wish to possess, as it is learnt by those to whom it is native."[17]

Hepp describes the genesis of the Natural Method in United States German teaching as follows:

Im Jahre 1865, während Heness einem Freunde die Vorteile des Anschauungsunterrichts auseinandersetzte, wie er in Süddeutschland angewendet wurde, um den Kindern zu helfen, ihren Dialekt zu verlieren und ihre Sprachweise zu verbessern, kam ihm der Gedanke, daß dieses Hilfsmittel auch angewendet werden könne, um die deutsche oder andere neuere Sprachen zu lehren. Ein halbes Jahr darauf verpflichtete er sich, die Söhne von mehreren Professoren von der Yale University so zu lehren, daß sie nach Ablauf eines Schuljahres von 48 Wochen mit 4-stündlichem, täglichem Unterricht an 5 Tagen der Woche, fließend deutsch sprechen würden. Darin hatte er solchen Erfolg, daß er eine Schule gründete, den Dr. L. Sauveur in seine Methode einweihte und ihn dann als Assistenten für die französische Sprache anstellte. Durch die Publikationen des Dr. Sauveur und anderer Lehrer, sowie durch zahlreiche Privat- und Sommerschulen ist dann diese Methode überall bekannt geworden.[18]

While a number of somewhat different "natural methods" have been proposed here and abroad, their common denominator appears to be "die Sprache so zu lehren, daß der Schüler gewissermaßen unbewußt die fremde Sprache lernen soll, wie das Kind seine eigene Muttersprache lernt."[19] According to Heness, the use of spontaneous, contextually connected questions and frequent use of realia and pictures to teach the meaning of vocabulary are the main techniques. Further, like modern proponents of the Natural Approach, he insists on the exclusive use of German in the classroom:

> One principle, however, must guide him [the teacher] throughout the course—he must never speak English. . . . He must withstand every temptation of exhibiting his erudition in grammar, philology, literature, etc., before his pupils are prepared to understand what he says in German.
> . . . My experience teaches me that by book we never can learn to speak. Speech, like music, is acquired by ear. . . . Therefore let us put aside the book, and use it only to read. In the natural order, reading and writing come after speaking, grammar and dictionary after reading and writing. . . . Grammar serves to correct mistakes, and the dictionary only assists in the recovery of words which cannot be recalled without it.[20]

Altschul, attempting to distinguish between the Grammar Method (also called formal, abstract, or analytical method) and the Natural Method (also called direct, imitative, concrete, or synthetic method) finds that the terms "abstract" (requiring rules and paradigms to be analyzed) and "concrete" (leading to subconscious acquisition without theoretical explanation) best express their differences.[21]

In 1869, about the same time that Heness and Sauveur advocated the Natural Method, Claude Marcel described his "rational method."[22] He spoke against using translation in foreign language teaching and advocated a skills sequence from "the skills of impression" (i.e., the receptive skills: reading and listening comprehension) to the "skills of expression" (i.e., the productive skills: speaking and writing). Communication without translation became the goal of instruction. Amazingly modern in his thinking, and predating psycholinguists such as Asher, Krashen, Postovsky, and Winitz by more than a century, he believed that development of the receptive skills led to language acquisition and emphasized a focus on meaning rather than form in language practice.[23] We have no indication, however, that Marcel's insights found large-scale acceptance in the teaching of German (or any other foreign language) at that time.

Other methodological experimentation of the time with a focus on German advocated an "Etymological Method"[24] and a "Mastery Approach" which limited vocabulary to two or three hundred words practiced in unending sentence recombinations.[25] According to Altschul, the "Meisterschafts-System" required from the learner "das Auswendiglernen einer großen Zahl von Sätzen, die er so beherrschen soll, daß, wenn einer der gelernten Sätze ihm in seiner Muttersprache gegeben wird, er augenblicklich den entsprechenden Satz der fremden Sprache vollkommen korrekt von sich geben kann." Altschul assures us that "Das Verfahren ist nicht so unsinning, wie es auf den ersten Blick scheinen könnte; empfehlen möchte ich es allerdings niemand."[26]

It appears that, initially, new methodologies focusing on development of the oral skills had a greater impact on foreign language instruction in the schools than in colleges. Levy gives us a clue as to why—in those dignified times (1878)—the Natural Method was not readily accepted by the professoriat:

> I have it from a very trustworthy authority that in some New England town a teacher of the "Natural Method" gambols around the room to express the idea *to run*. If this be the general case, school committees will no longer be called upon to deliver certificates of proficiency to teachers of Languages: this duty will devolve on P. T. Barnum.[27]

Still in 1909, in justification of the translation method on the college level, Bagster-Collins differentiates between methods and goals appropriate for secondary and post-secondary German instruction:

> Auf der Universität . . . wird man wenig Zeit für Sprechübungen finden. Dort muß der Lehrer sich mit dem Übersetzungsverfahren begnügen. In der Sekundärschule dagegen, wo der Kursus 3 oder 4 Jahre dauert, sollte man den mündlichen Gebrauch der Sprache als einen der grundlegenden Bestandteile der neusprachlichen Methodik betrachten.

Sounding amazingly modern he adds:

> Es ist meine Meinung, daß wir einen großen pädagogischen Fehler machen, wenn wir die ganze Grammatik in einem Schuljahre zu lehren versuchen. Die deutsche Grammatik ist ungemein schwer, sie ist viel zu reich an Formen, als daß die Schüler sie in einem Jahre bewältigen können. Sie brauchen viel mehr Zeit dazu und reichhaltige sowie mannigfaltige Übungen. Bei den jetzt herrschenden Zuständen lernen unsere Schüler nichts Gründliches. Es ist und bleibt nur verworrenes Zeug, was sie im Kopfe haben.[28]

In 1882 the anonymously published pamphlet entitled "Der Sprachunterricht muß umkehren!" by Wilhelm Viëtor had a major impact on modern language teaching in Europe as well as North America.[29] Published first in Heilbronn under the pseudonym of Quousque Tandem, the treatise strongly criticized the grammatical analyses of modern languages on the basis of paradigms relevant for the classical languages; it further criticized the deductive nature of grammar teaching, the mechanical learning of structural rules and vocabulary, and the lack of relevant content in the teaching materials. Viëtor rejected the collection of structurally similar but semantically unrelated sentences (a mainstay of the Grammar Translation Method as well as later of Audiolingualism) and insisted on systematic teaching of phonetics in early language instruction and on presenting vocabulary in thematic contexts of short authentic reading texts such as poems, folk tales, and other short narratives rather than in isolated vocabulary lists.

Walmsley has extracted the following teaching principles from Viëtor's writings:

(1) the foreign language must be spoken in the classroom;
(2) the native language can be used for translating into, for conveying the meanings of new words, and for putting questions about the content of the text. Translating into the foreign language as teaching/learning activity is, however, inappropriate;
(3) grammar teaching is to be inductive rather than deductive;
(4) the method is text-oriented, with conversation revolving around the content of a text rather than on free interaction among students.[30]

Most of Viëtor's principles were to be incorporated into the Direct Method, of which, after 1887, the Berlitz Method became a major proponent.

By the turn of the last century the Natural Method (at least in name) had fallen somewhat into disrepute among German teachers. Learned speaks of "abuses connected with the so-called natural method," apparently referring to the lack of grammar teaching in that approach, because he adds: "It is a well established fact in the experience of the best teachers that language must be taught and learned with systematic references to rules of construction."[31] And Hepp takes the stand that the Natural Method is unrealizable within the constraints of a regular classroom and "ließe einige der höchsten geistigen Kräfte des Schülers brach liegen, und die Resultate wären gering und unbefriedigend."[32] Major principles of the Natural Method were, however, incorporated in the Direct Method.

The Direct Method has appeared throughout the history of language teaching with slight variations and adaptations under a number of names: the Natural, Berlitz, Phonetic, Inductive, Mastery, or Conversational Method, and, more recently, as de Sauzé's Cleveland Plan.[33] Essentially, any method that avoids the learner's native language in the classroom as well as in the instructional materials can be called a "direct" method. Diller lists the following principles for modern versions of the Direct Method:

(1) exclusive use of the target language in instruction;
(2) step by step progression (grading by difficulty) in the introduction and use of vocabulary and grammatical structures;
(3) meaning of vocabulary and grammatical patterns taught through use in communication and explanation of new words and meaning mainly through paraphrase rather than translation;

(4) grammar taught inductively, though there can be conscious rule analysis after a phonetic or grammatical pattern is recognized;
(5) simultaneous teaching of all four skills, with writing serving as important reinforcement skill;
(6) mastery of the productive skills as basis for reading comprehension;[34]
(7) use of high-interest materials and techniques which promote constant student involvement and communicative interaction.[35]

Older forms of the Direct Method permitted more or less translation, more or less formal grammatical analysis, and varying emphasis on reading texts as the basis for instruction. But the general consensus was that the Direct Method was more appropriate for instruction in high schools than in colleges because high school students were younger and less capable of grammatical generalizations than students on the post-secondary level.

Although the Direct Method had apparently a sizeable following among German teachers by 1917, B. Q. Morgan, while acknowledging some value in that approach, calls for a reconsideration of translation as a language teaching device. His seven points in favor of translation must have expressed the attitude of many traditional scholars of that time. Morgan calls translation "our supreme disciplinary exercise" and "the mathematics of language study." To those who find translation a difficult or unnatural language-learning technique he responds: "[Learning] German is an arduous affair, and I distrust *a priori* the disciplines of any task which half of an average class can do without considerable error." He further calls translation "our supreme *cultural* or *aesthetic* exercise" and finds it

> almost the only literary exercise open to an elementary class . . . the principal contribution we can make to the student's knowledge and command of English . . . for we cannot teach German with any effectiveness to a generation that is innocent of the distinction between a participle and an infinitive, a prefix and a preposition, a pronoun and an adjective. It is in translation that such confusion of mind is most promptly and glaringly displayed, and can most readily be corrected.

Morgan also finds translation "the quickest, and frequently the only way of determining the accuracy of a student's preparation" and as a last point mentions "the almost inestimable value of translation in dealing with the very difficult problem of the German-American [who] . . . thinks he knows more than the teacher. . . ." He continues:

> for such pupils there is no more useful or salutary exercise than translation. . . . It offers incomparable opportunities for showing the pupil at the very outset just how limited and imperfect his knowledge really is. The chastening effect of strictly conducted translation on the cocksure boy whose grandmother came over in the 50's, and who has "a kind of a vague idea what it means," is a perfect godsend to the American-born teacher.[36]

When dealing with the history of foreign language methodology around the turn of the century, we cannot forget François Gouin. His *Art of Teaching and Studying Languages* had considerable impact on foreign language teachers here and abroad.[37] His observations have since been supported—at least in part—by psycholinguistic research.[38] Gouin observed that children often verbally describe the activities they are engaged in or which they are observing. This sequential description of particular acts became the basis of the Gouin Method. The approach was also called the Series (or Psychological) Method, because the utterances to be practiced were organized into series of sentences describing step by step a particular activity. For instance, a series might focus on the act of pheasant hunting:

> Der Hund sucht. Er sucht und sucht. Er wittert eine Kette Rebhühner. Er tut eine Kette Rebhühner auf. Er steht. Er geht auf den Befehl des Jägers vor. Die Rebhühner bemerken (sehen) den Hund. Sie fürchten sich vor dem Hunde. Sie fliegen auf. Sie fliegen davon. Der Jäger sieht die Kette Hühner davonfliegen. Er ergreift sein Gewehr. Er legt an (führt das Gewehr zur Schulter). Er zielt und zielt. Er drückt ab. Der Schusz geht los. Die Ladung trifft ein Huhn. Das Huhn fällt zur Erde.[39]

The serial arrangement of sentences had the advantage that the logical step-by-step organization of an exercise was based on a concrete, meaningful context which made it easy to recall from memory the events described.

The series descriptions were organized around the major topics of man, the quadruped, the bird, the reptile, the insect, the plant, and the elements. These topics were subdivided further, dealing, for instance, under the heading of man, with persons at various stages of life, in the home, in occupations or the arts, etc. Gouin divided his lessons into "objective" and "subjective" language practice. Objective language was that presented in the series; subjective language consisted of the language (directions, explanations, questions, praise, etc.) which accompanied the series description.

Gouin considered the verb to be the most important component of language and the focus of each frame within a series. These verbs were practiced by restating the series in different tenses or by using different subjects.

Initial language practice with the Gouin Method focused on oral recitation exclusively. After oral mastery the students were expected to write the series from memory. When, considerably later, the reading of literature was introduced, Gouin presented even the classics in a series format.

Gouin believed that full bilingual fluency could be achieved with 4000 of such series (ranging from eighteen to thirty sentences each) in from eight hundred to nine hundred hours of instruction. The language level of a twelve-year-old child could be reached in 1200 lessons or about three hundred hours of instruction. Handschin reports in 1912 that the Gouin Method or an adaptation thereof was used in some two hundred high schools and academies and a few colleges.

By 1900, well over a dozen different language teaching methods were described in the professional literature. Since instructional materials and program descriptions of that time are not easily obtained, it is difficult to surmise the influence, if any, these methodological innovations actually had on the German classroom. The main methodological conflict, however, was clearly between those advocating some form of direct method and those favoring grammar-translation—both groups grappling with a major question still unanswered: To what extent is adult (or adolescent) foreign language learning analogous to a child's acquisition of the mother tongue?

The Report of the Committee of Twelve, commissioned by the Modern Language Association of America and published in 1899, clearly subordinates the utilitarian aspects of foreign language study to "the higher ends of linguistic and literary" goals. "The process of learning to speak a foreign language has no educational value except as it is connected with, and grows out of, the improvement of the mind." The report reviewed the advantages and disadvantages of five teaching methods: the Grammar Method, the Natural Method, the Psychological Method (i.e., the Gouin Method), the Phonetic Method, and the Reading Method.

The Grammar Method was praised for providing "the best possible exercise" of reasoning abilities, but was criticized for neglecting the study of literary masterpieces and for being uninspiring for high school-age students. No redeeming features were found in the Natural Method, since any analogy between first- and second-language learning was rejected. Furthermore, according to the Committee, the Natural Approach "provides little discipline for the intelligence, it affords only the poorest kind of mnemonic training; it favors vagueness of thought and imprecision of expression and it sacrifices the artistic interest of language-study to a so-called 'practical' one." The Gouin Method fascinates students, trains the memory, affords insights into the life of a foreign country, and provides "in a reasonably short time a ready command over a large, well-arranged, and well-digested vocabulary." On the negative side, the Committee states that the Gouin Method "affords but little opportunity for the exercise of judgment" and neglects the aesthetic sense formed through literary study. The Phonetic Method is also criticized for overlooking the importance of literary education but praised for "giving pupils a ready and accurate control of the spoken language." Finally, the Reading Method purportedly enables the student to read "with the same kind of intelligence and enjoyment with which good classical scholars read Latin," but it is considered appropriate only for serious students.[40]

Then as now, it appears, the profession had problems in differentiating between the study of language and the study of literature, in setting appropriate goals, and in having unrealistic expectations of methods and teachers.

Without question, the first fifteen years of the twentieth century were the heyday of German instruction in America. About 5000 schools taught German to over 600,000 pupils.[41] Then came 1917 and America's involvement in World War I. Zeydel calls the collapse of German "the most disastrous pedagogic event of the period, perhaps of all times" (364). Twenty-two state legislatures and several cities forbade the teaching of German in public school, some going so far as to prohibit the speaking of German when more than a given number of persons were present. Later, all these laws were held to be unconstitutional, but in the meantime, irreparable harm had been done to the teaching of German and to foreign language teaching in general.

Despite the overwhelming setback to German teaching during World War I, publication statistics of that time indicate that teachers of German were "still the unquestioned leaders in methodology" in 1917.[42] During that year, the number of articles dealing with methodological questions surpassed that of any previous year. Ninety-two papers by seventy-seven different authors were published. Forty-three of these seventy-seven authors were German teachers who were responsible for fifty-one of the publications. *Monatshefte* (with twenty-four articles) runs a close second to the *Modern Language Journal* (with thirty-one articles) in numbers of papers published during that year.

Methodologically speaking, the years between the two World Wars were uneventful. In 1923 Handschin, a professor of German at Miami University, published his *Methods of Teaching Modern Languages*.[43] He calls both the Grammar and so-called "Natural" methods antiquated and labels his book "a course in our American approximation of the direct method" (62–63). According to Handschin, careful attention to pronunciation, inductive grammar, listening and speaking before reading and writing, little translation, and much use of realia are guiding principles. He points out, however, that the American version of the direct method is a compromise in that "it teaches formal grammar in the mother tongue and uses translation from and, in some cases, into the foreign language" (54). In other words, Handschin was a pragmatist and eclectic. He does, however, insist on the exclusive use of the target language by teacher and students except during formal grammar lessons. At the same time he warns against premature, unstructured oral production, and makes clear that his Direct Method is not the so-called Conversation Method, depending solely on oral work. He cautions that

> too much of it [conversation], to the slighting of thorough work in reading and writing, makes for superficiality, and taxes the aural memory only, thus neglecting the visual and graphic memory. . . . The result . . . is a smattering of inaccurate conversational ability which is soon lost and leaves nothing in its wake. Too fluent speaking on the part of pupils in the first months of a course is dangerous to pronunciation and grammar alike. (135)

Apart from the Direct Method, the only other method acknowledged by Handschin is the Reading Method. Definitions of various reading methods lack clarity and agreement, but Handschin apparently finds the practices described by M. Clarahan acceptable.[44] Techniques included reading aloud easy German stories—a sentence or two at a time—following a teacher's model—followed by comprehension questions and frequent translation. Grammar was explained only when necessary. Incidentally, Clarahan claims that students taught by the reading method performed decidedly better in grammar, pronunciation, reading comprehension, *and* speaking (though the latter skill was not formally tested) than students taught by the grammar method.

It is interesting to note—even though his Direct Method emphasizes the spoken language—that Handschin does not list oral proficiency among the three most important values of modern foreign language study. Five of the ten points listed emphasize foreign language study for the improvement of the mother tongue:

(1) Foreign language study [aids] in acquiring the ability to do purposive or abstract thinking . . . since . . . the greatest aid to thinking is linguistic ability.

(2) [It] yields the power to read French, German, or Spanish. . . . Reading is the objective of this instruction in the United States. One hundred percent of the pupils studying these languages need to learn to read them.

(3) The study of . . . literature yields a comprehension of and a power to interpret and to use the facts of history, life, institutions, art, religion, and politics of a foreign nation, which is not gained by historical study of translation merely.

(4) [Foreign language study] yields the ability to understand the spoken language and to speak it.

(5) [It] yields the ability to write the language.

(6) [It] yields a better comprehension of and power to use English grammar, including syntax.

(7) [It] yields a better comprehension of and a better ability to use English words.

(8) [It] yields the ability to use the language as a tool for the prosecution of other studies. . . .

(9) [It] yields the ability to interpret foreign abbreviations, phrases, and quotations used in English.

(10) . . . in common with other cumulative subjects, *if well taught* [italics mine], [foreign language study] yields general habits and ideals of the greatest value; e.g., the habit of hard and sustained application, systematic work, accuracy, and scholarly activity.[45]

Several developments helped a slow revival of German teaching in the United States, among them, in 1926, the founding of the American Association of Teachers of German (AATG). Zeydel chronicles other developments during that period, such as the compilation of word frequency lists, the development of prognostic tests, intensive summer schools, and programs abroad.[46]

In 1929 the controversial Coleman Report was published.[47] Its recommendations were motivated by the findings that only about two percent of those students who started the study of a modern foreign language in 1925/26 stayed through a four-year course of instruction in that language. For students of German the percentage was only .6 percent! The Committee warned that under these prevalent conditions it was likely that foreign language study would eventually be dropped from the program in all secondary schools except those which prepare especially for college, "unless it can be shown that there is a possibility of attaining values which will be measurable after graduation" (78–79).

Similar to recommendations made by E. S. Joynes in 1890,[48] and by the Committee of Twelve in 1899,[49] the Coleman Report found the reading objective the only possible and realistic goal after two years of instruction. "For any shorter course [than three years] the Committee declares we should advise the reading method, accompanied, however, by scientific training in pronunciation, drill in the rudiments of grammar and a moderate amount of oral practice."[50]

Methodological innovation started again in full force during the early forties when America, because of its involvement in a world war, suddenly found itself with a major scarcity of individuals able to communicate in any language but their own. In 1942 the Army Specialized Training Program (ASTP) and its Foreign Area and Language Study Curriculum (FALSC) started what Zeydel calls "the most dynamic period in the history of American foreign-language study" (47). In intensive instruction (six to nine months, fifteen contact hours per week) and small classes, using "native informants" as drill masters, thousands of military and civilian students achieved remarkable fluency in a spoken language. Linguists got into the act of developing instructional materials based on contrastive analysis of the native and target languages in question. Audiolingualism was born.

Beginnings of the Audiolingual Method can be traced back to the last decades of the nineteenth century and British linguists, such as Henry Sweet, Otto Jespersen, and, somewhat later, Harold Palmer.[51] Palmer believed that the best method for language learning does not require a student to reason, analyze, or theorize. Many of the practices he advocated in his Oral Method—ear training and articulation exercises, text gradation, receptive before productive skill order, choral work before individual response, and extensive use of pattern drills—were to become the mainstays of Audiolingualism.[52]

Audiolingualism is founded in structural linguistics and the behaviorist school of psychology which viewed language not as intellectual (i.e., requiring conscious thought and analysis or creative behavior), but rather as conditioned behavior. Language is viewed as a set of habits. Oral language now definitely gains primacy over the written word. Mimicry/memorization of "useful words and phrases," structurally seeded dialogues, and manipulation of pattern drills became the main teaching techniques—all following the stimulus/response paradigm of Pavlovian conditioning. Errors are to be "extinguished" immediately and language patterns are drilled until they become "automatic." Listening, speaking, reading, writing followed an obligatory sequence of presentation, regardless of a student's objectives or preferred learning style, and notwithstanding the fact that most adult second language learners are literate already and might like the written word as study aid.

The "Introduction" to *Spoken German: Basic Course—Units 1—12* by Jenni Karding Moulton and William G. Moulton provides some insights into early Audiolingualism.[53] The student is told that

> a native speaker is the only good source of first-hand knowledge of the pronunciation and usage of any language. . . . He should be neither over-educated nor too uncultured. . . . The native speaker is always right. There may be instances where this manual or the phonograph records indicate one pronunciation and the native speaker will pronounce something a little different. Always imitate the pronunciation of your Guide [the native speaker] rather than that of the phonograph records . . . (iv and vi).

As to the learning procedure, students are told:

> The leader will read the English out loud, and the Guide [native speaker] will pronounce the German twice, each time allowing enough time for you to repeat the German after him. . . . While you are listening to the guide, follow with your eyes the Aids to Listening.[54] When you repeat the words and sentences after the guide or phonograph records, repeat them loud—good and loud. Never mumble. It is absolutely essential that you repeat after the guide

or phonograph record each time, and that you imitate as closely as you can, and learn by heart what you have imitated. . . . In speaking German you should not first figure out what you want to say in English and then translate it into German, word for word. This will get you nowhere. You should apply, instead, the words and expressions you already know to the given situation. If you cannot immediately rattle off a word or expression to fit a particular situation, go on to another, or ask a question, but under no circumstances attempt to compose. As soon as you do, you lapse into English speech habits and stop learning German and German speech habits. . . . (v, vi, vii & 2)

Beginning in 1958, spurred on by the Russian launching of Sputnik, the National Defense Education Act (NDEA) funded institutes, language and area centers, language labs, fellowships, contracts for research, loans to non-profit private schools, research grants-in-aid to agencies, organizations, and individuals, all for the improvement of foreign language instruction in the United States to the tune of more than $43 million during 1958–60 alone.[55] The Audiolingual Method became the "American Method" of foreign language teaching.

Unfortunately, lacking small classes, highly motivated students, and the vast number of contact hours offered by the ASTPs, Audiolingualism did not show as successful a record in public education as that claimed by the army.

Already in 1963 criticisms were voiced about the practical application of the method in the classroom. Teachers and program supervisors found the approach time-consuming and the pre-reading period too long. English could not be eliminated entirely and grammar could not be left totally to induction. Materials were found to be inadequate and drills tiring.[56]

Cognitive psychologists and linguists of the generative/transformational school started questioning the habit formation view of language learning and by the early sixties a countermovement to Audiolingualism— Cognitive Code Methodology—was in full swing. Mental understanding and analysis of language rather than "automatic conditioning" are emphasized. The guiding principle for second-language learning becomes: what is not understood cannot be learned or retained, regardless of the amount of practice. Language is viewed as *creative* rather than conditioned behavior. Cognitive Code Methodology is, however, not a return to the Grammar Translation Method. While it emphasizes structural analysis and deductive rather than inductive understanding, the course objectives remain clearly those of the audiolingual classroom: mastery of the *oral* language and cultural understanding.

In 1968 the results of the Pennsylvania Foreign Language Research Project were published. This ambitious study attempted to establish empirically, once and for all, which of three language teaching methodologies—including a "traditional" (grammar translation) method and two variations of the "functional skills" (audiolingual) method—was superior.[57] Like other studies which have attempted to establish the superiority of one method over another, the Pennsylvania Project demonstrated that methodology, while important, is clearly not the only variable determining success in language learning. Variables such as student motivation, the language competence of the teacher, amount of language input, teacher personality, teacher energy, instructional time, and materials are difficult to control—as are the methodological treatments when a number of teachers are involved in a study.

In reviewing the history of German teaching and foreign language teaching methodology in general, one cannot avoid a feeling of pessimism for the future of the profession, for it appears that *plus ça change, plus c'est la même chose*. The problem with many teaching methods of the past *and* present is that they derive their dogma from a limited theoretical view of learning in general and of second language acquisition in particular. It is surprising (and depressing) how many language teaching methods have been created without taking into account existing research on language learning and without reference to what has been written before. The methodological "missionaries" take one linguistic, psychological, or even physiological aspect of language learning and attempt to build a complete method around it, without addressing the tremendous complexity of interacting factors affecting adult language acquisition. As Diller recognizes, foreign language methods in the United States did not have a linear development in which the creators of new methods attempted to correct the faults of the preceding ones.[58]

Scholars of the history of language teaching, in attempting to synthesize the many approaches, often point to a dual nature in the controversies raised by the various methodological movements. Some have seen the basic conflict between those who emphasize the oral nature of language and those who focus on grammatical analysis or the study of literature. Other conflicts are between those who see first and second language learning as identical processes and those who believe that the adult (or adolescent) learner with fully developed mental faculties—and already fluent in a language—uses different processes to acquire a foreign tongue. Krashen and Terrell see the major division between grammar-based and communication-based methods, one school emphasizing form (grammatical accuracy), the other meaning (fluency).[59]

Diller, who calls language acquisition "the most emotion-ridden and controversial aspect of linguistic theory," divides all teaching methods (past and present) into two distinct schools; the "empiricists" and the "rationalists."[60] The empiricists (behaviorist school) view language as a set of conditioned habits and advocate a methodology depending mainly on mimicry, memorization, and pattern drills (brought to glorified heights in the Audiolingual Method of the sixties); the rationalists—ranging from the Grammar Translation Method to direct methods—see language as rule-governed (rather than conditioned) behavior, insisting that students use the language creatively (rather than imitatively) from the first day of instruction. To quote again from George Ticknor's 1832 address:

> There are, no doubt, principles which may be ascertained and settled—principles which rest on the nature and laws of human faculties, and which it must, therefore, be important to understand rightly and to apply with judgment. Undoubtedly, too, experience and skill have long since discovered most of these principles, perhaps all of them; and established landmarks, which, pointing out the way others have trodden with safety or success, may prevent us, if we are wise, from making impossible experiments or falling into gross deviations.[61]

Thus far, judging by the number of contradictory premises and practices, the foreign language teaching profession still appears to be looking for a set of dependable principles.

Will there ever be *one* method for teaching German as a foreign language? Most educators today accept that different goals call for different teaching approaches. We still know relatively little about the process of second language learning by adults. If, however, *language proficiency* is the goal of instruction, then we do know some prerequisites which a sound methodology and syllabus of the future will take into account. Assuming functional language proficiency as the goal of German instruction and assuming a motivated learner, the methodology of the future will meet the following criteria:

- It will provide large amounts of comprehensible input (oral and written) in realistic communicative settings; this will require teachers who themselves are fluent in the language and who use the language not only as the content but also as the medium of instruction and classroom interaction.
- It will allow for priority attention to receptive over productive skills practice and will permit a limited "silent period" on the part of the learner rather than insisting—as do many methods—on immediate error-free production of language material which has not yet been acquired.
- It will insist on meaningful and contextualized language practice since only what is understood can be effectively assimilated and remembered.
- It will provide authentic language samples and develop strategies for their comprehension.
- It will utilize, as much as possible, inductive learning principles (self discovery), since such learning is often superior in terms of retention to rule memorization. It will, however, recognize the adult learner's need for conscious analysis and comparison.
- It will provide for interactive language practice and will not prescribe the teacher as the asker of all questions and the initiator of all communication.

- It will provide multisensory and multimedia approaches, recognizing that adult learners have different learning styles and can benefit from a variety of learning experiences not limited to the written or spoken word.
- It will allow for evaluation of content (comprehensible meaning) as well as form (accuracy).
- It will incorporate pragmatic language use (based on an analysis of notional/functional principles) with structural analysis and progression. It should be noted that I recommend the *incorporation* or joining of a notional/functional and grammatical syllabus. Since exposure time to the language is extremely limited when the language is taught in a formal instructional setting outside the target language culture, the development of pragmatic competence (getting across intended meaning), sociolinguistic competence (appropriateness of message for cultural context), and linguistic competence (accuracy) need to go hand in hand.
- It will provide for a worthwhile content, not just trivia clothed in unfamiliar linguistic structures.
- It will provide for a systematic, cyclical reentry and review of vocabulary and structures. Our expectations that students have "mastered" (i.e., can use without errors) linguistic structures just because they were "taught" in lesson X have proven to be unrealistic and have frustrated generations of language teachers and students.[62]

But even if one methodology could be devised which would meet all the above criteria, one factor outside the realm of methodology still needs to be dealt with before we can hope to increase our success rate in terms of developing language fluency on the part of large numbers of German students. That factor is *time*. Given the time allotment of the average high school or college language curriculum, overwhelming success cannot be expected of any method.

Notes

1 Emil Dapprich, "Die Methoden des modernen Sprachunterrichts," *Pädagogische Monatshefte* 1 (1899): 34.
2 L. G. Kelly, *25 Centuries of Language Teaching* (Rowley, Mass.: Newbury House, 1969).
3 Witness methodological innovations of the past two decades, such as Community Language Learning (also known as the Counseling/Learning Method), the Total Physical Response Approach, a revival of the Natural Approach, the Lozanov Method (also known as Suggestopaedia or Suggestive Accelerative Learning and Teaching), the Silent Way—not to mention efforts to individualize, intensify, humanize (e.g., the Confluent Approach), personalize, mediate, team-teach, group, clarify values and foster creativity in instruction.

4 Among them, Louis Viereck, "German Instruction in American Schools," *U. S. Bureau of Education: Report of the Commissioner of Education for the Year 1900–01*, 531–708; John A. Walz, *German Influence in American Education and Culture* (Philadelphia: Carl Schurz Memorial Foundation, 1936); Peter Hagboldt, *The Teaching of German* (Boston: Heath, 1940); and Edwin H. Zeydel, "The Teaching of German in the United States from Colonial Times to the Present," *German Quarterly* 37 (1964): 315–92; reprinted, in part, on pp. 15–54 of this volume.

5 Janet E. Hildebrand, "Methods for Teaching College German in the United States, 1753–1903: An Historical Study," diss., U. of Texas, 1977; Richard Helt and David J. Woloshin, "Where Are We Today? A Survey of Current German Teaching Methods in American Colleges and Universities," *Unterrichtspraxis* 15 (1982): 110–15.

6 Because of the difficulty of access, this study does not include a systematic examination of textbooks to investigate the extent to which various methodological movements were reflected in available teaching materials. Generally speaking, however, textbooks lag decades behind methodological discussions, and since it would be difficult, if not impossible, to find sales and user figures for these early texts, discussions in the professional literature will have to serve as indication of the acceptance or rejection of differing methodological schools.

7 See Note 5.

8 Quoted in Constantin Grebner, "Franklin als Jugenderzieher," *Monatshefte für deutsche Sprache und Pädagogik* 7 (1906): 7.

9 Klaus J. Bartel, "German and the Germans at the Time of the American Revolution," *Modern Language Journal* 60 (1967): 96–100.

10 E. H. Babbitt, "How to Use the Modern Languages as a Means of Mental Discipline," *Methods of Teaching Modern Languages*, ed. A. M. Elliott, Calvin Thomas, et al. (Boston: Heath, 1893) 125; cited in John J. Weisert, "Foreign Languages as Mental Discipline: A Survey," *German Quarterly* 12 (1939): 62.

11 S. L. Pressey, *Psychology and the New Education* (New York: Harper, 1933) 508; cited in Weisert 67. The controversy over whether certain subjects or learning activities improve mental faculties more than others continues. Recent animal research indicates that frequent exposure to certain tasks can alter brain structure.

12 G. J. Adler, *Ollendorff's New Method of Learning to Read, Write, and Speak the German Language; to which is Added a Systematic Outline of German Grammar* (New York: Appleton, 1850) iv.

13 Katharine Darrin, "German in the Class-Room," *School Review* 12 (1904): 559.

14 Arthur Altschul, "Über die natürliche Methode im deutschen Unterricht," *Pädagogische Monatshefte* 4 (1903): 323.

15 Jean Hepp, "Über natürliche Methoden beim Lehren neuer Sprachen," *Pädagogische Monatshefte* 1.2 (1900): 9f.

16 N. G. Dufief, *Nature Displayed in Her Mode of Teaching Languages to Man* (1804; 5th ed. Philadelphia, 1823), cited in Kelly 40.

17 George Ticknor, "Lecture on the best Methods of Teaching the Living Languages," delivered before the American Institute, 24 August 1832; rpt. *Modern Language Journal* 22 (1937): 19.

18 Hepp 10.

19 Hepp, *Monatshefte* 1, 3 (1900): 2.

20 Gottlieb Heness, *Der Leifaden* cited in Edmond A. Méras, *A Language Teacher's Guide* (New York: Harper, 1954) 35–36. Stephen D. Krashen and Tracy D. Terrell espouse similar practices in their *Natural Approach: Language Acquisition in the Classroom* (New York: Pergamon, 1983).

21 Altschul 321.

22 Claude Marcel, *The Study of Languages Brought Back to Its True Principles* (New York, 1869); cited in Kelly 40–41.

23 See, for instance, James J. Asher, "Comprehension Training: The Evidence from Laboratory and Classroom Studies," 187–222; Valerian A. Postovsky, "The Priority of Aural Comprehension in the Language Acquisition Process," 170–86; and Harris Winitz, "A Reconsideration of Comprehension and Production in Language Training," 101–40, all in *The Comprehension Approach to Foreign Language Instruction*, ed. Harris Winitz (Rowley, MA: Newbury House, 1981). See also Stephen D. Krashen, *Principles and Practice in Second Language Acquisition* (New York: Pergamon, 1982).

24 F. L. O. Roehrig, *The Shortest Road to German* (Ithaca, NY: Andrus, McChain, 1874).

25 Thomas Prendergast, *The Mastery Series, German* (New York: Appleton, 1870).

26 Altschul 327.

27 J. Lévy, "Thorough Method vs. Natural Method: A Letter to Dr. L. Sauveur" (Boston, 1878), cited in Kelly 11.

28 E. W. Bagster-Collins, "Beobachtungen auf dem Gebiete des fremdsprachlichen Unterrichts," *Monatshefte für deutsche Sprache und Pädagogik* 10 (1909): 217, 219.

29 Wilhelm Viëtor, *Der Sprachunterricht muss umkehren! Ein Beitrag zur Überbürdungsfrage* (Heilbronn, 1886.)

30 John B. Walmsley, "*Quousque Tandem:* Wilhelm Viëtor's *Language Instruction must Do an About-Face,*" *Modern Language Journal* 68 (1984): 37–44.

31 M. D. Learned, "When should German Instruction begin in the Public Schools?" *Pädagogische Monatshefte* 3 (1902): 89.

32 Hepp 4.

33 Emile B. de Sauzé, *The Cleveland Plan for the Teaching of Modern Languages* (1929; rev. ed. Philadelphia: Winston, 1959).

34 This principle contradicts recent adaptations of the Natural Approach which advocates the comprehension skills as basis for the productive skills. See Krashen and Terrell (Note 20).

35 Karl C. Diller, *The Language Teaching Controversy* (Rowley, Mass.: Newbury House, 1978) 72–86.

36 Bayard Quincy Morgan, "In Defense of Translation," *Modern Language Journal* 1 (1917): 236–40.

37 François Gouin, *The Art of Teaching and Studying Languages,* trans. Howard Swan and Victor Bétis (London: Philip, 1892); originally published as *L'art d'enseigner et d'étudier les languages* (Paris: Fischbacher, 1880).

38 See publications listed in Note 23.

39 Charles Hart Handschin, "A Historical Sketch of the Gouin Series-System of Teaching Modern Languages and of its Use in the United States," *School Review* 20 (1912): 170–75.

40 W. H. Rosenstengel, "Bericht des Zwölferkomitees der 'Modern Language Association of America'," *Pädagogische Monatshefte* 1 (1900): 11.

41 Zeydel (Note 4).

42 "Literature of Modern Language Methodology in America for 1917," *Modern Language Journal* 3 (1918): 36.

43 Charles H. Handschin, *Methods of Teaching Modern Languages* (Yonkers, N.Y.: World, 1923).

44 M. Clarahan, "An Experimental Study of Methods of Teaching High School German," *Bulletin of the University of Missouri,* Educational Series 1 (1913): vi.

45 Handschin (Note 43) 3, 5, 7, 8 & 9.

46 Zeydel (Note 4).

47 Algernon Coleman, *The Teaching of Modern Foreign Languages in the United States* (New York: MacMillan, 1929).

48 E. S. Joynes, "Reading in Modern Language Study," *PMLA* 5 (1890): 33–46.
49 *Report of the Committee of Twelve of the Modern Language Association of America* (New York: Heath, 1899).
50 Coleman 83; cited in Robert Herndon Fife, "The Reading Objective," *German Quarterly* 2 (1929): 83.
51 Steven Darian, "Backgrounds of Modern Language Teaching: Sweet, Jespersen, and Palmer," *Modern Language Journal* 53 (1969): 545–50.
52 Harold E. Palmer, *The Scientific Study and Teaching of Languages* (Yonkers, N.Y.: World, 1917).
53 Jenni Karding Moulton and William G. Moulton, *Spoken German: Basic Course—Units 1–12,* rpt. for the U. S. Armed Forces Institute by the Linguistic Society of America, 1944.
54 The Aids to Listening, incidentally, are attempts to transcribe pronunciation with conventional orthography, e.g., fer-TSAI-ung, FROI-lain, VOH ist dehr BAHN-hohf? DASS ist dehr BAHN-hohf, dort LINGKS. fer-SHTEHen zih? (19).
55 Zeydel (Note 4).
56 Theodore Huebener, "The New Key is Now Off-Key!" *Modern Language Journal* 47 (1963): 376–77.
57 John B. Carroll, "What does the Pennsylvania Foreign Language Research Project Tell Us?" *Foreign Language Annals* 3 (1969): 214–36.
58 Diller (Note 35).
59 Krashen and Terrell (Note 20).
60 Diller 2.
61 Ticknor 20.
62 For an elaboration on this topic see Renate A. Schulz, "Language Acquisition and Syllabus Design," *ADFL Bulletin* 15. 3 (1984): 1–7.

German and National Policy: The West Point Experience

CRAIG W. NICKISCH
United States Military Academy

After the Revolutionary War, George Washington and Alexander Hamilton suggested that Congress establish an engineering school, for among the critical needs of the new republic were mapping, fortification, and construction in the western territories. Congress founded the United States Military Academy in 1802, and challenged it to educate and train officer-engineers. West Point's curriculum also included humanistic elements; it was the answer to Thomas Jefferson's hopes for a national university.[1] The difficulties associated with beginning the teaching of German at West Point are quite remarkable, and subsequent successes illustrate the effects of changing trends in national policy and pedagogical doctrine.

German was first suggested for the West Point curriculum in March of 1808. In a letter to President Jefferson, Major Jonathan Williams made several suggestions for the fledgling academy, including a "french teacher and a german teacher [sic] in the Department of Engineering."[2] Those teachers were included because no suitable engineering text was available in English, whereas several existed in German and French.[3]

An alternate proposal, made by Major Joseph Swift, suggested an instructor of French rather than one of German. Many French officers were then serving as engineers in the United States Army, and Napoleon had replaced Frederick the Great as the military standard of success. Scharnhorst himself contrasted the Prussians with the French: "Alter, Schwäche, Unthätigkeit, Unwissenheit und Unmuth auf der einen Seite, Thätigkeit und Entschlossenheit auf der anderen."[4] Defeats at Jena and Auerstedt were responsible for Prussia's relatively poor military image between 1806 and 1815.

In 1812 Congress passed the Swift proposal, which made no mention of German, and untranslated French works became the texts for courses in advanced mathematics, engineering, and the sciences.[5] French was a daily subject, taught in the grammar-translation method; students were to pronounce it "tolerably" and translate "with accuracy."[6] Cadet Edgar Allan Poe had only a brief and unhappy sojourn at West Point, but he nonetheless ranked third of the sixty-seven members of his class in

French.[7] Cadets were not expected to learn the spoken language, but by 1840, earlier than in many American colleges, developing an ability to speak was an explicit instructional goal.

Meanwhile, Prussia had undergone a military renewal, which caused renewed American interest in her army's organization, doctrine, military academies and, as a practical matter, her language. Pressure to include the teaching of German at West Point increased as reports of Prussian military successes were added to those of German achievements in science and letters. When the curriculum was extended from four years to five, there was time to include German, and the subject was discussed as though decided. Cadet Robinson, class of 1858, wrote to his parents in 1854 that cadets in their last year would study "Elocution, composition, Spanish and German in addition to our course."[8] But when the fifth year arrived, German was not taught after all. The most likely explanation is that no additional faculty space was created, and at that time no member of the faculty could teach German.

As a result of the war with Mexico, however, Spanish was added in 1854.[9] The professor of French could also teach Spanish and did, although a Congressional Commission headed by Senator Jefferson Davis heard a former cadet testify in 1860 that "throughout the [language] course little care was taken to have me *apply* what I learned from print; . . . [I] have since learned more . . . from Mexican senoritas in two months than I did . . . at the Point in two years."[10] The commission considered recommending the teaching of German, but Davis became the President of the Confederacy. His report was not accepted in Washington.

The Board of Visitors is a group of distinguished citizens which is still constituted to evaluate West Point's programs, and its 1871 report reflected German successes in the Franco-Prussian War. The board "would gladly urge attention to . . . German, so far as may be practicable."[11] Since educators and national leaders have often sought to emphasize the humanistic element in West Point's educational experience, Goethe and Schiller may have contributed as much as did Gneisenau and Scharnhorst to that recommendation. But West Point had been too successful; its graduates had served the nation almost too well, and any suggestion that the curriculum might be improved came to naught. The Superintendent reported:

> The subjects of study at the Military Academy embrace all that is essential and nearly all that is necessary to the education of an officer of the Army. . . . [It cannot] reasonably be expected that any change . . . in the system of instruction would give any general result decidedly for the better.[12]

In February of 1872, the matter of introducing German was on the floor of the Congress as a joint resolution. Congressional reasoning is most interesting from the point of view of German-American studies:

> . . . the English and German languages are more generally spoken in the
> United States than any other tongue, and . . . during the late civil war em-
> barrassments frequently occurred in consequence of companies and regiments
> of Germans being commanded by officers who did not understand their lan-
> guage. The joint resolution therefore directs the Secretary of War to substitute
> the German language instead of the Spanish in the regular course of studies
> in the United States Military Academy, and cause to be employed one German
> professor and two German assistant professors for that purpose.[13]

A modification was suggested from the floor: ". . . on one of our frontiers,
extending many hundreds of miles, the Spanish language is spoken altogether. While the German language is undoubtedly of value as a branch
of study in the Military Academy, the Spanish language ought not to be
neglected."[14] The resolution was passed as modified, and West Point's
Superintendent reacted without delay, writing to the Secretary of War:
"That the German Language would be a very desirable addition to the
course of instruction, there is no doubt; but there is, as the course is
arranged, no time disposable . . . any considerable addition to the present
course could only be at a sacrifice. . . ."[15] The Superintendent expressed
other objections:

> The resolution, if correctly published, contemplates putting the instruction of
> the German language on a different footing from that of French or Spanish,
> and on a more expensive basis from any other branch, as if Germans only are
> to be employed. Officers of the Army, unless Germans, although as competent
> to instruct in German, as other languages, could not be detailed for the duty.[16]

Continued resistance to change, indicated by the finely drawn distinction between a "German professor" and a "professor of German," is
unmistakable. Congress passed the right resolution, but unfortunately did
so for the wrong reasons. Congress did not follow up its directive, and the
Academy did not begin to teach German, despite the explicit wording of
the resolution. National policy, as demonstrated by this episode, had little
effect on the curriculum when it was not espoused by policymakers in
Washington and also by the leadership at West Point. When, however,
the United States Army adopted the Prussian spiked helmet, the Academy's faculty wore it.

In 1879 the Board of Visitors, then openly critical of West Point's
hesitancy to change, requested "that the German language be substituted
for the Spanish as being one of the foremost languages of science in all its
branches, the military included, and as furnishing an excellent discipline
for understanding and writing English with intelligent judgment."[17]

Whether or not one subscribed to the board's theory of positive
transfer, discussion about the introduction of German was widespread in
1879. Letters from prospective instructors arrived at West Point: "In dem

Clevelander Anzeiger habe ich gesehen und gelesen, daß der Grundplan der Militair-Akademie abgeändert werden soll, so zwar, daß in Zukunft auch Unterricht in deutscher Sprache erteilt werden soll."[18] The writer had attended the Prussian Cadet School at Kulm, and went on to describe himself as "Im Dienst ganz Soldat! Außer Dienst ganz gebildeter Mensch!" Another applicant held a doctorate from Jena and was teaching in the Philological Institute in Rome. However, despite the widespread discussions and the board's unequivocal recommendation, the curricular *status quo* prevailed.

After the turn of the century, West Point faculty members were more keenly aware of the practical significance of German than was the school's administration. Another effort to introduce German came as the United States was drawn ever closer to the First World War. This time the language department itself proposed the teaching of German: "It is the opinion of the department [of foreign languages] that German should form an element of the course of languages. It will shortly submit a report on this subject, looking to the introduction of German on Sept. 1, 1917."[19]

West Point's officer-professors acted far more reasonably than other Americans, educators included, who at that time viciously attacked both the use and teaching of German in America. But the faculty's recommendation was lost in the wartime turbulence at the Academy, when the language department itself was disbanded for a short time. The experiences of the American Expeditionary Force during World War I demonstrated anew the practical value of languages, German included.

The teaching of German would next be suggested, again by the faculty of West Point, when the situation in Europe caused a thorough curriculum review in 1939. Significantly, the intellectual and political climate of that year was distinctly different from that of 1916. The many emigrants to the United States in the 1930s were, to be sure, vivid proof that all Germans were neither "Huns" nor National Socialists. Another factor, one demanding additional attention, is the particular constellation of professors at West Point. One senses that they were unusually thoughtful, perceptive officers who were eager to adjust to meet the needs of the nation.

The 1939 study recommended "a balanced and liberal education in the arts and sciences, to include . . . the possible introduction of German."[20] This suggestion from West Point met with agreement in Washington, and the study of German was launched in the fall of 1941, when 112 cadets began 109 hours of German instruction. The language requirement was reduced from six to four semesters.

A 1942 study group reported, in what may be the understatement of that decade, that the Army "must have officers with a knowledge of the foreign languages that are likely to be most useful."[21] In 1942 Portuguese was introduced, and quotas were established for each language. About

22% of the cadets studied German. Russian was added after World War II, and the War Department adjusted its quotas, based on projected national requirements. German's proportion was set at 16% and has since risen to 25% despite the addition of Chinese and Arabic to West Point's offerings. The figures are guidelines, however, and cadets are allowed free choice of language. In 1984 nearly a third (32.6%) of entering cadets selected German.

Two of the first German instructors, then-Captain Walter J. Renfroe, Jr. and Dr. Fritz Tiller, taught in the department for many years and were responsible for unusually progressive and effective pedagogy. In West Point's 1941 methodology ". . . considerable time and attention are devoted also to the lighter side of the study. . . . [Spoken German] is stressed from the beginning, and free composition, both oral and written, is practiced extensively. The history of the literature and of the civilization . . . is brought out in the texts for reading and in lectures."[22]

The "new oral method" was first tried in beginning German in 1945 and later extended to the other languages: ". . . even the very slight use of English found necessary [in the first ten lessons] was completely eliminated and [only German] was heard in the classroom for the remainder of the year. . . . Cadets actually learned to converse understandably in German."[23] The use of "sound recordings" dates from 1947, when they provided "recorded examples of lesson materials so that the cadets may thus be guided during their hours of preparation . . . [and] record their own version [in German] for immediate comparison with a recorded norm."[24] In the same year a Cadet German Club was founded. It still provides opportunities for the practical use of German outside the classroom. The German Club's success is such that it regularly counts over a hundred members.

An advanced German course has been taught since 1955, and in 1961 elective courses were introduced. In 1969 the Academy adopted "areas of concentration," the approximate equivalent of minors. German was one of those. In 1982 optional majors were added, and the foreign language requirement was reduced to two semesters for cadets in scientific fields and three for those in the humanities.

A cadet who now majors in German takes a rather standard curriculum, although course content is oriented, understandably, somewhat less to literature and somewhat more to political, cultural, historic, and military matters. An interdepartmental area of concentration in Foreign Area Studies, Western Europe, is heavily subscribed, too, for much of the United States Army is located in the Federal Republic and an officer is virtually assured of at least one assignment there. That of course plays a role in cadets' selection of German as a language to study; it also occasions infrequent queries from Washington, asking whether West Point should not teach German to every cadet—indeed, why the Academy teaches any language other than German and, perhaps, Spanish.

Reduction of the general requirement to fewer than four semesters caused concern in some quarters. An amendment to H.R. 6030 (1982) was offered by Congressman Paul Simon:

> The Secretary of Defense shall conduct a study on the feasibility of requiring each cadet . . . at the United States Military Academy . . . to study at least one foreign language for not less than two years and to increase existing requirements for foreign language study. . . .[25]

West Point, based on specialized curricular demands in mathematics, science, and engineering disciplines, declined to increase the basic language requirement. However, the goal of increased language study was reached after all; each cadet must study a language for two or three semesters, beginning at the appropriate level.

In many ways the history of attempts to introduce German at the Military Academy reflected the maturation of the nation itself. The teaching of German at the Military Academy resulted from specialized national interests, which were interpreted similarly in West Point and Washington. Since its inception in 1941, the teaching of German has reflected a creative tension between exposure and variety, between the requirements of a humanistic education and those of an increasingly complex world. West Point still produces officers with an extensive background in the sciences, but cadets now specialize in other disciplines as well, one of which is German.

Notes

1 Thomas J. Fleming, *West Point: The Men and Times of the United States Military Academy* (New York: Morrow, 1969) 15–16.
2 Major Jonathan Williams, "Report on the Progress and Present State of the Military Academy," a letter to President Thomas Jefferson, 14 March 1808, ms. USMA Library.
3 John R. McCormick, "History of Foreign Language Teaching at the United States Military Academy," *Modern Language Journal* 54 (1970) 1:319–23.
4 Max Lehmann, *Scharnhorst* (Leipzig: Hirzel, 1866): 361. Quoted from a letter to his son.
5 Robert Leo Doherty, "Foreign Language Study at United States Service Academies: Evolution and Current Issues," diss. Teachers College, Columbia U., 1982, ch. 3, p. 7.
6 *Annual Reports of the Superintendent of the United States Military Academy, 1802–1902* (West Point, NY: Office of the Printer, n.d. [1903?]) 131.
7 John Thomas Russell, *Edgar Allan Poe: The Army Years* (West Point, NY: USMA P.O., 1972) 14.

8 William G. Robinson, Letter to his Parents, 19 September 1854. USMA Library.

9 Sidney Forman, *West Point: A History of the United States Military Academy* (New York: Columbia UP, 1950) 136.

10 U. S. Senate, "Report of the Commission to Examine into the Organization, System of Discipline and Course of Instruction at the United States Military Academy at West Point," *Senate Miscellaneous Document No. 3,* Second Session, 36th Congress (Washington, D.C.: GPO, 1881) 300.

11 "Report of the Board of Visitors," *The Report of the Honorable Secretary of War* (Washington, D.C.: GPO., 1871) 4: 438.

12 "Report of the Superintendent," *The Report of the Honorable Secretary of War* (Washington, D.C.: GPO., 1872), 787–88.

13 "West Point Academy," *The Congressional Globe* 26 February 1872: 1217. The resolution was H.R. 104.

14 Ibid.

15 USMA, *The Superintendent's Letter Book* 2 March 1872, USMA Library.

16 Ibid.

17 "Report of the Board of Visitors," *The Report of the Honorable Secretary of War* (Washington, D.C.: GPO, 1879) 428.

18 C. Zacha, Letter to the Commander of the Military Academy, 16 October 1879. USMA Library.

19 "The Report of the Superintendent of the Military Academy," *War Department Annual Reports, 1916* (Washington, D.C.: GPO, 1916) 1195.

20 U.S.M.A., Department of Economics, "A Study of the Curriculum of the U.S.M.A. by the Academic Board," *Wartime History of the U.S.M.A.,* ts., 1946, Exhibit H, p. 6. USMA Library.

21 USMA, "Report of a Special Committee Appointed by the Superintendent, October 15, 1942," ts., 30 November 1942, p. 8. USMA Library.

22 USMA, *Information Relative to the Appointment and Admission of Cadets to the U.S.M.A., West Point, New York* (Washington, D.C.: GPO, 1941) 22.

23 USMA, *Annual Report of the Superintendent* (West Point, NY: 1947) 12.

24 USMA, *Annual Report of the Superintendent* (West Point, NY: 1948) 18.

25 U.S. Congress, "Amendment to H.R. 6030, As Reported Offered by Mr. Simon of Illinois," *Congressional Record,* Sec. 902 (29 July 1982), p. H4897.

One Hundred and Fifty Years of German at Princeton: A Descriptive Account

RUTH B. BOTTIGHEIMER
State University of New York at Stony Brook

Introduction

A comprehensive history of German as it has been taught in the United States since the arrival of the first German speakers more than three hundred years ago does not yet exist. When such a study is written it will be based, in part, on the institutional histories of many and widely varied instructional entities, from Dame Schools, where German rarely if ever was taught, to great modern state universities, and including women's colleges, sectarian academies, men's colleges, black academies and colleges both secular and religious, private and public foundations.

An overview of one hundred and fifty years of German teaching at Princeton University demonstrates a fluctuating sense of German as a discipline, a gradually shifting perception of the scholars who taught German language and literature, as well as a later slow decline of the proud self-confidence the discipline seemed to enjoy when German science and technology reigned supreme in the nineteenth century.

Perhaps it will surprise some readers that German as a discipline appears to be far more rigorously defined and taught today than it has been in the past, an unexpectedly optimistic conclusion that I have been able to draw from my study.

Princeton University is both typical and atypical within the American educational establishment. In its early years a small private college for educating young, white, primarily Protestant men, it now administers significant amounts of public monies as a medium-sized, private, coeducational, nonsectarian, integrated university. The general development in German language and literature instruction outlined here probably has parallels in other American colleges and universities, although the precise timing might vary from one educational institution to another in some respects and to some extent.

The Nineteenth Century: Creation and Consolidation

The institution later to be known as Princeton University was sparsely populated in the 1830s by a group of professors teaching theology, Greek,

Latin, and surveying. The first was a desideratum, the last a necessity for students, many of whom came from or were destined for an agrarian or frontier life. In those same years the college suddenly increased its total faculty to eight (it had been three in 1829!) and expanded its purview, adding chemistry, natural history, and modern languages.[1] Two "modern" subjects, chemistry and natural history, brought modern languages in their train not intentionally but fortuitously, for the degreeless chemist, Louis Hargous, also knew French, and "Mr. Benedict Jäger (who has charge of the Cabinet of Natural History) [gave] instruction in the German and Italian Languages" (1831–32, 4). Freshmen could now study the French or German languages in their first two years. By 1833 Jäger had acquired an A.M. and shifted his priorities when he became Professor of German and Italian, and Lecturer in Natural History, while Hargous was listed as Professor of French and Spanish. These neophyte modern language instructors were also responsible for freshman and sophomore instruction in Livy, Xenophon, Roman antiquities, Latin, English, Horace, Cicero, and Plato. Their paid duties seem, however, to have been different. Consistent with the fact that French was listed as part of the required recitations for freshmen and sophomores in 1833, instruction in that language did not incur extra charges, leaving us to infer that Jäger had to be paid to share his knowledge of German and Italian. In the following year, Jaeger (umlaut dropped) seemed to be principally involved with adding to the butterfly collection, but when Hargous departed in 1835, Jaeger became the Professor of Modern Languages and Lecturer on Natural History.[2] At that point the college bulletin noted that "Instruction in the French, Spanish, German, and Italian languages is given at the option of the student, without extra charge" (1835–36, 15). One marvels at Jaeger's sudden competence in three additional languages and wonders how he taught his classes.

The amalgamation of all modern languages contrasted clearly with the college's careful separation of ancient languages from one another at the same time. In the 1840s a continuing demand for modern languages, particularly French and German, was evident, which implies the informal preparation of Princeton's students for some contact with European culture, perhaps the grand tour which Henry James chronicles so sensitively later in the century.

The introductory level at which modern languages were taught also differed from the classics and was reflected in admissions criteria. In 1830 candidates were examined in English grammar, arithmetic, and geography—previously part of the freshman and sophomore curriculum—as well as on set texts in Latin and Greek, but not in any of the modern languages. Set examination texts in French and German would not become part of the admissions procedure until much later in the nineteenth century.

The instructional staff for modern languages remained in their posts at Princeton for much briefer periods of time than members of the philosophical or theological faculty, and for much of the nineteenth century the modern languages presented a picture of institutional indecision and individual transience. Nothing illustrates this better than the following train of events. The 1845–46 bulletin announced that Henry J. David had joined the faculty as "Teacher pro-tem, of the German Language." He was replaced by Frederick Perrin, who, as his name suggests, could and did teach both French and German. When he left, two "Teachers" were hired to replace him, I. Loewenthal, A.M. and Edward Dubuque (no degree listed) for German and French respectively (1852). Three years later G. A. Matile, LL.D., Lecturer on Civil History, had taken on German teaching, while Henry M. Baird, A.M., became Tutor in Greek and Teacher of French. In 1857 Matile, then Professor of History, had passed the pedagogical baton to Carl Langlotz, the new Teacher of German, who displayed remarkable staying power, being still listed nine years later in 1866.

Princeton's nineteenth-century catalogs often seem to suggest that the individual faculty member was viewed as more important than the subject he taught, a primacy of person over discipline well illustrated in the figure of Henry C. Cameron, A.M., who joined the faculty as Instructor in French in 1859. His competence in French was linked to a knowledge of history, in which field he rose to a professorship. But when he subsequently gained his Ph.D. (1866), he was abruptly transmogrified into a Professor of Greek and Instructor of French. A scant two years later he added an ecclesiastical facet to his identity, and as the Reverend Henry Cameron, Ph.D., he passed his French responsibilities on to a junior colleague.

As the Henry Cameron vignette well illustrates, it took quite a while for modern languages to be accepted as a coherent area of study rather than as something a faculty member might do in addition to other duties. In the 1840s, for example, lectures began to be organized systematically in various fields, but modern language courses remained unlisted as a form of instruction outside regular offerings. The college exhibited a certain schizophrenia about the importance of developing skills in modern languages, even though in theory these corresponded to other practical skills offered by the college, such as trigonometry with reference to its application to surveying and navigation.

Not until the 1870s was the subject matter of modern languages spelled out when French literature was made available from the first year onwards and German from the third year under a new Tutor in Modern Languages. Beginning in 1872, French was introduced into first year studies for all students, with both French and German available in the sophomore year, while in the junior and senior years modern languages were elective. At that point the college catalog published the names of set texts from which students were to study. Students of French read Otto's *French Conversation Grammar* and Bocher's *French Reader*; students of German in their junior year were treated to Otto's *German Grammar* and Whitney's *German Reader*. Seniors advanced to Otto's *German Conversational Grammar*, followed by *Egmont* and *Nathan der Weise*, while the second and third terms of the senior year were filled by lectures on the history of French and German literature combined. Further fine-tuning of the language curriculum in 1874 brought a "review of the irregular verbs" into the first term of the senior year, while the second and third terms addressed Lessing (*Minna von Barnhelm*), Schiller (*Die Jungfrau von Orleans*), and Goethe (*Egmont*) with lectures on the history of German literature—now separated from lectures on French literature—finishing up the year. In 1876 Lessing (*Nathan der Weise*), Schiller (*Piccolomini*), and Goethe (*Hermann und Dorothea*) moved into the junior year curriculum, and seniors used Adler's *Handbuch der deutschen Literatur* and heard lectures on the "History and Progressive Development of the French and German Languages."

The Beginnings of Literary Study

The history of German literary study at Princeton really dates from 1877, when course listings broadened considerably. In the senior year students could take up the *Nibelungenlied, Meister- und Minnesänger*, Lessing, and Goethe and his contemporaries. In the following year a doctoral program was instituted. *Two* professors of German now held forth, one in the School of Arts and one in the School of Sciences.

Until the mid-nineties an uncomfortable see-saw existed within the German and French faculties, both of which were split between the School of Arts and the School of Sciences. By the early 1890s the literature curriculum, whose offerings were far stronger in the School of Sciences, had settled into a track reflecting the biographical approach of contemporaneous literary criticism: "Lessing's Life and Works," "Schiller's Life and Works" and "Goethe's Life and Works." Philological interests dominated course offerings in the School of Arts with the addition of Middle High German, Old High German, Old Icelandic, Old Saxon, Gothic, and Anglo-Saxon in 1896.

The addition of a graduate program naturally enlarged the number and expanded the variety of courses offered. As the years passed, literature courses settled into the undergraduate curriculum, while graduate study revolved around Germanic philology on the German university model. The trend separating literature from philology was short-lived and ended when literature re-entered the graduate curriculum in 1912 with "Beginnings of New High German Literature" and "Literature since 1885."

Graduate offerings continued to move away from philology (despite the addition of a phonetics course in 1915) and towards literature, adding "German literature from the earliest times to the 14th century," but literary criticism made its first formal appearance not as a graduate course, but as an undergraduate offering.

This brief overview of course offerings at the undergraduate and graduate level conjures up images of the classroom and poses questions about how Princeton faculty might have taught these courses several generations ago. From time to time hints and clues emerge. For instance, a note in 1886 states: "The German itself being used, as far as time permits, in conducting the recitations" (1886–87, 67). But the use of German in the classroom seems to have lagged behind efforts among French instructors, who not only added racy material to the syllabus, like George Sand's *La mare au diable,* but did so with an express purpose: "idiomatic expressions and delicate shades of modern French construction are carefully noted" (1887–88, 69). The School of Arts added Koch's *Über die Bakterien* and emphasized reading, although "speaking the foreign idiom" was mentioned. The next specific mention of teaching methods appeared almost forty years later, in 1925, when "German [would] be generally used" in beginning and intermediate courses.

The distribution of teaching personnel is just as important as the teaching methods used. One might ponder the effect on language teaching of the following reversal. In the early 1930s language courses formed part of a system in which tenured professors acted as course heads directing a shifting population of junior faculty who bore the chief responsibility for teaching, but within a few years tenured professors had disappeared completely from lower-level language courses, all responsibility having been shifted to junior faculty, and with German no longer the language of instruction.

Analyzing faculty lists from the late nineteenth to the mid-twentieth century discloses a change indicative of important changes in the university itself. In the university's earlier years, a large permanent faculty had taught together with a smaller number of untenured men who rotated through fairly rapidly. In the late 1930s these proportions had reversed, with a small number of tenured faculty overseeing a large number of untenured men who rotated through at a slower rate. The faculty listing of 1939–40 exemplifies this tendency: two full professors, under whom were two assistant professors and five instructors. This modern pattern suggests a radical alteration in the university's sense of itself from the stable community of teachers and pupils of the early years of the nineteenth century to a teaching institution making the most efficient possible use of personnel.

Then as now, fellowships in the humanities were funded at lower levels than those in the sciences. The most lucrative, and presumably the most prestigious, were the Boudinot Fellowships. Established in 1873 and based on examinations in French, German, and history, they conferred $250 on each of three recipients.[3] In German the examination encompassed the history of literature from Klopstock to the death of Goethe; three dramas (*Nathan der Weise, Egmont*, and *Maria Stuart*), and one translation from English to German (but none from German to English). Subsequent examinations expanded the field to include "Luther to Lessing" (1876). The first holder, J. H. Scribner, used his award to study in Germany, but a remarkable number of early Boudinot holders remained at Princeton as junior instructors. Very few recipients opted to study abroad, especially after the fellowships' value was reduced in 1892 to $200 apiece. Another award, the Humphreys Prize, instituted in 1908, recognized the best examination on junior-level courses, 31–32 and 33–34, with a $40 prize. This award, too, was diminished when it became two separate prizes of $25 and $15 in 1920.

Organizationally, German existed for decades in what seems to have been an uneasy partnership with French within the Department of Languages and Literatures. Set up in the 1880s as one of four university departments, it embraced Greek, Latin, English, Rhetoric, Oratory, English Composition, and Modern Languages and Literature. Faculty and instructors, a division made in the listing of teaching personnel, seemed to teach according to their abilities and capacities, filling perceived needs insofar as areas of competence made it possible, but not according to a departmental structure which reflected a clear perception of the disciplines of language and literature study. In 1891 German began its separatist path when language groups were designated. A further reorganization in 1900 deleted Rhetoric and differentiated Modern Languages into German, French, Italian, and Spanish. In 1904 a radical reorganization broke the Division of Languages and Literatures down into Classics, English, and Modern Languages. Dividing itself into two sections, Germanic and Romanic, the Department of Modern Languages incorporated the previously separate Science and Arts language faculties into a single group.

One can infer changes in attitude of the college toward the teaching of German over the years from the way in which course listings appeared. In the early nineteenth century the instructor clearly dictated the subject matter. No evidence surfaces that the college felt any inherent necessity to offer one modern language rather than another. This was demonstrated particularly clearly in 1841 when A. Cardon de Sandrans replaced Benedict Jaeger. German disappeared along with Jaeger, the lapse obscured somewhat by identifying Sandrans as a "Teacher of Modern Languages." As long as Greek and Latin remained the handmaidens of theology, their association with the queen of the sciences ensured them a privileged place in the curriculum and pushed modern languages to the rear. Exemplifying this tendency, the college bulletin, which listed faculty members according to the importance of their subject, put Frederick Perrin (teaching French and German in 1849) into last position. When Carl Langlotz joined the faculty in 1858 as "Teacher of German" he, too, was placed at the end of the list, preceded even by the registrar. However, a little later in the century the Princeton curriculum had accommodated itself to modern concerns about science and mathematics, and the classical languages came to be regarded simply as another set of languages, whereas, with the center of scientific discovery and development manifestly in German universities, the German language came to be seen as a necessity.[4] Under the heading "Future Course of Instruction," the catalog in 1868–69 noted that "at the beginning of the next college year, the Course of Instruction will undergo some important changes recently ordered by the trustees." Among others "the Sophomore Class will have one weekly exercise in Natural History and one in Modern Languages (French or German)."[5] During the 1870s French and German were systematically incorporated into the course of study, part of a general shift in priorities which stuffed Biblical literature into a catch-all "Courses not included in any of the preceding departments" in 1911, a move which dethroned theology, the former queen of the curriculum. Philosophy now reigned supreme, followed by oriental languages, classics, modern languages and literature, and English, but even this hierarchical remnant fell to simple alphabetical listings in 1932, suggesting that at last subjects were broadly perceived as valid in and of themselves rather than in relationship to a central body of knowledge, be it theology or philosophy.

Admissions requirements and language requirements for graduation offer yet another approach for assessing the position and stature of German language and literature within the university in those years. A school to prepare candidates for admission to Princeton opened its doors in 1873. Thirty-eight eager scholars from the South and the Midwest immediately filled all available places and settled in to perfect their Greek and Latin. But modern languages, which played no part in these young scholars' course of study, soon acquired greater prominence. In 1890 applicants could offer a knowledge of either French or German for admission to the College of Sciences, French having been required since 1886, while for advanced standing in modern languages, some knowledge of French or German was deemed desirable, but no examination was required. In 1892 the bulletin announced that beginning in 1894 the Arts College would also require an examination in elementary German or French, in addition to Latin or Greek, which were still required. The examination itself required the translation of fifty pages of easy prose from Grimm's *Märchen* or Meissner's *Aus meiner Welt*. The extent to which the Grimms dominated this aspect of German shows up in alterations made to this requirement. In 1903 Grimms' *Märchen* were replaced by Andersen's fairy tales, but Wilhelmi's farce about the Grimms, *Einer muß heiraten* was added![6] When the CEEB examinations became available for admissions testing in 1915, the College of Arts required English, mathematics, Latin, and Greek for admission, while the College of Sciences required English, mathematics, Latin, and French or German, with the German examination adapted to the proficiency of those who had studied it in school 2–3 years. In 1917 the proficiency examinations added oral and aural components "with a view to encouraging the secondary schools to lay greater emphasis on pronunciation and ultimately of requiring an oral test on the modern languages for admission" (1917–18, 95). Consisting of dictation, simultaneous translation, and answering questions in the language, by 1925 the oral/aural test determined advanced placement, with failure redirecting the student to a freshman course. Only fifteen years later (1940) the language scene had altered immeasurably. Gone was the brave intention to encourage secondary schools to emphasize spoken German and French; undergraduates might be admitted with one language at level three or two languages at level two, the equivalent of meeting the requirement for a reading knowledge. Indeed, the language requirements for graduation aimed no higher. In 1940–41 proficiency was spelled out as "an adequate foundation for acquiring a satisfactory reading knowledge." This statement both characterized and ended more than a century of German at Princeton. In succeeding years the entire approach departed from this hallowed paradigm.

World War I and Its Aftermath

World War I marked an educational as well as a social and historical turning point in the perceived relevance of the study of German. The "Study of German Institutions" and "Military German," courses which were added (fall of 1918) to the undergraduate curriculum, assisted the war effort as part of officer training. At the same time, however, both graduate enrollment and faculty availability were diminished by the requirements of armed service; four courses were dropped "temporarily" in the graduate curriculum, with courses being offered in alternate years for the first time beginning in 1919. The disappearance of the survey course in literature from graduate offerings suggests a higher level of preparation among graduate students entering the program, a conclusion borne out by the addition of more highly specified course content such as "The Novel" and "Literature since 1885" in the following years. Because of war service, the German faculty diminished from eight to three from 1915 to 1919; by 1921 there were four, and by adding two instructors in 1925, the faculty rose to six, still only three-quarters of its pre-war strength and a bellwether for the following two decades of declining popularity and enrollments.

At the end of the nineteenth century it had seemed self-evident that educated men and women would enjoy at least a passing familiarity with German, but twenty-five years later it was necessary to spell out clear reasons for doing so: in 1925 the Department of Languages and Literatures, of which German formed a part, offered plans of study supported by a rationale. All options were "designed to provide not only training in literature and language study, but to interpret one of the great European civilizations or some important period," with a minimum of six courses in the department required. Meanwhile the graduate enrollment appears to have continued to decrease, for three courses—"German Literature since 1885," "Historical German Grammar," and "Introduction to the Study of Old German Literature"—were dropped into the category "in case of sufficient demand" (1926), while at the same time graduates were allowed to take certain undergraduate courses for graduate credit. Three years later Gothic was co-listed with the Department of Oriental Languages and Literatures, further contracting course offerings.

Mid-1930s catalogs reveal a changing sense of individual courses. In addition to the material to be explored, the aims of undergraduate courses were clearly stated. In this same period, graduate courses also became increasingly specific in title and content: two semesters of "German Prose Fiction" became "The Romantic Period" and "The German Lyric."

The World War II Years and After

During and after World War II the teaching of German at Princeton University differed in every respect from that of the preceding century. If there was a single cause, it surely resided in the shift of the ethnic complexion of the Department of Modern Languages and Literatures. Every division—French, German, Portuguese, Russian, and Spanish—hired more and more native speakers, but this was particularly the case among the Germanists. This single fact made itself felt in departmental organization, staffing, the distribution of personnel, visiting scholars, the curriculum, and even in teaching aims and methods.

The curriculum of World War II looked very different from that of the World War I years. Instead of the language departments looking at the culture and institutions of the national enemy Germany, as they had done in a gentlemanly way during World War I, the university as a whole threw itself into the military effort by incorporating courses in lubricating military vehicles and overhauling engines under ROTC supervision. In the Germanic division, however, courses revolved not around military German, but instead around Goethe. Of the five courses offered from 1943–45, three took Goethe as a reference point: "Goethe's Life and Works," "Goethe's Faust," and "German Literature since Goethe's Death."[7] The anachronism of viewing German literature through a periscope directed at Goethe emerges from the course description of "German Literature since Goethe's Death," which described itself as dealing with literature "in the last hundred years," generously conferring an extra decade on Goethe's lifespan! One also notes that, although the town of Princeton had more than its share of refugees from the Third Reich, only four appeared, and then very briefly, on the published list of teaching staff of the department.[8] And finally, enrollments and departmental size increased after World War II, a trend opposite to that following World War I.

It is interesting and perhaps instructive to look closely at the composition of the German teaching faculty at Princeton from the earliest year for which data are available, 1819. Very roughly, one may characterize the teaching of German at Princeton in the nineteenth century and in the twentieth century up to World War II as a task undertaken by American-born tenured faculty members as well as by their usually American-born juniors. There were individual exceptions, naturally, but like the rest of the faculty, the language departments consisted predominantly of native-born Americans in those years. From the 1890s (when all languages had been lumped together in a single department) the various linguistic disciplines seemed to cohabit relatively serenely. When "modern languages" split off from oriental and classical languages, they divided gracefully into the Romanic and Germanic divisions, and graciously alternated precedence; "Germanic" came first in the undergraduate course listings, while in the graduate listings "Romanic" opened the listings. In the 1930s, 1940s, and 1950s, however, as French-, Spanish-, Italian-, Russian- and German-born instructors and tenured professors entered departmental ranks, they may well have brought traditional national animosities with them. "Romanic" continued to precede "Germanic" in the graduate catalog, but "French" maintained its primacy in the undergraduate listings by putting all the modern languages offered there in alphabetical order—with French firmly in the van.[9] More importantly, the French division dominated the chairmanship of this department over a twenty-year period, with a relatively brief appearance by a representative from the German section in the 1930s; for a long period thereafter, no full professor represented German interests. But by 1950–51 four regular members comprised the German section of the Department of Modern Languages and Literatures, most or all of whom were German-born. When the department formally separated into the Department of Germanic Languages and Literatures, the nine-member department was predominantly German-born, although the instructors and assistants in instruction were predominantly American-born.

A dramatic expansion in the Department of Modern Languages in 1946–47 created a department of three full professors, four associate professors, eleven assistant professors, and twenty instructors. Further expansion in 1947–48 resulted in two new categories, part-time instructors and part-time assistants. This many soldiers needed a general, and in 1948, after many years without a full professor in German, one arrived at Princeton, but no associate professors appeared until one of the assistant professors was promoted and tenured the following year.

Relatively little changed in the next few years until the newly formed Department of Germanic Languages and Literatures came into independent existence.[10] At this point, two opposing tendencies in staffing became apparent. At the senior level, American-born senior scholars were hired into the department, while at the lower levels, it was primarily German native speakers who were promoted and tenured. The final result was that ultimately native speakers of German moved into tenured positions which became available because of retirements or moves, creating eventually a department whose tenured component was composed principally of German-born native speakers.

A second direction in hiring procedures began in 1972, when the German faculty added its first regularly hired female.[11] Further hirings in 1973 (Instructor), 1974 (Lecturer), 1976 (Lecturer), 1979 (Assistant Professor), 1980 (Professor), 1981 (Lecturer), and 1985 (Assistant Professor) insured the presence of one or more women in the department. Thus from the point in 1972 when the United States Department of Health, Education and Welfare reportedly exerted pressure on the university to move toward a faculty that was ten percent female and six percent minority, the German Department took measures to cooperate.[12]

The distribution of personnel within the department followed a predictable course in the years after World War II. The most recently hired junior faculty generally took on responsibility for two areas: beginning and intermediate language instruction and the lowest level non-language course, "Contemporary German Society."

The curriculum shows the greatest change after 1950. The immediate postwar years retained a reliance upon Goethe as a central figure from which all other literature was dated. When a sixth course was introduced in 1945 to join those mentioned at the opening of this section, it was called—characteristically—"Selected Readings from Goethe to Thomas Mann." But this marked the final moment of such devotion. The next year, the two-semester course, "German Literature since Goethe's Death," was renamed "German Literature of the Nineteenth Century" and "Modern German Literature," although the second semester of "German Literature in the Eighteenth Century" reintegrated Goethe's name in "The Age of Goethe and Schiller." A further name change the following year changed "German Literature from Goethe to Thomas Mann" to "Fundamental Aspects of German Literature," while another new course, "The History of German Thought: Reformation to Present," made its appearance. These alterations, small and inconsequential in themselves, reveal profound changes in the way department members defined their subject. As Goethe's domination of Germanics diminished, other perspectives opened. By 1949 Goethe remained in the title of only one course, with thematic approaches beginning to be explored ("The Individual and Society in German Literature"). "Relevance" appeared to be anathema in the postwar years, for whereas a course on German society had appeared in the last year of World War I, the first course to address a similar subject after World War II waited a full decade after the invasion of Normandy to make its debut. "Introduction to Germany," offered in English, outlined "factors such as geography, history, culture, customs, religion, sociological and political conditions which have played their part in the evolution of modern Germany." On the language side courses expanded and were differentiated into "Beginner's German," "Intensive Intermediate," "Lower-Intermediate," "Upper-Intermediate," "Advanced," and "Studies in German Language and Style."

Both language and literature courses were offered in ever more closely defined units in the 1960s and 1970s. As the century wore on it was certainly natural to differentiate twentieth-century literature and thought. "Expressionism," "Origins of Modernism," "Modern German Poetry," and "Intellectual History of Germany" appeared in 1969 for the first time. At the nadir of general interest in German as a major, course titles seem designed to entice, for instance, "Rebellion, Reaction and Realism," a good deal peppier than its former title, "Aspects of German Literature." Such disparate offerings made it possible to outline three separate areas of concentration within the department beginning in 1973: German Civilization, German Literature, and German Language, to which a fourth was added a few years later, German Linguistics. The extensive list of courses did not necessarily reflect higher enrollments, for of the eighteen courses in literature and civilization listed for 1978–79, only nine were actually offered in that year, a relatively minor increase over the six courses given in the 1940s.

Instructional aims and methods both showed considerable change during the postwar years. This can best be followed by looking closely at course descriptions for entry and exit language courses, outlines of the major, and comments on graduate education. In 1958–59 German 101–102 was described as it had been for several years: "Introduction to phonetics, essentials of grammar, composition, graded readings. For students with no previous study of German. Prepares for 105. Three hours of class, three hours of drill per week for two terms.'' The following year a different set of desiderata appeared: ''This course aims at an early command of German through the *spoken* language. The course meets six hours: three times a week in small drill groups for intensive oral practice and tape work; and three times in larger class sections for grammar-analysis and reading.'' This course description lasted twelve years. In 1971 a different organization of class time aimed at the same goals: ''This course aims at an early command of German through the *spoken* language. Limited to fifteen students. Five hours of grammatical analysis, drill, and oral practice, one additional hour in the language laboratory.'' A final shift in the statement of aims (1976) again emphasizes the traditional skill in foreign language acquisition, reading ability: ''This course aims at an early command of German by developing four skills: hearing, speaking, reading, and writing. Oral-aural practice, oral and written exercises, grammatical analysis in classes of fifteen students. Covers all fundamental syntactical forms and enables students to read and speak moderately difficult German. Five classes, one one-hour laboratory.'' In these shifts the German department followed trends set in the teaching profession as a whole, beginning with methods employed at the then United States Army language facilities in Monterey and continuing with an echo of language teaching methods developed in the broader American language teaching community.

The linguistic demands of the exit course also suggested an increasing rigor: ''Reading and analysis of literary and expository texts, with discussions and occasional brief lectures in German. Outside reading in German. Satisfies the language requirement and serves as prerequisite for upper-class German courses. Prerequisite: 105 or CEEB score of 600.'' The ''occasional brief lectures in German'' presumably prepared the student for courses counting towards a major in German, where they could expect to hear far more German.

As more and more native speakers filled teaching positions in all sections of the Modern Languages Department, pressure for teaching in the language of the course material had been building. In 1943–44, the following announcement preceded French literature and civilization courses: ''In all upperclass courses . . . provision will be made for at least one preceptorial to be conducted in French.'' In the following year the use of French was extended to the lectures themselves with these words: ''Courses in French literature and civilization will be in French, preceptorials in English or French according to the students' desires and capabilities.'' German quickly followed suit, adopting the French formula as its own: ''Courses in German Literature and Civilization. Lectures will be in German, preceptorials in English or German according to the students' desires and capabilities.''

In 1959 the university changed the format in which it presented itself to the public. To the undergraduate and graduate catalogs it added a third publication which offered general information about the university. Each department thus had the opportunity to introduce itself and to outline its aims. German offered this distinctly interdisciplinary message: "Departmental work in the German language and literature is intended to provide a comprehensive view of German culture through a study of the chief representatives of German arts and letters as well as history and philosophy." As an aid to approaching German culture, a summer work program had been instituted: "Departmental students are offered an opportunity of paid summer-work in German industry, which is designed to bring the student into closest contact with German life and institutions."

The union of German arts, letters, history, and philosophy into a broadly defined major in German culture, however, subsequently broke down into much smaller, more narrowly defined units. Beginning in 1971, potential German majors chose among three areas, each with a specified purpose:

> Area A: *German Civilization* aims at providing an understanding of contemporary Germany and its historical background through the study of writers, artists, and thinkers, as well as of political issues.
> Area B: *German literature* focuses on major periods and forms of German literature with emphasis on literary criticism and the socio-political context.
> Area C: *German language* concentrates on the history and structure of the German language.

In this narrower focus, the major followed the lead taken by the courses themselves.

The avowed aims of the graduate program took the same path. In the 1960–61 Graduate School Announcement, graduate study was broadly defined with reference to scholarly methods and to the material which graduate students would address:

> Graduate instruction in the Department of Germanic Languages and Literatures is designed to acquaint the student with the aims and methods of scholarship, to develop an intelligent appreciation of literature, and to make him an effective teacher. The special purpose of graduate work in this field is to provide the student with a thorough understanding of German culture, its language and literature, and its relationship to the whole of Western Civilization.

Seven years later the purpose of graduate education was redefined for the 1967–68 Graduate School Announcement: "Graduate instruction in the Department is designed to enable the student to become an effective teacher and a productive scholar in the field of German language and literature." Although learning how to become a productive scholar is inherent in the process of seminar learning, the acquisition of teaching skills is not, but no formal course addressed the special problems which a graduate student might encounter in his or her teaching either language or literature. This omission was addressed in the catalog, though not in the curriculum, for later editions added the following: "The department endeavors, as a matter of policy, to give each graduate student supervised experience in undergraduate teaching and regards such training as an integral part of the Graduate Program." In subsequent years, at least one term of supervised teaching experience was stipulated as a requirement for the Ph.D. degree, while the candidate's own proficiency in German was expected to be of a sufficiently high degree to speak extemporaneously in German in a final public oral examination which was "to make a final estimate of the student's abilities as a scholar and critic and to determine his or her effectiveness in oral discourse in both English and German."

The foregoing material outlines how a single department presented itself and its subject matter over more than a century. Aims may have differed from results; in the university catalogs the tips of many icebergs appear whose extent and dimensions further study might clarify. Institutions have relatively short memories. How things were, even a brief time ago, is soon forgotten, and new generations of participants in the teaching process imagine that the past trails off into a uniform otherness from the change they seek to initiate themselves. This study has left many tantalizing questions that I hope a subsequent scholar will want to take up to illuminate the precise relationships between personalities, policy, and the teaching process.

Notes

1 I have pursued this subject not as a historian but as a literary critic. My text has been the annual bulletin of the college. A historian would have sifted through the notes of faculty meetings, examined enrollment lists, scrutinized budget allocations, and might also have scoured surviving evidence for clues about the social origins and subsequent career trajectories of students, faculty, and administrators. As a literary critic I have taken a different route, partly because I did not wish to invest the enormous amount of time burrowing into mountains of records to find coherent patterns in infinite bits of disparate data which an institutional history would have required. I have taken the route at once the most and the least obvious, the 160 years of annual publications in which the university presented itself to itself and to its public. This sole source reveals the university's stance on a number of issues, although it does not lay bare the divisions and disputes which preceded new directions taken. But just as what people *do* indicates their beliefs far more surely than what they *say,* so here patterns of corporate beliefs and intentions appear which can be inferred, analyzed, and understood with perhaps the same conclusions that a historian might have reached using resources appropriate to him or her.

2 This fact suggests that extra charges for learning German turned students away, for the bulletin continues to note that there is no extra charge for French and Spanish instruction.

3 At the same date the university catalog lists analogous fellowships in the sciences conferring $600.

4 The speed with which this accommodation could be made surfaces in the change in course names. "The Relationships of Science, Philosophy and Religion" (1865–66) became "The Harmony of Science and Revealed Religion" (1866–67), which in turn changed to "Evidences of Natural and Revealed Religion" two years later (1868–69).

5 The "others" in this case include the history of philosophy, political economy, English language, English literature, organic and applied chemistry, modern history, the science of language, French language and literature, and German language and literature.

6 The catalog suggested that satisfactory preparation for this examination could be furnished by the two year MLA course. It would be interesting to compare what this course covered with what is required for advanced standing today.

7 The other two were eighteenth-century literature and Romanticism.

8 An illustrious, and unlisted, refugee, Thomas Mann, accepted a guest professorship, whose duties he describes not as formal classroom teaching but consisting principally of occasional lectures. He touches on this in the essay, "Sechzehn Jahre": "Aber meine Verbindung mit der Universität, als Gastprofessor, legte mir sanfte Pflichten auf: Öffentliche Vorträge und solche für fortgeschrittene Studenten, über Goethe's [sic] *Faust* und *Werther,* über Freud, über die Geschichte des europäischen Romans, sogar über den *Zauberberg* wurden ausgearbeitet." His brief stay in Princeton ended in the spring of 1940 when he moved to Brentwood, California. See Thomas Mann: *Autobiographisches,* ed. Erika Mann (Frankfurt: Fischer, 1968) 267–70.

9 This observation may appear to be based on trivial information, but the order and extent of information presented in the university's catalogs corroborates this hypothesis.

10 In his autobiography Benno von Wiese paints a memorable (but largely unflattering) portrait both of the department at this transitional point in its development and of the university itself. See *Ich erzähle mein Leben* (Frankfurt: Insel, 1982) 279–87.

11 Directly after World War II, the department had hired two female refugees for a single year.

12 *Prospect,* 1.2 (1972): 5.

Domesticating the Revolution: The Kindergarten Movement in Germany and America

JEANNINE BLACKWELL
University of Kentucky

For most of us, kindergarten calls up memories of harmless fun, Graham crackers, and milk. The kindergarten has become such an accepted, uncontroversial institution of American primary education that we would hardly think of it today as an agent of social change or as a radical philosophical experiment. But just as those innocent Graham crackers are themselves the product of a populist health movement in nineteenth-century America—Sylvester Graham's self-curing vegetarianism, which was later absorbed into the mainstream of American nutrition—so the kindergarten comes from a long tradition of radical experiment and popular agitation for institutional change. In its nineteenth-century origins, the kindergarten was not only a social movement led primarily by women in Germany and America and a vehicle for the furthering of women's education; it was also the embodiment of revolutionary democracy. As such it was regarded suspiciously by both the autocracy and the bureaucracy of Prussia. Indeed, the kindergarten was prohibited by the Prussian minister of education von Raumer on 7 August 1851 as atheistic, revolutionary, and destructive of the family.

How can we explain the threat which this happy little institution implied for the Prussian state? What place did it have in the traditions of German education and philosophy? How did it begin, why and how was it brought to America, and why did it thrive here? To explain the successful transplanting of this German educational institution in America, we must look at its roots in German idealism and republicanism.

Friedrich Froebel (1782–1852, figure 1), the founder in 1840 of the first kindergarten, was a product of the worst and best of the German cultural tradition. The son of a stern widower who was a Protestant theologian in Ilmstadt near Weimar, Froebel had very strict and needlessly confining primary schooling; he was ignored by most adults around him. A troublemaker in his confirmation class, he was considered by his teachers a lazy daydreamer. Meanwhile, he had lots of time to play by himself out of doors, discovering nature. The introspective recluse studied topography, geology, and languages at Jena and Göttingen. There he came

Figure 1. Friedrich Froebel reprinted from Ruth Baylor, *Elizabeth Palmer Peabody: Kindergarten Pioneer* (Philadelphia: University of Pennsylvania Press, 1965), facing p. 132.

across books by Fichte, Schiller, and Comenius, and through them he worked out his own philosophy of education. He carried his patriotic, nature-oriented philosophy further by working as a private tutor from 1803–1815, and by fighting with the Prussians in the Wars of Liberation. *Selbsttätigkeit* (self-activity), his notion both of self examination and self-motivated, autonomous action in learning the world, was the key to his educational plan.[1]

Developing himself in nature as a forestry apprentice, botanist, and surveyor, he began to see his life in organic metaphor: the bud, given sunshine and nourishment, becomes the rose. Froebel draws, of course, on a long literary tradition of the mind as a flower or a growing plant, but makes the practical application of the Romantic imagery by demanding actual sunshine and light for the human seed of intellect. "So erschien mir das Naturstudium, die Naturforschung als der Grund- und Eckstein, um auf einer anderen Stufe der Lebenserscheinungen über die Gesetze und den Gang der Menschenentwicklung, Menschenbildung, Menschenerziehung klar und sicher zu werden" (105). In accepting nature and introspection as the source of personal growth, he allied himself with Pietist thought, but the individualistic, nonconformist thrust of his teachings placed him squarely with the Romantics. Neither idea could be successfully executed without a heavy dash of German idealism. Froebel believed that humans can pull themselves out of their degradation by sublime effort, exposure to color, light, and nature. Froebel describes the process in his autobiographical notes. "Ein Kind, das ganz freithätig und freiwillig Blumen sucht, sie hegt und pflegt, um sie seinen Eltern, seinem Erzieher zum Strauß und Kranz zu winden, kann kein schlechtes Kind, kein schlechter Mensch werden. Ein solches Kind kann leicht zur Liebe, zum Dank, zur Erkenntniß seines väterlichen Gottes geführt werden, welcher ihm solche Gaben giebt und wachsen läßt, und damit seinen Eltern und sich selbst als froher Geber Freude zu machen" (92). Here Froebel gives outline to his sentimentalized view of childhood innocence, his advocacy of natural play; he then carries his theory of childlike religion to iconoclasm, which would later endanger the movement: "Ich schließe daraus, daß das naturgemäß geleitete Kind keiner positiv-kirchlichen Form bedarf, weil das liebend gepflegte und darum sich stetig und kräftig entwickelte Menschen- und Menschheitleben, also auch das ungetrübte Kindesleben, an und für sich ein christliches ist" (93).

Using this organic metaphor for early childhood, Froebel expanded his theory of "Kinderkultur" in his reading of three pedagogical philosophers who attempted to establish schools for older children: the seventeenth-century Czech Comenius, author of the first primers, the German nationalist philosopher Fichte, and the Swiss pedagogue Pestalozzi, with whom he worked and studied in 1805 and 1808–10. Froebel's kindergarten differed from the experimental infant schools established by Robert Owen in Great Britain or the *salles d'asile* of Jean Denis Marie Cochin in France: these social reformers attempted to correct the dehumanizing effects of early proletarianization by providing rudiments of education for poor, uncared for children whose parents worked in mills. The aim in part was to eliminate the social evil of criminal children. Froebel's kindergarten did not aim simply to get children off the street, to stop them from carousing, and to make them clean and quiet. Froebel wanted the kindergarten to lead children to love beautiful things through play; he believed that children might teach themselves the lessons of beauty and harmony by playing with color and form. Schiller's collection of letters, *Über die ästhetische Erziehung des Menschen,* profoundly influenced Froebel's thought. From Froebel's writings and kindergarten plans it is apparent that Schiller's fifteenth letter was a cornerstone of the kindergarten, as well as of Froebel's other pedagogical undertakings. Schiller states that humanity is most wholly itself when it learns beauty through play. For Schiller, playing with beauty creates a dynamic and harmonizing synthesis between material and spiritual human nature, rendering people most receptive to beauty, to the moral ideal which incorporates harmony, and thus to the final goals of humankind. Froebel, in essence, took Schiller's theory and made a practical program for the aesthetic education of humankind, beginning with K-12.

Froebel's kindergarten began, then, firmly rooted in the tradition of idealistic German philosophy and of utopian pedagogical experiment. Just as important for the further development of his movement was the mood of the times in the 1820s and 1830s. Already at the *Hambacher Fest* of 1832, Germans were chafing under the bit of autocracy. The call to the *Fest* served as a model for Froebel's appeal of 1840 for the establishment of a national system of kindergartens, which was addressed to the women of Germany.[2] In this appeal he called for the establishment of a *Kindergarten Aktiengesellschaft,* in which patriotic mothers would buy stock for Germany's children. This same combination of quixotic entrepreneurism and patriotic radicalism continued through the fluctuating life of the movement.

In this call for the national kindergarten and in his later writings, Froebel laid out his radical theory of child education. His program today sounds simple, harmless, and familiar.

1. Children are naturally constructive and destructive, and they play naturally. Instead of stopping them from playing alone and with each other, their play should be directed so that the children analyze their own play and draw conclusions about shape, use, and morality from this activity. Thus children learn to ask questions and come up with their own explanations instead of simply tearing things apart out of curiosity.

2. Froebel stressed the importance of physical development for children, insisting on the need for movement, space, fresh air, light, and bright colors. In a continuation of his organic metaphor, the kindergarten should truly be a garden "where children can grow." He wanted the children outside every possible minute, exercising, marching around, taking field trips, dancing, or gardening. We can see this in the plan of the Kindergarten (figure 2) expounded by Caroline Progler in Geneva, in an 1870 paper translated by kindergarten supporter and teacher Mrs. Horace Mann.[3] There are playrooms and workrooms for each of the classes, individual garden plots for each child, a large open lawn with trees for dancing and exercising, and vestibules for clothing and storage.

3. Children learn by teaching themselves the laws of harmony and form, and therefore are taught to sing and to manipulate geometric forms

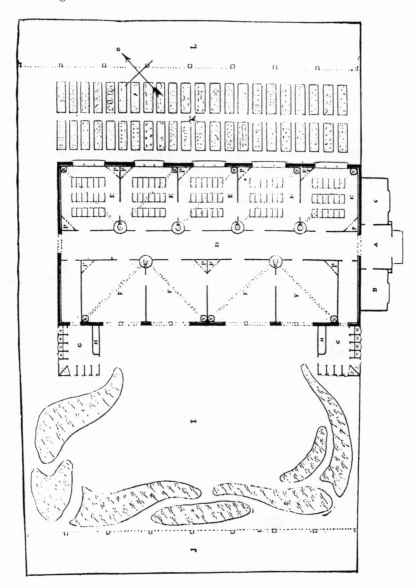

Figure 2. Floorplan of the Kindergarten, reprinted from *Papers on Froebel's Kinder-garten, with Suggestions on Principles and Methods of Child Culture in Different Countries,* ed. Henry Barnard (Hartford: American Journal of Education Press, 1890), p. 775.

in increasing difficulty and refinement as they get older. The 20 "Gaben" ("gifts") of Kindergarten play are the basis for these skills. Many of them are still among the creative playthings found in preschools and homes today (fourteen are illustrated in figure 3), including the first tinker toys: skeleton forms for building, made of cork cubes and pointed wires, which strike terror in the heart of today's parent. Stress was placed on the manipulation of primary colors and classic geometric shapes, on increasing levels of difficulty up to pattern perforations and clay modeling. The Froebelian method was very strict in this order of presentation, and in the types of designs children could make: geometric, harmonic, and by the book.

4. The Froebelian kindergarten drastically revised contemporary thinking on how children learn. It assumed that, in a social world, children need *more* than the family for training—they need their own social institutions for developing the best sense of utopian community. He thereby undermined the "natural" role of motherhood. Froebel felt that women should run the kindergartens, but under strict training programs and under

Figure 3. Fourteen of the twenty "Gaben" (gifts) of Kindergarten play, reprinted from *Papers on Froebel's Kindergarten, with Suggestions on Principles and Methods of Child Culture in Different Countries,* ed. Henry Barnard (Hartford: American Journal of Education Press, 1890), pp. 776–781. (Figure continues on next two pages.)

1st GIFT   2nd GIFT
Soft balls   Geometric shapes suspended
in primary colors   from strings

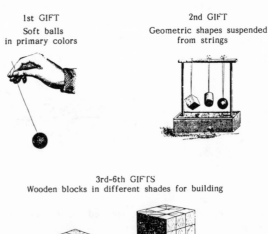

3rd-6th GIFTS
Wooden blocks in different shades for building

7th GIFT
Flat geometric shapes: squares,
obtuse, equilateral and right triangles

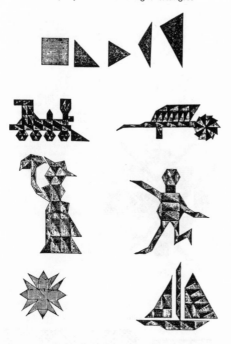

8th GIFT
Sticks in various lengths for laying

9th GIFT
Rings and half rings for laying

10th GIFT
Ruled paper or slateboard for drawing

13th GIFT
Square ruled paper for folding and cutting

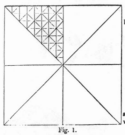

Fig. 1 represents the ruled paper before being folded.

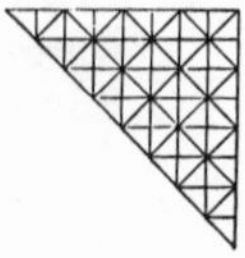

Fig. 2
Fig. 2 is one of the triangular surfaces which is on the outside when folded.

Fig. 1.

Fig. 3 represents this same surface with cutting marks applied.

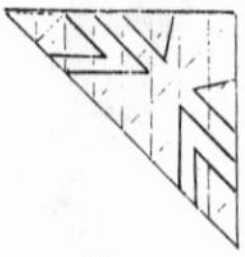

Fig. 3.

Fig. 4 is the same design when cut and mounted.

Fig. 4.

14th GIFT
Strips of colored paper for weaving

15th GIFT	16th Gift
wooden slats for laying and building	jointed wooden slats for geometric design

19th GIFT
Cork cubes and pointed wires for construction

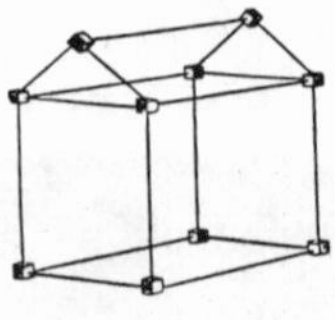

the control of a national pedagogical theory. The kindergarten thus undercut the private sphere theory of early childhood education, professionalized the raising of children, and provided an argument for the specialized training of women outside the home.

The theory of the kindergarten was thus a product of German idealism, innovations in pedagogical theory, and the rise in German national spirit. As such it should have been a noncontroversial addition to the improvements in state organization contemporaneous with the Stein reforms, the consolidation of governments during the Napoleonic occupation, and the rise in school attendance and literacy which began in the early nineteenth century.[4] In practice, however, the kindergarten took on other more threatening aspects in central German governments of the 1830s and 1840s.

First, its nondenominational character undermined the hold of parochial instruction in public schools. In Prussia and the German states, it meant a direct, local confrontation with the parish clergy, who saw their confirmation classes dwindle and propagation of religious ideas undermined. Very frequently the clergy condemned the local attempt at a kindergarten as evil, demonic, or atheistic. During the confrontations with local church leaders, more and more kindergarten supporters, who tended to be upper-class, idealist young women, such as Malwida von Meysenbug, Bertha Meyer Ronge, and Margarethe Meyer Schurz, became critical of established religion.

Second, the kindergarten encouraged autonomous action and thought in small children and put ideological power into the hands of leaders who were critical of Prussian autocracy. Froebel's experimental schools at Blankenburg and Keilhau reconfirmed suspicions: students did all the maintenance and farm work, ate a vegetarian diet, had long hair, and did not honor the Prussian uniform. Froebel educated his two nephews, Karl and Julius, who were firebrands and atheists in the 1840s and became the warning examples of what free education could do. In his memoirs, Julius Froebel insists that the radical reformist nature of his uncle's institutions made them unwelcome under the Prussian regime, with or without his own radicalism.[5] The prohibition caused others to rally around the beleaguered movement and to embrace it as part of the suppressed revolution of 1848. Indeed, it was a challenge to the hierarchy, because of its female leadership, anti-authoritarian national structure, and negative stance toward the Prussian state and organized religion. Thus it was included in the harsh mass prohibitions of 1850–51, which also forbade women from participation in public political meetings.[6]

The supporters of Froebel included many of the *freie Gemeinden,* the Freethinker groups which had formed after the enforced fusion of the Reformed and Lutheran churches into the *Evangelische Kirche* in 1822.

Unhappy both with the State church of Prussia and with the Catholic church, liberal republicans began to establish *deutsch-katholische* or *frei-denkende* congregations which advocated liberal reform and social action as practical, active, Christianity.[7] In many beliefs and community activities, they were similar to the Unitarian congregations in pre-civil war America, which bred abolitionism and the American women's rights movement.

A second group to align itself with the kindergarten movement consisted of German organizations supporting women's rights or women's education, ranging from the *Lette Verein* to Louise Otto-Peters' *Bund deutscher Frauenvereine*.[8] They spread from groups demanding access for women to university study and teacher training colleges to the most timid and patriotic voluntary nursing organizations. They glorified woman's natural domestic role on the one hand while demanding her professionalization and specialization on the other: women needed competent "natural" professionals in early childhood education, children's doctors, family legal experts, and administrators of schools, hospitals, nursing homes, servant training schools, and employment agencies. Female role specialization was thus its own cause and effect: the undermined and specialized role of "natural" motherhood bred the new professions, one of the most popular of which was kindergarten teaching. Many of the leaders of the German women's movement—Louise Otto-Peters, Henriette Goldschmidt, and Auguste Schmidt—were strong proponents of the kindergarten in their journals.

The kindergarten found a base in the political climate of pre-revolutionary Germany, but its association with these progressive groups was also its temporary downfall. Froebel himself died soon after the prohibition. Many of his more radical followers had gone to Hamburg, where Karl Froebel and Emilie Wüstenfeld established a training school for kindergarten teachers in close association with the Freethinker church. The school was closed in 1851, and many of its students had to go into exile: Margarethe Meyer Schurz, Bertha Meyer Ronge, and Malwida von Meysenbug went to England. Even under suppression, however, they began to use their skills in exile: Bertha Meyer Ronge established a kindergarten in Manchester, England; Johanna Kinkel wrote *Songs for little Children* in London, 1852; and Malwida von Meysenbug applied the Froebelian principles as a governess to Alexander Herzen's children in British exile.

The Kindergarten in Exile

The kindergarten, compared to the larger republican institutions demanded by the 1848ers, was a small, simple, mobile arrangement: it required only

Figure 4. Margarethe Meyer Schurz. Courtesy of Watertown, Wisconsin, Historical Society.

a teacher who could read and sing, some bits of paper and cork, a room, and children. It is not surprising, then, that the kindergarten was the only lasting institution among those transported with the exiles to England and then to America. A first attempt to establish a Froebelian elementary school was made in 1838 by Froebel's student Caroline Frankenburg in her short-lived private German language school in St. Louis.[9] Due to a lack of students and financial support, she returned to Germany for further work and study. Twenty years later she did run a successful kindergarten in Germantown, Pennsylvania, and lived in America until her death. The first successful kindergarten in the United States was established by Margarethe Meyer Schurz (figure 4), whose sister Bertha Meyer Ronge had

Figure 5. Elizabeth Palmer Peabody. Courtesy of The Schlesinger Library, Radcliffe College

established the first kindergarten in England, and whose brother Adolph Meyer, a wealthy merchant in Hamburg, had bankrolled several kindergarten undertakings. Both sisters had studied at the Froebelian school in Hamburg. Margarethe and her husband, the revolutionary leader and exile Carl Schurz, had moved the family to Watertown, Wisconsin, a German settlement, and here in 1856 Margarethe started up a small class composed of her children, their cousins, and friends. The experiment would have remained a family enterprise if her idea had not found reinforcement among other of the 1848 exiles: Adolf Douai attempted to start his own kindergarten, based on his reading of Froebel, in Hoboken in 1861, with the support of his associate, radical editor Karl Heinzen, and Maria E. Zakrewska, one of the first woman physicians and an associate of Elizabeth Blackwell.[10] Julia A. Sprague began a kindergarten in Boston with the encouragement of Karl Heinzen. Douai wrote several books on the kindergarten and primary primers in the tradition of Comenius' *Orbis Pictu*[11]; he established a kindergarten training school in New York and convinced Peter Engelmann of the Deutsch-Amerikanische Akademie that there should be a kindergarten teachers' training school in the academy in Milwaukee. The Douai kindergarten failed with little public notice, and he became convinced that only women could effectively lead the Froebelian pre-schools.

The kindergarten would have remained an old world remnant of the exile community, taught in German, if a connection to educational leaders in the English-speaking community had not been established. Margarethe Schurz brought the kindergarten to the attention of Elizabeth Palmer Peabody (figure 5), the tireless translator and supporter of liberal causes, whose indirect association with the Brook Farm experiment and whose teaching in Bronson Alcott's infant school had prepared her for radical experiment in education.[12] Elizabeth Peabody embraced the idea and threw all her formidable energies behind it. She convinced her sister, Mary Peabody Mann, and her brother-in-law, Horace Mann, of its worth, and set up in 1858 her own kindergarten and teacher training school. She started the first English language kindergarten in Boston in 1859. The idea spread through Peabody's intellectual connections to New York, Davenport, and Philadelphia. Her long correspondence with Henry Barnard, the first U. S. Commissioner of Education, led to his "conversion" to kindergartens and his inclusion of many important articles in his periodical, *The American Journal of Education*. Horace Mann, the successor to Barnard's post, again gave moral, if not financial support, to early childhood education in the public schools. The Manns were already aware of the excellence of German schools from their 1843 trip to Germany, inspired by the Cousin report on instruction.[13]

Publicity was a crucial factor in the spread of kindergarten doctrine to the Midwest and the frontier. Barnard's *American Journal of Education*, Engelmann's normal school organ *Monatshefte*, Peabody's *Kindergarten Messenger* and other publications, and the emerging International Kindergarten Union, which eventually merged with the National Education Association, provided a basis for the spread of the kindergarten as an americanized institution.[14]

Later emigration of women trained in Froebel institutions enhanced the direct influence of the German movement in America. Mathilde Kriege and her daughter arrived in New York and came to Boston to assist in Peabody's training school while she was in Germany, studying Froebel's method and developing contacts with other kindergarten supporters. Johannes Kraus came to Texas in 1848, later joining Maria Boelte, later Kraus-Boelte, at her seminary for kindergartners in New York in 1873. The Kriege women, Maria Kraus-Boelte (figure 6), and Elizabeth Peabody

Figure 6. Maria Kraus-Boelte reprinted from *Pioneers of the Kindergarten in America,* prepared by the Committee of Nineteen
(New York: Century, 1924), facing p. 80.

trained over 3,000 women as kindergarten teachers in their lives and
thereby established the faculty for the American movement. There were
privately run kindergartens in New York, Boston, Washington, Milwaukee, Philadelphia, St. Louis, and Baltimore—frequently in cities with large
German educational establishments—by the 1870s. Emma Marwedel, a
German immigrant, founded a kindergarten first in Washington, D.C., and
then established the movement on the West Coast in 1876. Her most
famous student, Kate Smith Wiggin (figure 7), led the Silver Street kindergarten in San Francisco from 1881.

Money was always a problem. Douai's kindergarten failed not only
because of his lack of expertise, but also because of a shortage of funds

Figure 7. Kate Douglas Wiggin reprinted from Agnes Snyder, *Dauntless Women in Childhood Education, 1856–1931* (Washington, D.C.: Association for Childhood Education International Press, 1942), p. 88.

and German-speaking pupils; Elizabeth Peabody was constantly on fund-raising trips and ventures to support her school. Her bookshop in Boston, a gathering place for the *Dial* group of Transcendentalists, her brother-in-law Nathaniel Hawthorne, and the Concord School of Philosophy, was such a moneymaking venture. She went on lecture tours, as did the abolitionists and supporters of women's rights, and thus spread the gospel of the American kindergarten. The movement received a considerable boost from the interest of entrepreneur toymaker Milton Bradley, who smelled a profit to be made, and developed and marketed the kindergarten "gifts" in America with Peabody's encouragement.[15] They had previously been handmade by the kindergarten workers, or imported from Europe. Now they could be mass marketed, and the burgeoning market of educational and ladies magazines in post-1860 America provided a willing public for these goods. Gradually a market developed for the handbooks for teachers and mothers. Froebel's works were translated and popularized in English: his *Mother-Play* went through at least sixteen editions, while *Education of Man* saw twenty editions before 1912. *The Student's Froebel* became a handbook in normal colleges throughout the United States, and if Michigan State University's dog-eared and underlined copies are any indication, they were used extensively. To supplement seed money for her San Francisco kindergarten, Kate Smith Wiggin wrote children's stories based on the "new education": *The Story of Patsy, Marm Lisa,* and *Rebecca of Sunnybrook Farm* were products of her fund-raising efforts. The kindergarten movement thus set the theme for modern children's literature in America.

Peabody's extensive correspondence with the unconvinced William T. Harris, superintendent of the St. Louis Public Schools, finally achieved results, and he agreed to allow Susan Blow, a student of Kraus-Boelte and an independently wealthy kindergartner, to establish kindergartens in St. Louis under the aegis of the public school system in 1873. It was no doubt beneficial to the American movement that Harris, a later U. S. Commissioner of Education, received his doctorate from Jena and admired the German school system. Meanwhile, Felix Adler, a German immigrant with a doctorate from Heidelberg, leader of the American branch of the Freethinker Church and President of the Society of Ethical Culture, established kindergartens in the West. Much of his support came from the German Jewish community in California and New York. He was the first to connect kindergartens with supporting charities, and thus the California preschools took money from the Hearst Foundation and the Stanford Endowment. Philanthropic and influential American-born women—Pauline Agassiz Shaw, Lucretia Willard Treat (Emma Willard's granddaughter), and even Louisa May Alcott assisted in kindergartens. By 1882 there were 500 kindergartens in the United States, with 1,000 teachers and 20,000 pupils. By 1901, less than twenty years later, there were 5,107 kindergartens with almost 10,000 teachers and 243,447 pupils.[16]

The devotion of the old guard leadership to the increasingly stylized Froebelian principles took on the features of a religious cult. By the 1880s Froebelian orthodoxy and unorthodoxy became an issue as women borrowed the name to start schools of their own in various cities, and as the sale of books and toys became a source of profit. Professional accreditation of kindergartners was called for by the orthodox group, which started the International Kindergarten Union in 1870. These leaders brooked no variation from the specifics of the Froebelian method as expounded by Countess Berta von Marenholtz-Bülow, the principal spokesperson of his ideas from 1861 on.

One of the issues in the generational battle for hegemony was German influence on the training of teachers, and strict adherence to the original Froebelian model. This model had become increasingly conservative in the years of prohibition: advocates of the kindergarten tended to be aristocratic women who took on progressive teaching methods for their privately educated children; with the rise of Bismarck and a conservative nationalism to replace the republican nationalism of 1848, the cutting edge of the kindergarten's radical patriotism was dulled. With the rise of normal schools for elementary teachers in Prussia and the German states, kindergarten methods were gradually introduced. When von Raumer was replaced as Minister of Education in 1861, aristocrats were able to have the kindergarten reinstated. Leadership roles in the movement were then assumed by aristocrats and mainstream educators in Germany.

As the first generation of American exile kindergartners retired from the educational front, younger American women whose education had proceeded under the influence of Darwinian biology, genetics, and modern psychology came to the fore in the 1890s. Patty Smith Hill, a fifth generation "daughter" of Elizabeth Palmer Peabody, later professor of early childhood education at Columbia, is an example of the new breed. Following the lead of Alice Putnam in Chicago and Anna Bryan, her own teacher in Louisville who had collaborated with John Dewey, she called publicly for a revision of kindergarten principles.[17] These leaders rejected the close handwork of the Froebelian gifts, while accepting the larger objects of play; they investigated motor ability and physiological capabilities measured by age and thus could predict more exactly which activities would tire children and which would help them grow. They stressed the importance of exercising the creative urge through free sketching and freehand drawing rather than copying of designs and the necessity for children to escape geometric forms to create their own pictures. They felt that the Froebelian method was tied to the examples and atmosphere of European small village life and that American children needed to have that method adapted to fit their urban, industrial existence. The original illustrations from Froebel's *Mother Play* display the idyllic German village world they were rejecting as an American model (figure 8). Here we see mother and child in an idealized, Germanic medieval setting, the mother in a long gown playing with the child amid simple trades of carpentry and agriculture. The glorification of the Germanic past, which served a real political function in Froebel's mid-century republican ideal, was merely quaint in turn-of-the-century America: it did not give children what they needed to know about their environment. I need only mention the anachronism of the kindergarten at Hull House in Chicago, where the children of industrial

Figure 8. Illustrations from Friedrich Froebel, *Motherplay and Nursery Songs,* ed. Elizabeth Palmer Peabody, trans. Josephine Jarvis (Boston: Lothrop, Lee & Shepard, 1878; here the 1906 edition).

workers from over twenty-five different language areas learned about German barnyards. Even today the tendency is still present in preschools to sentimentalize and ruralize childhood experience from "Old MacDonald Had a Farm" to picture lessons with animals.

Needless to say, the revisionists won in many areas and a closer correspondence of task and subject matter to child ability and age was established. More emphasis was placed on expression of the child's own creative urges, rather than memorizing or copying patterns from others. Above all, with the rise of Freudian psychology, the sunny, bucolic world of the children's garden became a nostalgic dream of adults, rather than active, radical pedagogical theory. The kindergarten joined the ranks of other established German educational imports—graduate school, technical-vocational school, and the physical sciences—as mainstream Americana.

How, then, was the kindergarten revolution domesticated? In Germany, the national ideal was rendered harmless and unrevolutionary by economic and political unification through conservative forces. Increasing urbanization and universal primary education in both Germany and the United States rendered the question moot: the *Gärten* became playgrounds, small and standardized, the radical import of education for all became accepted procedure in the primary levels. Support of the kindergarten as sound pedagogical method by aristocratic and other wealthy women rendered it respectable as a bourgeois educational institution. The churches reasserted their claim on early childhood education by establishing their own kindergartens, thereby undercutting the religious radicality of Froebel's message. The Freethinkers waned in importance in Germany as well.

In the United States, the "revolution" was domesticated from its arrival in the 1850s. It was thoroughly compatible with the prevailing educational philosophies of the day: the haphazard, necessarily experimental, and frequently egalitarian schools of American prairies and plains in the time of westward expansion provided fertile ground for kindergarten work. Emerging industrialization, with more women in the urban workforce, made the kindergarten less a radical experiment than a financial and social necessity. It was supported by capitalists, entrepreneurs, and philanthropists who had a vested interest in seeing it thrive. It was English-speaking and thus did not hold the same threat as the workers' leagues and other groups accused of divisiveness and lack of patriotism. It had, above all, no *American* associations with radical politics. The kindergarten leadership did not overlap with the women's rightists, the abolitionists, or the socialists, even if certain leaders were sympathetic. The kindergarten lost its original "melting pot" ideology and was run by various interest groups: churches, industries, philanthropic organizations for the poor or foreign-born, and privately for profit. By 1917, the kindergarten had been so thoroughly assimilated into American culture that it was possibly the only German-American institution to remain unscathed by American chauvinism during World War I.

The kindergarten seemed even more harmless after the rise of newer, more radically permissive theories of learning from John Dewey and Maria Montessori. Yet like the theories of Dewey, Montessori, and the later free schools, kindergarten theory foresaw the idea of massive social reorganization through teaching little children to think, act, and feel differently. To see how radical this idea still is today, we have only to look at the controversy surrounding daycare in America, and to observe the outrage at the Green Party of the 1980s and their ideas on childraising, eating, and personal life. An irony of history makes those 48ers timely again: when they immigrated to America in the 1850s, the older, more conservative German-Americans ridiculed them as "die Grünen," the greenhorns. The transforming, uprooting nature of play, of physical activity, and of personal, childlike autonomy which characterized the early kindergarten movement is still with childraisers and radicals in Germany and America today. Their spirit can be summed up in a modern phrase that turns around the notion of "domesticating the revolution," rendering it not harmless but rather a matter of everyday praxis: the personal is political.

Notes

1 Friedrich Froebel, "Aus einem Brief an den Herzog von Meiningen," *Gesammelte pädagogische Schriften,* (1862–63; rpt. Osnabrück: Biblio, 1966), 1.1: 106. Further page references in the text are to this edition.

2 Ferdinand Winther, "Appeal to the Women of Germany in 1840," trans. in *Diesterweg's Wegweiser* (1876), *Papers on Froebel's Kindergarten, with Suggestions on Principles and Methods of Child Culture in Different Countries,* ed. Henry Barnard (Hartford: American Journal of Education, 1890) 83.

3 Caroline Progler, "Kindergarten Buildings and Grounds," in Barnard 769–74.

4 See Rudolf Schenda, *Volk ohne Buch: Studien zur Sozialgeschichte der populären Lesestoffe, 1770–1970* (Frankfurt: Klostermann, 1970) 44; Rolf Engelsing, *Analphabetentum und Lektüre: Zur Sozialgeschichte des Lesens in Deutschland zwischen feudaler und industrieller Gesellschaft* (Stuttgart: Metzler, 1973) 56, 91–93, 98–99, 101; Albert Ward, *Book Production, Fiction, and the German Reading Public, 1740–1800* (Oxford: Clarendon, 1974). Schenda estimates literacy roughly at 15% in 1770, 25% in 1800, and 40% by 1830.

5 Julius Froebel, *Ein Lebenslauf: Aufzeichnungen, Erinnerungen und Bekenntnisse,* 2 vols. (Stuttgart: Cotta, 1890) 1: 26.

6 Prussian Vereinsgesetz 1851, Paragraph 8.

7 A description of this social action in the congregation, women's seminary, and Kindergarten in Hamburg can be found in Malwida von Meysenbug, *Memoiren einer Idealistin* (Berlin/Leipzig: Schuster & Loeffler, 1875) 1: 298–359.

8 Margrit Twellmann, *Die deutsche Frauenbewegung: Ihre Anfänge und erste Entwicklung, 1843–1889,* vol. 1 (Meisenheim am Glan: Hain: 1972) & vol. 2 (Kronberg: Athenäum, 1976). A thorough summary of the involvement of German women activists in the kindergarten in Germany is found in Ann Taylor Allen, "Spiritual Motherhood: German Feminists and the Kindergarten Movement, 1848–1911," *History of Education Quarterly* 22 (1982): 319–40.

9 The first kindergartens in America are described in Edward W. Hocker, "The First Kindergarten Teacher," *American-German Review* 8 (1942): 9; Elizabeth Jenkins, "How the Kindergarten found its way to America," *Wisconsin Magazine of History* 14 (1930): 48–62; Elizabeth Jenkins, "Froebel's Disciples in America," *American-German Review* 3 (1937): 15–18; and Kurt F. Leidecke, "The 101st Year of the Kindergarten," *American-German Review* 7 (1941): 6–8.

10 On Adolf Douai and Karl Heinzen see Eitel Dobert, *Deutsche Demokraten in America: Die Achtundvierziger und ihre Schriften* (Göttingen: Vandenhoeck & Ruprecht, 1958); Albert Faust, *The German Element in the United States: With Special Reference to its Political, Moral, Social, and Educational Influence* (New York: Steuben Society, 1927); Carl Wittke, *Against the Current: The Life of Karl Heizen, 1809–1880* (Chicago: U of Chicago P, 1945); Carl Wittke, *Refugees of Revolution: The German Forty-Eighters in America* (Philadelphia: U of Pennsylvania P, 1952); see chapter 20, "Learning and Letters."

11 See three works by Karl Adolf Douai, *The Kindergarten: A Manual for the Introduction of Froebel's System of Primary Education into Public Schools; and for the Use of Mothers and Private Teachers* (New York: Steiger, 1871); *Adolf Douai's Series of Rational Readers, Combining the Principles of Pestalozzi's and Freobel's Systems of Education* (New York: Steiger, 1872); *Kindergarten und Volkshochschule als sozial-demokratische Anstalten* (Leipzig, 1876).

12 Ruth M. Baylor, *Elizabeth Palmer Peabody: Kindergarten Pioneer* (Philadelphia: U of Pennsylvania P, 1965).

13 John A. Walz, *German Influence in American Education and Culture* (Philadelphia: Carl Schurz Foundation, 1936); on Victor Cousin's report, see p. 14; on the kindergarten, pp. 35–43.

14 Peabody and Mary Tyler Peabody Mann also published Mrs. Horace Mann and Elizabeth P. Peabody, *Moral Culture of Infancy and Kindergarten Guide: With Music for the Plays* (New York: Schemehorn, 1870); Elizabeth P. Peabody, *Lectures in the Training Schools for Kindergartners* (Boston: Heath, 1888).

15 Elizabeth Palmer Peabody, "Brief Notice of the Kindergarten in America," Barnard 14.

16 Albert Bernhardt Faust, *The German Element in the United States: With Specific Reference to its Political, Moral, Social, and Educational Influence* (New York: The Steuben Society of America, 1927) 2: 238.

17 The debate was played out in several publications of the International Kindergarten Union and its committee to resolve theoretical differences, in which there were dissenting reports. Patty Smith Hill's "Second Report" in *The Kindergarten: Reports of the Committee of Nineteen on the Theory and Practice of the Kindergarten* (Boston: Houghton-Mifflin, 1913) lays out the criticisms from the new generation. Direct confrontation of the aging Maria Kraus-Boelte against Patty Hill and Nina Vandewalker is found in *The Sixth Yearbook of the National Society for the Scientific Study of Education* (Bloomington, IL: Public School Book Publ. Co., 1907), part 2.

The Dawn of Teaching German in the Public Schools: A Study of *Der amerikanische Leser,* Cincinnati, 1854

TED E. FRANK
University of Texas–Arlington

By the late nineteenth century the teaching of German in the American public educational system was regarded as both a right and an obligation. U. S. Commissioner of Education W. T. Harris reminded a Cleveland, Ohio, audience in 1890 that children of immigrants, like all other children, should be educated in the best institutions of the country and become "Americanized" in the free spirit of public school classrooms. But beyond this basic right, these children had another: the right to be taught the language of their forebears as well as English, and public school officials bore the responsibility to have this teaching carried out in American classrooms. Harris pointed out that for some time after establishing themselves in America, immigrants maintain a close relationship with their families still in the mother country and correspond with them frequently. To preserve such family ties and to participate in relationships with German-speaking family members, children of German immigrants must learn two languages. If these German-American children learn only English, they have little or no part in maintaining relationships carried on through correspondence. The children are consequently cut off from their roots, a situation that could result in misfortune, Harris speculated, even eventual catastrophe. Basic for all youth, the Commissioner believed, are a knowledge of ancestry and a consciousness of one's history. Immigrant children are no exception. The benefit these children would derive from a familiarity with their ancestry and a consciousness of their history, as well as from maintaining communication with the oldest members of their family still in Europe, would contribute to their maturity and their becoming respected American citizens. In concluding his address, Harris urged his audience to guarantee the well-being of their communities by supporting the teaching of German, particularly in those areas where the number of immigrants from Germany was on the rise in the 1890s. "A class of immigrants who had no desire to preserve a relationship with their family stock," Harris warned, "would bring calamity upon the community into which they come."[1]

By the time Harris' speech publicly recognized the need for teaching German in American schools, other educators and public officials had been concerning themselves for some years with the need for proper textbooks for that instruction. In 1881, for example, H. A. Rattermann, the editor of *Der deutsche Pionier* (a national monthly published in Cincinnati, Ohio), questioned the suitability of textbooks then being used for teaching German in America. Speaking before the delegates to the "Deutsch-Amerikanischer Lehrertag," Rattermann lamented the fact that "die deutsche Sprache hierlands an Kinderkrankheiten laboriert, wovon eine der Mängel an praktischen Schulbüchern ist."[2] Without proper textbooks for the teaching of German, Rattermann prophesied, there could be no future for the language in the United States and consequently no understanding by Americans of Germans and their *Weltanschauung*. The German people, their culture, and their attitudes could only be understood, Rattermann argued, through the German language. Essential to teach it were attractive and interesting textbooks.

Half a century before Commissioner Harris and Editor Rattermann voiced their opinions, public officials and school teachers alike had recognized the need for the teaching of German in American classrooms and for suitable textbooks to teach it. Those citizens of the 1830s and 1840s had consequently undertaken the job of introducing German into the then recently founded schools supported by public tax funds. After German became a required part of the curriculum of the public schools, one of the teachers' tasks was the writing of textbooks to teach the language. That task was soon fulfilled by the issuing of a series of graded German readers, the first such series to be written and published in the United States for use solely in American public schools wherever German was taught. Entitled *Der amerikanische Leser*, the series consisted of three volumes and an introductory primer, the latter separately entitled *Das amerikanische A-B-C Buch*. A group that identified itself only with the pseudonym GERMANNS wrote these four textbooks and had them published in Cincinnati, Ohio in 1854. According to their imprimatur, all four books were expressly written "für die öffentlichen Schulen in Cincinnati."[3] There they enjoyed a marked success.

Their use was, however, not limited to the Cincinnati schools. The four textbooks were widely distributed and widely used for several decades after their first printing. I have recently found copies of them in private and public collections in Michigan, Illinois, Indiana, and Texas, as well as in Ohio. Penciled markings by students and teachers in these particular copies indicate their having been used in classrooms in these states as late as 1900.

An analysis of the contents of these four German textbooks as well as their methodology is the chief concern of this paper. Before I begin this analysis, it is essential, however, to set the books in their proper historical context by looking briefly into the background of German instruction in American public schools, with particular emphasis on Cincinnati, and especially into the aims of teachers and the problems they and other citizens encountered when German was first taught there.[4]

German in Cincinnati Public Schools

The first discussion of establishing public schools in which German would be taught took place in Philadelphia in 1783.[5] Such schools did not, however, become a dominant force in American education until well into the next century. One of the earliest public school systems in the United States to offer German instruction to its students was that of the city of Cincinnati, in 1840. Then the fifth largest city in the United States, Cincinnati had a German-speaking population of at least one-third its total figure, a percentage that had remained almost constant since the city's founding in the 1780s. Already in 1825 the citizens of Cincinnati had established a public school system supported by their taxes. This system, adopting many recommendations from Calvin E. Stowe, patterned itself after the Prussian system of public schools and soon became a model for other cities, cities both young and old—the older and larger New York and Boston; the younger and smaller Chicago and St. Louis.[6] Other cities set up similar instructional systems that included German after it had found a secure place in the curriculum of Cincinnati's public schools. Thus, the textbooks on which this paper focuses were written, published, and used in a city that was a nineteenth-century leader in American educational policy as well as in the teaching of German in the United States.

After the 1825 opening of public classes in the traditional "three r's" for all children in Cincinnati, private German classes for the city's German-speaking children were sponsored by churches in the city. These classes were gradually combined into the privately funded *Emigranten Schule* which functioned as the city's German language learning center until 1837.[7] At that time the Presbyterian Church, the sponsor of the school, forced its particular creed into the school's curriculum with the result that German Lutheran and Catholic parents refused to allow their children to continue attending the school. That brought a temporary halt to the teaching of German in Cincinnati. The deep desire of German immigrants in that city as well as in other cities of the Midwest and the East to see German instruction in the public schools is perhaps best shown by the German convention held in Harrisburg, Pennsylvania in 1837. Delegates from five states including Ohio approved three resolutions that they hoped would initiate the teaching of German in public schools: (1) that German be recognized as a second state language next to English; (2) that German be taught in the tax-supported public school system of each state; (3) that German normal schools be established in order to provide qualified teachers for the German classrooms in the public schools. Not until three years after the convention, however, was German added to the public school curriculum in Cincinnati, and only then after arduous struggles on the part of concerned citizens.

The person probably best remembered for adding German to this curriculum was August Renz, known locally as "Notar Renz." An immigrant to Cincinnati in 1836, Renz led the local committee that demanded a place in the public school curriculum for the teaching of German to German-speaking children. After the closing of the *Emigranten Schule,* Renz chaired a meeting of German-American parents at which he is said to have spoken in his native Swabian dialect: "Was brauchat mer eigena Schula z'gründa; zahlet mer doch Taxa für d'öffentlicha Schula. Mer wollet verlanga, dasz in d'öffentlicha Schula d'deutscha Spracha g'lehrt wird."[8] Those at the meeting agreed with Renz. For three years thereafter, he and a committee of nine other citizens pressed the school authorities to fulfill their demands for German instruction in the city's public schools.

The committee met with strong opposition from the public school trustees in particular, but other Anglo-American citizens as well rejected its demands at that time. Not discouraged, however, the committee pressed on and succeeded two years later in convincing the trustees to offer German instruction temporarily in one of the city's public schools. Instruction in German gained a permanent place in the city-wide curriculum a year later, however, when the Legislature of Ohio passed an act that read, in part: "The Board of any district shall cause the German language to be taught in any school under its control, during any school year, when a demand therefore is made in writing by seventy-five freeholders, resident of the district, representing not less than forty pupils, who are entitled to attend such schools, and who, in good faith, desire to study the German and English languages together. . . ."[9]

On the basis of this law the Cincinnati public school trustees agreed to add German to the standard curriculum and to be responsible for teaching the language. Yet they did not respond by adding it to the subjects taught in all the city's public schools. Instead, they opened a special school, the so-called "German-English School" in the basement of Cincinnati's Lutheran Church. There, on 1 September 1840, one Joseph Hemann assumed responsibility for teaching children—most of them of German parentage—German and English orthography and grammar, and also writing and reading in both languages. Hemann's goal, the trustees made clear, was to ready the German-speaking children to enter the regular English public schools in the shortest possible time. There they would learn arithmetic, geography, and other subjects in English. Because a large number of the city's German-speaking citizens wanted their children taught in both their mother tongue and in the "foreign" tongue, English, a second German-English school had to be opened two months later—in November 1840. The total enrollment of these two schools stood officially at 427. As Zeydel points out, however, truancy was a serious problem in those days before attendance laws were invoked; hence the average daily attendance in German classes was probably about 200 (31). By the 1850s, when the daily attendance of children learning German climbed to about 1,200, the course organization for the German classes and their approaches to language teaching became standardized in most of the public schools throughout the city. According to Zeydel, "there was one teacher in the smaller schools who gave instruction in both German and English. The larger schools either had special teachers of German or developed the so-called 'parallel-class system' in which all the students were taught a half-day alternately by an English and a German teacher up to and including the fourth grade"(30). Handschin states, in his historical account, that in later years "German instruction in grades 1 through 4 did not exceed nine hours per week. From the fifth to the eighth grades, forty-five minutes to one hour a day were given to German."[10] By the 1860s, nonetheless, German was being taught in ten school districts to more than 3,500 students, and in the 1870s there were some 10,000 students studying German. A large percentage of these were children of Anglo-Americans who recognized the advantage of learning to speak and write German in the thriving Ohio city in which more immigrants from Germany were regularly arriving. By the 1880s the practice seemed permanently established. Superintendent John B. Peaselee of the Cincinnati Public Schools enthusiastically approved German instruction: "To those who oppose German instruction in our public schools let me say," Peaselee remarked, "that the statement that its cost is great has been shown to be without foundation . . . , that the belief that the study of the German language retards the progress of the children in English has been completely overturned by statistics, that the assertion that this is America and therefore we ought to teach the English language only is not worthy of notice, and the claim that the study of German tends to Germanize our pupils and make them less loyal to our own country is not borne out by facts. . . . I not only believe thoroughly in the German departments of our schools, but I am convinced that it would be better for the intellectual development of our pupils if they all studied the German language in connection with English."[11] Peaselee's approval of studying German in public schools was to no small extent the result of the convictions and work of August Renz and his committee some forty years earlier. Until the political effects of World War I caused German instruction to decline in Cincinnati (as in schools throughout the nation), the city's classrooms remained the stronghold of German instruction in the United States. Even as late as 1917 some 175 teachers taught German in Cincinnati.[12]

Der Amerikanische Leser

As soon as German secured a firm foothold in Cincinnati's classrooms, its teachers undertook the task referred to earlier: the writing of textbooks suitable for teaching German to children, textbooks intended solely for teaching those children who already spoke German as their mother tongue at home. Until that time German textbooks published in America had been written primarily for another type of student—the adult English speaker who wanted to learn German as a second language. A German reader had been available for such students since Charles Follen had published his *Deutsches Lesebuch für Anfänger* at Harvard College in 1826. Two years later a grammar had also become available when Follen supplemented his reader with his *Practical Grammar of the German Language.* Prior to these entries into the American textbook market, teachers and students had relied on German textbooks from Germany and England. Follen's texts were followed by similar readers and grammars by other American educators, among them W. H. Woodbury and Bernard Roelker. Common to all of these books were their contents and methodology, both of which were selected for speakers of English who had no previous knowledge of German. For literary content each reader drew from classical German authors, from Lessing down to the more nearly contemporary writers of the early nineteenth century. Grammar sections presented traditional rules and drilled them. Passages for translation from German to English and English to German offered an opportunity for students to apply these rules and to recognize structures in the foreign language similar to those in their mother tongue. In sum, Follen, Woodbury, Roelker, and other authors intended their textbooks for the then available market—the college classroom market at Harvard and other Eastern establishments as well as that of the numerous private tutors teaching German to adults. These books had not been intended and were inadequate for the new and expanding public school market of the 1850s. They had not been written for children of German immigrants who had already learned to speak German before enrolling in school.

Without adequate textbooks, Cincinnati's teachers of German in the 1840s faced a serious obstacle to effective teaching. They attempted to overcome it by selecting, mostly at random, various pedagogical materials for classroom use and by improvising presentations of these materials. Such variety of materials and approaches resulted in uneven teaching and learning of German in the schools throughout the city. A multitude of different requirements and standards of performance existed, and this multitude produced much dissatisfaction on the part of parents, teachers, and school trustees. In 1853 a reorganization of the German classroom curriculum was undertaken in an attempt to overcome this dissatisfaction. Among changes initiated at that time were those of selecting (1) a common textbook and (2) a uniform course of study for each level of German instruction. The course included the alphabet, spelling, grammar, reading, writing, composition, and declamation in German. To make it possible, new textbooks were written for each level of German instruction. The reorganization proved successful enough to dispel doubt about and dissatisfaction with the teaching of German in the public schools. German became a regular and rewarding part of the Cincinnati curriculum. Rufus King, President of the Cincinnati School Board soon after the reorganization called German "that link" without which all family and social ties between the old and the new countries are lost.[13] For him as for other citizens, German instruction was finally well warranted (which is to say, worth the taxpayers' money). The most important feature, perhaps, of the total reorganization was the series of new textbooks called *Der amerikanische Leser*.

The first of these, written by the group calling itself GERMANNS, is entitled *Das amerikanische A-B-C Buch: kurze und leichte Lautir- und Buchstabirübungen*. Eight inches by six inches in size, it includes 30 pages, each containing several woodcuts to illustrate the letters of the alphabet and the individual words assigned to that particular page. The textbook is a primer, and as such was intended for six-year-olds in first grade who had been taught German as their mother tongue. No English is used in the book. The names of household items, animals, birds, family kindred, and other such words as children of this age group were likely to have learned in their everyday speech comprise the German vocabulary. Connected narratives are not a part of the book's contents. What the primer does in its opening section is to present the entire alphabet by means of objects designated by words that begin with the twenty-six letters of the alphabet. In a second section the *Laute, Umlaute, Doppellaute,* and *Mitlaute* are presented with several illustrations. The book's final section, containing approximately 500 individual, unconnected words, gives beginners at the task of formally learning to read their mother tongue ample opportunity to practice sight reading. If the book's title is to be considered a source of information as to how to use the book, then students were supposed to master the spelling of these words. This was evidently to be done orally. The art of reproducing any of these 500 words in written form was not expected of students using this primer. Nor were other demands made by the authors. They gave no additional practice exercises in the book, nor did they give any additional suggestions for using or not using the book. Each teacher was responsible for teaching its contents by using his/her own best pedagogical methods. The teacher's goal was presumably to create conditions in which each child could develop a solid basis of good articulation, inflection, accent, and stress, goals that all good teachers intended their students to achieve whether through specific training, osmosis, or natural ability.

Der amerikanische Leser, Erstes Buch, another 8″ by 6″ volume that follows the *A-B-C Buch,* contains 110 pages, an increase of 80 pages over the primer. Written for seven- or eight-year-olds, this first reader was intended to teach them not only to read but also to write German. The contents of the book are graded in difficulty and they aim throughout, according to the "Vorwort," "das Interesse des Kindes zu wecken und seine Aufmerksamkeit zu fesseln." The preface notes also that the reader is modeled after the English classroom reader by William H. McGuffey (also published in Cincinnati), which at the time of the appearance of this *erstes Buch* had already been used in U.S. schools for several years. Apparently much impressed by McGuffey's title, *First Eclectic Reader,* the authors calling themselves GERMANNS decided that they would entitle their textbook a "Leser" rather than the standard "Lesebuch."

In this "reader" (and "writer") for seven- and eight-year-olds, pages 7 through 17 called for the student to write down, first, individual letters of the alphabet, then combinations of them, and, finally, whole German words. Most of these words were common knowledge to seven- and eight-year-olds and were merely a slight extension of the vocabulary in the *A-B-C Buch.* Occasionally, to illustrate a certain letter or sound, a decidedly American word creeps into the traditionally German list. One such word is "Ypsilanti," a city in Michigan, used to illustrate uppercase *Y.* Pages 18 through 20 list single, two-syllable words for mastery in reading, pronunciation, spelling, and writing. A handsome woodcut, taken with permission from McGuffey's reader, illustrates several of the words in the lists. Fifteen pages of especially tricky words then follow, words that were intended to correct faulty pronunciation habits some of the children had undoubtedly acquired from use of dialects in their homes. Special emphasis here is on producing the correct sounds of vowels, dipthongs, and consonant clusters. One series of lines for practice in pronunciation is

> Wilhelm lockt die alte Katze seiner Tante.
> Er steckt sie zu dem Huhn in den Kasten.
> Die böse Katze beiszt das Huhn.
> Aber das Huhn hackt der Katze ein Auge aus.

Prose and lyric reading selections, beginning with passages four or five lines in length, follow these pronunciation exercises and continue to the end of the book where their length may extend to twenty or more lines. Each of these readings focuses on a simple topic familiar to the child, such as "Das Haus," "Das Steckenpferd," or "Die Mühle," or on topics with more suggestive titles such as "Der kleine Otto zu Hause." Some of the later, more difficult readings in the *erstes Buch* illustrate concepts perhaps new to the child, such as "ein Aal" as contrasted to "ein Wurm." Several readings are of a religious nature. Both the didactic value of these readings and their value in teaching specific language points clearly played important roles in the selection of religious passages for inclusion in the book. Generally, each of these contains a moral that serves to shape a child's behavior. The syntax of all the readings through page 41 is that of simple statements and questions. From page 42 to the end of the book, compound sentences with relative and other subordinate clauses frequent the readings. The length of these compound sentences increases, as does the complexity of their grammatical structures, as the book progresses. All four cases, the present and past tenses of the subjunctive and indicative, and the usual other parts of speech are introduced in these pages. By the concluding pages of the book, the German-speaking seven- or eight-year-old was reading such sentences as this: "Es war noch ein Glück, dasz der Arzt die Nadel bald wieder herausbrachte, sonst hätte das Kind unter groszen Schmerzen sterben müssen" (77). To test the childrens' comprehension of the selections, the teacher was to ask German questions provided in the text and based on the content of each selection. These questions are demanding, wholly as demanding as a child's capacity to understand that content.

From a critical standpoint, we note that the reader lacks a systematized or in any way regulated build-up of vocabulary. One supposes that the authors' aim was merely to confront young students with as many different and useful words as possible. If a word count of the reader were carried out, it would yield probably 3,000 or more German words. The book's emphasis is on variety of vocabulary and syntax. Such variety, the authors undoubtedly anticipated, would encourage avid learners to go on to tackle the remaining two readers of the series enthusiastically.

The first of these, *Der amerikanische Leser, Zweites Buch*, contains 160 pages of reading selections more challenging than those in Book I. The sources of the new readings are, as stated in the book's "Vorwort," "die deutsche Jugendliteratur." Among the 72 selections are 54 narratives, 16 poems, 1 Biblical Psalm, and 1 dialogue. They are again graduated in length and display in their content pleasant and practical wisdom easily grasped by eight- or nine-year-olds. Several of the narratives focus on religious and moral themes and hence add to the childrens' growing sense of personal values as introduced in the first reader. Sample titles of the selections suggest their intent: "Das dankbare Kind," "Der verlorene

Geldbeutel,'' "Das gestohlene Pferd,'' "Der schöne Eichbaum.'' More difficult selections include such titles as "Unterschied zwischen Sparsamkeit und Geiz,'' and "Weise Anwendung der Jugendzeit.'' Copious woodcuts, again borrowed from McGuffey, illustrate several titles.

Each of the reading selections commences with a list of fifteen or more of the most difficult words in the selection. According to instructions from the authors, these words were to be repeated frequently in written and oral work—as vocabulary exercises and spelling drills to increase students' facility in German. Each reading ends with six or more well formulated questions that require a complete understanding of the content. The questions also challenge students to infer correct answers rather than merely to copy or summarize statements given in the narrative itself. No grammatical explanations are offered in this book.

The first narrative in the second reader is grammatically and stylistically complex, containing both relative and subordinate clauses, the present and past subjunctive, and all tenses of the indicative. Full familiarity with this grammar was expected of students from previous use of the language. Grammar was not apparently considered a subject to be explained and taught here; that task was separate. By the end of this second reader, a full range of grammatical structures and syntax was in daily use, with the result that the third and final reader in the series focused on providing the German-speaking ten- or eleven-year-old with an extensive vocabulary and broad understanding of it in his/her mother tongue, a tongue that at that age was being supplemented more and more, according to curricular regulations, with classroom instruction in English.[14]

Der amerikanische Leser, Drittes Buch, with some 260 pages of text, has as its purpose: (1) to enhance students' language ability; (2) to develop their intellectual taste; (3) to widen both their knowledge of language and the world; and (4) to make them cognizant of the good, the useful, and the beautiful in themselves and their world. "Kein Buch gibt der Jugend so verschiedenartigen Stoff zum Nachdenken und erweitert ihren Ideenkreis so sehr, als ein zweckmässiges Lesebuch,'' the authors wrote in the "Vorwort.'' This text's selections were excerpted or, in some cases, copied in full from the best childrens' literature available in Germany in 1854. By "best,'' the authors no doubt meant literature that awakened understanding, sharpened judgment, and provided nourishment and joy for the mind and heart. Among the authors included in the prose and lyric selections are Johann Paul Hebel, Krummacher, Bürger, the Grimms, Schiller, Herder, Gessner. Book III contains fewer biblical or otherwise religiously oriented stories than the preceding two books. In their place are anonymous tales about the Greeks, Romans, and *Germani,* as well as fairy tales and myths. In all selections the didactic function is evident. Each reading, as in the previous books, starts out with a list of difficult words and ends with several challenging questions that review the content. Vocabulary in this reader goes beyond everyday usage; terms drawn from history, mythology, science, and metaphysics are included. A word count would reveal a range of several thousand German words. Book III was intended to challenge the German-speaking students in upper public school classes with a wide range of vocabulary and intellectual discernment before they moved on into classrooms in which instruction proceeded in English only.

Rarely represented in this third reader or in the previous ones are selections that focus on America, the students' homeland, selections that might have widened student understanding of the country from the standpoints of German or German-American authors. Book III contains only two such selections: a three-part reading entitled "Die Entdeckung von Amerika durch Christopf Kolumbus," and a two-part narrative by Benjamin Franklin. Book II has only one such selection, which briefly recounts General LaFayette's role in the War of Independence. The lack of emphasis on American history and American writers was presumably not of concern to the authors. Such oversights, however, set a trend in German-American textbooks that continued for several decades. To such lacunae as these W. A. Rattermann specifically referred when, in his 1881 address mentioned above, he charged that German language instruction in the nation's classrooms was suffering from a lack of adequate, even proper teaching materials. "Unsere hiesigen deutschen Schulen sind keine amerikanisch-deutschen Schulen," Rattermann charged, "sondern bewegen sich ganz in dem Gang der europäisch-deutschen Schulen."[15] In Rattermann's view, the continental emphasis in German textbooks published for use in the United States was debilitating. Such books were filled with German-authored selections and/or with European-inspired content, both of which, in his words, "haucht den hyperloyalen Duft über Gott, König, und Vaterland"(8). In the Republic of the United States of America such typical Prussian/German concepts and values were not suitable pedagogical themes for youth learning German, Rattermann argued. A new spirit, an American spirit, had to infuse the German textbooks. And that spirit was to come from a greater use of the writings of German-American authors and from a wider use of American history with particular reference to the contributions of German-Americans. Rattermann's proposals could certainly have been adopted, at least in part, by the group GERMANNS in 1854. More than likely, though, these men and women were themselves recent immigrants to the United States and as such not sufficiently acquainted with German-American history or its writers to include them in their three textbooks. Instead, they simply followed their own continental training and interests when they wrote the three volumes of *Der amerikanische Leser.*

This initial venture into the field of textbook writing, editing, and publishing was followed by a second series of two readers entitled *Lesebuch für amerikanische Volksschulen, Erster Teil* and *Zweiter Teil*. These appeared in 1863 from the same Cincinnati publisher as the first series. A cursory review of them shows that they rectify only some of the content deficiencies of the first series. Analyses of these two books and an investigation of any other German language texts used in the Cincinnati classrooms together with *Der amerikanische Leser* go beyond the scope of this paper. But when these additional analyses are completed, we will have a much wider appreciation of the historically important work for the teaching of German in the United States carried out by a group of dedicated German teachers, parents, interested citizens, and public school trustees in Cincinnati in the 1840s and later. Their interest, commitment, and achievement eventually fixed the nature of the curriculum of German in American public schools for several decades. The series of readers called *Der amerikanische Leser* was especially successful in establishing the teaching of German on a pedagogically sound basis. The task of writing textbooks that might be an improvement on these trailblazing readers awaited their successors.

Notes

1 As quoted by Louis Viereck in "German Instruction in American Schools," *Report of the Commissioner of Education for the Year 1900/01* 1: 548.
2 H. A. Rattermann, *Die deutsche Sprache in der amerikanischen Schule* (Cincinnati: Mecklenborg & Rosenthat, 1881) 1.
3 As stated on the title page of each of the volumes (Cincinnati: Wilde, 1854).
4 I am indebted especially to the following sources: Charles Hart Handschin, *The Teaching of the Modern Languages in the United States*, U.S. Bureau of Education Bulletin No. 3, (1913); E. W. Bagster-Collins, "History of Modern Language Teaching in the United States," *Studies in Modern Language Teaching* (New York: Macmillan, 1930); Louis Viereck, "German Instruction in American Schools," *Report of the U.S. Commissioner of Education, 1900/01*, 1; Edwin H. Zeydel, "The Teaching of German in the United States from Colonial Times to the Present," *Reports of Surveys and Studies in the Teaching of Modern Foreign Languages* (New York: MLA, 1959–61); also: Edwin H. Zeydel, "The Teaching of German in Cincinnati: An Historical Survey," *Bulletin of the Historical and Philosophical Society of Ohio* (1962) 30.
5 The term "public school" is here meant to designate any school supported by public tax funds and hence open to every child of the community regardless of the parents' social position.
6 C. E. Stowe was selected by the Ohio Legislature to spend a year in Europe observing European schools at first hand, observing especially their methods of instruction. After his official report to the legislature on his return to Ohio, many of his recommendations

were put into effect in the state's public schools. See his *Report on Elementary Public Instruction in Europe Made to the Thirty-Sixth General Assembly of the State of Ohio, 1837.*

7 Viereck (557) states that in 1831 more children attended private German schools than the city schools of Cincinnati, probably from 400 to 1500 children, and that this pattern continued for a number of years because the public schools were inferior in instruction.

8 F. H. Röwenkamp, "August Renz: Ein Vorkämpfer für das deutsche Schulsystem in Cincinnati," *Der deutsche Pionier* 6 (1874): 76.

9 John B. Shotwell, *A History of the Schools of Cincinnati* (Cincinnati: School Life, 1902) 289.

10 As quoted by Zeydel 293.

11 From an address Peaslee delivered at the National German American Teachers Association in Chicago in 1889, quoted by Zeydel 36.

12 Of interest here, perhaps, is a comparison of German instruction in Cincinnati with that in other U. S. cities having a high German-speaking population. E. W. Bagster-Collins (15) points out that "German was introduced into New York's school system in 1854, in Chicago and St. Louis in 1865, Cleveland in 1870 and Baltimore in 1874. . . . By 1867 Milwaukee had over 5000 children attending private schools as against 7000 in public schools, and we may assume that for the most part German was the language of instruction."

13 Shotwell 301.

14 Shotwell (293) states that "the pupils of the advanced German-English class were to be promoted to the proper English public schools after a biennial course, or sooner if they passed a satisfactory examination in English. By the adoption of this plan a three-years' course was secured for the German pupils, in accordance with which German and English were taught alternately."

15 Rattermann 7.

Mark Twain's German Language Learning Experiences

URSULA THOMAS
University of Wisconsin–Madison

> Drill—that is the valuable thing. Drill—drill—drill—that is the precious thing. For, from drill comes the automatic, and few things in this world are well done until they can *do themselves*. If teachers would but drill—drill—drill in the language! But God never made a language-teacher out of a sane person yet. When He can't get an idiot He won't play.[1]

The sense of that quotation might have been expressed in a foreign-language methods book of the twentieth century, but its wit is unmistakably Mark Twain. It is a notation he made in a journal from the year 1894, almost forty years after he had begun his first language study.

The chief published evidence of Mark Twain's acquaintance with and knowledge of German is the much-quoted "Awful German Language," Appendix D of *A Tramp Abroad;* however, study of that essay raises many questions. The first and most important is familiar from the Watergate hearings: How much did he know, and when did he know it? There are others: How did he learn German, and where did he begin his study? What was his attitude toward foreign languages and their learning? What was his attitude toward foreign cultures?

An answer to the question "How much did he know and when did he know it?" has been given in a monograph by John Krumpelmann, *Mark Twain and the German Language,* published in 1953.[2] Krumpelmann's monograph prompted a review in *English Studies,* Amsterdam, 1954, which may indicate the results of Krumpelmann's study: " 'Mark Twain's peculiar brand of humor,' " says the reviewer, "may console 'those who have no talent for foreign languages,' but it seems unnecessary to 'publish in a scientific and elaborate study every particular step on a road leading to . . . next to nothing.' "[3] Since 1953, however, significant materials have been published, materials which shed more light on Mark Twain's experience with and attitudes toward foreign languages and their study. Two of these publications are particularly worthy of mention, namely, *Mark Twain's Notebooks and Journals,*[4] thus far two volumes, which comprise all of the extant jottings from 1855 to 1883, and Alan Gribben's *Mark*

Twain's Library: A Reconstruction.[5] The latter is helpful because it lists three beginning German grammars which predate Mark Twain's first real study of German. The notebooks afford insight into his day-to-day impressions, his observations of people, and fleeting ideas for use in formal writings, along with such mundane things as laundry lists and appointments. Most important from the standpoint of the present investigation is that Mark Twain frequently used these same notebooks for foreign-language exercises, including lists of idiomatic phrases and their translations, copied passages from literary works, and attempts to write his own sentences. These sentences are reminiscent of those that teachers in all times hear and see. Here is one example, leaving out the false starts: "[Die Baronin] war sehr reich, aber ihrer Mann, der Baron, wer auch reich war, hat ihrer gelt squandered in gambling & dissipation, so ist die arme Weibe nun geltlos & hat zwei Kinderlein mit bringen ihrer alte heimat zu. Ihrer Mann hat sie grausam treated."[6] In addition, at those times when he was most actively endeavoring to learn a language, his character sketches and thumbnail descriptions of surroundings were peppered with individual words from that language.

To the German teacher familiar with Mark Twain's "Awful German Language" it may be surprising to hear that the first language he seriously attempted to learn was French, at the age of twenty while working on the Mississippi. The first extant notebook has a series of seven French lessons, consisting mainly of vocabulary lists with English equivalents. They abound in spelling mistakes and the wrong use of accents and other diacritical marks characteristic of Mark Twain's written foreign languages. Perhaps this carefree attitude toward the written form of the foreign language goes back to his school days, of which he says in his autobiography: "Although good spelling was my one accomplishment I was never able to greatly respect it."[7]

The young Clemens had laid out space for eleven French lessons in this first notebook, but headings for eight through eleven are all that remain. However, he apparently went on with his studies and kept up interest in French for several years, for in the third notebook, kept in the winter of 1860–61, there are entries which indicate a much more advanced knowledge of the language, including fairly extensive passages from Voltaire's *Dialogue Entre un Plaideur et un Avocat.*[8] For several years there is also frequent use of a French word or phrase in the midst of a note in English or in a letter to some family member.

It is not clear whether Clemens ever had formal instruction in French, either in a class or with a tutor. The first lessons look as though he had started with something like a phrase book. A note in the first journal, "Get mon Francais lecon,"[9] indicates that he may have been working from unbound sheets. Much later, in Notebook 8, kept from May to June of

1867, there are full conjugations of the past, the future, and the conditional of the verb *parler*.[10] This was evidently part of his preparation for his first trip to Europe, at a time, incidentally, when many Americans were planning to go. He wrote: "I am afraid the French language will not be spoken in France much this year. I shall feel mighty sick if, after rubbing up my rusty French so diligently, I have to run the legs off myself skirmishing around Paris, hunting for such a sign as 'Ici on parle Français.' "[11]

Unfortunately there is no informal day-to-day record of Mark Twain's first encounter with French as spoken in France because that critical notebook, the one he kept in the summer of 1867, has been lost. His travel book, *The Innocents Abroad,* is the only source of these first impressions, which were apparently much more favorable than later ones. Of the language he said only: "Occasionally, merely for the pleasure of being cruel, we put unoffending Frenchmen on the rack with questions framed in the incomprehensible jargon of their native language, and while they writhed, we impaled them, we peppered them, we scarified them, with their own vile verbs and participles."[12] But he and his friends traveled as mere tourists, sightseeing and making admiring and deprecatory comparisons with American life as tourists are always likely to do.

Much later, when the Clemens family had made long sojourns in Europe and Sam especially would have liked to be able to settle down quietly at home in America, his reactions were quite different. Mrs. Thomas Bailey Aldrich reported visiting them in Paris and said of Mark Twain that he was "very busily engaged in wrestling with the French language, which he said was illiterate, untenable, unscrupulous, for if the Frenchman knew how to spell he did not know how to pronounce—and if he knew how to pronounce he certainly did not know how to spell."[13]

Mark Twain did not become seriously involved with German until the spring of 1878, in preparation for an extended trip to Germany. He was already in his early forties, an age at which it is well known to be very difficult to learn a foreign language, especially with the amateurish methods he had, we must assume, employed to learn French earlier. Albert Bigelow Paine, Mark Twain's idolizing amanuensis and first biographer, says of this time that the Clemens family "entered into the study of the language with an enthusiasm and perseverance that insured progress. There was a German nurse for the children, and the whole atmosphere of the household presently became lingually Teutonic. It amused Mark Twain, as everything amused him; he acquired a working knowledge of the language in an extraordinarily brief time, just as in an earlier day he had picked up piloting. He would never become a German scholar, but his vocabulary and use of picturesque phrases, particularly those that combined English and German words, were often really startling, not only for their humor, but for their expressiveness."[14] This uncritical judgment of Mark Twain's prowess in learning languages is offset by his daughter Clara's much later assessment of his knowledge of German: "Father read German very well and had moods when he could command his tongue to utter many of the words he had memorized. At other times he would make no attempt to speak anything but English, and if Viennese ladies and gentlemen who called were unable to speak anything but German, great misunderstandings took place as to what the topic of conversation really was. The American thought it was noted politicians, and the Viennese knew it was pigs."[15]

Except for the presence of the German nursemaid, Rosa, it is not known exactly what materials and learning aids were used, or whether there were classes to attend or a tutor employed during those months preceding the first trip to Germany. If we go by his experience learning French, however, we can assume that Mark Twain probably started by purchasing a grammar and studying by himself. This impression is reinforced by a note made while he was in Germany: "The idiotic fashion in America of teaching pupils only to read & write a foreign language . . . There may be a justifiable reason for this. God knows what it is. Any fool can teach *himself* to read a language—the only valuable thing a school can do is to teach how to *speak* it."[16] In a letter to his friend William Dean Howells of 27 June 1878, written about two months after his arrival in Germany, he commented: "Drat this German tongue, I never shall be able to learn it. I think I could learn a little conversational stuff, maybe, if I could attend to it, but I found I couldn't spare the time. I took lessons two weeks & got so I could understand the talk going on around me, & even answer back, after a fashion. But I neither talk nor listen now, so I can't even understand the language any more."[17]

The two weeks of classes taken in Germany may be the only formal instruction in German that Mark Twain ever had. The next question is, then, what books did he have at his disposal?

In the first place there is a book by Heinrich Gottfried Ollendorff,[18] whose grammars and readers in French, German, and Italian were very popular in the middle of the nineteenth century. No copy of Ollendorff is listed in the reconstructed library, but Mark Twain mentions him several times in his notebooks and once in a published work. Since this was a name with which he was already familiar, as he probably used his grammar at some time to study French, he may very well have begun his first serious study of German with it.

Ollendorff's grammar was first published in England. The American edition was revised by G. J. Adler and published by D. Appleton and Company. The copy at my disposal was published in 1858, and it is probably essentially the same one available to Mark Twain.

This beginning book consists of 103 lessons, followed by a "Systematic Outline of the Different Parts of Speech, their Inflection and Use," the contribution of Adler. The first lesson, covering five pages, presents the alphabet and rules of pronunciation. Each of the remaining lessons treats one concept of grammar in the form of tables, along with brief statements of rules and observations. Vocabulary is presented in the form of brief sentences arranged in columns, English on the left, German on the right. Exercises consist of sentences based on the grammatical principle introduced in that lesson. From exercise to exercise there is some review of grammar concepts and vocabulary, but it is only occasional and incidental to the practice of each new concept.

There are some remarkable features in the order of presentation. The author offers only masculine and neuter nouns at the beginning of the book, and with those he covers everything about adjective declension, pronouns including the interrogative and indefinite, numerals, comparatives, and noun plurals, using only the verb "haben" in the present and, occasionally, the form "ist." This brings us to Lesson 24, where he introduces the infinitive form of the verb and the expressions "Haben Sie Lust" and "Haben Sie Zeit," with the notation that "Lust" and "Zeit" are feminine nouns. From Lesson 24 on he deals with verbs, throwing both simple and compound, including separable and inseparable verbs, into Lesson 25. All the intricacies of verb and preposition are then presented, lesson by lesson, including all the passive, beginning in Lesson 55 with the example sentence "Ich werde geliebt." At last, in Lesson 78, we come upon the feminine, and in this and the following exercises a few sisters as well as brothers, soup and nuts as well as meat appear. But throughout the book masculine and neuter nouns dominate over feminine. Finally, in Lesson 90, comes that bugbear, the subjunctive, and the book ends with a "Recapitulation of the Rules of Syntax."

In attempting to construct a simple system, the author created possible confusion. For example, in the thirteenth lesson, which treats the plural, after clearing away the nouns ending in -el, -en, -er, -chen, and -lein, he states as Rule 3: "In all cases of the plural masculine substantives take -e, and neuter substantives -er, and soften the radical vowels a, o, u, into ä, ö, ü."[19] Adler's outline of grammar at the end of the book has a succinct but complete statement of the rules for forming the plural, but in the lessons themselves nothing more is said about it until the introduction of the feminine in Lesson 78, and then only feminine nouns are treated. Since there is no German-English or English-German vocabulary, the learner could have difficulties finding what he needed to translate the copious exercises into German.

Ollendorff was not, however, the only book available to Mark Twain, as indicated by Gribben's reconstruction of his library. He mentions three grammars predating 1878: *Ahn's Complete Method of the German Language,* adapted by Dr. P. Henn,[20] W. H. Woodbury's *New Method of*

Learning the German Language,[21] and a *German Conversation-Grammar* by Dr. Emil Otto.[22] All three available for me are in essentially the same editions which Mark Twain owned. Ahn is meant for use in grade schools, from the fifth through the eighth grades, while Woodbury mentions high schools and academies in his quite lengthy introduction; Otto does not indicate anything about his teaching philosophy or the targeted users of his book. All three books include both a German-English and an English-German vocabulary.

All three start out with an introduction to German script, both print and handwriting, and a guide to pronunciation which is much more comprehensive than that in Ollendorff. Ahn has the most extensive guide of all, with example words in very large type and interlineated translations of these vocabulary words. There are thirty pages of unconnected words before students see a complete sentence, and the first sentences are also set up with interlinear translation. In this book the interlinear English is

Reading Exercise.

Die Biene und die Taube.   The bee and the dove.

Eine durstige Biene, welche zu einer Quelle hinab-
A   thirsty   bee,   which   to   a   well   de-

gestiegen war, um zu trinken, wurde von dem strömenden
scended   was, in order to drink, was   by   the   streaming

Wasser fortgerissen, und wäre beinahe ertrunken.   Eine
water   carried away and was   nearly   drowned.   A

Taube, welche dieses bemerkte, pickte ein Baumblatt ab
dove   which . this   perceived, picked a   (tree-)leaf   off

und warf es in das Wasser.   Die Biene ergriff es und
and threw it into the water.   The bee   seized   it   and

rettete sich.
saved   herself.

Nicht lange nachher saß die Taube auf einem Baume
Not   long afterwards sat . the dove   on   a   tree

und bemerkte nicht, daß ein Jäger mit seiner Flinte auf
and perceived not,   that · a hunter with his gun   at

sie zielte.   Die dankbare Biene, welche die Gefahr
her aimed.   The :hankful bee   which   the   danger

erkannte, in welcher ihre Wohlthäterin sich befand, flog
recognised, in which her   benefactress herself found,   flew

hinzu und stach den Jäger in die Hand.   Der Schuß
near   and stung the hunter in the hand.   The   shot

ging daneben und die Taube war gerettet.
went aside,   and the dove   was saved.

Figure 1. Ahn's *Complete Method of the German Language*

not fractured. For example, "Wie befinden Sie sich?" is translated as "How do you do?" and "Haben Sie meinen Garten gesehen?" as "Have you seen my garden?"[23]

Otto, after a detailed discussion of pronunciation, including rules of accent (some of which must have been confusing to the beginning student), gives an interlineated reading exercise of three pages consisting of two fables. The first sentence reads: "Eine durstige Biene, welche zu einer Quelle hinabgestiegen war, um zu trinken, wurde von dem strömenden Wasser fortgerissen, und wäre beinahe ertrunken." This sentence is interlineated thus: "A thirsty bee, which to a well descended was, in order to drink, was by the streaming water carried away and was nearly drowned" (figure 1).[24] Who knows? Perhaps this teaching device gave Mark Twain the idea for his English rendering of German word order, for instance the famous de . . . parted passage from "The Awful German Language."

In all three books the only exercises offered are translation exercises. Thus groups of sentences in German illustrative of a certain grammar point alternate with groups of sentences in English to be translated into German. Sometimes Ahn even mixes English and German sentences thus, and without explanation as to what the pupil is to do with them: "What are these girls doing? Sie nähen. Are these singing-birds or birds of prey? Was für eine Frage! Singvögel sind sehr klein und Raubvögel sind sehr groß. Is this gentleman an Englishman? Nein, mein Herr, er ist ein Amerikaner" (figure 2).[25]

In Woodbury and Ahn, explanations of grammar are kept to a minimum and exercises force the students to practice the point in question, although the vocabulary introduced within a few lessons seems to the twentieth-century teacher to be excessive, and almost inevitably grammar concepts not yet explained are incorporated into the sentences to be translated into German.

97.   grün, green

What are these girls doing? Sie nähen. Are these (birds) singing-birds or birds of prey? Was für eine Frage! Singvögel sind sehr klein und Raubvögel sind sehr groß. Is this gentleman an Englishman? Nein, mein Herr, er ist ein Amerikaner. Where are your brothers now, Mr. Stern? Sie wohnen jetzt beide in London. Are these apples ripe, uncle? Nein, mein Freund, diese Aepfel sind nicht reif; sie sind noch so grün wie Gras. What kind of a garden is this? Ich glaube, es ist ein Obstgarten. There is a flower-garden, too. How beautiful these gardens are!

Figure 2. Otto's *German Conversation–Grammar*

Otto, on the other hand, tries to teach all the complexities of grammar to the beginning student. Imagine if you can our forty-three-year-old humorist confronting the following passage in Lesson Three (if, indeed, he got that far). I quote fairly extensively because only thus can one get the full impact of the explanation.

> Declension of Substantives. The German grammarians are not yet agreed on the division of the nouns substantive into declensions, and on the number of these. Some adopt 6, others 5, others again 4 or 3, and even 2 declensions only. This division, however, is quite arbitrary; indeed, in this matter there is much irregularity in German. The reason is, that the language was practised and cultivated by different tribes in various ways before a grammar existed, which was then obliged to accept matters as they were, and to make the best of them. Notwithstanding, there are two fundamental ideas, on which declension is principally founded, viz. the *gender,* and the *number of syllables,* and though the arrangement presents occasional deviations and exceptions, this system offers really far less difficulty than any other division.
>
> We consider therefore that each of the three genders has its own mode of inflexion, and further that the masculine gender admits of three different forms of declension, the feminine of one, and the neuter also of one.
>
> Hence we adopt five declensions, the three first of which comprise the masculine, the fourth the feminine, the fifth the neuter substantives, exceptions not included.
>
> Our distribution has the great advantage of enabling the learner, on seeing any substantive, accompanied by its article, to refer it to its proper declension. This is not to be attained by any other method.
>
> In consequence we state as follows:
>
> (1) the first declension comprehends all *masculine* and *neuter* nouns ending in el, er, en, chen and lein.
>
> (2) the second comprehends all *masculine* words ending in e, and most foreign masculine substantives having the accent on the last syllable.
>
> (3) The third contains all *monosyllabic masculine* words and those of two syllables ending in ig, ich and ling, and some words of foreign origin in ier, ar, etc.
>
> (4) To the fourth belong all the *feminine* substantives.
>
> (5) To the fifth all *neuter* substantives not ending in el, er, en, chen and lein (see 1).[26]

Following this explanation Otto presents a complete table of endings (figure 3). One can imagine how useful such a chart would be, especially in the third lesson! Moreover, it is followed by ten "general hints," which the author says "may facilitate" the study of the declensions, which will be given one by one in the following lessons.

No wonder Mark Twain made snide remarks: "In early times some sufferer had to sit up with a toothache, and he put in the time inventing the German language."[27] "Never knew before what Eternity was made

Table of the endings of the five declensions.

Singular.

	masculine.			feminine.	neuter.
	I.	II.	III.	IV.	V.
N.	— -	— e	— -	— -	— -
G.	— ß	— en	— eß (ß)	— -	— eß (ß)
D.	— -	— en	— (e)	— -	— (e)
A.	— -	— en	— -	— -	— -

Plural.

	I.	II.	III.	IV.		V.	
N.	⌣*)-	— en	⌣ e	⌣ e	— en	— e	⌣ er
G.	⌣ -	— en	⌣ e	⌣ e	— en	— e	⌣ er
D.	⌣ n	— en	⌣ en	⌣ en	— en(n)	— en	⌣ ern
A.	⌣ -	— en	⌣ e	⌣ e	— en	— e	⌣ er

Figure 3. Otto's *Complete Conversation–Grammar*

for. It is to give some of us a chance to learn German."[28] The following passage from the year 1897, written after he had been struggling with German for almost twenty years, must not be omitted: "It is easier for a cannibal to enter the Kingdom of Heaven through the eye of a rich man's needle than it is for any other foreigner to read the terrible German script."[29]

Mark Twain not only expressed his exasperation at the complexities of learning German; he also had some practical advice, comparing that task to learning to ride a bicycle, which, like studying German, he tried to do as an adult. He wrote:

> The steps of one's progress are distinctly marked. At the end of each lesson he knows he has acquired something, and he also knows what that something is, and likewise that it will stay with him. It is not like studying German, where you mull along, in a groping, uncertain way, for thirty years; and at last, just as you think you've got it, they spring the subjunctive on you, and there you are. No—and I see now, plainly enough, that the great pity about the German language is, that you can't fall off it and hurt yourself. There is nothing like that feature to make you attend strictly to business. But I also see, by what I have learned of bicycling, that the right and only sure way to learn German is by the bicycling method. That is to say, take a grip on one villainy of it at a time, and learn it—not ease up and shirk to the next, leaving that one half learned.[30]

To return to the spring of 1878, the Clemens children were taught at home by a German nurse, Rosa, who then accompanied the family to Europe. After their arrival the two daughters, Susie, age six, and Clara, age four, were subjected to strict discipline as far as language was concerned. Mark Twain described one reaction to it in a letter to his friend Howells: "Poor Susie! From the day we reached German soil, we have required Rosa to speak German to the children—which they hate with all their souls. The other morning in Hanover, Susie came to me (from Rosa, in the nursery), & said, in halting syllables, 'Papa, wie viel Uhr ist es?'— then turned, with pathos in her big eyes, & said, 'Mamma, I wish Rosa was made in English.' "[31]

The methods used in the family were successful with the children, but so far as I am able to determine, Mark Twain never commented on age as a factor in the language-learning process. He did observe the results in the case of his youngest, Jean: "When she talks German, it is a German talking—manner and all; when she talks French she is French—shrugs and all, and she is entirely at home in both tongues. She is getting a good start in Italian and will make it her property presently."[32]

I suspect that Mark Twain might have approved of many of the recent innovations in language-teaching methods, although from his perspective some of our books might seem watered-down. He would have seen the reason for teaching the student to suit the gesture to the word. He would have applauded the breakdown of material to be learned into small steps. He might even have responded enthusiastically to a computerized program, though with his burdens and worries it might have become too time-consuming. He would tell teachers to teach their pupils to *speak* the language, and above all: "Drill—that is the valuable thing. Drill—drill—drill!"

Notes

1 Albert Bigelow Paine, *Mark Twain's Notebook* (New York: Cooper Square Publishers, 1972) 236.

2 John T. Krumpelmann, *Mark Twain and the German Language* (Baton Rouge: Louisiana State University Press, 1953).

3 Quoted in Thomas Asa Tenney, *Mark Twain, A Reference Guide* (Boston: G. K. Hall, 1977) 209.

4 *Mark Twain's Notebooks & Journals,* ed. Frederick Anderson et al., vol. 1 (1855–1873), vol. 2 (1877–1883) (Berkeley: University of California Press, 1975). Michael B. Frank and Kenneth M. Sanderson worked with Anderson on volume 1, and Lin Salamo and Bernard L. Stein on volume 2.

5 Alan Gribben, *Mark Twain's Library: A Reconstruction* (Boston: G. K. Hall, 1980).

6 *Notebooks & Journals* 2: 66–67.

7 Charles Neider, *The Autobiography of Mark Twain* (New York: Harper & Row, 1975) 220.

8 *Notebooks & Journals* 1: 51–53.

9 Ibid. 36.

10 Ibid. 238.

11 Franklin Walker and G. Ezra Dane, eds., *Mark Twain's Travels with Mr. Brown* (New York: Knopf, 1940) 236.

12 Samuel L. Clemens, *The Innocents Abroad* (New York: Harper, 1869) 1: 106.

13 Lillian Aldrich, *Crowding Memories* (Boston: Houghton Mifflin, 1920) 229–230.

14 Albert Bigelow Paine, *Mark Twain: A Biography* (New York: Harper, 1912).

15 Clara Clemens, *My Father, Mark Twain* (New York: Harper, 1931) 192.

16 *Notebooks & Journals* 2: 184.

17 *Mark Twain–Howells Letters, The Correspondence of Samuel L. Clemens and William D. Howells, 1872–1910,* ed. Henry Nash Smith and William M. Gibson, 2 vols. (Cambridge, Mass.: The Belknap Press of Harvard University Press, 1960) 1: 237.

18 G. J. Adler, *Ollendorff's New Method of Learning to Read, Write, and Speak the German Language* (New York: Appleton, 1858).

19 Ibid. 22.

20 P. Henn, *Ahn's Complete Method of the German Language* (New York: Steiger, n.d.) Mark Twain's copy was published in 1873; the copy available to me has only a handwritten date 1876.

21 W. H. Woodbury, *A New Method of Learning the German Language, embracing both the Analytic and Synthetic Modes of Instruction: Being a Plain and Practical Way of Acquiring the Art of Reading, Speaking, and Composing German* (New York: Ivison, Blakeman). Mark Twain's copy is dated 1864; the one available to me 1855.

22 Emil Otto, *German Conversation-Grammar, A New and Practical Method of Learning the German Language* (New York: Holt). Both Mark Twain's and my copies bear the date 1864.

23 Henn 30–31.

24 Otto 16.

25 Henn 78.

26 Otto 25–27.

27 Paine, *Mark Twain's Notebook* 141.

28 *Notebooks & Journals* 2: 121.

29 Paine, *Mark Twain's Notebook* 346.

30 Mark Twain, *What Is Man? and Other Essays: Taming the Bicycle* (London: Chatto & Windus, 1919) 288.

31 *Mark Twain–Howells Letters* 1: 228.

32 *Mark Twain to Mrs. Fairbanks,* ed. Dixon Wecter (San Marino, Calif.: Huntington Library, 1949) 269–70.

Language and Culture in German Textbooks from the Amana Colonies in Iowa

FRITZ H. KÖNIG
University of Northern Iowa

The Amana Colonies are a cluster of seven Hutterite villages with a total population of about 1,700 in the vicinity of Cedar Rapids, Iowa. They were founded in 1854 by immigrants of mostly Hessian and Swiss stock under the leadership of their spiritual leader Christian Metz. Until 1932 these communities adhered to an economic system which was based on Christian Socialism, that is, all means of production, such as fields, buildings, tools, animals, small factories, etc., were communal property.

With a growing liberalization of religious rules, Americanization of younger generations, and changes in the national economy after World War I, the basis for cooperative farming fell apart; the communal property arrangement was succeeded by a corporate one and shares were issued. Because of their unique architecture, manufactured artifacts, German cuisine, music, and other cultural traditions, the Colonies today are a thriving tourist attraction.

In recent years some efforts have been made in the Colonies to preserve cultural heritage. Among other things, a museum was established. In the spring of 1983 my colleague Reinhold Bubser and I inventoried the German textbooks at the museum. Many of the textbooks were present in two or three different or parallel editions. These books have several traits in common: all were in use from the 1880s until after World War I; all were printed in German in Amana in several editions especially for the pupils of the communities of true inspiration ("Gemeinden der wahren Inspiration"), as the Colonies referred to themselves; all are anonymous (two prefaces are simply signed: the teachers). Mental property seems to have been just as communal as the physical and the issue of copyright did not matter.

As in most fundamentalist schools, education in the Amanas at the time before World War I was confined to reading, writing, arithmetic, and a fair amount of religion. The children entered school at the age of five and finished at twelve or thirteen. The teachers were recruited from talent within the community. They were appointed by the leaders, sometimes against their own will and frequently lacking formal education. The basic

Erſtes

Lehr= und Lesebuch

für die

Schuljugend

in den Gemeinden

der wahren Inſpiration.

Neu aufgelegt im Jahr 1889,
in
Amana, im Staat Jowa.

Figure 1. *Erstes Lehr- und Lesebuch* title page. Courtesy of The Amana Historical Society

instructional aid for all academic endeavors (except arithmetic) was the reader, which was available on three levels. These texts, however, were designed to do far more than teach reading, writing, and praying skills; they also tried to convey basic natural science, history, geography, and ethics. Above all, they tried to render a consistently Christian *Weltanschauung*.

Three of the books examined are readers for different levels. One is entitled *Erstes Lehr- und Lesebuch*[1] another is entitled *Lese- und Lehrbuch*, without reference to level, but with the subtitle "Hilfsmittel zur Anleitung und Fortbildung in einigen Zweigen der bürgerlichen Wissenschaften";[2] a third with roughly the same structure as the second is called *Lehrreiche Erzählungen für geübtere Schüler.*[3] It is quite clear that these three readers, though they were put together in the Amanas, were based on German models, though we have not as yet been able to find the models. Some of the stories in the readers are still with us today in German elementary school readers, or at least they were present in the late forties. However, large sections were introduced into these readers which take life in the United States into account and thus there exists an interesting dichotomy between German and American cultural traditions and points of view.

A fourth book is entitled *Deutsch-Amerikanische Arithmetik.*[4] Language, the units of measurement used, and multiplication and division techniques indicate an American model. Finally, there was a book which in all likelihood was written in the Amanas, for it caters to spiritual requirements for young people and thus had to take the special theological foundations of the Amana Community into account. It is called *Kinder-Stimme* and bears the following explicatory subtitle: "Anleitung zum kindlichen Lob und Tugend-Übung der Kinder durch Trieb des Geistes verfasset von Einigen, die nach dem kindlichen Geist Christi in Aufrichtigkeit des Herzens sich sehnen."[5] Those who seek sincerity of the heart are obviously the members of the community of true inspiration, namely Amana. The book is a combined prayer book and hymnal, providing prayers and songs for all occasions in a child's life. What we encounter in the prayers is a type of fundamentalist mysticism with a tangible heaven and hell and the added belief that God not only in Biblical times but even today inspires people to speak His word and will. Although it is repetitive, exhibits bad language usage, employs forced rhymes, and thus makes for very tedious reading, this book is nevertheless essential if one wants to develop a feeling for the spiritual life of the Amanas, for the psychological setting, and for the general cultural environment. In this context another important tool to the understanding of life in the Amanas is the now defunct annual publication *Inspirations-Historie*—a chronicle, relating in detail the year's events: births, deaths, marriages, church-related items, members gained or, more often, lost to the community, accidents, and miracles that happened to one of the brothers or sisters.[6]

Today these readers are interesting cultural history. Quite apart from the fact that it is engaging to view the world through the eyes of the more educated members of the Amana Colonies, that is, the teachers, during the first quarter of this century, conclusions can also be drawn with regard to acculturation processes; the problem of keeping one's heritage alive in relatively new and different surroundings; the problem of bilingualism in a semiliterate setting; the problem of perpetuating religious fervor in an increasingly complacent society.

Kinder = Stimme

oder

Anleitung zum kindlichen Lob

und

Tugend = Uebung der Kinder,

durch

Trieb des Geistes verfasset

von Einigen,

die nach dem kindlichen Geist Christi in Aufrichtigkeit
des Herzens sich sehnen.

Zum sechstenmal aufgelegt.

Gedruckt in A m a n a, im Staat Jowa,

1906.

Figure 2. *Kinder-Stimme* title page. Courtesy of The Amana
Historical Society

Of the three readers at hand, the first one (level I) consists of 132
pages (a table of contents is missing). In lieu of a preface there is a general
admonition to the pupils to be good, to behave, to honor teachers and
parents, to practice Christian love and self-denial, and above all to love
and praise God.

The first section is a reading exercise addressing chiefly the problems of homonyms in German in alphabetical order. The exercise is close to the minimal pair-type exercises routinely done in modern phonetics classes. As a language teacher today I would find the exercise problematic because there is a general confusion of phonemes and graphemes: words that differ only graphically are juxtaposed although by induction one would expect phonological differences. Frequently words appear under one letter, for instance "Eiche" and "eigen" under *e*, although /ç/ and /g/ are contrasted and no vowels at all. The orthography corresponds to the 1870s and 80s. The first edition of the book dates from 1889.

Next follows a section entitled "Lesestücke und einfache Darstellung aus der Naturgeschichte." These are six simple descriptions of animals. Section 3 personalizes, so to speak, the general descriptions, for six animal anecdotes follow. That the animals come first might be construed as a clever pedagogical strategy because most children like animals. With some logic then follow other parts of nature (each contained in a one- or two-page composition): "The Earth," "The Air," "The Four Seasons," "The Sun," "The Plants," etc., until we reach a climax in the middle of the book: "The Human Being"—first body, then soul.

The fourth section is entitled "Erzählungen aus dem Leben," but "God and Man" would describe the content of the little stories more accurately. They are all of an edifying nature and culminate in a set of moral aphorisms ("Denksprüche").

The final section is a "Deutsche Sprachlehre" which, one presumes, the good Amana teachers borrowed from another German grammar. The terminology is German. Ten word categories are discerned.

A. Es gibt im ganzen zehn Wortarten:
(1) Das Hauptwort (noun) z.B. Haus, Woche, Sohn.
(2) Das Zeitwort (verb) = gehen, arbeiten, suchen.
(3) Das Beschaffenheitswort (adjective) = groß, neu.
(4) Das Fürwort (pronoun) = ich, du, dieser, wer;
(5) Das Zahlwort (numeral adjective) = zwei, einige;
(6) Das Geschlechtswort (article) = der, die, das;
(7) Das Umstandswort (adverb) = hier, jetzt, bald;
(8) Das Bindewort (conjunction) = und, aber;
(9) Das Verhältnißwort (preposition) = in, auf, durch;
(10) Das Empfindungswort (Interjection) = ach, pfui! (122)

As a concession to America, the English equivalents appear in parentheses.

No *Sprachlehre* would be complete without syntax. The authors of this reader felt the same and managed to take care of the problem on six pages. After the syntax, the *Sprachlehre* has to be applied: there are suggestions on how to write descriptive prose and how to write letters. The sample letters deal with Amana business reality.

Thus this first reader introduces the children to the sounds of words, nature, the universe, God, German grammar, and business letters. They are now ready for life in the Amanas, especially if they simultaneously complete the arithmetic text.

The second reader from the year 1908 functions not only as reader but also, as the preface explains, as a textbook of "einiger gemeinnütziger Wissenschaften," such as "Naturlehre" (=earth science), "Naturgeschichte" (=zoology) and "Geographie" (=an amalgam of geography and history). It was probably used on a higher level than the first one. There is also an appendix in which eleven compositions of variable content are presented in German: George Washington—Benjamin Franklin—Abraham Lincoln—Gaslight—Paper Manufacturing—Glass Manufacturing—A Rare Gratitude—Socrates—The Spartans—The Invention of the Printing Press, and, finally, The Cotton Industry.

The first part of the reader, earth science, is the shortest section of the book. It should be noted that there is almost a complete absence of references to the United States. Though there is talk of volcanoes and hot springs, natural phenomena which are in abundance in the United States, only European examples are given.

The second part, zoology, is very different in this respect, as great care is taken to describe the conditions in the United States in general and in Iowa in particular. Although it is clear that this part, like the earth science chapters, was lifted from other German texts, the teacher (or teachers) who were responsible for zoology tried very hard to adapt the material to local United States conditions and environments. The hedgehog is described, yet we are told right away that it is not native to Iowa. For many animals, such as bears, the exact geographic habitat is indicated. The American zoologist Audubon is quoted twice as many times as his German counterpart Brehm. Frequently, and especially as far as species native to the United States are concerned, names do appear in English in italics. Sometimes, as for instance in the case of squirrels, the different kinds appear only with their English names. The presentation of the animals varies from a purely descriptive approach to an anecdotal approach of the type "Once upon a time two Negroes in Kentucky encountered a wolf. . . ." The chapter on kangaroos starts with these words: "Cook, auf seiner ersten Reise im Jahre 1770. . . ."

In traditional fashion the animals are still accorded some human qualities. The fox is sly, the lion is the king of the animals, the tiger is courageous. Or they are compared with each other: "was der Tiger für Asien, ist der Jaguar für Amerika." On the other hand the American puma is only "ein erbärmlicher Abklatsch" of the African lion.

A certain amount of cruelty also manifests itself. At one time we hear "wenn ein Tiger den Elefanten angreift, stampft derselbe ihn oft zu Brei." Or wolves are captured in a most cruel manner and bludgeoned to death.

The marten is valuable and therefore "trägt er ein wertvolles Fell zu Markte, das ihm oft genug über die Ohren gezogen wird." In a physics experiment a sparrow is placed under a glass bowl then the air is pumped out and the bird dies in the vacuum.

On the other hand, there is a long paragraph admonishing students not to torment animals. Also, there is a surprising amount of environmental concern, ranging from exhortations not to damage trees and disturb the forest to the disapproving remark about the "stumpfsinniger Grönländer" who mistreats his sled dogs. Even today, when one travels to the Amanas, a fair amount of forest can be noted, a rarity in an area where farmers otherwise remove trees with a passion.

Apart from animal names, the German is High German. In the entire text I found only two Americanisms: "Die Eichhörnchen laufen an der Fenz entlang" and "Kapitän McCowen von der V. St. Armee." Where possible German names are used, although at times very unusual ones, especially as far as animal categories are concerned; a few examples: "die Zahnarmen," "die Scharrtiere," "die Schwielensohler," "die Hornträger." Pronghorns are "Gabelgemsen," martins are "Purpurschwalben," and we learn a lot about "das Armadill" and "das Kloakentier." On the other hand, English names are kept wherever advisable, as in the case of the different kinds of American squirrels mentioned earlier. A whippoorwill remains the same in German, as do the muskrat and the civet cat. Some trees, such as cottonwood, box elder and hickory, also keep their names in German. But we do have in German a "Moostier" (loan translation from the English "moose") although a perfectly good German name exists, namely "der Elch." "Die Buchnuß" (likewise a loan translation of "beechnut") exists in High German as "die Buchecker." Only mammals and birds are considered in the zoology chapter.

The part on geography contains a general section on physical geography, followed by a description of America, that is, the United States (Canada is never mentioned). Of interest is the division of human beings into "Wilde, Halbwilde, Halbzivilisierte und Zivilisierte Nationen." This, applied to America, yields the following result:

> Wilde, die bloß von Jagd und Fischfang sich nähren, in schlechten Hütten leben, und überhaupt die unterste Stufe in der menschlichen Gesellschaft einnehmen. Hierzu gehören die Indianer Amerikas, die meisten Neger und der größte Teil der Bewohner Australiens . . . 4) Zivilisierte Nationen, worunter man alle europäischen und die meisten amerikanischen Nationen rechnet; doch sind auch unter ihnen die Grade der Zivilisation noch sehr verschieden. (174–75)

Otherwise the Indian is described here as the "noble savage." He is intelligent, cruel, and brave. His saving grace is his belief in one superior being (a fact, and this is of course not mentioned in the book, which makes him uniquely suited for Christianity).

A description of the United States government follows. We learn that in order to become a state in the union a territory needs a minimum of 60,000 men over 25. One may vote at age 21, immigrants may vote after five years. And then we hear why the people of the Amanas find the United States so attractive: no nobility, no social class system, general freedom of speech and the press, and most importantly "ein aber noch schätzbareres Gut ist die allgemeine Religionsfreiheit." Last but not least, a good business sense is in evidence: "Amerika ist der erste Handelsstaat der Welt, nach England."

A brief history of the United States yields no surprises, with the possible exception that there is no mention of fellow German immigrants, not even of the more famous ones who fought in the War of Independence. The Civil War receives short shrift. The reader states very laconically that slavery was abolished and that Negroes received the same rights as whites. Iowa is the only state described in more detail. Here too a physical and a historical overview comes first, followed by an outline of the state government. The authors struggled with the state offices and had largely to retain the English names or Germanized versions thereof: "der Lieutenant Governor"; "der Auditeur," "der Gerichtsclerk," "der Recorder," "der Coroner." I was proud to find my own university mentioned in this book from 1908 as "die Staatsnormalschule in Cedar Falls."

The rest of the Americas is dealt with very swiftly. The Antilles are summed up in the following sentence which has either a structural, a logical, or a racial problem, or all of the above: "Vortrefflich gedeihen hier in den Plantagen die sogenannten Kolonialwaren, vor allem Zuckerrohr und Kaffee, dann auch Baumwolle, Kakao, Tabak, Piment oder Nelkenpfeffer, u.s.w., daher denn freilich auch eine Menge Neger" (202).

The description of Mexico is a little more extensive. But the rest of Central America occupies one single page (more or less a list of the republics) and all of South America occupies two pages. By comparison Belgium yields two and a half pages, The Netherlands, three.

The look at Europe starts in the north with the Scandinavian peninsula. Nothing to report from there but beautiful countryside. Russia is next and, somewhat to our astonishment, we read that the Russian is a good businessman but that the country struggles with terrible religious chaos. Now we come to the southeast (this is a circular approach to European geography): the Balkan countries. There are only two: Turkey and Greece. Current problems, and God knows there were some in 1908, are not addressed. The emphasis is on the historical, mainly how the poor Greeks succumbed to the wild Turks and how Constantinople was lost to the world in 1453. "Aber der rohe Eroberer [Muhamad II], lange nicht

zufrieden, dachte seine Rosse sogar in der römischen Peterskirche zu
füttern." Thus we arrive at the next point of interest: Italy. Here again,
history is important, especially the history of the early Christians and the
martyrs. The pope is introduced and described very diplomatically, yet
not without a note of disapproval (please note the verbs and especially the
two subjunctives!):

> . . . er ließ sich "heiliger Vater" anreden, wie Jesus in seinem Gebet (Joh.
> 17,11) seinen himmlischen Vater nennt, gab sich für den Stellvertreter Jesu
> Christi auf Erden aus, setzte bald den Bischofshut und bald die Königskrone
> auf sein Haupt, gab seine Füße den Bischöfen und sogar den Königen zu
> küssen, nahm zwei Schlüssel in die Hand, zum Zeichen, daß er die Schlüssel
> des Himmelreichs habe, und ließ zwei Schwerter vor sich her tragen, um
> anzudeuten, daß er das Recht habe, in Kirche und Staat zu regieren (224)

The Spanish are proud, nationalistic, and have a majestic language.
In their long history the inquisition seems to be the most noteworthy item
to the textbook authors.

Now we come to the heart of the matter, namely France and Germany.
France occupies five pages. First, there is an enthusiastic description of
the landscape and the climate, reminiscent of the old German adage "wie
Gott in Frankreich leben." But as soon as we come to the history we
realize that all is not well in France. We learn that the French, in the
seventeenth and eighteenth centuries, cunningly supported protestantism
in Germany but suppressed it with fire and sword in their own country.
Louis XIV had "ungerechte Vergrößerungspläne" and consequently,
"grenzenlose Schmach hat damals Deutschland von den Franzosen er-
duldet, welche am Oberrhein wie Mordbrenner hausten, in Speier nach
Schätzen wühlend die Särge der Kaiser aufbrachen und ihre Gebeine
zerstreuten." Neither did the Amana teachers care for "das Lasterleben
am Hof und die tolle Verschwendung." The French Revolution is not seen
in a very positive light either: "sie war ein verhängnisvolles Chaos. . . .
1804 kam *endlich* [italics mine] das Kaisertum." But soon we find "die
geknechteten Völker erheben sich gegen die Unterdrücker," and "die
tollkühne Kriegserklärung Napoleons III" is a recent memory. Not only
are the French a political nuisance, but France is also the cradle of atheism.

The greater importance of Germany is indicated by the fact that its
description, like that of the United States, occupies seven pages. From a
distance, that is, in retrospect from their position in Iowa, the authors
have rare insight into the German national character: no nation is as split
up as the German nation. "Stammesbewußtsein" traditionally has
superseded "Volksbewußtsein." Instead of treasuring the great German
fatherland, the Germans admire all things foreign "und äffen alles Auslän-

dische nach." This, of course, is a somewhat precarious statement considering the Iowa source.

Nevertheless Germany is the great fatherland, the home of inventors, the country where even the lowest social classes receive education. The history of Germany starts with the Romans, who were miserably afraid of the German warrior: "der hünenhafte deutsche Krieger mit seinen großen blauen Augen, seinen rötlich blonden Haaren, wenn er mit Schlachtgeheul auf den Römer losstürzte . . ." From here on, the only way is up. The Slavs get conquered, Poland, Denmark, and Italy are vassal-states. "Das neue römische Kaisertum war des alten nicht unwürdig." Alas, the downturn comes with the Thirty Years War. "Von der Zeit ab mischten sich Fremde in Deutschlands Angelegenheiten, vor allem die Franzosen." And so it goes until 1870, when France's alleged envy over German unity and prosperity leads to the declaration of war. But "einig und daher mächtig zerschmetterten die Deutschen mit furchtbaren Schlägen die Kräfte des alten Erbfeindes auf dessen eigenem Boden." At the end of the chapter, just as Iowa was emphasized in the United States, Prussia is accorded two pages of its own, the only one of the German states to receive this special attention.

Great Britain, finally, receives benign neglect, being seen more or less as an extension of Germany. After all, the Angles and Saxons were German and so are the present-day Hanoverians.

Three continents are still missing: Asia, Africa and Australia. Asia consists of Siberia (the tsar's Gulag Archipelago is mentioned) and of China where Buddhism is rampant: "Der Buddhismus ist ausgeartet, besteht nur noch aus einigen abergläubischen Meinungen und leichteren Zeremonien." The Arabs are brave, generous and hospitable. Turkey isn't what it used to be. Palestine is the land of Biblical history. India is missing, and Japan has just begun, with the aid of the United States, to turn into a country with some commercial potential. Africa consists chiefly of Egypt and the Sahara and "Einförmigkeit ist der Charakter Australiens." It is very surprising that there is absolutely no mention of colonies, either of United States or German ones. Even Britain is discussed without reference to the Empire, which, after all, in 1908 had reached its pinnacle.

It is evident that the anonymous authors, i.e., the Amana teachers, reflect in their texts the state of knowledge of the turn of the century. They apparently use German textbooks as a source, but they strive to make the necessary adjustments to their new surroundings. Sometimes they are successful in this attempt, sometimes not. Politically they exhibit a split conscience: they are Americans, yet they sympathize with their country of origin to which, obviously, strong ties exist. However, both the United States and Germany, or actually the entire outside world, are a secondary consideration. What matters is their own community (for them the center of the universe), and in that they have not strayed far from the original model of their society. World War I and the sweeping abolition of any second language teaching had its impact on the Amanas, yet ways were found to circumvent laws and German continued to be taught (although after the war mainly during the summer months). Many of the older generation in the Amanas still have a working knowledge of German (or dialect versions thereof). The real change came in 1932 and it was not a cultural or a linguistic one, but economic in nature.

Notes

1 *Erstes Lehr- und Lesebuch für die Schuljugend in den Gemeinden der wahren Inspiration* (Amana, Iowa: n.p., 1889).

2 *Lese- und Lehr-Buch für die Schuljugend in den Gemeinden der wahren Inspiration als Hilfsmittel zur Anleitung und Fortbildung in einigen Zweigen der bürgerlichen Wissenschaften* (Amana, Iowa: n.p., 1908).

3 *Lehrreiche Erzählungen und verschiedene andere Lesestücke zum nützlichen Gebrauch für geübtere Schüler in den Gemeinden der wahren Inspiration* (Amana, Iowa: n.p., 1912).

4 *Deutsch-Amerikanische Arithmetik,* anonymous (Amana, Iowa: n.p., 1886).

5 *Kinder-Stimme oder Anleitung zum kindlichen Lob und Tugend-Übung der Kinder durch Trieb des Geistes verfasset von Einigen, die nach dem kindlichen Geist Christi in Aufrichtigkeit des Herzens sich sehnen* (Amana, Iowa: n.p., 1906).

6 *Inspirations-Historie: oder verschiedene Aufsätze und Erzählungen von dem Werk des Herrn in den Inspirations-Wegen und Führungen* (Amana, Iowa: Amana Society, 1884).

From Genesis to Convention: Literary Criticism as a German-American Institution

RICHARD SPULER
University of Houston

This essay delineates some of the parameters of literary scholarship related to *Germanistik* in nineteenth-century America.[1] Since this topic remains relatively unexplored, some methodological problems should be made explicit. One of them is common to any "narrative" act; namely, the question as to where to begin and end the story, and why. Of special importance in this regard is the context in which parameters appear as relevant: I will place the discussion within a frame of reference outlined by the emergence of the American university and issues pertaining to the professionalization of literary scholars and scholarship in the latter third of the nineteenth century.

A second problem concerns the scope of the presentation. At least four different perspectives seem possible. The first, and narrowest, would involve a diachronic account of successive generations within *Germanistik*. This approach would ignore essential contextual factors and would result in a largely positivistic exercise. Another viewpoint would place *Germanistik* within its immediate academic context—the American university and the role of the humanities and the liberal arts within American intellectual affairs. A third approach might, in addition, try to account for the historically significant dimensions of the extensive German-American community, placing *Germanistik* within the set of functions made relevant by this additional sociopolitical and cultural context. Fourth, one can relate real and perceived functions of *Germanistik* in America to those of *Germanistik* in Germany at the same time. Since many scholars of German in America were German-born and/or educated in German universities, questions of methodological and/or ideological interplay become pertinent. Heuristically, these different domains need to be isolated and assigned their relative dimensions, although our sense of historical depth will come only with a differentiated sensitivity for where and how they overlap and interrelate. The four perspectives I have outlined here will become relevant to varying degrees throughout this essay.

Finally, a third methodological problem concerns what could be called the "fallacy of disinterested discourse." With this term I mean to draw attention to the kinds of questions that need to be asked in order to understand the historically significant and, from today's perspective, meaningful issues involved in the study, teaching and interpretation of German literature within the American academic enterprise and beyond. Or should our interest be merely antiquarian? Clearly, there is a choice.

Reception theory, as Peter Hohendahl and others have noted,[2] generated new impulses for considering the history of literary criticism (as *Literaturwissenschaft* or *Literaturkritik*). The formulation of different questions—a shift of epistemological paradigms—resulted in a different hermeneutic situation. Previous questions—those emanating from within a convention of thought which viewed literature primarily in terms of production aesthetics, questions which could ask only for those answers already sanctioned by the paradigm or concept of literature in force—have in many instances simply lost their theoretical interest. (But not for purely theoretical reasons, to be sure!) The consequence of asking different questions—those more concerned with the institutional base of literature and its manifold issues rather than with more or less close readings of isolated texts—has been a substantially changed view of the history of literary criticism, at least within the academic branch of German literary scholarship (*Literaturwissenschaft,* as distinct from *Literaturkritik*).

Much could be said from a German-American perspective about the changes within the shifted focus of interest of reception theory, and as far as the German and the American versions of this "school" acknowledge each other, I refer to the essay by Robert Holub in *The German Quarterly.*[3] But since I have at least implied the presence of Hans Robert Jauss by speaking of paradigms in literary criticism, I will—just to present two sides of the picture—also mention the name of Stanley Fish, whose model of interpretive communities points in a similar direction. In his book about the classroom text that some of us have and some of us don't, Fish notes that "once we give up the essentialist notions that inform a demonstration model—the notion that literature is a monolith and that there is a single set of operations by which its characteristics are discovered and evaluated—we are free to consider the various forms the literary institution has taken and to uncover the interpretative strategies by which its canons have been produced and understood."[4]

In this regard, much work is still needed in the area of *Literaturkritik,*[5] but I will direct my comments toward the sphere of academic literary criticism and try to consider it from a slightly different angle. Discussing the institution and institutionalization of literary criticism from a German-American perspective presents an opportunity not only to examine particular modes of inquiry into the nature and function of literature within its institutional contexts, but to expand this analytical model to account as well for what we might call the "transfer of culture," a term used by Jürgen Herbst in his work on *The German Historical School in American Scholarship*.[6] In addition to questions we have come to expect about our critical assumptions, about conventions of writing, reading, and interpreting, it will be necessary to conceive of synchrony and diachrony in a way that allows for the interplay of multiple—and in this instance, foreign— cultural institutions. My focus will be the institutionalization of *Germanistik* in America in the nineteenth century.

I will begin *in medias res* by positing a distinction, in the nineteenth century, between the pre-institutional and the institutionalized practice of literary criticism in America dealing with German literature and ideas. Such a distinction, offhand, begs the question of precisely what factors constitute an institution of this sort in the first place. Let us consider this question first in terms of *discourse*. The kinds of topics and how they are talked about at professional conferences (the MLA, for example) is one notable instance where it is clear who is talking to whom (even if what is being said is not always so clear): it is scholars talking to each other. For the topics of these sessions, their particular interest and argot, we are situated within a history of conventions (both figurative and literal) that exert a distinct kind of generic pressure. In his work on *Theory and Practice,* Jürgen Habermas suggests that "Only when certain domains of discourse are *institutionalized* to such an extent that under specifiable conditions a general expectation exists, that discursive conversations will be initiated, can they become a systematically relevant mechanism of learning for a given society."[7]

Habermas' description of institutionalized discourse offers some points of departure for determining the framework of the institution of literary criticism, practiced by Germanists, as it emerged during the nineteenth century in America. The "systematically relevant mechanism of learning" in this instance involves several factors: the growth of German departments (among the modern languages per se) within academic institutions; the advent of the Graduate School of Arts and Sciences (a largely German educational import originating at Johns Hopkins in 1876); and the appearance of professional organizations and scholarly journals which provided the ascending specialist with a locus of identity, a qualitatively different kind of scholarly *persona,* outside the bounds of the university.[8] The institutional framework under consideration here evolved with the American university after the Civil War. Debates from then until the turn of the century revolved around rival concepts of higher learning, notions of discipline and piety, intellectual license, utility, the roles of research and the advancing scientism, and finally, of liberal culture in America.[9] Of special importance is the so-called "Germanization" of American higher

education in the last decades of the nineteenth century. Impelled by notions of *Wissenschaft* and academic freedom, and encouraged by the flow
of students to Germany and back, the American university gradually
incorporated professional education and the requisite professionals. These
influences tell as much about the indigenous growth of the American
university as they do about its cultural debt.

The institutionalization of literary criticism did not take place only
within the admittedly peripheral field of German Studies. As Laurence
Veysey writes in his diligent and illuminating book on *The Emergence of
the American University:* "The modern languages first appeared as distinct
fields of study during the seventies and eighties . . . not even the classics
were taught from a literary standpoint in the mid-nineteenth-century college. Except for such isolated pioneers as John Bascom at Williams and
James Russell Lowell at Harvard, the study of literature as such was new
in the American academic world after 1865. Indeed, in 1870 Noah Porter
termed the tendency the 'New Criticism'."[10]

Porter's term is suggestive, but here I can only cite it as still another
feature giving definition to the emerging institutionalization of academic
literary criticism. I would hasten to add a qualification gleaned from Stanley Fish: "The change from one structure of understanding to another is
not a rupture but a modification of the interests and concerns that are
already in place; and because they are already in place, they contain the
direction of their own modification."[11] Before considering the particular
"institutional nesting" (Fish) of literary criticism after 1870, then, I will
look briefly at the pre-institutional phase mentioned above.

William Charvat's study of *The Origins of American Critical Thought,
1810–1835* shows that the commonly held attitude toward literature did
not condone rebellion of any kind against the existing social and economic
order. Literature should avoid derogatory statements and immoral in-
nuendos. Art in general was considered suspect because, in Charvat's
words, "amusement was considered a loosener of moral fiber in that it
made men forget duty."[12] Furthermore, the conventions of literary criticism in this pre-institutional phase preferred optimism to gloom, sanctioned the intelligible but not the mystical or the obscure, and shunned
egocentricity and sentimentalism. In Charvat's words, the literary critic
of the first third of the century "felt it a duty to repress any writer who
tended to disrupt the political, economic, and moral *status quo*."[13]

Most important, however, is the fact that most of the people talking
and writing publicly about literature in general or German literature in
particular during the first half of the nineteenth century were not literary
critics by profession or training. The activities of Longfellow, Emerson,
and Margaret Fuller are of course well known. Their work with German
literature at least sustained, if not actually animated, the critical reception

of German ideas on the part of American intellectuals. But they and others carrying on this discussion talked in the absence of an institutionalized discourse structured by the presence of the university and professional education in a specialized field. As Edwin Zeydel notes in his history of the teaching of German in the U.S., "theologians, lawyers, and men of many other professions could become Germanists overnight in those days."[14] True that most periodicals of consequence advanced more or less critical opinions of German literature, enough to lead one modern scholar of the history of German culture in America, Henry Pochmann, to claim that "everyone who had charge of . . . a literary department had to take note of German literature"[15]—but the academic superstructure was absent.

To the extent that specialization among literary critics was only just emerging in the 1870s, the kind of criticism practiced then exhibited certain "shared exemplars"[16] with that of its predecessors. For one, it had no truck with representations of attitudes and behavior which threatened the status quo. This is clear enough in the histories of German literature which began to appear within American scholarship around 1870. For another, as the introductory remarks to almost all of these works make explicit, they refrained from scholarly paraphernalia in order to remain accessible to as large a public as possible. But the general interest in German literature and ideas present (or at least thought to be present) among the public at large in the first half of the nineteenth century no longer obtained, and the realm of the "Dichter und Denker" was soon to become the province of Germanists and educated but nonacademic German-Americans.[17] The literary histories themselves reflect—in their style and in their concept of history—this structural change in the literary public sphere. While the earlier criticism published in intellectual journals and literary magazines was grounded on the prevailing notions of cultural discourse (*Räsonnement*), the later histories of German literature occupied an uncomfortable position between the advancing demands of professional specialization and the larger social realities which promoted the mass distribution of culture and aimed largely at catering to, while at the same time creating, a consumeristic need for entertainment. These histories, as a consequence, are replete with several interesting contradictions: in the midst of the (nearly unquestioned) approbation of German scholarship within the emerging American university,[18] these works shied away from the conventions of German scholarship and its ideals of thoroughness and comprehensiveness. Instead they generally aimed, as one work of the time stated, "at nothing more ambitious than to give an outline of the growth of German literature."[19] The typical work proceeded from biographical sketch to plot summary occasionally interspersed with commentary. History clung relentlessly to chronology. As a result, German literary history appeared as a parade of great (and less great) personages. From birth to death of the poet, from first work to last, literary history revealed itself ultimately as something rather convenient and simple; it was, in fact, just one thing after another. Before specialization among literary critics became advanced (it was recognized as a problem already in 1896 by Kuno Francke, the most prominent Germanist of the time), one can witness a phenomenon similar to that of the *Gartenlaube* in Germany, where "Literary criticism was offered only in the form of author portraits in which the literary as well as ideological processes were personalized."[20]

With the institutionalization of the university came the prescription of a uniform curriculum ("no accident," notes Jürgen Herbst, "but the conscious and deliberate result of a philosophy of education prevalent in nineteenth-century America").[21] For academic literary scholarship, this uniformity translated into the prescription of classics forming the literary canon. The canonization of literary works and authors went hand-in-hand with the changing image of the literary scholar as it evolved under the forces of specialization. As poets became prophets, literary scholars became their distinguished proxy. "Literary criticism," wrote Richard Hochdoerfer, a Germanist, in 1904, "is the indispensable concomitant of literary production, supplying the reader as well as writer with a standard of judgment. However wide the range of the poet's license, there are some fixed principles governing artistic creation which he cannot pass by unheeded. Writers, as a rule, are also good critics, and the literary critic, if not taking first rank as a poet, must have poetic feeling and power. Literature and life are linked by the poet, the interpreter of life; the worth of the genuine critic depends upon the same faculty of interpretation, the lack of which disqualifies him even as a judge in aesthetics."[22] In lieu of *creative* authority, the literary critic presented an appeal to a *legislative* authority grounded upon an elitist notion of affiliation. For Germany, meanwhile, Gunter Reiss has shown that "the image of the poet-prince [*Dichterfürst*] unmistakably betrays—already in its choice of words—the 'process of feudalization' which proceeded rapidly within bourgeois society of the latter third of the 19th century."[23]

This occasional parallel drawn to the German context—that is to say, to the situation in Germany at roughly the same time—is not intended to illustrate or suggest similar developments in the societies at large or within the microcosm of the universities. More immediately, any parallels point to the largely unquestioned esteem for German scholarship within the institutionalized and professionally sanctioned literary criticism of German Studies in America at the turn of the century. This esteem effectively closed off serious debate with German critics. Admittedly, in some instances this reliance was a matter of convenience: in the years of its academic infancy (the 1870s), American histories of German literature exhibited a decidedly anti-academic character, even though they depended heavily upon German critical sources for their observations. Later, the openness toward German scholarship and its larger implications (a latent and cultivated Wilhelminian ideology) began to evidence a coincidence of interests.[24] But here I need to return more closely to my topic, "From Genesis to Convention: Literary Criticism as a German-American Institution." I have dealt with the genesis; now I will direct my attention toward the convention.

Again, convention here should be understood both figuratively and literally, in its abstract and concrete manifestations. Few conventions among literary scholars (not just Germanists) are more firmly etched in our institutional memory than the MLA, one hundred years old in 1984. During my research on this topic I discovered a text that allows me to talk about both the figurative and the literal, the abstract and concrete manifestations of conventions at the same time. I have in mind the presidential address delivered at the Annual Meeting of the Modern Language Association in 1896, held—where else?—in Cleveland. The speaker was Calvin Thomas, a noted German scholar, whose edition of *Faust* became a standard work and who also published a lengthy book on Schiller as well as a history of German literature.[25] The title of his address was "Literature and Personality,"[26] and it offers an interesting possibility to explore the dimensions of literary criticism from a German-American perspective. I intend to focus on the interpretive conventions invoked by Thomas. As Steven Mailloux has recently defined this term, "Interpretive conventions . . . are group-licensed strategies for constructing meaning, describable in terms of conditions of intelligibility. These conventions provide the mechanism for the acceptable and approximating translation in the interpretive process; they are the grounds not only for producing interpretations but also for accepting them."[27]

I will try to condense Thomas' arguments along these lines. First, he acknowledges the lack of a term like *Literaturwissenschaft* in English and regrets the restricted application of the word "science," with which people associate "not so much the grand ideals of carefulness and love of truth, as rather the particular methods employed, and the kind of accuracy aimed at, in the study of physics and biology" (299–300). He notes the "division of sentiment" separating philologists from men of letters (in materialistic rather than idealistic terms we could speak of a "division of labor"). In fact, Thomas does assume "that there is such a thing as literary science" (301), but in the search for truth he resists the gravitational pull "in the direction of the amorphous *Abhandlung* which is apt to be true but not interesting" (301).

Why scholarly work should interest as well as advance knowledge derives from Thomas' view of literature "as the product and the expression of personality" (301). Accustomed to viewing things "under the aspect of development" (302), Thomas remains "a good enough determinist" (308), but he is not ready to discount "one's judgment, if one has such a thing," nor "one's opinion, provided the opinion has been carefully formed according to the evidence" (304). Thus, despite his positivist bias, he warns against being "misled by the analogy of natural phenomenon" (*sic, 304*).

Thomas shows an awareness of the limits of epistemology: "the critic's opinion," he writes, "can settle nothing for those who do not agree with him" (306). In order to make sure that understanding does not become a problem, he projects consensus as a function of morality by requiring the "faithful record of [the critic's] honest feeling." He adds: "It is of course essential to this view of the matter that the critic be honest in reporting the state of his mind" (306).

The apparent lurch from the objective to the subjective paradigm[28] is deceptive, since Thomas reinforces the constraints placed on the critic's discretion by the accompanying notion that "one's taste in literature is very largely a matter of national and individual peculiarity" (306). While the distinct shape of Thomas' "theory" remains elusive and seems at times self-contradictory, his concept of the hermeneutic situation remains decidedly teleological and thus he acknowledges as legitimate scientism's enterprise of advancing knowledge toward eventual complete understanding.

In 1896, Thomas appears to stand in the cusp of another shift of paradigms: positivism was becoming ossified, and in the name of liberal culture humanists sought to rescue, from within the institution of literary studies, the integrity of the human mind. As Laurence Veysey shows, "The word 'culture,' in its humanistic context, had several fairly distinct connotations: aesthetic, moral and emotional, and social," but above all "culture was closely tied to literary and artistic standards."[29] Important in this regard, too, are the social assumptions contained within the notion of culture as understood by humanists of that time: "The cultivated person was a 'lord,' even if only figuratively; he was a gentleman." Not all humanists were comfortable with the implications of this attitude, and "the pronounced tendency in this direction revealed itself in a sense of alienation from the dominant (industrial) patterns of American life."[30]

This sense of alienation discloses, I think, a significant moment in the history of *Germanistik* in the United States,[31] one which relates past and present. In this regard, it becomes important to detail the formulation and modification of what Samuel Weber—through the work of Charles Sanders Peirce—refers to as "habits" which "depend upon collective traditions and the institutions through which they transmit and reproduce themselves." The "institution of specific interpretations"—be they in literary criticism or academic literary scholarship, in the context of German, American, or German-American perspectives—will necessitate "the interpretation of specific institutions."[32]

Notes

1 Earlier versions of this article were read in the Special Session on "The Institution and Institutionalization of Literary Criticism: A German-American Perspective" at the Annual Meeting of the Modern Language Association in Los Angeles in 1982, and at the conference on "The Teaching of German in America: The Historical Perspective" in Madison, WI, April 1983. The current essay rests to a large extent on my *"Germanistik" in America: The Reception of German Classicism, 1870–1905* (Stuttgart: Heinz, 1982), but it attempts to explore new points of departure by highlighting different methodological problems than those discussed in my book.

2 See Peter Uwe Hohendahl, "Prolegomena to a History of Literary Criticism," in *The Institution of Criticism* (Ithaca/London: Cornell University Press, 1982) 224–41.

3 Robert C. Holub, "The American Reception of Reception Theory," *German Quarterly*, 55(1982): 80–96.

4 Stanley Fish, *Is There a Text in This Class?* (Cambridge: Harvard University Press, 1980) 368.

5 See Hohendahl 240.

6 Jürgen Herbst, *The German Historical School in American Scholarship: A Study in the Transfer of Culture* (Ithaca: Cornell University Press, 1965).

7 Jürgen Habermas, *Theory and Practice,* trans. John Viertel (Boston: Beacon, 1973) 25.

8 See the discussion in Herbst 40.

9 These are some of the topics treated at length by Laurence R. Veysey, *The Emergence of the American University* (Chicago: University of Chicago Press, 1965).

10 Veysey 182.

11 Fish 319.

12 William Charvat, *The Origins of American Critical Thought, 1810–1835* (New York: Barnes, 1936) 15–16.

13 Charvat 7.

14 Edwin Zeydel, "The Teaching of German in the United States from Colonial Times to the Present," *Reports of Surveys and Studies in the Teaching of Modern Foreign Languages* (New York: MLA, 1961) 291. See also this volume 34.

15 Henry Pochmann, *German Culture in America: Philosophical and Literary Influences, 1600–1900* (Madison: University of Wisconsin Press, 1957) 491.

16 See Thomas Kuhn's extremely influential work, *The Structure of Scientific Revolutions,* 2d ed. (Chicago: University of Chicago Press, 1970).

17 Wolfgang Heinsohn, for example, has written that in America, by "1870 the idea of the superiority of German literature, scholarship, art, thought, and philosophy had, indeed, become a myth. This myth survived largely from the cliché of 'Dichter und Denker,' which although maintained still in some groups, had lost its 'popular' appeal." "The Reception of German Literature in America as Exemplified by the *New York Times,* Part I: 1870–1918," diss., New York University, 1974, 168.

18 Victor Lange, for example, has maintained that "If we cast a glance at the volumes of
    Monatshefte prior to the First World War, we shall be struck by the curious mixture in
    almost every issue, of labored pedantry and the unquestioned assumption that the teaching
    of German should be motivated by a passionate and unswerving attachment to the
    values—political, philosophical and literary—that were then held in Germany: pride in
    the German imperial power, reverence for the idealism which German artists and thinkers
    appeared to defend against all corrosion of public and private life by the alien forces of
    materialism and, most emphatically, the example which this sum of superior aspiration
    offered for the missionary work of American teachers of German." "Thoughts in Sea-
    son," in *German Studies in the United States: Assessment and Outlook,* ed. Walter F.
    W. Lohnes and Valters Nollendorfs (Madison: University of Wisconsin Press, 1976) 11.
19 Helen S. Conant, *A Primer of German Literature,* 6th ed. (New York/Cincinnati/Chicago:
    American Book, 1878) vii.
20 Hohendahl 239.
21 Herbst 26.
22 Richard Hochdoerfer, *Studies in German Literature* (Chautauqua, N.Y.: Chautauqua
    Press, 1904) 235–36.
23 Gunter Reiss, *Materialien zur Ideologiegeschichte der deutschen Literaturwissenschaft:
    Von Wilhelm Scherer bis 1945* (Tübingen: Niemeyer, 1973) 1: xviii (my translation).
24 I think my own work has confirmed the suspicion voiced by Jeffrey Sammons, "daß
    dieser in die amerikanische Germanistik importierte Komplex der wilhelminischen Ideo-
    logie, sollte er einmal richtig erforscht werden, einige unerfreuliche Aspekte zutage
    bringen würde." "Die amerikanische Germanistik: Historische Betrachtungen zur ge-
    genwärtigen Situation," *Germanistik international,* ed. Richard Brinkmann et al. (Tü-
    bingen: Niemeyer, 1978) 107.
25 See Thomas, ed., *Faust* (Boston: Heath, Part 1, 1892; Part 2, 1897); Thomas, *The Life
    and Works of Friedrich Schiller* (New York: Holt, 1901); and Thomas, *A History of
    German Literature* (New York: Appleton, 1909).
26 Calvin Thomas, "Literature and Personality," *PMLA* 12(1897): 299–317.
27 Steven Mailloux, *Interpretive Conventions: The Reader in the Study of American Fiction*
    (Ithaca: Cornell University Press, 1982) 149.
28 Irving Babbitt, as one example, remained skeptical of these efforts: "The humanist who
    at present enters college teaching should not underestimate the difficulties he is likely to
    encounter. He will find a literature ancient and modern controlled by a philological
    syndicate, a history dehumanized by the abuse of scientific method, and a political
    economy that has never been humane. . . . From the outset the orthodox political econ-
    omy has been humanitarian rather than humane. The end of man, as it views him, is not
    the attainment of wisdom but the production of wealth. It therefore tends to reduce
    everything to terms of quantity and power and, as an offset, resorts to various mixtures
    of altruistic sympathy and 'enlightened self-interest'." *Literature and the American
    College* (Boston/New York: Houghton, Mifflin, 1908) 144–45.
29 Veysey 184.
30 Veysey 189.
31 See the article by David Bathrick, "On Leaving Exile: American *Germanistik* and its
    Social Context," Lohnes and Nollendorfs 252–57; and the article by Henry J. Schmidt,
    "The Rhetoric of Survival: The Germanist in America from 1900 to 1925," 165–175 of
    this volume.
32 Samuel Weber, "Closure and Exclusion," *diacritics* 10.2 (1980): 46.

The Rhetoric of Survival:
The Germanist in America, 1900–1925

HENRY J. SCHMIDT
Ohio State University

The documents that chronicle the history of German studies in the United States between 1900 and 1915—the professional journals, the publications for specialists and for mass audiences, the speeches and memoirs—reveal an apparently healthy, self-confident profession. Seen in retrospect, conditions were indeed enviable. Since the late nineteenth century German had been considered the second language of the Republic, and by 1915, twenty-four percent of all public high school students were taking German, compared to nine percent in French and two percent in Spanish. (Today the high school enrollment in German is 1.5%.) The teaching of German was actively supported by the newspapers, organizations, churches, and financial enterprises of what was then the largest ethnic group in the United States: in the year 1910 over eight million Americans were either German-born or of German parentage. The teaching profession itself seemed firmly united behind its primary objectives: to preserve the German language and to transmit the cultural heritage and moral idealism of Wilhelminian Germany.

Under such circumstances, one would expect to find a profession complacent in its success. The question therefore arises why, long before the outbreak of World War I, instructors of German were so strident and immodest in their praise of all things German. Book-length studies, countless speeches and essays extolled the German national character and its allegedly formative influence upon the development of American democracy. Explicitly or implicitly, Germans were considered superior to other nationalities in qualities ranging from discipline and thoroughness to the love of music, family, and pets. A simple rearrangement of the familiar catalogue of virtues exposes, through contradiction, its fundamental meaninglessness: the Germans turn out to be a proud, humble, serious, light-hearted folk; they are daring and obedient, manly and soulful, aristocratic defenders of democracy and individualistic defenders of the collective will. Clearly this rhetoric signifies something beyond its vapid substance. As I intend to demonstrate in this paper, such chauvinistic utterances signify an intense struggle for legitimacy: a struggle for professional recognition within the academic sphere and for a secure position for German-Americans within American society.

German immigrants who taught at American universities helped popularize the concept of the professor as spiritual leader. Like their colleagues in other fields, Germanists at German universities regarded themselves as high priests of culture, as builders of character, as interpreters of ultimate moral values. These academic mandarins, as Fritz K. Ringer calls them,[1] were a homogeneous social class: male, affluent, Christian, politically conservative. They defended their privileged status against the less well educated masses as well as against women, Jews, and foreign influences by claiming to be the guardians of the nation's cultural heritage, which they fashioned into an instrument of support for the monarchy.

Around 1900 the American university was not unreceptive to an educational ideology of this sort because it, too, subscribed to a trickle-down theory of culture. The American-born Germanist Marion Dexter Learned, for example, urged the educated German classes to unite with American academicians in order to ensure that German culture would be represented by German-American intellectuals instead of by "German communities representing the uneducated classes," where the German element was "so objectionable, not only to the English population, but to the better German classes as well."[2] His comment reflects the antagonisms within the German-American community between the so-called "soul" Germans and the "stomach" Germans. Academic humanists attempted to distinguish themselves not only from the uneducated but also from plutocrats, the well-born, and the military on the basis of their classical learning. The prestige and authority deriving from a classical education implied the mastery of a prescribed set of subjects as well as familiarity with the prevailing canon of classical works. In order to fulfill their mission to influence the moral upbringing of American students, Germanists had to find models for spiritual uplift within their own cultural heritage. In doing so, they were obliged to confront the traditional dominance of Greek and Latin classicism and to compete in the educational marketplace against Anglo-American, French, and Hispanic cultural missionaries—a competition that has in fact never ceased. This pursuit of academic territory was reflected in an essay published as early as 1887 by Julius Goebel, who attempted to put the teaching of idealism on a German footing: "It is a wrong assumption of some of the classic philologians . . . that 'idealism' can only be attained by the reading of the ancient classics. Would not a careful study of Schiller's 'Anmut und Würde' or 'Aesthetische Briefe' enrich the mind of the student at least as much as one of the easier dialogues of Plato?"[3]

As literature emerged as a curricular commodity, culture was similarly instrumentalized. Kuno Francke, for example, considered his efforts to establish a Germanic Museum at Harvard in 1903 "als eine Notwendigkeit, wenn das von mir vertretene Fach sich gegenüber dem alles überwiegenden englischen und französischen Einfluß dauernd behaupten sollte."[4] Germanists justified their cultural expansionism by insisting that they were operating in an intellectually backward country. Charles J. Hexamer, the American-born president of the Deutschamerikanischer Nationalbund, said in 1915 that "no one . . . will ever find us prepared to step down to a lesser *Kultur*; no, we have made it our aim to draw the other up to us."[5] His polemic was motivated by ethnic protectionism; as Goebel remarked in 1910, the primary target group of the cultural chauvinists was the second and third generation of German-Americans: "Es gilt nur, . . . sie zurückzuholen vom Versinken in eine niedrigstehende Kultur und, an Stelle der feigen Scham über ihre Herkunft, den berechtigten Stolz zu setzen."[6] The solidification of ethnic ties would assure a constant and possibly expanding clientele for educators, the clergy, the German-language press, and for any entrepreneurs who profited from the maintenance of German identity.

Unsurprisingly, therefore, the spirit of "am deutschen Wesen soll die Welt genesen" within the German-American community was often as intense as in the Fatherland itself. To promote ethnic goals, Germanists spoke out against Prohibition, Puritanism, women's suffrage, American materialism, mass culture, and—most important of all—against Germany's enemies. While German-language newspapers sold German flags and pictures of Kaiser Wilhelm to their readers,[7] the editor of *Monatshefte für deutsche Sprache und Pädagogik*, the official journal of the Nationaler Deutschamerikanischer Lehrerbund, devoted a full page in 1913 to congratulating the Kaiser upon the twenty-fifth anniversary of his coronation.[8] Even Kuno Francke, the leading Germanist of his time and an opponent of ethnic extremists in his own camp, was moved to confess that he thought the Kaiser to be a combination of Richard Wagner's Parsifal and the Nietzschean superman.[9] Already in 1900 Francke had described the German struggle for cultural dominance in terms of a holy war.[10] Little wonder, then, that this crusading spirit eventually caused some Germanists to welcome the outbreak of hostilities in 1914. Heinrich Hermann Maurer announced in *Monatshefte*: "Wir wollen den Sieg Deutschlands. . . . Wir brauchen den Sieg Deutschlands als Bürgschaft dessen was uns hier bitter not tut: des sieghaften Einflusses einer überlegenen deutschen Kultur."[11]

When the war began, many Germanists continued to defend the German cause. (Others holding different views either did not attempt to voice their opinions or were not granted a forum, as far as I have been able to determine.) The greatest threat to their ethnic status lay in America's pro-British bias. In response, prominent academicians from America and Germany spoke to mass meetings and thousands of copies of books and pamphlets were distributed in order to counter stories about German army atrocities, to justify the invasion of Belgium, and to protest against mis-representations of the German position in the American press. American Germanists helped revive the ancient fear of the "barbaric Slavic hordes" overrunning the Fatherland and its culture. But as anti-German sentiment grew, so did the willingness of German-Americans to cast off their ethnicity and disappear into the Great Melting Pot. The Deutschamerikanischer Nationalbund campaigned desperately against such assimilation; those who differed from its extremist views were branded as traitors. Kuno Francke, for example, incurred its wrath when he publicly rejected its political lobbying efforts, appealing instead for cultural diplomacy. He argued that if the Nationalbund had limited itself to the cultivation of German music, literature, and art, the American public would have been more receptive to its cause.[12] His idealistic stance reflected the tendency among academic humanists to defend their interests in terms of morality and fair play rather than political expediency, thereby rendering them vulnerable to the charge of naiveté.

After 1914, the German-American community was split essentially into four camps: the pro-Germans, the pro-Americans, the neutralists (out of religious conviction or the desire for anonymity), and the socialists, who opposed the war from the start as a manifestation of capitalistic imperialism. Germanists who continued to publish had two options: they either lent their expertise and rhetorical skills to the battle for German ideals being waged by *Monatshefte* and the German-language press, or they published "neutral," "apolitical" scholarship in the pages of *PMLA*, *Modern Language Notes*, *The Journal of English and Germanic Philology*, and *Modern Philology*. The nationalists continued to mine the classics for confirmation of the German cause. Thus the German people were seen as being on the verge of fulfilling the prophecy of *Nathan der Weise*'s para-ble,[13] Goethe and Schiller were employed as heroic prophets of a mighty German national state,[14] but Heinrich Heine was cast aside as "ein mo-ralisch haltloser Mensch."[15] "Neutral" scholarship had an entirely differ-ent goal, namely, to legitimate German literary criticism and philology as academic disciplines governed by principles of scientific objectivity.

At this time, American *Germanistik* was not dominated by one par-ticular school of criticism; the eclecticism of critical method in fact resem-bles that of the post-World War II era, as a small sampling of article titles, all published during the war, will indicate: "Kleist at Boulogne-sur-mer," "Goethe's Theory of the Novelle," "English Translations of *Werther*," "Isoldes Gottesurteil," "The Influence of Hans Folz on Hans Sachs," and "Concerning the German Relatives 'Das' und 'Was,' in Clauses De-pendent upon Substantivized Adjectives, and upon Neuter Indefinites, as Used in Schiller's Prose." On the whole, World War I had no visible effect on journals of "pure" research. Whereas *Monatshefte* disappeared completely from 1918–1920 and did not resume its monthly publication until 1928, these other journals, having shielded their scholarship from the war, were able to continue publishing without interruption. In fact, they regularly contained comparative studies by Germanists, which appear to have had a function antithetical to the cultural separatism of *Monatshefte*. The comparatists attempted to *integrate* German literature into European culture, to strengthen its bonds with other national literatures. It is revealing that even during a period of protracted hostility, English and Germanic philology would willingly coexist under the roof of the same journal, especially considering that the journal's long-term editor and one of its most prolific contributors was Julius Goebel, who was also one of the most rabidly militant, anti-Semitic, unreconstructed German nationalists on the academic scene.[16] Obviously, the integrationist and segregationist alternatives were by no means mutually exclusive; numerous Germanists besides Goebel practiced both simultaneously. I would theorize that their adaptability is paradigmatic for the institutionalization process of German studies in America: the profession attempted to acquire recognition and status through several institutionalized modes of discourse at the same time. Historical events proved nationalistic rhetoric to be in the last analysis a transitory and ineffective method of achieving institutional permanence. The future, in short, belonged to assimilation.

The first major setback for the pro-German campaign in the United States was the sinking of the Lusitania in May 1915. Thereafter German teachers began to lower their collective profile, and voices critical of rabid partisanship were heard, even in *Monatshefte*.[17] Looking beyond the war's end, German teachers began to realize that their professional stability was now at odds with their cultural identity. Especially after the United States declared war on Germany in April 1917, the profession underwent a full-scale ideological metamorphosis. This transformation is most vividly recorded in *Monatshefte*. In early 1915, a prominent contributor had ended an article about the war with the words, "Und darum Heil und Sieg den deutschen und österreichischen Waffen auf dem Wasser und unter dem Wasser, auf dem Lande und in der Luft";[18] by May 1918 the journal was advising its readers—now in English rather than in German—about survival techniques in the classroom. In a lengthy article titled "Adjusting Instruction in German to Conditions Imposed by the War," J. D. Deihl urged that teachers "combine a sympathetic appreciation of the values of German with an uncompromisingly American opposition to those forces in Germany which have helped make this war possible." He instructed teachers to employ "Yankee ingenuity and grit" as they readjusted their classroom procedures, for in his opinion, the profession could afford to be optimistic: "there is no reasonable doubt that the present war will stimulate to a hitherto undreamed-of degree the interest in modern foreign language study.''[19] The wholesale substitution of pro-Americanism for pro-Germanism becomes less startling the more one realizes that the patriotic attitude has not changed at all, merely its content.

In self-preservation, teachers cast about for "safe" literary texts. Thus Deihl recommended Heyse, Fouque, Eichendorff, and Chamisso and urged that instructors emphasize literature's formal and stylistic beauties.[20] Textbooks that glorified Kaiser and Fatherland were removed, and one German teacher in Cincinnati was commended by his Superintendent of Schools for censoring "with absolute fidelity" textbooks he himself had written.[21] Literary criticism in *Monatshefte* underwent a similar transformation. For example, in May of 1916 C. H. Handschin published an essay on "Gottfried Keller und Deutschland" in which he eulogized Keller as a "Seher des Germanentums.''[22] While having to argue around the inconvenient fact that Keller was Swiss, Handschin nevertheless saw in him "die Hauptmerkmale des deutschen Charakters: Treue, Ehrlichkeit, Gründlichkeit, Fleiß und Gemütstiefe.''[23] Less than two years later, Handschin published another article on Keller in *Monatshefte*, but this time the subject was "Kellers Tierliebe.''[24] Keller was now no more nor less than a "passionierter Tierfreund.''[25] Although I cannot prove that the changing *Zeitgeist* affected Handschin's perspective, the contrast is symptomatic of the profession's reaction to the war.

But the profession's shift of allegiance must also be seen against the background of the anti-German hysteria that seized America after it entered the war. The spirit of vengeance was directed at anything and everything German, from Beethoven and Schiller to hamburger and sauerkraut. University professors were dismissed for unpatriotic utterances, and textbooks were burned at public ceremonies. Linguistic chauvinism was as rabid among the anti-Germans as among the pro-Germans: German was denounced as a barbarian language "in which it is impossible to think clearly,''[26] a language whose sound "reminds us of . . . the driving of about 100,000 young French, Belgian, and Polish women into compulsory prostitution.''[27] As a consequence, the teaching of German was banned outright in approximately half the states of the Union. The precipitous drop in student enrollment decimated the ranks of the profession and, although I cannot prove this conclusively, apparently traumatized the mandarins of American *Germanistik*. The profession was under fire not primarily because of its cultural aspirations and humanistic ideals but because it taught the German language. To comprehend the consequences adequately we must consider briefly the institutionalization of foreign culture studies as a whole in the American university up to that point. The best indicator of this development is its main journal, *PMLA*. Its earliest issues after its founding in 1884 contain a mixture of pedagogical and philological research, as well as literary criticism. But as universities increasingly emphasized professional training and allowed the graduate school to rise to a dominant position, these disciplines divided into well-defined areas of specialization. Philology eventually gravitated from *PMLA* to other journals. Pedagogical studies disappeared from *PMLA* before the turn of the century, and in 1902 the pedagogical section of the MLA was eliminated. In his Presidential Address to the MLA in 1914, the Wisconsin Germanist Alexander Hohlfeld applauded this development, claiming that it had been necessary "to repress narrowly and specifically pedagogical interests." He hailed the "final victory of scholarship" and praised those "who, in this struggle for supremacy, held high the banner of learning."[28] Note that pedagogy is excluded from "scholarship" and "learning." Pedagogues retaliated by expanding their own organizations and founding the *Modern Language Journal* in 1916. As a result, the MLA's remaining hierarchy that set the standards of professional achievement was dominated by a highly specialized elite of literary critics.

But this state of affairs did not jibe with the expectations of American society—a difference of opinion that still prevails today. Whereas the humanist aspired to influence moral values and instill ideals, society demanded training in functional skills.[29] When many Germanists—those who still held jobs, that is—were reduced to teaching "der-die-das" to small classes, the true base-superstructure relationship of the profession in America was revealed. The self-image of the Germanist as an intellectual leader never again reached its inflated prewar proportions because never again could enrollment be taken so much for granted. Falling enrollment, in other words, tended to reduce class distinctions in German Departments and in the German-American community.

To be sure, not every Germanist chose the course of self-protective adaptation. Kuno Francke and other regular contributors to *Monatshefte* made a virtue out of necessity by conjuring a new myth out of the ashes of the old myth of German invincibility. Since the Germans had failed to achieve grandeur in victory, they were to be allowed grandeur in martyrdom, idealized as a folk with a superhuman ability to endure suffering. This theme occurs in much of Francke's inspirational poetry, which was published regularly in *Monatshefte* and in American newspapers. His poem "Deutsches Volk," which appeared on the first page of the January 1917 issue of *Monatshefte,* is typical of the genre; I quote the final stanza:

> O du Volk, schicksalsgestählt,
> O du Volk, gnadenerwählt—
> Neue Menschheit hast du begründet,
> Neuen Glauben hast du entzündet,
> Mitten aus Schrecken und Donner der Schlacht
> Hast du den Heiland der Zukunft gebracht!
> Deutsches Volk![30]

Elsewhere he wrote that German history and culture were branded with a "Signatur des Tragischen," causing the Germans to endure a recurrent *Götterdämmerung* out of which they would again arise to new heights of idealism.[31] Meanwhile, other Germanists and the German-language press blamed the war on Germany's rulers who, it was claimed, had led the German people astray. This scapegoat deflected attention from their own complicity, and once again the moral superiority of Germans—and by extension, German-Americans—was assured. By focusing, as before, on spiritual rather than material values, the revisionists were able to hail the end of the war as a victory of American ideals while at the same time urging their audiences to protest Germany's so-called dishonor at Versailles.

Between 1920 and approximately 1925 a number of former cultural crusaders and ethnic politicians attempted to rebuild their prewar influence and prestige. In German studies, this brief Age of Restoration was spearheaded once again by *Monatshefte*. Publishing almost exclusively in German again, *Monatshefte* resurrected the definition of the German teacher as a missionary for the German language, *Geist,* and culture. That the journal chose this form of coming to terms with the past may be attributable to its founding editor, Max Griebsch, who was appointed in 1899, was still in office after the war and would remain until 1934—an editorship of thirty-five years. In his preface to the first *Monatshefte* yearbook in 1920 he announced: "Das Jahrbuch soll die Kunde ins Land hinaus tragen, . . . daß unser Glaube an die Sache, die wir vertreten . . . nicht erschüttert ist."[32] The laws of competition in the educational marketplace appeared to have reinstated nationalism as an acceptable quality; Griebsch noted approvingly that French and Spanish teachers were producing textbooks imitating the prewar *Im Vaterland,* one of the favorites of the book burners.[33] To underscore its ideological heritage, *Monatshefte* created a series called "Sie waren unser" to commemorate the extremists who had fought for the German cause. For further moral support, a regular feature called "Stimmen von drüben" broadcast the political opinions of those German academics who were nostalgic for the Second Reich. With a sigh of relief, contributors welcomed back the old values: "Also doch—der unverwüstliche Idealismus, das deutsche Pflichtgefühl: arbeiten und nicht verzweifeln."[34] A Führer-ethos predominated, and the rhetoric was at times frighteningly prophetic: "Was jetzt als ein stilles Säuseln vernehmbar ist, wird dereinst als ein Sturm, als reinigendes Gewitter über das Land fahren. Das Gesunde wird über das Kranke und Abgelebte siegen, der Gemeinsinn über die Selbstsucht, der Geist der Wahrheit über den Irrwahn der Lüge."[35] But no contributor was able to match the brazen unrepentance of Julius Goebel in 1922: "Die Zeit [wird] kommen, wo man uns danken wird, den wahren Geist der Republik vom Untergang gerettet zu haben

. . . mir persönlich scheint es, daß wir im Lob des Deutschen im allgemeinen ziemlich bescheiden gewesen sind."[36] A further indication of the political direction behind this campaign appeared in a polemic in the same yearbook against "die durch die Idee der proletarischen Internationale verblendeten Arbeitermassen." The conclusion: "das Heil liegt nicht im Internationalen, sondern im Nationalen!"[37]

But the ethnic lobbying of yore and the calls for the mystic rejuvenation of the German spirit lacked popular support. Although many German-Americans may well have shared the pro-German sentiments of the *Monatshefte* contributors, they now preferred to remain within the national consensus, avoiding public attention and criticism. In German studies the moderates began to prevail, and *Monatshefte* again lowered its volume. After the Supreme Court ruled in 1923 that the ban against teaching German was unconstitutional, German departments accelerated their rebuilding of language programs, and by 1932 the mission of the profession had become, according to Alexander Hohlfeld, "zielstrebig verfolgte deutsch-englische Vermittlertätigkeit."[38] Literary scholarship steered clear of political issues, and German culture was converted into an inoffensive commodity. Claiming to fear a repetition of past errors, the profession took little note of the cataclysms occurring in Europe during the 1930s and 1940s; the impact of World War II was appraised primarily in terms of its effect on pedagogy. Having limited its objectives to strictly academic concerns, the profession, according to Henry C. Hatfield and Joan Merrick in 1948, "failed to make what might have been its greatest contribution in a period of crisis: the interpretation of the German mind to a puzzled nation."[39] I believe their criticism is justified, for the profession had indeed overreacted to the chauvinistic excesses of an earlier era. Its revulsion for politics created a legacy of exclusivity, a preoccupation with aesthetics and existentialist philosophy that survived long into the postwar period.

Notes

This article originally appeared in *America and the Germans: An Assessment of a Three-Hundred-Year History*, eds. Frank Trommler and Joseph McVeigh (Philadelphia: University of Pennsylvania Press, 1985) 2: 204–16.

1 Fritz K. Ringer, *The Decline of the German Mandarins: The German Academic Community, 1890–1933* (Cambridge, Mass.: Harvard University Press, 1969).
2 Marion Dexter Learned, "The 'Lehrerbund' and the Teachers of German in America," *Pädagogische Monatshefte*, 1.1 (1899): 13.

3 Julius Goebel, "A Proposed Curriculum of German Reading," *Modern Language Notes,* 2 (1887): 26.

4 Kuno Francke, *Deutsche Arbeit in Amerika* (Leipzig: Felix Meiner, 1930) 41.

5 Frederick C. Luebke, *Bonds of Loyalty: German-Americans and World War I* (De Kalb: Northern Illinois University Press, 1974) 100.

6 As quoted by G. J. Lenz in excerpt form from Julius Goebel's article "Die Zukunft des Deutschtums in Amerika" in the 75th *Jubiläumsausgabe* of the *New Yorker Staatszeitung* in *Monatshefte für deutsche Sprache und Pädagogik,* 11 (1910): 154.

7 Carl Wittke, *German-Americans and the World War (With Special Emphasis on Ohio's German-Language Press)* (Columbus: Ohio State Archaeological and Historical Society, 1936) 31.

8 *Monatshefte für deutsche Sprache und Pädagogik* 14.6 (1913) frontispiece.

9 Kuno Francke, *A German-American's Confession of Faith* (New York: B. W. Huebsch, 1915) 6.

10 Kuno Francke, "Goethes Vermächtnis an Amerika," *Pädagogische Monatshefte* 1.2 (1900): 6.

11 Heinrich Hermann Maurer, "Wir Deutschamerikaner und der Weltkrieg," *Monatshefte für deutsche Sprache und Pädagogik* 16 (1915): 42.

12 Kuno Francke, "Die Deutschamerikaner, die Harvard Universität und der Krieg" (1915, n.p.), reprinted in Kuno Francke Papers, Harvard University Archives. See also *Deutsche Arbeit in Amerika* 68.

13 Clara L. Nicolay, "Die Kinder des Ringes," *Monatshefte für deutsche Sprache und Pädagogik* 17 (1916): 89.

14 Julius Goebel, "Goethe und Schiller," *Pädagogische Monatshefte* 2 (1901): 357.

15 O. E. Lessing, "Neuere Literaturgeschichten," *Pädagogische Monatshefte* 4 (1903): 42.

16 See, for example, his *Das Deutschtum in den Vereinigten Staaten von Nord-Amerika* (München: Lehmanns, 1904).

17 See for example Paul E. Titsworth, "The Attitude of the American Teacher of German toward Germany," *Monatshefte für deutsche Sprache und Pädagogik* 17 (1916): 195–96.

18 Ernst Voss, "Zum Weltkriege," *Monatshefte für deutsche Sprache und Pädagogik* 16 (1915): 73.

19 J. D. Deihl, "Adjusting Instruction in German to Conditions Imposed by the War," *Monatshefte für deutsche Sprache und Pädagogik* 19 (1918): 128–34.

20 Deihl 131, 134.

21 "Umschau," *Monatshefte für deutsche Sprache und Pädagogik* 19 (1918): 236.

22 C. H. Handschin, "Gottfried Keller und Deutschland," *Monatshefte für deutsche Sprache und Pädagogik* 17 (1916): 155–61.

23 Handschin 155.

24 C. H. Handschin, "Kellers Tierliebe," *Monatshefte für deutsche Sprache und Pädagogik* 18 (1917): 71–74.

25 Handschin 72.

26 Knight Dunlap, "Value of German Language Assailed," reprint from *The New York Times* in "German Department," William Oxley Thompson Papers, Ohio State University Archives.

27 "Throw Out the German Language and All Disloyal Teachers," published by the American Defense Society; quoted in Luebke, *Bonds of Loyalty* 216.

28 Alexander R. Hohlfeld, "Light from Goethe on our Problems," *PMLA* 29 (1914): lxxiii.

29 Richard Ohmann's comment about teaching English composition pertains equally well to elementary courses in foreign languages: "the part of our job that justifies us to others within and outside the university is the part we hold in lowest regard and delegate to the least prestigious members of the profession." Richard Ohmann, *English in America: A Radical View of the Profession* (New York: Oxford University Press, 1976) 243.

30 Kuno Francke, "Deutsches Volk," *Monatshefte für deutsche Sprache und Pädagogik* 18 (1917): 1.

31 Kuno Francke, *Die Kulturwerte der deutschen Literatur von der Reformation bis zur Aufklärung* (Berlin: Weidmannsche Buchhandlung, 1923) 623.

32 Max Griebsch, "Begleitwort," *Monatshefte für deutsche Sprache und Pädagogik* (*Jahrbuch* 1920): 1.

33 Ibid. 3

34 F. Klaeber, "Stimmen von drüben," *Monatshefte für deutsche Sprache und Pädagogik* (*Jahrbuch* 1920): 37.

35 Ibid. 39.

36 Julius Goebel, "Das Recht auf die Muttersprache und ihre Erhaltung," *Monatshefte für deutsche Sprache und Pädagogik* (Jahrbuch 1922): 24.

37 Heinrich Maurer, "Der Kampf um das Deutschtum in Amerika in seiner kulturgeschichtlichen Bedeutung," *Monatshefte für deutsche Sprache und Pädagogik* (*Jahrbuch* 1922): 73.

38 Alexander R. Hohlfeld, "Eine Hauptaufgabe der Deutschen in Amerika," *Monatshefte für deutschen Unterricht* 24 (1932): 11.

39 Henry C. Hatfield and Joan Merrick, "Studies of German Literature in the United States, 1939–1946," *Modern Language Review* 43 (1948): 354.

The First World War and the Survival of German Studies: With a Tribute to Alexander R. Hohlfeld

CORA LEE NOLLENDORFS
University of Wisconsin–Madison

No period in the history of teaching German in America has had more long-term and far-reaching consequences than the First World War. The "war to end all wars" very nearly ended all German teaching in this country as well. And yet this era and the activities of the leading Germanists of the time have scarcely been investigated.

In the first section of this paper the immediate results of the war itself are outlined: the public policies and social attitudes which led to extensive cutbacks in German-language programs throughout the country. The second section focuses on Alexander R. Hohlfeld, Chairman of the Department of German at the University of Wisconsin, and on the leading role which he played in the struggle for the survival of German Studies.

Public Policies and Social Attitudes Toward the Teaching of German

"The United States is now at war with the imperial government of Germany and not with the German language or literature," wrote P. P. Claxton, United States Commissioner of Education, in 1917.[1] Although this declaration seems obvious to us today, some believed at the time that the teaching of German in the nation's educational institutions should be prohibited. The California State Board of Education condemned German as "a language that disseminates the ideals of autocracy, brutality, and hatred."[2] Not only the subject matter but also the teachers were included in such attacks. An Iowa politician claimed that "ninety percent of all the men and women who teach the German language are traitors . . . ."[3] One school district after another banned the teaching of the German language, and a number of states passed laws to the same effect. In 1918 an organization called the American Defense Society published a list of honor of fourteen states which had eliminated German language instruction, and stated that sixteen other states were considering similar action.[4]

The study of German in American schools suffered a blow from which it never recovered. The effort to "Americanize the foreign element in the United States" by curtailing the study of German was originally directed by private or semi-public patriotic organizations, among others the National Security League, the Council for National Defense, the American Defense Society, the National Chamber of Commerce, and the National Board for Historical Service. Soon, however, governmental agencies were also involved. Faced with the awkward situation of leading a nation to war within a few months of having won reelection to the presidency as the man who "kept us out of war," Woodrow Wilson created the Committee on Public Information—the CPI or Creel Committee, as it was known—to wage war for the minds of men, the "conquest of their convictions," largely by means of the dissemination of patriotic propaganda pamphlets.[5] The Bureau of Education at first resisted all attempts to propagandize through the schools, and its director, P. P. Claxton, urged that German be maintained as part of the school curriculum. Within a short period of time, however, he yielded to pressures and began to cooperate with both the National Board for Historical Service and the CPI in the distribution of materials for "war study" courses in the nation's schools. Not only public schools but also a number of colleges and universities required attendance at such war issues courses, and books appeared on the market to satisfy the new demand for patriotic propaganda. Throughout the years 1917 and 1918 one can discern a steady increase in the influence of this patriotism movement, from which the attempt came to rid the country of all things German, including the German language.

The pressure that was applied to have German language instruction discontinued was extremely successful throughout the United States. Eventually, all states passed laws concerning the language issue, although some did not have their legislation in place until after the end of the war. Most such laws dealt with *all* foreign languages, but in Ohio, Louisiana, and several other states, it was explicitly the German language which was at issue. Several states, including Oregon, Wisconsin, Idaho, and Maine, continued to allow foreign languages to be taught as subjects but required that English be the language of instruction in all public schools.[6] What the state governments did not proscribe was often banned by local school boards. In Madison, Wisconsin, for example, where in 1900 two-thirds of the population were foreign-born or children of at least one foreign-born parent, and nearly half of these claimed Germany as their country of origin, German instruction, previously available throughout the city's elementary schools, was totally eliminated.[7]

Some of the laws banning German language instruction in public schools were directed only at the elementary level. The Nebraska Foreign Language Statute, for example, which was challenged (1923) in a famous

case before the Supreme Court, prohibited the teaching of foreign languages to pupils who had not yet passed the eighth grade, presumably on
the grounds that one could thereby assure that English would be the
children's mother tongue.[8] However, the situation was not much better at
the high school level. In Madison the number of high school German
classes dropped from fifteen to two.[9] These reductions were made admin-
istratively, but this was a result of both school board policy and decreased
demand for German on the part of students.

Decreased demand, "voting with one's feet," had even more to do
with declining German enrollments at the nation's colleges and universities. A quick check of some sample university curricula at this time shows
that foreign language requirements remained strong. Despite this, however, German was losing ground at an alarming rate. At Harvard, for
example, the school known at the time as having the least restrictive
undergraduate program and offering its students maximum freedom to
choose their own courses, it was decided in 1909 that all students must
pass an "oral" reading test in either French or German. For Harvard, the
First World War resulted in an increase in the number taking freshman
German, as many students were no longer able to study German in secondary schools. At the same time the war "[reduced] deplorably the
attendance at advanced courses [in German]," while both French and
Spanish experienced increased enrollments at this level.[10] At Yale, new
requirements presented for approval in April of 1917 and approved in May
of 1917 included mandatory study of either French or German, but it is
also reported that because of attitudes during the war "the study of German
very nearly ceased."[11] At the University of Kansas there was no specific
foreign language requirement between 1908 and the mid-1920s, although
breadth requirements were such that most students took a language.[12]
Nevertheless, the German Department there was strong in the years before
the war, and the German Club large and active. However, beginning in
1917 German enrollments in Kansas—as elsewhere—plunged. The University of Wisconsin continued through the war era to require 32 credit
hours in two foreign languages for the Bachelor of Arts degree, counting
both high school and college credits, despite the recommendation of a
University Survey Report of 1914 that the foreign language requirement
be dropped.[13] In 1916 the faculty did approve a program leading to the
new degree of Bachelor of Philosophy, in which foreign language was
required neither for admission nor for graduation, but this option was not
popular and did not survive long.[14] The Wisconsin German Department
statistics tell the story of the war's effect most dramatically. In the year
1916–1917, 1400 students had been taught German by 25 members of the
instructional staff; in the year 1918–1919, only 180 students enrolled in
German, and all but eight of the 25 staff members had been let go.[15] The

language requirement remained the same, and while the German Department was decimated, French and Spanish grew stronger.[16] The pattern was similar throughout the United States.

Thus, although the United States was not at war with the German language, it was being defeated handily and on all fronts. Faced with these facts, we ask: What was the purpose of eliminating German language instruction here? What possible reasons could be advanced to make this seem advisable? Should not the country have argued, as did Commissioner Claxton, that

> when the war is over . . . we shall probably have much more intercourse with the German people . . . than ever before . . . . For practical, industrial and commercial purposes we shall need a knowledge of the German language more than we have needed it in the past.[17]

Why did such rational arguments fall on deaf ears?

Leaders in this country feared Germanism and pro-German sentiment within America as the United States entered the war on the side of the Allies. They identified allegiance to Germany with the perpetuation of German culture, German traditions, and the German language, and they hoped that through Americanization, total assimilation of the foreigners, they could unify the many disparate elements which made up the population. Three distinct groups, all having German connections, came under attack: (1) German-born immigrants in the United States and their immediate descendants; (2) persons suspected of being part of a propaganda or even conspiracy effort against the United States, "The Tentacles of the German Octopus in America," as one writer put it,[18] which included not only spies and saboteurs, but also the foreign language press, German exchange professors, and so on; (3) German-educated American academicians who, together with their German-born or German-American colleagues, were to be found in great numbers, not only in German departments, but throughout American universities, and who supposedly shared with them their love of Germany and their pro-German sentiment.

Let us take a look at these groups individually, beginning with the German immigrants and their descendants. It is easy to forget today that the American melting pot—if one accepts the worn-out image—had not been cooking very long at that time. Indeed, toward the end of the nineteenth and the beginning of the twentieth century the country was becoming less rather than more homogeneous because of the large recent influx of newcomers from many countries. The 1910 census reported that one-third of the American population in that year had either been born abroad or had at least one parent born abroad.[19] The largest single element among the immigrants was the German element. Not unnaturally, the German-Americans were banding together to a certain extent in common-interest organizations such as the National German-American Alliance. They were voting together on certain issues, such as prohibition, which they opposed, not only because of their drinking habits but also because of their financial interests in American breweries. Further, during the period of America's neutrality toward the war in Europe, they contributed sizeable funds to help the German cause. On top of this, the Kaiser himself was quoted as claiming control over the German-American part of the population, as in this statement from a 1908 speech, reported in the *New York Times:* "Even now I rule supreme in the United States, where almost one half of the population is either of German birth or of German descent, and where three million voters do my bidding at the Presidential elections. No American Administration could remain in power against the will of the German voters . . . ."[20] This point of view was also seen in the following statement by Heidelberg historian Hermann Oncken: ". . . if the German who intends to remain there [in America] does not become a citizen, he has . . . no influence of any kind on the conduct of the nation's political affairs. He must become an American; he is permitted, however, and can and ought in heart, thought, nature, and act to remain a German."[21] Americans wondered where the loyalty of the German-Americans really lay.

The continued use of the German language was blamed for the incomplete assimilation of German immigrants:

> . . . the possession of [German language and German culture] alone is sufficient to prevent the process of Americanization.[22]

> Of all the German conspiracies which have been directed against America, the most serious has been that insidious *Kultur* movement which has been quietly conducted through . . . the continued use of the German language.[23]

> No man of German descent can become thoroughly American while retaining allegiance to the German language . . . .[24]

Such was the feeling in America, and the German language fell victim to it. People paid no heed to signs of the allegiance of the German immigrants to their new country: to the fact that by 1910 more than ninety percent of them had taken out first papers toward naturalization, to the fact that they served in the war and shared this country's fate. The German language simply had to go. German-Americans themselves, anxious not to seem traitorous, often willingly joined the movement against the use of German. For example, interest among Wisconsin German-Americans in private and parochial schools where German was the language of instruction fell to the extent that nearly all of them were closed. Many German-Americans had their names legally changed to English-sounding ones. Many families who had spoken German in their homes until the First World War then consciously switched to English. This effort in all probability had no effect whatever on the outcome of the war, but the German language did succumb.

The second group which came under attack for seditious pro-German activities was much smaller than the German-Americans as a whole. However, as it included official representatives of the German government, exchange professors, and other public figures supposedly under the direct control of German interests, it was a newsworthy group. Names were named, and attacks were vicious. It was claimed that these people were here purposefully to keep Germanism alive in America—or were selling out to the Germans for the same reason. There were, to be sure, incidents of sabotage, particularly involving the destruction of a number of factories in the eastern part of the United States. But not all complaints against members of this group were justified, and a good deal of what appeared in print against them ranged from unsubstantiated to silly. As the attempt here was to sever connections with Germany, and this touches only peripherally on the question of German language instruction, I shall cite only a few examples. However, this group, those presumed responsible for a pro-German propaganda effort in the United States, is important for an understanding of the mood of the times.

It was held, for instance, that the German language press in America was supported by financial interests from Germany and that a number of American newspapers also had considerable financial or other ties with the German cause.[25] Postmaster General Albert Sidney Burleson was empowered by Congress to require all foreign-language newspapers to submit in advance of publication English translations of all political or war-related articles. These costly procedures and delays forced many such newspapers to close. This was another blow to the use of German in this country. All publications, foreign and English alike, were subject to possible censure by the Postmaster General, who was authorized by the Espionage Act of June, 1917, to suppress traitorous materials by banning them from the mails. Burleson seems to have had a rather broad understanding of the scope of his work.[26]

Academic freedom in America took giant steps backward during the First World War era. One example involves Count Johann von Bernstorff, the German ambassador, who left his post in Washington in February, 1917, just before the United States declared war. The University of Wisconsin, under considerable pressure to prove that it was not a "Germanized" institution as many were claiming, retracted an honorary degree which it had bestowed on him in 1910.[27] Unfortunately, the von Bernstorff event was not an isolated one. The University of Nebraska dismissed three professors for "believ[ing] in internationalism, imped[ing] the sale of liberty bonds, and criticiz[ing] their more patriotic colleagues."[28] The University of Minnesota dismissed the chairman of the Department of Political

Science for having stated that he did not wish to see "the Hohenzollerns
. . . wiped out root and branch";[29] he was, by the way, reinstated as
Professor Emeritus twenty years later. President Nicholas Murray Butler
of Columbia University withdrew academic freedom from members of the
University staff for the entire duration of the war.[30] But perhaps the most
extreme instances of such abuse were the attacks against Hugo Münsterberg, Professor of Psychology at Harvard. In 1916 he undertook to present
the German case to the American public—this was during the period of
America's loudly proclaimed neutrality. Rumors spread that he was in the
German Secret Service and that the pigeons his daughter fed in his back-
yard were carrier pigeons taking messages to spies.[31] A wealthy Harvard
alumnus, according to newspaper reports, threatened to annul a bequest
of $10 million unless Münsterberg were dismissed. Münsterberg was a
German citizen but had been at Harvard well over twenty years at this
time. It is to the credit of Harvard and its President, Abbott Lawrence
Lowell, that they supported Münsterberg, stating that the "University
cannot tolerate any suggestion that it would be willing to accept money to
abridge free speech, to remove a professor or to accept his resignation."[32]
But such a stand was the exception rather than the rule.

Americans at this point were also having some difficulty interpreting
their own history. The fact was that America had been at war twice against
England, but never against Germany. If one taught the American Revolution and failed to stress the role of the Hessian mercenaries in that war,
then one was pro-German and a teacher of *Kultur*.[33] William Herbert
Hobbs, a professor of geology at the University of Michigan, well known
as a teacher of patriotism during the war years, became irate over lectures
on the history of the American Revolution delivered by one W. W. Florer,
a member of the German Department in Ann Arbor. Hobbs writes: "In
one of [Florer's] statements he even claimed that our American Revolutionary fathers drew their inspiration from Schiller, who at the time was
seventeen years of age."[34] The German-American Historical Society, incorporated in 1901, came under attack for its work, "the investigation,
collection, and publication of material relating to the history and culture
of Germans in America . . . ."[35]

The American patriotism movement attempted to neutralize the effect
of such—as it thought—pro-German distortions by producing new distortions of its own. George L. Knapp, in a work published by the American
Rights League in 1918, addresses the question of the attitude of the English
during the American Revolution as follows:

> Our school histories tell us of the strong pro-American stand of Burke and
> Fox, but they do not tell us that the sentiments of these intellectual giants
> were shared by hosts of lesser men. Yet such was the case. The war was

forced on the colonies by the Tories, and by the King as foremost of Tories; but the great majority of the non-Tory population of Britain deplored and condemned it.[36]

The distribution of this idea was so successful that it appears in the 1920s as an item of American faith in *The New American Credo* by George Jean Nathan. According to him, Americans believe "That at the time of the American Revolution everybody in England was in favor of giving the colonies their liberty and that the war only took place because of the obstinacy of the King, who was very pro-German."[37]

The third group in America under attack for its pro-German sentiment was much broader than most of us today might suspect. Indeed, American academicians as a group and American institutions of higher learning as a whole were thought in some circles to be pro-German. Today, only a rare American student spends part of his years of study abroad, then usually returns home to finish his degree at a university here. Until World War I, however, it was not at all unusual for American students to take their graduate degrees at German universities, no matter what their field, but particularly in the sciences, mathematics, and psychology. After all, American universities were still rather young. The first earned—that is, not honorary—Ph.D. degree in America was awarded in 1861 by Yale University, but although the number of institutions which offered the doctoral degree increased rapidly (25 by 1876, the year Johns Hopkins was organized primarily for graduate studies), graduate students remained rare in most schools, and even the philosophy of what should constitute a graduate education was not universally agreed upon.[38] Thus American academicians were often German-educated.[39] In addition to this, arrangements for an exchange of professors between German and American universities were set up and carried out during the years immediately preceding America's involvement in the war.

Undoubtedly, the German influence in American universities was real and strong. In the Mathematics Department at the University of Kansas in the year 1909–1910, for example, two of the five staff members who held the Ph.D. degree had received it in Germany, in 1903 and 1909, respectively. Two of the other three had only honorary degrees, but one of these had studied mathematics in Germany for two years.[40] At the University of Wisconsin some of the most illustrious members of the staff were German-trained, including two historians, the first full professor of sociology, the chairman of the Department of Chemistry, and the director of the School of Pharmacy.[41] Charles R. Van Hise, President of the University during the World War I years, though himself a product of the University, had strong sympathies for the international movement among universities and welcomed the first national convention of university Cosmopolitan Clubs to Madison in December of 1907.[42] Former American students at German universities joined together in 1902 to form the Union of Old German Students,[43] and later a similar organization was founded called the German University League.[44] Similarly, German Clubs and German Houses on American college campuses spoke not only to the interests of German majors. German universities were so important for American education that one writer even urged the establishment of a German University in America.[45]

These three groups—the German-Americans, the pro-German propagandists, and the German-educated American academics—had something in common: knowledge of the German language and the desire to see it taught in American schools. As Americans drew together in the war effort, the German language and the possibilities which knowledge of German opened up to Americans were viewed with increasing suspicion. Those who knew German and/or had studied in Germany presumably also harbored pro-German sentiments. I have a notion that such views were furthered by the content of textbooks used for German language and literature instruction in this country, but this goes beyond the limits of this paper. My question is what happened to German language instruction during this era and why. Turning against the German language was equated in the American mind with Americanization of the U.S. population and the creation of a national feeling, a national allegiance, a national unity, which had to that point been lacking.

I wish to make one final observation: the First World War was not solely responsible for the decline in German language teaching in this country. The war merely accelerated a process which was already at work. It is reported, for example, that in Wisconsin "with the establishment of high schools, particularly after 1875, the teaching of foreign languages in the grades was gradually discontinued, and as a rule with little or no opposition."[46] The argument used apparently was that too much foreign language would handicap the students in learning English. In 1889 the Wisconsin Legislature passed the Bennett School Law, which mandated school attendance for all children between the ages of seven and fourteen and required that instruction must be in the English language. Although this law was repealed several years later, and German-language parochial and private schools in Wisconsin were strong at least to the time of the First World War, a gradual movement toward universal use of English is clear. In 1905 Alexander R. Hohlfeld of the University of Wisconsin reaffirms this trend, observing that German language instruction seems on firm footing only in American high schools and colleges—not in private or parochial German schools nor in American public elementary schools.[47] Indications are that there had been a tendency toward reduction in German language instruction, at least in the elementary schools, long before the beginning of the World War.

Historians agree that this much, at least, the World War did for the United States: it forged it into a nation. Charles Hirschfeld writes:

> A new American nation came into being during the war. The intense experience greatly furthered the nationalization of American life and gave the American people a real sense of unity. . . . And there was a cost—in illiberalism, intolerance, and the suppression of freedom of speech and opinion . . . . The nationalization of American life did not take place without great injury to American democratic ideals. But the hysteria which prevailed was precisely an indication of the extent and intensity of the wartime departure from the traditional American norms. . . . America, in short, was being welded into a new nation by the pressure of international crisis and war . . . .[48]

The history of the teaching of German during the First World War reflects this process of Americanization very well. The situation was unique and did not occur again. Some twenty years later, hostilities led once more to an outbreak of war between Germany and the United States. But immigrants from Germany in the 1930s were seen as refugees, outcasts who were forced to turn their backs on their homes in Germany and flee for their lives. They did not represent outposts of German culture and nationalism within a country whose own sense of national unity was not well developed—as had been the case during the time of the First World War. Rather they were German exiles who could be absorbed into a strong, unified American nation. And—as we all know—foreign language learning in the United States was stressed during World War II.

At least to some extent, this changed attitude toward the teaching of German must be attributed to the way Germanists dealt with the situation at the end of the First World War. They examined their role within the American education system, adjusted their programs to the changed circumstances, and set about the task of rebuilding from the bottom up. The real leader in the German teaching profession's struggle for survival between the two World Wars was Alexander R. Hohlfeld. The second part of this paper addresses his contribution.

Alexander R. Hohlfeld and the Struggle for Survival

Alexander R. Hohlfeld had come to the University of Wisconsin in 1901, and by the time the United States entered the First World War he could claim much of the credit for having built a strong German Department in Madison. The Department had a respected graduate program and a large undergraduate program. In the year 1915–1916 it taught 9.5% of the total number of student credit hours in Letters and Science—a surprising figure when compared to today's 1.6%.[49] Hohlfeld had been instrumental in founding the Carl Schurz Memorial Professorship at the University (1911); and he had helped to organize the University's German House (which opened in 1914). On the national level, Hohlfeld had served as President of the MLA for the year 1913. The First World War demolished what he had spent his life developing. Correspondence between Hohlfeld and Dean E. A. Birge of the College of Letters and Science for the years 1917 through 1919 reveals the major problem of the time: retrenchment and reorganization of the Department along much more modest lines.[50]

Hohlfeld faced an additional problem at that time: the active and vicious Germanophobia in the United States, which was victimizing even the most loyal German-Americans. Hohlfeld, an American citizen of German birth and education, was particularly open to attack because of his profession, the teaching of German language and culture, subjects then viewed as subversive. Hohlfeld might have had troubles even had he stuck his head in the sand or hidden in his office on the Wisconsin campus. But students, colleagues in the profession, and fellow German-Americans looked to him for leadership, and he responded in ways which the American press followed eagerly and with bias and prejudice. Not only did his department lose great numbers of students; his personal integrity was also under attack.

A case in point concerns the address delivered by Hohlfeld at the graduation ceremonies of the National Teachers Seminary in Milwaukee on 20 June 1918 (see the following paper in this volume). This was a formidable assignment in view of the fact that the graduates faced a job market far less promising than anything which has been known since. The Teachers Seminary itself was in jeopardy, and a few months later the Wisconsin State Board of Examiners withdrew its accreditation and thus sealed its doom.[51] Hohlfeld's remarks address the question of the stand to be taken by German-Americans at the bewildering point in history to which they had come. Urging pride in their German heritage as well as patriotism toward their new homeland, Hohlfeld sees promise for the future only if they do their part in the war effort.

Hohlfeld's words were misquoted in newspaper accounts, and a considerable row ensued. Complaints crossed the desk of University of Wisconsin President Charles R. Van Hise. C. R. Fish of the Wisconsin History Department sent Van Hise a newspaper report of the speech with the note: "I enclose a report of Hohlfeld's address in Milwaukee. If it is true it is bad stuff. . . . He is courageous, but his citizenship isn't worth shucks, and he is certainly a danger to the University."[52] The President of the Board of Regents of the University also wrote Van Hise concerning Hohlfeld's address: "The address . . . as reported . . . is one which might much better not have been given. . . . I think it is very unfortunate that Professor Hohlfeld should continue to give public expression to his personal sentiments, and I imagine that the best thing that could happen to him would be to have a large, heavy weight placed upon him which would prevent his breaking out into print from time to time."[53]

The issue of the Milwaukee speech was just one of several incidents for which Hohlfeld was attacked in the press during the first half of 1918. Despite these attacks, he was busy with two projects, each with political overtones. The first, an effort in which he and several other leading members of the German-American community collaborated, proposed a collective statement, "a nation-wide declaration" of the position of German-Americans. This, it was hoped, might "stem the tide of popular feeling" against them.[54] To Hohlfeld's disappointment, the effort came to naught. The second, more narrowly related to interests of the German-teaching profession, resulted in a resolution and a motion proposed by Hohlfeld and adopted at a May, 1918, meeting of the Association of Modern Language Teachers in Chicago. The resolution recognizes the responsibility of teachers of German in "win[ning] back public confidence" by proving "that the sympathetic and effective teaching of the language and literature of our present enemy is in no way incompatible with the most whole hearted Americanism—an Americanism which includes the active and loyal support of the government in the prosecution of the war to victory . . . ."[55] The motion directs the Chair of the German section to appoint a committee of five "to consider carefully the situation of the study and teaching of German in our territory as it is being affected by the war and to help guard the legitimate interests of our work and profession with special reference to the spirit of the loyalty resolution adopted as [sic] this meeting."[56] These moves represent an attempt to help teachers adjust to the war situation; and they form an impressive beginning of Hohlfeld's fight for the survival of German Studies in America after World War I. President Van Hise of the University of Wisconsin congratulated Hohlfeld on his resolution and motion, stating warmly: "Both seem admirably formulated for the purpose for which they are intended. I hope that the committee appointed under the second resolution will be an active one, for I feel that wise work by a patriotic committee along the lines of the resolution is necessary."[57] The influential former Regent of the University of Wisconsin, Thomas E. Brittingham, sitting in his lovely home on the western edge of Madison, now the home of the University's President, also heard of the Hohlfeld resolutions and wrote to Van Hise: "Now [Hohlfeld] is ready to be launched on the platform—I do hope he will go and too [?] under the auspices of the University—In his talks eliminating any reference to the teaching of German but simply arousing and creating patriotism."[58]

The idea of "launching" Hohlfeld, even into a career of giving patriotic addresses, one may find amusing, but Brittingham certainly did not
have any feeling for Hohlfeld's intention if he thought Hohlfeld could be
persuaded to stop talking about the teaching of German. By the end of
1918 the war was over, and German programs in America lay defeated
and in ruins. Hohlfeld, a man of great vision and leadership capabilities,
began launching his efforts to rebuild.

His first concern was the low enrollment in German courses at the
University and in public schools and colleges and universities throughout
the country. As he fully realized, without strong enrollments at many
levels, teachers would not be needed, and without the need for teachers,
university undergraduate and graduate programs could not survive. At
Wisconsin enrollments in German courses increased rapidly: from 180 in
the fall of 1918 to more than 1000 in the fall of 1923, and more than 1580
in the fall of 1927. By 1927 there were for the first time more individual
enrollments in German than there had been before the United States' entry
into the war. However, as the total enrollment in Letters and Science had
roughly doubled in the same period, this still represented approximately
a 50% overall loss in the German Department's share. The strength of the
pre-war German program in Wisconsin and of those members of the faculty
who had remained undoubtedly helped Hohlfeld's home department to
bounce back, but evidence exists also that he was continually using his
own influence to gain help from the administration: he protested cuts in
office and classroom space, urged the reintroduction of elementary German in the University High School, and informed his Dean's office of
German Department statistics showing growth.[59]

However, as before, his involvement extended far beyond his own
campus. Because the war came to an end, the committee of five to study
the situation of German studies did not become reality, but very quickly
Hohlfeld was looking for another way to organize German teachers to
share statistics and other information and thus support each other in their
attempts to rebuild.[60] At an MLA meeting in Chicago (December 1920), a
small group which Hohlfeld had helped to organize proposed a study of
the status of German language instruction in high schools throughout the
central, western, and southern districts; simultaneously there was a similar
effort to canvass the eastern region.[61] In connection with this study, Hohlfeld sent out 150 questionnaires in January, 1922.[62] The project quickly
turned into something more major. In December of the following year, a
group of twenty-four modern language teachers, including Hohlfeld, held
a conference in Atlantic City. They adopted a report which urged an
investigation of the teaching of modern foreign languages in America and
recommended a plan for such a study. The Carnegie Corporation supported this Modern Foreign Language Study, as it was called, and the

American Council on Education agreed to sponsor it. A Committee on Direction and Control was appointed, which included twenty respected educators and teachers in various languages from the United States and Canada, among them Hohlfeld. Eight regional districts were set up in order to gain information at local levels and to sound out local opinions and circumstances. The Modern Foreign Language Study, the work of which extended roughly from 1924 to 1930, produced an eighteen-volume opus which appeared under the title *Publications of the American and Canadian Committees on Modern Languages.*[63] It is impressive even today.

I do not know to what extent Hohlfeld was behind the movement to consider the question of the study of German in America as part of the larger topic of the study of foreign languages in general, but he certainly approved. From the beginning, Hohlfeld and others promoted the study of foreign languages to aid the cause of German, and vice-versa. They argued that in many instances German had not been replaced with another foreign language, and that no foreign-language study at all was detrimental to communities.[64] Similarly, Hohlfeld later expressed reservations about the founding of both the *Germanic Review* and the AATG, arguing that Germanists would do better to join together with representatives of other modern languages rather than become a group unto themselves.[65] I personally feel that from many points of view his philosophy on this matter was correct and that it is to the detriment of our programs that many Germanists, particularly at the college level, remain isolated from their colleagues in other foreign language fields.[66]

Hohlfeld's second effort in the area of strengthening the study of German at all levels was a mobilization of what we would call "outreach" activities to assist German teachers and their programs by providing supportive services through the German Department in Madison. This assistance was made available in Wisconsin and throughout the country and included the following:

(a) The German Service Bureau, established in Madison during the academic year 1928–29 to lend teaching materials, such as slides and other visual aids, and to give advice and help to teachers of German. Eventually regular Service Bureau Notes appeared in *Monatshefte,* and in 1937 the Bureau even offered a catalogue of loan materials on hand. Despite a modest beginning, usership increased phenomenally, and by the year 1934–35, 2000 letters and parcels were being sent out annually to "practically all parts of the country."[67]

(b) A bulletin of the University of Wisconsin entitled "The High School Course in German," written originally by M. B. Evans and long out of print, was issued anew in 1929 and made available free of charge. Further, a new edition of the popular *Deutsches Liederbuch* appeared in 1931.[68]

(c) Summer study trips to Germany, which had been offered earlier but were interrupted by the war, were made available again, the first in 1922. University credit was offered for these trips, and the clientele included not only university students but also teachers who needed more experience with German language and culture.[69]

(d) In the early 1930s the Department even added radio broadcasts to its statewide outreach effort, sometimes with fifteen-minute, sometimes with half-hour weekly programs.[70]

These efforts, of course, represented the work of many members of the Wisconsin German Department, but Hohlfeld was behind and in the midst of them. In the fall of 1929, for example, Hohlfeld and two other members of the Department collaborated to present a series of German extension lectures in Milwaukee, and in the spring semester of 1930 he continued alone, lecturing there once a week on *Faust*.[71] Milwaukee is 90 miles from Madison, and there was an extra effort involved in adding these lectures to his full schedule at home.

The third effort we can attribute to Hohlfeld during this period of reconstruction was a move to stress teacher-training programs for graduate students in the German Department. Hohlfeld was personally involved, giving part of his time to the School of Education to help with the training of future German teachers.[72] But he also played another part in the development of teacher training at Wisconsin. As a trustee of the National German-American Teachers Seminary in Milwaukee through its long period of dormancy after the end of the war, he was instrumental in the resolution of its problems, first through what was considered a temporary transfer of its work to the campus in Madison in 1927, and later through a permanent arrangement, which brought all of its assets, not an inconsiderable amount, to the Madison campus in 1931. The University pledged to continue the work of the Seminary both in teacher training and in the Seminary's journal, the *Monatshefte für deutsche Sprache und Pädagogik*, forerunner of the present *Monatshefte*.

Hohlfeld's interest in teacher training was a lifelong commitment, which antedated the war and long outlived the immediate postwar pressures to boost teacher-training efforts.[73] Nearly ten years after his retirement Hohlfeld was involved in rather serious altercations with the German Department concerning the use of the Teachers Seminary Fund. He also feuded with R. O. Röseler, editor of *Monatshefte*, for having turned the journal into a journal for literary scholarship, rather than keeping its emphasis on matters of pedagogy as agreed with the Seminary.[74] Hohlfeld's energy as ex-chairman was surpassed only by his energy as chairman, but this is another topic altogether.

Hohlfeld's fourth effort to promote the survival of German studies was an attempt to improve the quality of offerings to students of German in his own department. First came the revival and reorganization of the German House, which had been closed in 1918 but reopened in 1923.[75] Financial problems beset the House, and there was the perpetual headache of filling its rooms, which were rented to women students.[76] To combat these problems and provide some measure of financial support, the German Department formed an organization called Friends of the German House.[77] Hohlfeld also set out to find additional financial support for graduate students. As early as January 1918, he wrote to President Van Hise that he hoped to "secure from some Milwaukee friends of our department a number of scholarships and fellowships for the study of German for the next few years [and] . . . thus . . . to tide over the difficulties."[78] A similar effort along these lines was the establishment of the Hohlfeld Memorial Fund, a fund-raising effort managed by B. Q. Morgan, whose stated objective was to honor Hohlfeld on the occasion of his sixtieth birthday in December of 1925. A separate fund was the Hohlfeld Memorial Scholarship, which was established when Hohlfeld's youngest son, a geologist-explorer, drowned in Peru in 1925, at the age of twenty-five.

The fifth and final item to be mentioned concerns a new direction in literary scholarship with which the work of Hohlfeld and his students became identified. He was convinced that American German Departments have a unique mission, and he emphasized their potential as centers of cross-cultural literary studies. Altogether, Hohlfeld directed some twenty-five dissertations which fell into the category of what he called the "Wisconsin Project of Anglo-German Literary Relations."[79] Among these are titles such as "German Literature in American Magazines 1846 to 1880," or "The Attitude of the *Grenzboten* toward English Literature," or "Goethe's Lyric Poems in English Translation—Prior to 1860," and "— After 1860," or "The Reception of Goethe's *Faust* in England in the Second Half of the Nineteenth Century"—titles which illustrate to some extent the type of work the project meant to include.[80] Similar directions in research were later initiated by Hohlfeld's disciples at other major universities, by Lawrence M. Price at Berkeley, B. Q. Morgan at Stanford, and Harold S. Jantz, first at Clark and then at Johns Hopkins. Hohlfeld's contention was that an American German Department should be just that. Its work, beyond that of foreign-language teaching, should be to relate German culture to the culture of this country. Why? Because it is a thing of inherent value to the United States. In keeping with this philosophy Wisconsin introduced a course on German literature in translation as early as the Spring of 1921 in order to serve the American student with limited knowledge of German language and culture; and for similar reasons, members of the German Department in the early 1920s undertook research work which had to do with translating German poems into English.[81]

Hohlfeld retired in 1936, three years before the beginning of World

War II and five years before the United States entered that war. This time there was no major outbreak of Germanophobia in the country. As a matter of fact, the usefulness of German language studies was widely recognized, and many American Germanists, including several from Wisconsin, lent their expertise to the war effort. Members of the German teaching profession had recovered, slowly but steadily, by examining their role in American education, by offering assistance to fellow teachers, and by building strong programs to produce strong new members of the profession for the future. Hohlfeld was one of the foremost leaders in these efforts. Perhaps one of his finest achievements is that he successfully led the struggle for the survival of German studies in America after the First World War.

Notes

1 In a letter to W. S. Covert, Principal of a Long Island high school, 22 June 1917. The letter was reprinted repeatedly and became the subject of much controversy. See *The New Republic*, 2 March 1918: 146; *Monatshefte für deutsche Sprache und Pädagogik* 19 (1918): 58–59; George Creel, *How We Advertised America* (New York: Harper, 1920) 444–47.

2 Lewis Paul Todd, *Wartime Relations of the Federal Government and the Public Schools 1917–1918* (New York: Columbia University, 1945) 73.

3 Todd 73.

4 *Monatshefte für deutsche Sprache und Pädagogik* 19 (1918): 274.

5 Creel 3.

6 La Vern J. Rippley, *The German-Americans* (Boston: Twayne, 1976) 123–24; Wallace H. Moore, "The Conflict Concerning the German Language and German Propaganda in the Public Secondary Schools of the United States, 1917–1919," diss., Stanford, 1937.

7 David V. Mollenhoff, *Madison: A History of the Formative Years* (Dubuque: Kendall/Hunt, 1982) 417, 426.

8 Robert T. Meyer v. State of Nebraska, 262 Sup. Ct. 1044 (U.S. Supreme Court, 1923).

9 Mollenhoff 417.

10 *The Development of Harvard University, 1869–1929*, ed. Samuel Eliot Morison (Cambridge: Harvard University Press, 1930) 70–71, 83, 85.

11 Brooks M. Kelley, *Yale: A History* (New Haven: Yale University Press, 1974) 347; George W. Pierson, *Yale: College and University, 1871–1937* (New Haven: Yale University Press, 1952) 1: 474.

12 Clifford S. Griffin, *The University of Kansas: A History* (Lawrence: University of Kansas Press, 1974) 306–07, 546.

13 *Report upon the Survey of the University of Wisconsin: Findings of the State Board of Public Affairs and Its Report to the Legislature* (Madison, 1915) 32.

14 Merle Curti and Vernon Carstensen, *The University of Wisconsin: A History, 1848–1925* (Madison: University of Wisconsin Press, 1949) 2: 317–19.

15 Alexander R. Hohlfeld, "The Wisconsin Project on Anglo-German Literary Relations," document in the University Archives, dated 1949, p. 8. The figures given here are slightly

different from those given in Curti and Carstensen (2: 324), but I cannot explain this, since Curti and Carstensen cite the Hohlfeld document as their source (2: 323).

16 Curti and Carstensen 2: 321–22.

17 See Note 1.

18 Earl E. Sperry, *The Tentacles of the German Octopus in America*, National Security League, Patriotism through Education Series, no. 21, 1917.

19 David M. Kennedy, *Over Here: The First World War and American Society* (New York: Oxford University Press, 1980) 24.

20 Gustavus Ohlinger, *Their True Faith and Allegiance* (New York: Macmillan, 1917) xiv–xv. Quoted in the preface by Owen Wister.

21 William H. Hobbs, *The World War and Its Consequences* (New York: Putnam, 1919) 152.

22 Hobbs 201.

23 Hobbs 193–94.

24 Gustavus Ohlinger, *The German Conspiracy in American Education* (New York: Doran, 1919) 108.

25 Hobbs 136–40, 264–67.

26 Kennedy 75–77.

27 Curti and Carstensen 2: 119.

28 Richard Hofstadter and Walter P. Metzger, *The Development of Academic Freedom in the United States* (New York: Columbia University Press, 1955) 497.

29 Hofstadter and Metzger 497.

30 Hofstadter and Metzger 499.

31 Samuel Eliot Morison, *Three Centuries of Harvard, 1636–1936* (Cambridge: Harvard University Press, 1965) 453.

32 Hofstadter and Metzger 502–03.

33 Hobbs 153–54.

34 Hobbs 154.

35 Ohlinger, *The German Conspiracy* 71.

36 George L. Knapp, *Britain and America*, American Rights League, Bull., No. 41, Feb., 1918: 8. Quoted by Hobbs 391.

37 George J. Nathan, *The New American Credo: A Contribution toward the Interpretation of the National Mind* (New York: Knopf, 1927) 190.

38 Griffin 174–75.

39 For information on the history of American students seeking education at German universities, see Starr Willard Cutting, "Modern Languages in the General Scheme of American Education," *Monatshefte für deutsche Sprache und Pädagogik* 19 (1918): 25–34.

40 G. Baley Price, *History of the Department of Mathematics of The University of Kansas, 1866–1970* (Lawrence: Kansas University Endowment Association, 1976) 122–23, 777–88.

41 Professors William L. Westermann, Dana C. Munro, Edward Alsworth Ross, Louis Kahlenberg, and Edward Kremers.

42 The published report of this convention is amusing. For example, a student representing Japan states: "I want to learn all about American commercial methods, so that I may teach them to my people at the University of Tokio." See Louis Lochner, "Cosmopolitan Clubs in American University Life," *Review of Reviews* 37 (1908): 316–21.

43 Ohlinger, *The German Conspiracy* 29–30.

44 Ibid. 96–97.

45 Ibid. 86–87.

46 Conrad E. Patzer, *Public Education in Wisconsin* (Madison, 1924) 68. "Issued by John Callahan, state superintendent."

47 Alexander R. Hohlfeld, "Die Zukunft des deutschen Unterrichts im amerikanischen Unterrichtswesen," *Pädagogische Monatshefte* 6 (1905): 239.

48 Charles Hirschfeld, "The Transformation of American Life," *World War I: A Turning Point in Modern History,* ed. Jack J. Roth (New York: Knopf, 1967) 74, 77–78.

49 John F. Cook, "A History of Liberal Education at the University of Wisconsin, 1862–1918," diss., University of Wisconsin, 1970, 354.

50 See Series 7/14/2, Box 2, file on E. A. Birge, University of Wisconsin Archives.

51 The history of the National German-American Teachers Seminary can be found in Series 7/14/10 of the University of Wisconsin Archives.

52 Note from Prof. C. R. Fish to President Van Hise, dated July 6, 1918. Series 4/10/1, Box 67, file on A. R. Hohlfeld, University Archives.

53 Letter from Theodore M. Hammond to President Van Hise, dated June 24, 1918. Series 4/10/1, Box 67, file on A. R. Hohlfeld, University Archives.

54 From the speech cited above. See also letter from Hohlfeld to Professor Otto Heller, dated 16 February 1918; and letter from A. R. Hohlfeld to President C. R. Van Hise, dated 18 February 1918. Both letters are in Series 4/10/1, Box 67, file on A. R. Hohlfeld, University Archives.

55 Dated 4 May 1918. Series 4/10/1, Box 67, file on A. R. Hohlfeld, University Archives.

56 Series 4/10/1, Box 67, file on A. R. Hohlfeld, University Archives.

57 Letter from Van Hise to Hohlfeld, dated May 14, 1918. Series 7/14/2, Box 13, file on C. R. Van Hise, University Archives.

58 Handwritten note from Thomas E. Brittingham to Van Hise, dated 17 May 1918. Series 4/10/1, Box 67, file on A. R. Hohlfeld, University Archives.

59 Letter from A. R. Hohlfeld to President E. A. Birge and Dean G. C. Sellery, dated 6 August 1920 (Series 7/14/2, Box 2, file on E. A. Birge); letter from A. R. Hohlfeld to President E. A. Birge, dated 28 May 1920 (Series 7/14/2, Box 2, file on E. A. Birge); reports from Series 7/14/2, Box 1, file on Annual Reports to the Dean—also letter from A. R. Hohlfeld to President Birge, dated 18 February 1919 (Series 7/14/2, Box 2, file on E. A. Birge), and letter from A. R. Hohlfeld to Dean G. C. Sellery, dated 15 January 1920 (Series 7/14/2, Box 12, file on G. C. Sellery), among others. All are in the University Archives.

60 Letter from A. R. Hohlfeld to S. W. Cutting, Chairman, Department of German, University of Chicago, dated 29 January 1919 (Series 7/14/2, Box 3, file on S. W. Cutting, University Archives).

61 See A. R. Hohlfeld to S. W. Cutting, 8 December 1920 (Series 7/14/2, Box 3, file on Cutting, University Archives), and other items in this file.

62 A. R. Hohlfeld to S. W. Cutting, 13 January 1922 (Series 7/14/2, Box 3, file on Cutting, University Archives).

63 A short history of the work of the Modern Foreign Language Study is given in Vol. 18 of the *Publications of the American and Canadian Committees on Modern Languages,* which appeared under the title *A Summary of Reports on the Modern Foreign Languages,* by Robert Herndon Fife (New York: Macmillan, 1931) 1–10.

64 In an undated draft of the proposed communication to school superintendents, probably from October of 1921 (Series 7/14/2, Box 3, file on S. W. Cutting, University Archives).

65 Concerning the *Germanic Review,* see letter from A. R. Hohlfeld to R. H. Fife, dated 18 January 1925 (Series 7/14/2, Box 5, file on Fife, University Archives); concerning the AATG see letter from A. R. Hohlfeld to William R. Price, dated 24 November 1926—also memo from A. R. Hohlfeld to six people, whose names appear on it, dated April, 1927 (both in Series 7/14/2, Box 1, file on AATG 1926–1932, University Archives).

66 Today this idea is espoused most notably by David P. Benseler of Ohio State University. See "The American Language Association: Toward New Strength, Visibility, and Effec-

tiveness as a Profession," *Our Profession: Present Status and Future Directions,* ed. Thomas H. Geno (Middlebury, Vt.: Northeast Conference, 1980) 142–56.

67 German Department *Newsletter,* December, 1935, 2. Series 7/14/00-3, Box 1, University Archives.

68 "The High School Course in German," manuscript prepared by Joseph Dwight Deihl, ed. B. Q. Morgan, was offered to anyone who wrote the University Editor for it. The *Deutsches Liederbuch* edition was prepared by Max Griebsch and B. Q. Morgan; it had first been issued by a German Department committee in 1906. See German Department Newsletters of April, 1929, 1, and November, 1931, 2. Series 7/14/00-3, Box 1, University Archives.

69 In 1926 B. Q. Morgan took his third such tour to Europe (German Department *Newsletter,* 1926–27, 1: 1. Series 7/14/00-3, Box 1, University Archives); his first tour after the end of the war had gone in the summer of 1922 (letter from B. Q. Morgan to A. R. Hohlfeld, 22 March 1922, and other letters from that Spring. Series 7/14/2, Box 14, file on B. Q. Morgan, University Archives).

70 Radio broadcasts are first mentioned in the German Department Newsletter of November, 1932, 2, and repeatedly thereafter. Series 7/14/00-3, Box 1, University Archives.

71 German Department *Newsletter,* April, 1930, 2. Series 7/14/00-3, Box 1, University Archives.

72 Letter from A. R. Hohlfeld to President E. A. Birge, dated 13 July 1919. Series 7/14/2, Box 2, file on E. A. Birge, University Archives.

73 See, for example, the address Hohlfeld delivered as President of the MLA on 30 December 1913, "Light from Goethe on our Problems," *Fifty Years with Goethe 1901–1951* (Madison: University of Wisconsin Press, 1953), 315–38, especially 326–31.

74 See Series 7/14/10-2, file on Röseler-Hohlfeld Feud, University Archives.

75 Hohlfeld, "The Wisconsin Project" 6.

76 See German Department *Newsletters,* Series 7/14/00-3, Box 1, University Archives. Rooms were full in the fall of 1927. In November of 1931 it is reported that "while some rooms are vacant we have not been as adversely affected by the depression as might have been expected." Recipients of the *Newsletter* are repeatedly asked to help advertise the German House and suggest names of students who "would be desirable members of the German House."

77 Organized in the Spring of 1926. German Department *Newsletter* 1926–27, 1: 1 (Series 7/14/00-3, Box 1, University Archives).

78 Letter from A. R. Hohlfeld to President C. R. Van Hise, dated 12 January 1918. Series 7/14/2, Box 13, file on Van Hise, University Archives.

79 These are listed in Hohlfeld, "The Wisconsin Project" 19–21.

80 Written by Martin H. Haertel, Lawrence M. Price, Lucretia V. T. Simmons, Stella M. Hinz, and Heinz S. Bluhm, respectively. See note 79.

81 See letter from A. R. Hohlfeld to the Library of Congress, dated 20 November 1923, and form letter directed to various libraries, dated 1 February 1924. Both letters are in Series 7/14/6, Box 1, file on A. R. Hohlfeld 1910–1925, University Archives.

Alexander R. Hohlfeld, 1865–1956

Address by Professor Alexander R. Hohlfeld, University of Wisconsin, to the Graduating Class of the National Teachers Seminary at Milwaukee on Thursday, 20 June 1918

On 20 June 1918, Alexander R. Hohlfeld of the University of Wisconsin addressed the graduating class of the National Teachers Seminary in Milwaukee, whose official name had until 1918 been the Nationales Deutschamerikanisches Lehrerseminar. His task was staggering. What was he to say to the graduates, the five women and two men, whose education had prepared them to teach German in a country where the German language and culture had been labeled morally unacceptable? What was he to say to the others in attendance at the graduation ceremonies, mostly members of the German-American community, whose loyalty to their new homeland was under constant question and whose own positions and sentiments—as Hohlfeld fully realized—were perhaps not clearly defined?

Hohlfeld, himself a German-American of German birth and training, did not seek an easy way out. His speech contains no hollow platitudes or empty promises to those who received their diplomas that day. It does not avoid the political issues and realities of the time. On the contrary, Hohlfeld seems to have used the occasion to search his conscience and make a bold and open declaration of his own position. He carefully outlines the factors which had caused difficulties for the German-Americans: (1) the fact that most of them had held pro-German sympathies during the period of America's neutrality toward the war in Europe and could not change their convictions from one day to the next upon America's entry into the war; (2) the lack of understanding or consideration shown by most Americans toward the difficult position in which German-Americans found themselves; and (3) the fanatic attacks on the part of many Americans against members of the German-American community, treatment which Hohlfeld terms "injustice" and "unmerited abuse." He argues that German-American resentment to this unfair treatment has caused them to overlook the changes in Germany's position, where the war had become a war of aggression, and that of the United States, where President Wilson's war aims "[look] with faith and vision toward a just and stable ordering of the international affairs of the world." Hohlfeld urges German-Americans to maintain a pride in their heritage and in their contribution to the greatness and success of their new homeland. But he urges them at the same time to a patriotic and unrestrained support of America's war effort, stating that only if "we German-Americans do our part" in the struggle, will there be any possibility of rebuilding "some of the things dear to us and, we are convinced, of value to our country."

Hohlfeld's speech is patriotic. At the same time it is so forthright in its consideration of the difficulties of the German-Americans and the resentment and intolerance with which they had been treated that it was probably inevitable that Hohlfeld should be attacked for it. *The Milwaukee Journal* of 21 June 1918 published a lengthy account under the headline "Ill-Treated, He Complains: German Teachers Told Wave of Hatred is against Them: Prof. Hohlfeld, Trustee of German Teachers' Seminary, Excuses Efforts in Behalf of Germany Prior to U.S. Entering War." Quoting at length from Hohlfeld's speech, *The Milwaukee Journal* also shortened, summarized, and reworded the text, resulting in at least one serious misquotation and a general misrepresentation of Hohlfeld's position. But the protests did not stop there. Theodore M. Hammond, President of the Regents of the University of Wisconsin, and Professor C. R. Fish of the Department of History both wrote to Charles R. Van Hise, President of the University, concerning Hohlfeld's address as it had been reported in the newspapers.[1] The *Milwaukee-Herold,* one of Milwaukee's German-language newspapers, on the other hand, also published an account of Hohlfeld's speech under the title "Der Geist der Zeit," fully recognizing its patriotic intent and character (22 June 1918).

Hohlfeld's speech was courageous. It was also very timely and is interesting to us today as a historical document. Beyond this, however, it has a timelessness characteristic of all great addresses and contains a message of lasting validity for all students and teachers of multi-national and cross-cultural disciplines.

Never before published, this address can be found in the University Archives of the University of Wisconsin in Madison.[2] It is a typewritten manuscript containing many handwritten additions and changes, as well as numerous typographical errors and other small mistakes. The text is reproduced here in full, with obvious small errors corrected.

CORA LEE NOLLENDORFS

Members of the Graduating Class,
Friends and Patrons of the Seminary,
Ladies and Gentlemen:

It was not my good fortune to be present at the graduating exercises of the Seminary a year ago. I cannot, therefore, make any comparison, based on real knowledge, between the general atmosphere and spirit of your gathering then and of our gathering tonight. We were in the World War then as we are in the World War now; and I can take it for granted that this supreme fact colored and inspired the utterances of your speakers then as it is bound to be the fundamental and predominant note in the thoughts and feelings of every one of us today.

And yet, what a difference, what an enormous difference between today and a year ago! The very fact that the faculty of the Seminary requested me—and I feel convinced that their request was a wise one—to deviate from the natural and time-honored custom of this institution and make my remarks to you tonight not in German, but in English, this apparently insignificant fact alone, I say, is symbol and proof of the profound change which we all have lived through during the past twelve months.

Two things, I feel sure, not even the wisest and most farsighted among us foresaw at that time: first, the gigantic and almost superhuman proportions of the undertaking, no doubt without parallel in all the annals of history, upon which our nation had set forth and which only gradually unfolded itself to us in its far-reaching claims upon each and every citizen, rich and poor, young and old, native-born and foreign-born, men and women, body and soul, in short, its claims upon all we have, and all we are; and second, the furious wave of hatred and suspicion which, despite the earnest warnings of some of the voices of wisdom and courage and without regard for fairness or for truth, has been let loose against large groups and numberless individuals of that German-American population to which belong most of us assembled here tonight, and against all interests, no matter how restrained and legitimate, in German language and literature, music and art, scholarship and education, which this institution traditionally has tried to foster in a spirit of patriotic service, and as an unselfish contribution to the national life of our country and its people.

These two things have profoundly affected the lives and destinies of every one of us, and, aside from all other minor factors of more local or personal nature, it is they which explain why our gathering of today is bound to be suggestive of infinitely more complex problems and infinitely more exacting issues than your first war commencement of a year ago.

As long as our own country had not entered the war, the great mass of Americans of German birth and descent—and, hence, in all probability almost all of you to whom I am now speaking—had been sympathizing with the Central Powers, especially with Germany, in what appeared to us as a titanic struggle for self-preservation against apparently overwhelming odds. It was not merely the voice of blood or race, strongly as we felt its impelling call, that we followed, blindly and without reason or without weighing the evidence before us; but we saw in the war as it had broken out in Europe the terrible and perhaps inevitable result of long years of national rivalries, suspicions and intrigues of which all the European nations had been guilty and whereby Germany and her ally had finally been forced into a position of exasperated self-defense against a powerful ring of relentless enemies openly avowing their purpose of crushing and dismembering their antagonists.

I am inclined to think that, even then, however, most of us, although distinctly pro-German in our general sympathies, were consistently opposed to the idea of a peace of annexation and spoils for either side in the conflict. Just because we were willing to grant that Germany was justified in her plea of self-defense, for that very reason we were decided to take her by her word and to demand that her actions should unmistakably prove the honesty of her contention. We therefore hoped—and fain would hope even now—that in Germany the liberal and democratic forces, to which as Americans with American instincts and ideals of government we were bound to pin our faith, would assert themselves triumphantly over the strongly entrenched elements of reaction and aggression. Thus we were not hoping for a German peace, but for a peace of justice and of international conciliation, for a settlement that would not merely lay the foundation for future wars, but which would bear within it at least a reasonable promise of a lasting and genuine peace among the nations of the world.

We also believed that such an end might be attained more certainly if our country were to exercise its powerful influence in the role of a great neutral arbiter rather than as an immediate participant in the war itself. Thus we hoped that America might stay out of the conflict as long as such a course was compatible with our national honor and safety.

The question now is not whether that position, which we then took, has been proved right or wrong by the subsequent course of events, but merely whether it was honestly taken and sincerely based on views not foreign to the best traditions of American life and thought. That that was the case we unhesitatingly maintain, pointing to the fact that many prominent Americans of non-German descent, who could not possibly be suspected of purely racial prejudices, analyzed the situation as it then existed as we did, and took the same stand that we took.

As long, therefore, as the momentous question of peace and war hung in the balance we claimed the right and duty belonging to the responsible citizen of a democratic commonwealth, of voicing our convictions. We used, as best we knew how, the freedom of petition, press, and assembly vouchsafed to us under the constitution, in the interest of peace. For all this, which has now become past history but which only later generations will be able to judge impartially and dispassionately, we have no apologies to offer; no one has any right to demand any.

But now came the first great turning point. We were bound to admit that we had had as full and fair a chance as could be expected under the circumstances to voice and defend and urge our views; but, when the final test in Congress came, the other side, which, from equally strong and sincere convictions, had from the beginning taken the opposite stand, was shown to be overwhelmingly in the majority. As citizens of America, to which we owed our undivided and unconditional allegiance and patriotic devotion, we all of a sudden found ourselves at war with Germany, which we instinctively loved as the land from whose people we had sprung.

Truly a tragic and soul-trying situation; especially in view of the fact that for almost three years our emotions had all been attuned to a definite and convinced stand which we were now no longer permitted to maintain and that there were no foreign forces threatening our shores against which all of us would have leaped with a bound and with all the fervor of true patriots.

For a while many of us no doubt were stunned. To be sure, we recognized instantaneously and confessed unflinchingly the immediate consequences resulting from the decision that had gone against us: the necessity of loyally supporting the majority will of the nation and the measures adopted by the government for carrying on the war. With negligible exceptions, we were prepared to render service, to yield our children, to bear the burdens of taxation, to do all the government required of us to help win the war.

Our feelings and convictions, however, it is needless to say, we could not change from one day to the next. Sentiments cannot be dictated to at will, and we should not have deserved much respect and certainly would not have proved the most desirable qualities of heart and character if we had been capable of any such presto change of what we are wont to call instincts and conviction. In fact, any sound psychologist—and what leader of public opinion can afford not to be a sound psychologist?—will have to admit that the best and most loyal American citizens of German blood and ancestry will inevitably exhibit, and continue to exhibit, in regard to many matters connected with the war, different intellectual and emotional reactions from those of their fellow citizens not of German descent. The more ungrudgingly this right would have been granted to us, the more quickly and unreservedly we would have been able to merge ourselves in the general consciousness of the country in regard to the great undertaking in which we had engaged.

But unfortunately no such understanding or consideration was shown us or, to be just, it was accorded to our difficult position only in some sporadic cases by men of real vision and true insight. The loudest voices of the day were those of men with narrow outlook and fanatic intolerance. Through their unbridled and unjust denunciations born of arbitrary suspicion and instinctive hatred a golden opportunity was, if not lost, at least dangerously delayed. Suspicion bred resentment, rancor called forth exasperation, persecution led at best to sullen silence, but no progress was thus made in winning over hearts and feelings.

This has brought me to that second element which, as I have said before, has tended to produce so great a change between conditions as they were a year ago, and as they are now: the unjust and often fanatic attacks against loyal citizens merely because it is German blood that is flowing in their veins, as well as against the German language and everything German, no matter how remote it may be from the war policies of the German government against which we are fighting.

This unfortunately is not a matter of past history. We are in its very midst, and the wave has not yet spent its initial violence. In some form or other this state of affairs affects directly and keenly almost every one of us in our social and business relations; it affects especially the work of an institution like the German American Teachers Seminary and the life plans of these very students, who, by dint of hard and devoted work, have successfully completed their course of study and prepared themselves for a career as teachers of German.

This is neither the place nor the hour to attempt an analysis of this bewildering phenomenon, although to the future historian it will be an interesting task to examine into all of its causes and impartially distribute blame and responsibility. I do not mean to say that we German-Americans can claim to be wholly without fault, but if in some respects we erred and if individuals among us even may have erred grievously, all this stands in no proportion to the fury of public recrimination and resentment that has descended upon us. We know, most of it is inseparable from war as such; much is the result of the very democracy of our institutions; we also know and admit that the government itself is not responsible for this state of affairs—yea, men close to the government have tried and are still trying to stem the tide of the worst abuses and of the most dangerous hysteria, and President Wilson has always been careful to differentiate those things against which we have taken up arms from those that are outside, and should remain outside, the pale of our warfare against Germany.

For all of that, the sad fact remains—as I see the situation—that in consequence of so much injustice and unmerited abuse many of our best German-Americans, especially those who were born abroad, were hardened to an attitude of protest and resentment to such a degree as to remain insensitive to the enormous changes which, since our entry into the war, have taken place in the international situation. The situation—we cannot and must not blind ourselves to that fact—is at present vastly different from what it was in August, 1914, or in April, 1917. In fact, it is so different that if we had been confronted with it from the start, I feel convinced that our attitude would have been very different, too, in many respects. A few high points must suffice here to indicate what changes I have reference to.

Russia, that awful stumbling block for any theory of a war of democracy against autocracy, has been eliminated from the combination of anti-German forces; the rest of the Allies, under pressure, no doubt, from our side, have seen fit to modify their original imperialistic war aims as they stood revealed through the secret treaties published by the Bolsheviki; Germany, far from being in the precarious position of a nation fighting for her self-preservation, seems quite to have passed under the sway of those of its leaders that stand for military aggression, reactionary politics, and imperialistic expansion; and, last not least, through President Wilson's memorable messages delivered at the beginning of this year the fear was dispelled that our entry into the war would merely help the Allies to achieve selfish objects of aggression and expansion. No matter what one's attitude might be toward some of the details of this broad formulation of our war aims, so much was certain that in all those fundamental aspects on which the President dwelt with unmistakable vigor, his was a program that actually looked with faith and vision toward a just and stable ordering of the international affairs of the world.

Such far-reaching changes in the original situation demand of us, it seems to me, more than the unquestioned will to do our full duty in the support of the war. They demand that in their light we should critically re-examine our original attitude and earlier judgements and make all necessary adjustments courageously and openly.

I for one, at any rate, regret it deeply that a collective and truly imposing expression of the position of German-Americans was not brought about some time early this spring when conditions would have seemed ripe for it. That a feeling of the desirability and value of such a manifestation lived among some of our best elements, I know. But, leaderless as we have been, nobody seemed to be able to find the freeing word of compelling power and irresistible convincingness. Among the efforts made, I wish to call to your attention at least that stirring little book of Hermann Hagedorn, *Where Do You Stand?*, in which alone I found that mingling of sincere love and sympathy with a stern insistence on the inevitable demands of the hour that to me rang true and that alone can hope to succeed where harsh coercion and unfeeling denunciation are bound to remain powerless if not to do more harm than good. It is not necessary to subscribe to all the views of the author in order to feel that the general spirit of his appeal was of the right kind, and I would urge each one of you who has not already done so to read that little book and solemnly ask himself the question: Where do I stand?

Whether a nation-wide declaration on our part would have done much to stem the tide of popular feeling, I do not know. I should have liked to see it done even if it had not produced any such result. At present, I fear, there is nothing that we can do as German-Americans that will prove of help. When Professor Kuno Francke, who in the early stages of the war was held up to us as a model citizen, did try in public print to give an honest man's reply to Mr. Hagedorn's question he was brutally vilified and cynically ridiculed as a disloyal citizen and little better than a traitor.

What then shall we do under these circumstances? I have only one answer, and I address it not only to you, my young friends, but to all of you who are proud and not ashamed to be American citizens of German ancestry.

Continue to be proud of your blood and conscious of the worth of what men and women of your blood have been doing and are doing today for the greatness and success of this our country which we desire to see as strong, as united, as beneficent in its service to mankind as the most favored of nations has ever been. In this spirit, rise above the distress of the hour and do not let your grievances, severe as they may be, dampen the ardor of your patriotism, and trust to your future vindication. Continue to do your full duty as loyal citizens, and more than that full duty, which the country asks of you to help win the war, and do it ungrudgingly. Do not fasten your eyes so much on the flaws and defects as on the virtues and promises of this our country. On the contrary, try to deepen and purify your Americanism by going to the fountain heads of what is best and truest in American ideals and aspirations. Steep yourself, now more than ever, in the thoughts of men like Lincoln and Emerson, of Lowell and Whitman, and of just those of our great figures of thought and action which have best personified true Americanism. Apply these standards in a fair, but critical and unbiased way to an estimate of the ideals and institutions of modern German life. Do not let the great achievements of the German genius in so many fields of human endeavor blind you to short-comings and anach-ronisms in just those spheres of political and social life that are so dear to the American heart. If there is much that America has learned or could still learn from Germany, emphasize now the fact that also Germany has a great deal to learn from America. The movement toward political free-dom or what broadly we call democracy, and the idea of an international organization in some sort of a universal league of nations are the two pillars on which the best men of all countries more and more base their hopes for a better future of the world. Both of these ideals are typically American and foremost in all our discussions of the issues of the war; both have met with but little favor in those circles that control the political destinies of Germany. Let us hope that through our struggle and victory they may be made triumphant the world over and help usher in a new era of life here and abroad.

Only if in this struggle—as in the past great crises in our national life—we German-Americans do our part manfully and unreservedly in a spirit of consistent Americanism, do I see any hope that after peace is restored, in the time of reconstruction, we may be able to rebuild some of the things dear to us and, we are convinced, of value to our country.

Let me express the fervent wish that this time may not be too far off and that it may be granted to all of us to see this happy day and to contribute to the realization of these our hopes and prayers.

Notes

1 For more concerning this, see pp. 186–87 of this volume.
2 In the General Correspondence file of President Charles R. Van Hise (Series 4/10/1, Box 67, file on A. R. Hohlfeld, University of Wisconsin Archives).

Speaking and Teaching German in Iowa during World War I: A Historical Perspective

REINHOLD K. BUBSER
University of Northern Iowa

Settlement by German Immigrants in Iowa

The rich soil and the wide-open prairie of Iowa attracted settlers from various ethnic groups: the German contingent was one of the largest. In the decade between 1850 and 1860 the population of Iowa almost doubled. There had been a considerable influx of citizens from New England and the Middle States, as well as of foreign citizens, especially from the various German states, Scandinavia, Holland, and the British Isles. The Federal Census of 1860 showed that more than 38,000 Iowa citizens had come from the German States, compared to about 11,000 from England and 28,000 from Ireland.[1]

German settlements were concentrated in the counties bordering on the Mississippi River. In these five counties, the German-speaking people around 1895 reached almost eighty percent of the total population, while more than 40 out of almost 100 counties in Iowa had been settled by immigrants of German descent at a rate of twenty-five to forty-nine percent.[2] At one time, school children in Iowa read in their history books that "so many Schleswig-Holsteiners settled in Scott County that it has been called a new Schleswig-Holstein."[3] In addition, three distinctly German-speaking settlements in Iowa were able to preserve their language and heritage to a larger degree and for a longer time than any other group, largely due to their religious orientation and relative group cohesiveness. Most notable are the Amana colonies, the Amish-Mennonite settlements in Kalona (Washington County), Oelwein (Fayette County), Independence (Buchanan County), and the Low German communities of Schleswig (Crawford County), Holstein (Ida County), Mt. Carmel, and Breda (Carroll County).[4]

The period between 1850 (when the major influx of settlers began) and 1914 was characterized by continuous German language usage in many towns and villages throughout Iowa. Churches, parochial schools, social organizations, and cultural societies retained the native language as a means for most of their communications and interactions. The first generation immigrants also shaped the period culturally and economically. The native language appeared in newspapers such as the daily *Der Demokrat,* published in Davenport and edited by August P. Richter. This particular newspaper enjoyed the widest circulation of all foreign-language newspapers in the state. German was taught as an academic subject in high schools and institutions of higher education, leading to the claim that German had become the most popular foreign language in the state's high schools.[5] To prepare teachers properly in a more "universal public education," the teacher training curriculum at Iowa State Normal School (Cedar Falls) included foreign language education in Latin, Greek, German, and French.[6]

With the onset of the United States' engagement in World War I (6 April 1917), however, speaking a foreign language or clinging to transmitted customs was considered a disloyal act from which serious legal, social, and even physical consequences could arise. Communicating in English became the language litmus test for loyalty to the new country. Consequently, the German-American communities, as well as most other immigrant groups, particularly those in Iowa, were left with no choice but to abandon the inherited ways of communicating and socializing.

1918 and the Effects on Foreign Languages in Iowa

The entry of the United States into the war also marked the passage of federal legislation such as the Espionage Act, which required that all foreign-language publications take a pro-American stand or refrain from publishing. In addition, the emergence of war-related social and economic undertakings tested and demonstrated the loyalty of the immigrants. Included in these programs were: war bonds, liberty bonds and victory loans; patriotic organizations, such as the American Legion and the "Lincoln Patriotic Army"; and civilian councils, including the "Council for Defense" and the "Patriotic Investigation Council."[7] Where the so-called "hyphenated Americans" failed to cooperate with these patriotic organizations or responded slowly or inadequately to their call for the purchase of war bonds, they were coerced into submission through threats, intimidation, and castigation.

The governor of Iowa during the war years, William Lloyd Harding, a lawyer and Republican politician, issued a proclamation (23 May 1918) banning the use of all foreign languages.[8] This state edict has also become known as the "Babel Proclamation." The stress of international conflict led to a decline in the application of reasonable measures and in the principle of the United States as a melting pot for people of all nations. In Iowa the government specifically corroborated the hostile sentiments of the general populace by passing a decree that was designed to abolish the

A Proclamation

To the People of Rock Valley:

Whereas, W. L. Harding, Governor of the State of Iowa, having issued by PROCLAMATION the following rules regulating the use of *Foreign Languages;* your attention is hereby publically called to same and you are earnestly requested to co-operate in this patriotic attempt to promote peace and harmony and to assist in the WINNING of the WAR by strictly observing these rules which should obtain in IOWA during the war:

1. English should and must be the only medium of instruction in public, private, denominational or other similar schools.

2. Conversation in public places, on trains and over telephones should be in the English language.

3. All public addresses should be in the English language.

4. Let those who cannot speak or understand the English language conduct their religious worship in their homes.

                                    By Order of the Mayor
                                    C. W. JACOBS (Acting)
F. F. COCROFT, Clerk.

Dated Rock Valley, Iowa, June 1, 1918.

Figure 1. "Babel Proclamation"

study of foreign languages in the state. The war and reports of atrocities in Europe amplified anti-German emotions in the United States. The final phase of the war also produced the culmination of growing chauvinism in the general populace and the manifestation of widespread xenophobia. Governor Harding acquired the dubious distinction of being the only head of state in the United States who had made the speaking of a foreign language a criminal act. Some municipalities copied the governor's decree and disseminated it in their local newspapers (see figure 1). For the duration of the war, the declaration specified that English must be the only medium of instruction in public, private, or denominational schools. All conversations in public places and all public addresses had to be conducted in the English language. Finally, the ban decreed: "Let those who cannot speak or understand the English language conduct their religious worship in their homes."[9]

Since the language ban did not single out German, the other immigrant segments of the state felt that they were unduly punished for actions of others over which they had no control. While very few Iowans would have argued with the governor's action if it had been directed solely towards the German-speaking contingent, they were unwilling to submit to the state's law when it applied to them. Scandinavian and Dutch settlements in particular felt that they had been indiscriminately included and persecuted by the government's action. The "Babel Proclamation" provoked the wrath of teachers, preachers, and average citizens. In their letters to the editors of local and state newspapers the affected citizens protested against the government's decree. They resented the calling into question of their patriotism when they felt they had contributed more than their fair share by buying liberty bonds and war savings stamps, and had supported the Red Cross and YMCA.

Letters in the newspapers and editorials raised serious questions about the efficacy of the proclamation: Does the use of the official language bar disloyal thoughts? Will the language ban help to win the war? Other writers deplored the lack of clarity in the language ban; in their opinion the edict was susceptible to wide differences of interpretation. Most agreed that the government had overstepped its authority because Iowa was not under martial law and all effective orders had to be issued in accordance with civil authority. An editorial in the *Des Moines Register* warned of the consequences of the governor's action: ". . . nothing but mischief is going to come from an attempt here in Iowa to do what the Russian czar was never able to do, and what the emperor of Austria with the backing of Germany was never able to do. . . . What has happened here in Iowa to warrant an action the federal government has never considered necessary?"[10] An article in the *Cedar Rapids Gazette* condemned the language order as "unfortunate because unnecessary and because it fastens upon him [Governor Harding] the charge of playing politics. . . . It will be charged that Governor Harding, fearing that he had estranged the German element by former orders, sought to appease that element by proof that he meant to treat all foreign language citizens alike—to make no exception of them."[11]

Those who favored the Proclamation reasoned that the use of foreign languages was the biggest factor keeping the United States from melting into one great nation. Consequently, they felt that the governor's ban on foreign languages acted as the "blender" by precipitating the inevitable process of integration, whereas to continue the use of foreign languages would only have reinforced the clannishness of the community and "created in this country the same conditions, from which the parents fled to America."[12] Similarly, Lafayette Young, head of the Council on Defense, argued that "the study of the language prejudices the mind in favor of the people of that country . . ."[13] The Sac county newspaper found this statement rather absurd and raised the question whether the study of English prior to the Civil War tended to perpetuate slavery. In a resolution addressed to school administrators the Iowa Council on National Defense demanded that schools stop teaching German because "it is against every patriotic interest. This language assists in keeping our people apart while unity is necessary if the republic is to continue. It is no sacrifice to anybody to discontinue the teaching of German."[14] The resolutions by patriotic groups and the state government had a severe effect on several German teachers: in May of 1918 twenty-seven German teachers were released from their jobs in Davenport.[15]

The immediate effect of the edict on the study of foreign languages in Iowa defies a clear assessment since the ban was not carried out uniformly. Records indicate that foreign languages continued to be taught and used in some schools, colleges, and churches. Despite the order of the State Superintendent of Public Instruction to abolish the teaching of German in all Iowa schools, the city schools in Cedar Falls continued German language courses, practicing the acquired knowledge by translating President Wilson's speeches into German. On the other hand, the enrollment in German courses at the college level decreased to the point of extinction.

The outlawing of foreign languages was followed by a campaign of book burning described in the *Des Moines Capital:* "The Hohenzollern propaganda in public school books used here has been sent to the dirt pile. When the students returned from their summer vacation today all reference to the Kaiser Bill and his aggregation had been depleted [sic]."[16]

The word German had to be eliminated from signs, buildings and company names. Towns changed their names: Guttenberg once again became Prairie-la-Porte. The "German Savings Bank" turned into the "American Savings Bank," and German measles were called "liberty measles." German language newspapers folded; names were changed or anglicized.[17]

Those who were caught speaking German in public were attacked and rebuked. Often violators of the language ban were denounced by telephone operators or party-line users. Private citizens took it upon themselves to enforce the language proclamation. Painting a house yellow was a frequently used means of punishing a person for having spoken a foreign language.[18]

Ministers of German descent became the most frequent targets of violent actions, especially if they held services in German. In many cases, their churches had parochial schools attached to them which had in the past helped maintain the homogeneity of the ethnic group. Many parochial schools closed for the remainder of the war and services were held in English "to allay the mob spirit."[19]

Antagonism against Germans easily turned into harassment of all other ethnic groups as well. Even though Holland had to be considered an anti-German country, the "Holland Christian School" in Sully (Jasper County), which was holding classes in Dutch, was burned to the ground.[20]

Representatives of other ethnic groups openly defied the language ban and continued to preach and pray in their native tongue. They argued that no power on earth had the right to dictate what language they used in their religious services. During an address at the Memorial Day patriotic meeting at the Grand View College, a predominantly Danish institution, the minister defiantly used the Danish language to dedicate the service flag, representing the former students who were in the military service against Germany and her allies: "We are here to dedicate the service flag. I am not using the English language in compliance with the recent proclamation of our governor. I believe this proclamation to be unjust, unlawful, unconstitutional, and even pro-German in effect if not in intention."[21]

While ethnic groups of Scandinavian or Dutch descent found it easy to resist the language ban, small ethnic contingents with a predominantly German heritage, like the "Society of True Inspirationists" or "Amanas," had little choice but to submit to the governmental decree.

Historical Perspective of the Amana Colonies

Communal Amana had retained most of the cultural traditions from the year 1714, when this Pietist sect was established in Germany by Eberhard Gruber (1665–1728) and Johann Rock (1678–1749). After a period of decline, the "Community of True Inspiration," was revived under a new leader, Christian Metz. Intolerance towards their religious views in the early days of the movement's existence caused the Inspirationists to leave Hessen, cross the Atlantic, and buy land in the vicinity of Buffalo, New York, in 1843. Shortly thereafter, between 1854 and 1864, in order to escape the high land prices in the Buffalo region and the growing temptations of city life, the whole group gradually moved to its present location.

Around the turn of the century each of the seven villages had its own public school operated with state funds and subject to state laws. The teachers were members of the Community but were educated at institutions of higher learning, like any other teacher in the state of Iowa. Students between the ages of five and fourteen had to attend school six days a week and 52 weeks a year. The school curriculum consisted of three distinct categories: (1) the *Lehrschule,* where formal learning took place; (2) the *Spielstunde,* when the children played German games; and (3) the *Arbeits-*

schule, where instruction in handicrafts and trades was given. Only male teachers taught in the *Lehrschule,* while some women worked at the *Arbeitsschule* as "working teachers."

The governor's ban on the usage of German demanded rapid adaptations to the evolving conditions. Beginning in May 1918, church services consisted of Bible reading and hymn singing, in German nonetheless, with the congregation sitting in silence for the remainder of the service. Since very few people other than the colonies' leaders could speak English, German remained the language for daily communication. Although German textbooks had to be exchanged for English editions by the fall of 1918, the instruction for beginners continued to take place completely in German.[22] In the more advanced classes students learned German and English on a parallel basis: "The English texts of the United States History, Physiology, and Geography [were] translated into German; and the German texts of the other branches [were] translated into the English paragraph by paragraph."[23]

The use of the German language was an essential ingredient in the preservation of the homogeneity of the Amanas since it served to provide religious and cultural instruction and thereby helped to maintain the relative isolation of the group from secular influences: "Reasons for remaining in the community were especially strong in the Society's first two or three decades in America when, situated in a foreign culture, the community provided both familiarity—customs, language, faith, relatives, and friends—and security in form of food, clothing, shelter, and employment."[24] The "Babel Proclamation" severely curtailed the teaching of German in the Amana communities and, to a lesser degree, it affected the cultural and religious traditions and the cohesion of the communities which had always been challenged from the outside. As a result of the language ban, however, the use and instruction of German in the Amana schools never returned to the prominent position held before 1918.

Long-range Effects of the "Babel Proclamation"

At the end of World War I in November 1918, the damage to foreign language use and study had been paralyzing, even though Governor Harding's edict was later declared unconstitutional by the State Supreme Court. Nevertheless, on 10 April 1919, the 38th General Assembly enacted yet another law "requiring that instruction in secular subjects in all schools in Iowa, public or private, had to be in the English language. Foreign languages could be taught above the eighth grade only. To further the Americanization of all Iowans, the Assembly also passed a law requiring citizenship instruction to be given in all schools."[25] Ironically, on the national level, President Woodrow Wilson had previously recommended that, for the Fourth of July celebration in 1918, naturalized citizens of the United States give patriotic speeches in their native languages.[26]

While we cannot argue that the historical and political events after 1914 were the direct cause of the decline or abolition of foreign language use and study—especially German, it is quite evident from the records that these events accelerated the demise of foreign languages in the state and facilitated the assimilation of relatively small religiously oriented groups of German descent into the societal mainstream. Through these internal political decisions, coupled with Germany's involvement in two world wars, the study of the German language in the State of Iowa lost its leading position.

The study of foreign languages in Iowa today reflects the same trends that persist nationwide. A survey conducted in the 1974–75 school year indicated that in public and private schools the study of Spanish (18,290 students) ranks before French (9,355 students) and German (5,542 students).[27] Whether or not this trend is the direct result of the "Babel Proclamation" remains open to speculation.

Notes

1 *Studies in Iowa History* (January 1970) 66–67.
2 Cf. James R. Dow, "Deutsch als Muttersprache in Iowa," in *Deutsch als Muttersprache in den Vereinigten Staaten,* (Wiesbaden: Franz Steiner, 1979)1: 91–117.
3 T. P. Christensen, *The Hawkeye State* (Iowa City: Athens Press, 1956) 78.
4 Dow 97.
5 Christensen 78.
6 William C. Lang, "Higher Education in Cedar Falls: Town and Gown in the First Hundred Years," *The Palimpsest* 64. 3 (1983): 72.
7 The *Des Moines Register,* 1 June 1918: 2, reported from New York: "To conduct a campaign of patriotic education in the industrial centers of the country and to co-operate with the government 'in vigorous prosecution of the war' the Lincoln Patriotic army was organized here today with Gen. Coleman du Pont as its commander in chief."
8 William L. Harding, "Iowa War Proclamation," *Iowa and the War* 13 (July 1918): 45–46.
9 "Orders German Language Out Of All Schools In Iowa," *Des Moines Register,* 26 May 1918: M–10.
10 "Iowa Should Act," *Des Moines Register,* 30 May 1918: 6.
11 "Harding's Language Order," reprinted in the *Des Moines Register,* 29 May 1918: 6.
12 *Des Moines Register,* letters to the editor, 4 June 1918: 4.
13 Nancy Ruth Derr, "Iowans during World War I: A Study of Change under Stress," diss., George Washington University, 1978, 466.
14 Derr 467.
15 Ibid. 470.

16 Ibid. 465.

17 Nancy Ruth Derr, "The Babel Proclamation," *The Palimpsest* 60.4 (1979): 103.

18 Derr, "Iowans" 281.

19 Ibid. 474.

20 Ibid. 475.

21 "Danish College Dedicates Flag," *Des Moines Register*, 31 May 1918: 3.

22 Derr, "Iowans" 246.

23 Bertha M. H. Shambaugh, *Amana, The Community of True Inspiration* (Iowa City: State Historical Society, 1908) 208.

24 Jonathan G. Andelson, "The Double Bind and Social Change in Communal Amana," *Human Relations* 34. 2 (1981): 120.

25 *Acts and Joint Resolutions Passed at the Regular Session of the 38th General Assembly of the State of Iowa*, (1919) 219.

26 Leola Allen, "Anti-German Sentiments in Iowa during World War I," *Annals of Iowa* 42 (1974): 421.

27 Karl Odwarka, "German in the Iowa Schools," *Die Unterrichtspraxis* 10. 1 (1977): 85–90.

From New York to Philadelphia: Issues and Concerns of the American Association of Teachers of German between 1926 and 1970

GERHARD WEISS
University of Minnesota

The American Association of Teachers of German was founded in 1926 in the hope that such an organization would rejuvenate and strengthen the teaching of German on the high school and college levels after the erosions suffered as the result of the First World War. The organization was modeled after the eminently successful American Association of Teachers of Spanish, which had helped to propel that language to a major place in the American school curriculum. While skeptics were disturbed by yet another "national" language organization sapping strength from the foreign language profession as a whole, its proponents spoke eloquently of the common cause that united all teachers of German in their attempt to reestablish their language as a subject of cultural and economic importance for American students.

The development of the AATG is closely intertwined with the fate of the study of German since the 1920s. An examination of the early years offers interesting vistas of the struggle of our profession. Many of the issues debated then are still with us today. The AATG has not resolved them, but it has offered a forum for their discussion.

Compared to the American Association of Teachers of Spanish (founded in 1917), the AATG is a relative latecomer. However, by some stretch of the imagination one might establish an ancestry that leads back to the nineteenth century, to the time when German became a major instructional subject in American schools. That was the time of massive German immigration and the period when German began to dominate the fields of science and technology. The first call to form an association came from the teachers of the Cincinnati Public Schools who, in November of 1863, proclaimed: "Säumet nicht, werte Amtsbrüder, den ersten Schritt zu tun, und aus der Isoliertheit, in welcher Ihr Euch befindet, herauszutreten und uns die Hand zu reichen zu einer allgemeinen Verbrüderung des deutschen Lehrerstandes Nord-Amerikas."[1]

The actual realization of this dream did not occur until a few years later. The *Louisville Anzeiger* of 22 March 1870 reported:

Trotzdem die Deutschen, denen die Erhaltung ihrer Muttersprache in diesem
Lande am Herzen liegt, allerorts deutschamerikanische Schulen gegründet
haben, um ihre Sprache auf die kommenden Generationen zu übertragen,
damit die kulturgeschichtliche Mission des deutschen Elements erfüllt werde,
so läßt sich dennoch nicht leugnen, daß die gemachten Anstrengungen nicht
entsprechende Resultate zur Folge hatten. Insbesondere liegt dies an dem
Mangel einer Organisation der deutschen Lehrer, deren vereinzelte Tätigkeit
nach keiner Richtung hin befriedigen kann. Eine feste Organisation der Lehrer
und Schulfreunde tut darum not, und durch jährliche Versammlungen . . . soll
dieselbe vorerst angebahnt werden. (*Monatshefte* 19: 218)

We can see how strongly the nationalistic spirit that prevailed in Germany
at that time had also permeated the teachers of German in this country.
The federation of teachers that now evolved had as its goal the teaching
of the German language and literature alongside the dominant English, the
education of truly free American citizens, the furtherance of a "natur-
gemäße (entwickelnde) Erziehung in Schule und Haus" and the protection
of the intellectual and material interests of German teachers in America
(*Monatshefte* 19: 219). The journalistic enthusiasm of the *Louisville Anzeiger* suggests a case of severe cultural jingoism. A newly formed organization, the Nationaler Deutschamerikanischer Lehrerbund, held annual
meetings, usually in the Midwest, especially in cities like Milwaukee and
Cincinnati. One of its *Jahrestagungen* even took the members to Berlin
(1912) where they were cordially received by German educators and officials. The association also published a journal, *Pädagogische Monatshefte*, later to be called *Monatshefte für deutsche Sprache und Pädagogik*,
the precursor of our present *Monatshefte*. Both the organization and its
journal fell victim to changing times and especially to the anti-German
climate during and shortly after World War I.

While the Lehrerbund had been founded to meet the challenge of an
ever-increasing interest in German, the American Association of Teachers
of German (its English name is also significant), on the other hand, was
organized to prevent the total disintegration of the teaching of German,
which had already been so badly eroded that only a few high schools and
colleges still offered it. In 1914–15, more than 265,000 high school students
studied the language; ten years later, in 1925, this number had shrunk to
a mere 32,870. German, once in first place as foreign language, now had
fallen to a pathetic third. French comprised 56%, Spanish had rapidly
increased to 39%, and German had dropped to a dismal 4.4%.[2] The phenomenal growth of Spanish following the war had been ascribed by many
foreign language teachers, in part at least, to the activities of the newly
formed American Association of Teachers of Spanish. The teachers of
German hoped to duplicate this success with a similarly dynamic organization.[3] It was not methodological concerns but rather the need for survival

that prompted the teachers of metropolitan New York to come together at Columbia University on 18 December 1926. They were following an earnest invitation:

Wenn unserm Lande der deutsche Unterricht mit seiner weittragenden Bedeutung für unsere kulturelle und wirtschaftliche Entwicklung erhalten bleiben soll, dann bedarf es des einmütigen Zusammenstehens der Lehrer dieser Sprache, ganz gleich in welchem Staate unseres Landes, in welcher Anstalt und in welcher Stellung sie ihre Berufstätigkeit ausüben. (*GQ* 12: 21)

The new organization was to bring together the high school teacher and the scholar in a "great national blending of all teachers of German."[4] Its aims were "to spread the knowledge of German in this country by increasing the efficiency of the teaching of German (*GQ* 1: 4). This "efficiency," a somewhat unhappy word, the founders believed could be achieved through a psychological and curricular renewal. Psychologically, teachers would be rejuvenated through "strength in numbers." If a large number of German teachers banded together, they might regain their self-esteem, their self-confidence, their energy. They could shake off their sense of isolation and frustration. But even more important was the emphasis on the curricular renewal, to make it reflect the "new Germany." The writing of new textbooks had to be encouraged (*GQ* 1: 5): "Now that Germany presents a wholly new face, now that some of the greatest masters of modern prose have appeared there, should we be doing our duty unless we insisted on the publication of texts more modern and hence more vital to our students than those we have been thumbing for decades?" The founding manifesto concluded with these stirring words:

Knowledge of German, as every intelligent person admits, must once more become a vital factor in our national life. A large body of excellent teachers of German can in signal fashion help to bring this about. And such a group working shoulder to shoulder with teachers of other languages will be in position to do its share towards fulfilling that ideal dear to the heart of every one of us: to make American culture richer and more many-sided than any in history. (*GQ* 1: 6)

The founding document is an emotional exercise rather than a blueprint for precise action.

From its very beginning, the AATG avoided ideologies of method. It was concerned with *what* could be achieved, not *how* the teacher wanted to achieve it. It encouraged experiments, but not the espousal of "the one and only way." In the first major statement on German language teaching, teachers were warned against too narrow a methodological view. Not only would they grow old before their time, but they would live in a paradise of ignorance: "It may safely be said at the present time that nothing in the teaching of modern foreign languages is fixed. The greatest need, especially for the German teacher, is to keep an open mind for the new and to experiment intensively in order to find new ground. If he does that, he need have no fear of a lack of students of German."[5]

The newly organized AATG was immediately attacked from various sides, less on disciplinary grounds than because it was considered by some a threat to the harmony of the entire language teaching profession, as a duplication of efforts at a time when all should be standing together. Others feared that an association bringing together high school and college teachers would soon break apart. Pessimists envisaged an early death of the organization or, worse, a total disarray of all established language societies. B. Q. Morgan, then editor of *The Modern Language Journal,* seriously questioned the necessity of yet another organization in an editorial, appropriately titled "E Pluribus Unum." Would it not be better if we had "first, a national association of modern foreign language teachers and a national journal for the country as a whole; second, a modern language association and a modern language bulletin in every state; third, local associations for one or more languages wherever, as in large cities, they can be readily established and maintained"?[6] Despite his initial doubts, B. Q. Morgan later became one of the most important leaders of the AATG and was elected to Honorary Membership.

Morgan's structure for an association of Modern Language teachers was precisely the framework the AATG envisaged for itself: a national organization based on strong local chapters, a federal system rather than a centralized one. And, in spite of the concerns that continued to be voiced, the association began to grow. In 1932 Robert Fife, then president of the AATG, was able to report:

> The predictions made several years ago that the foundation of separate associations . . . would bring disunion and disaster have not been fulfilled . . . the recent work of the American and Canadian Committees on Modern Languages brought out clearly the fact that there is no cause for rivalry among teachers of the several modern languages . . . and that the fear that one would decay if another flourished is groundless. It is also clear that the selection of a foreign language for the schools and colleges does not lie in the hands of modern language teachers but depends on public interest and local situations.[7]

The fact that enrollments were down in any one foreign language was not so much the result of heavy competition, but rather of a totally changed environment. Fife's words deserve to be quoted in some detail:

> We are in the midst of a period of intensive review and reconstruction in curriculum and methods in secondary education. The great era of expansion in high schools and colleges . . . is now at an end, or very nearly so. In 1931, for the first time in our national history, the number of pupils in the elementary schools in the United States declined absolutely, keeping pace with the decline

in the national birth rate. . . . It is no mere guess to say that we are entering on a period of intensive study of objectives, materials, and methods of instruction to meet the new situation, for public opinion is bound to force an increasingly severe examination of all the curriculum subjects for their social and ultimate scholastic value. . . . Nowadays it has become impossible to show convincing results by following the old paths. The students in high school and colleges are a less select group than in 1914. Their education interests are much more complex and the time allowed for modern languages has grown shorter. (*GQ* 5: 52–53)

Fife's comments show how the problems confronting German teachers over fifty years ago are not so very different from those we are facing today. They reinforce the concept that the AATG was founded to strengthen an academic discipline that had importance in its own right within a totally American environment. German had ceased to be an immigrant language. It is also significant that some of the most vocal early leaders of the AATG were native born Americans, devoid of ethnic links to German speaking countries.

The concerns of the profession were manifold. There was an ongoing debate concerning standardized tests to improve foreign language instruction in the secondary and elementary schools, and there was no agreement "what the secondary school or college student of average intelligence should know after one, two, or three years' study of . . . German."[8] The wastefulness of language instruction was also a matter of grave concern because few students continued their studies beyond the first or second year. Of 32,870 students enrolled in German in public schools during 1925, 20,020 were in their first year, 10,282 in their second, 2,381 in their third, and only 187 in their fourth year.[9] While these statistics may be in part a reflection of the immediate postwar years (who, after all, took German in 1921?) the drop is greater than such circumstances could explain. The figures reflect a trend which has continued to trouble American education ever since.

It is one thing to identify the problems, still another to do something about them. From its beginning, the AATG attempted to guide its members and to take an active role in the nitty-gritty of the teaching of German. Indeed, during the formative years of the organization, matters of pedagogy were of primary concern and were shared equally by teachers on the secondary level and some of the major professors at leading universities. Camillo von Klenze, Robert Fife, B. Q. Morgan, Frederick Heuser, E. W. Bagster-Collins, Charles M. Purin, A. R. Hohlfeld are but a few names of leaders in the profession who became fully identified with the cause of teaching German in America. It was a time, after all, when the concept of "research university" with all its implications of "publish or perish" had not yet been developed, when the teaching of languages at the college level was shared by the entire faculty, and not yet relegated to the teaching assistants.

Many of the leaders of the fledgling AATG came from the German Department at the University of Wisconsin, and there was serious discussion of making *Monatshefte* the official journal of the new association. When these negotiations came to naught, the AATG established its own publication, *The German Quarterly,* as a means of communicating with its members.[10]

Published for the first time in January 1928, the *Quarterly* was designated a "clearing house" and an opportunity to "show that we have something worthwhile to say in the cause of education. The forty-eight pages of space should easily be filled each issue with articles that are stimulating by their quality."[11] *The German Quarterly* has since reached the point of middle-age spread by increasing the number of its pages almost four-fold; it has also changed its focus, but it has remained an excellent reflection of the status of the profession. During the first ten years of the journal, pedagogical concerns were predominant. Articles on how to teach language, how to present an adequate picture of contemporary Germany, how to deal with a literary text in the classroom, outnumbered purely scholarly papers in a ratio of approximately 2:1.

The same was true at annual meetings of the Association. Limited in those days to one day, usually as an adjunct to the MLA conventions, the concerns of the profession took precedence over the purely scholarly debate. A sample of topics from the first eight years of the AATG will give us an idea of the issues of the time, and we can see that some of these issues have lost none of their currency today. Repeatedly we encounter special sessions dealing with the "Uniformity of Grammatical Nomenclature"; others address problems in the training of secondary school teachers, examine the teaching of third and fourth year college German, discuss how one can make the schools language conscious, offer advice—"Creating Interest in the Study of German," "The First Vital Week of Beginning German," "Selection of Candidates for the Teaching of German," "Methods of Teaching of German," "Language Achievement and its Testing," "Kulturkunde bei der Darbietung idomatischer Ausdrücke," "The Function of the Course in Civilization," "The Teacher of German and the Teaching of *Kulturkunde,*" "Der Deutschlehrer und die Volkskunde," and, finally, "Das deutsche Plakat im Deutschunterricht."[12] In the evenings, the conventioneers were sometimes treated to samples of new German films as, for example, in 1937, when immediately before the festive dinner the teachers were able to enjoy the movie *Orphan Boy of Vienna.*

A review of the articles in *The German Quarterly,* of the programs of the annual meetings, and of the growing number of chapter reports reflecting grass-roots involvement shows that the AATG was very much concerned with the establishment of standards where there had been none before: What competency should one expect of the teachers? What goals should be established for the classroom? What tests would be most suitable at what level? What should be the role of literature? How much should one stress *Landeskunde?* Wishing for norms, however, did not produce them, and as soon as some were suggested, they were hotly debated, bitterly fought over, and in the end—usually ignored. After all, the AATG was able only to make recommendations; it never had the power to enforce. A case in point is the vigorous battle in connection with the setting up of a minimum standard vocabulary list, the AATG's first major undertaking.

The idea for this project was conceived at the constituent assembly of the AATG in Madison, Wisconsin, in December 1931. A committee under the chairmanship of B. Q. Morgan began its task. A mimeographed list, based on the Morgan-Kaeding *German Frequency Word Book,* was presented to the membership at the first annual meeting of the Association at Yale University in December of 1932. The draft was accepted in principle, and a refined list was further debated the following year.[13] The final list consisted of the 2400 basic words of the *German Frequency Word Book,* "reduced by a 4:1 vote to about 2000 words." Added were two small groups of "utility words," especially useful in beginning classes stressing oral instruction. The committee believed that a vocabulary list had now been established containing the words that "every college student will know at the end of his fourth semester, every high school pupil at the end of his fourth year" (*GQ* 7: 88). Words for two-year high school and one-year college courses were printed in bold type. The committee advocated the adoption of the list for three reasons: "1. The need of a standard vocabulary for German is long-standing and insistent. 2. The present list . . . is probably as good as . . . any committee would produce. 3. The nation-wide adoption of *any* good list will result in all the major benefits that could be expected from the acceptance of a 'perfect' list. What is needed is *agreement:* The committee believes it has furnished the profession an acceptable basis for it" (*GQ* 7: 89). Hardly had the list been accepted at the Annual Meeting in St. Louis when the New York City chapter protested vehemently and passed a resolution requesting that "no list be promulgated as the official Word List of the AATG until voted upon by the various Chapters of the AATG."[14] We witness here a perfect example of the frequently recurring conflict between the "States-Righters" and the "Federalists." New York's objection aroused the ire of the national president, Alexander Rudolph Hohlfeld—a strong supporter of central power—who responded in righteous wrath that "it is self-evident that a subdivision of the Association cannot constitutionally act as a sort of board of review for a constitutionally valid action of the Association as a whole."[15] The list, commercially published, was later critically reviewed in *The German Quarterly* by Otto Schinnerer, who found many weaknesses but admitted "without doubt, all textbook makers, no matter how they may personally feel about it, will henceforth rush to join the bandwagon, as some have already done. It is only by such universal adoption in practice that the real advantages or shortcomings of such a list can be ultimately determined" (*GQ* 7:89). Certainly, the AATG was never able to canonize the vocabulary list, and even its *imprimatur* was in no way binding for teachers or textbook authors.

The vocabulary list is but one example of early AATG activities. It is the only one that won a certain measure of success. Others were attempts at determining teacher qualifications, the establishment of classroom standards through nationwide tests, and attempts to achieve a consensus as to what should be taught. Most of these concerns remained bottled up in committees or were subjects of debate at the annual meetings. The minutes of the executive council meetings and of the business sessions, as well as the pages of *The German Quarterly,* are eloquent witness to this intense exchange of views. The desire to establish norms, however, never overcame the inherent anarchy of the American educational system.

Another problem which plagued the AATG from the very beginning (and which continues to do so) is the relatively small percentage of German teachers who actually join the organization. In 1933 A. R. Hohlfeld pleaded with his fellow-teachers of German to become members: "Especially in the central, western, and southern states there are many hundreds of teachers who, in fairness to themselves, can no longer afford to deny us their support and their co-operation. The Association needs them as they surely need the Association in order that both may profit by that consciousness of strength that comes from united experience and united council."[16] In 1950, President Günter Keil exclaimed: "Many high school teachers of German, especially those teaching in smaller communities, may not even know of the existence of our Association, or if they do, do not realize how much we need their cooperation and how much they, in turn, will benefit by our support."[17] Membership was never spectacular. As the statistics published in the *Quarterly* reveal, the AATG began with sixty teachers in 1926, rose to 140 by the following year, reached almost 1000 by 1940, passed the 1000 mark in 1950, rose to 1333 by 1958 and then, *mirabile dictu,* ascended, together with *Sputnik,* to 3200 by 1961, 4000 by 1962, to over 7,000 by 1970, at which point it began to level off. It has never been possible to obtain the exact number of active German teachers in this country. However, when we consider the mailing lists available at AATG headquarters, we find that less than half of those listed are actual members of the association. The reasons for this discrepancy are many.

Some teachers are only marginally involved in German instruction, others "never join anything"; some belong to other AATs, others may have other reasons. After all, nothing compels a teacher to join the AATG since it is not a union or regulatory association.

In the 1930s and early 1940s, the AATG was confronted with another issue, infinitely more complex than matters of membership or pedagogy: the relationship of the German teacher, the interpreter of German culture, to the political developments in Nazi Germany. While numerous attempts were made to take an official stand against the developments in Hitler's Germany, the association remained basically neutral and even tabled resolutions that might be considered "controversial." (Susan Pentlin's article in this volume discusses this issue in some detail.)

To be sure, the AATG never followed the "party line." As early as 1937, Theodore Huebener insisted that one should differentiate between Germans and Nazis. Articles in *The German Quarterly* point to the deterioration of the German language in the new *Reich* (for example "Volk und Führer," 11: 4ff.). At national meetings, and in the *Quarterly,* authors who were no longer acknowledged in Germany were studied with the same diligence as before. The AATG proved that it had become, indeed, an *American* association, concerned with the teaching of German language and literature, and that it was not an ethnic society beholden to the *Vaterland*. This was true not only on the national, but also on the local level. Chapter reports make interesting reading, telling us of some of the authors in exile who met with the German teachers, discussed their views of contemporary Germany literature, or read from their latest works. The AATG offered them a forum and contributed significantly to the preservation of a positive image of German culture.

The AATG came through the war relatively intact. In contrast to the aftermath of World War I, the teaching of German in America was not in shambles. There was no anti-German mass hysteria. While German as a high school subject had suffered considerable losses, government-sponsored programs for the military (ASTP) gave a new impetus to language teaching and area studies on many campuses. There was a strong interest in applied language skills; speaking and communicating were emphasized over reading. The AATG took an active part in these changes. In November 1944 B. Q. Morgan proposed a "Blueprint for Action" for the postwar years. He assumed that "(a) Modern foreign languages will hold an increased amount of public attention; (b) Foreign relations . . . will be stressed and cultivated; (c) Speaking knowledge of foreign languages will be . . . recognized as important." To meet this challenge, Morgan recommended that "significant utterances in favor of foreign language study by prominent citizens other than language teachers" should be collected and that "carefully worded statements" should be presented to school boards, principals, superintendents, PTA chapters, etc. He also suggested the forming of a pressure group to lobby for foreign languages. In addition to the political thrust, Morgan demanded that only competent teachers be certified and that oral proficiency be included in teacher certification. Teachers should have "time enough to do a good job. This implies permission to conduct third and fourth year classes despite reduced enrollment." He also noted that "Two years is not enough, and no other western nation acts as if it were. The practice of scheduled language classes of different levels in one period (e.g., German 1 and 2) is to be especially condemned." Teachers should be encouraged to study abroad and money should be made available for realia, phonograph records, books, etc. Morgan concluded his "Blueprint" with an emphasis on the strengthening and broadening of foreign language teaching: "Oral and aural is the new—or renewed—requirement. To produce this, school boards must provide (a) competent teachers, (b) adequate time."[18]

This "Blueprint" and the postwar conditions were the signal for action. What B. Q. Morgan had proposed was very much in line with what was written in the journals or taught in the Colleges of Education. The AATG accepted the challenge and embarked on many new projects as well as continuing and strengthening some of the old. The Service Center in Philadelphia, a joint endeavor between the AATG and the NCSA, provided films, slides, tapes and other realia to the membership and kept its stock up-to-date. The main thrust, however, remained the actual improvement of instruction and the old AATG dream of becoming involved in the certification of German teachers. The concerns brought out a problem that had been anticipated by critics at the very beginning, but had not been an issue before the war: communication between the high school teachers among the membership and the college professors became more and more difficult. Each group felt that the other was oblivious to its unique problems, that the literary scholars were arrogant, or the high school teachers were ignorant. Each side accused the other of "running the show." Actually, the proportions of the two groups have shifted slightly. In 1950, the ratio was two college teachers for every one from high school; in 1963, the ratio had changed so that more than half the membership came from the secondary level. Today, the ratio is 4:3 in favor of the high schools. In response to this problem, and in recognition that the association had obligations to the pedagogues as well as the Germanists, Eberhard Reichmann, with funding from the Stiftung Volkswagenwerk, developed a new journal, devoted entirely to the issues of the classroom. *Die Unterrichtspraxis* was an immediate success and was accepted as "an additional periodical of the Association" by membership vote at the Annual Meeting in December 1968.[19] It has been a major voice of the profession ever since.

Most of the projects in which the AATG has been engaged since the war have been directed toward the stimulation of interest and the improvement of the teaching of German primarily on the secondary school level. However, in the period of Sputnik-expansion, elementary schools began to introduce foreign languages. In 1959 there were 62,000 such students learning German in the grades, 40,000 of whom were in Military Dependents schools and 15,000 in radio or TV courses.[20] The AATG established a FLES-Taskforce which designed guidelines and developed materials for elementary school programs. It was particularly difficult to reach the FLES teachers because many of them were not German teachers at all, and some did not even know the language. They had to learn along with their students, who frequently surpassed them. In spite of the efforts of the task force, and of many dedicated teachers, the whole FLES concept never really took hold. By the early 1970s it had almost ceased to exist.

If FLES was a failure, other projects were not. Particularly successful was the development of a nationwide German contest for high school students offered for the first time in March of 1960. The test has since become a major motivating factor and is an excellent tool for establishing certain minimum standards of achievement. In the first year, 3,316 students participated; by 1974, the number had surpassed 16,000, and it has remained high ever since. The tests are not only used for the award program; they have also become a useful instrument of evaluation for colleges and universities.

The concept of evaluation brings us back to the setting of standards and norms, the favorite theme of the AATG. The postwar period is full of attempts to make progress in these areas. For years a committee was engaged in developing a "Guide for a German Major" which, however, never saw the light of day. The *Minutes* of the 1961 Annual Meeting record "it appears that work on the *Guide for a German Major* seems to have come to a stand-still in mid-course . . . ."[21] More exciting and more controversial were the attempts to become involved in teacher certification. In 1963 it was proposed to include a clause in the by-laws advocating that the Association take an active part in the licensing of teachers of German. While the recommendation was not passed, it was finally incorporated in the findings of the National Symposium on the Advancement of the Teaching of German in the USA, held in Philadelphia in December 1967 under the chairmanship of Victor Lange. This symposium, in many ways a continuation of the "Blueprint for Action," suggested "that the professional organization of teachers of German in the United States publish a set of standards for the training of teachers of German at the elementary, secondary, and college levels . . . ." It further recommended that "proficiency documents" be designed to be conferred on those teachers "who have reached the defined professional standards." The Philadelphia symposium offered the strongest articulation of what was and is needed to improve the quality of language instruction in general and the teaching of German in particular. It addressed not only aspects of teacher training and certification, but also sketched course contents at various levels, stressing "the importance of continuity as paramount to the success of German studies," and spoke of "the basic aims to be achieved at the various stages in the unbroken sequence of German studies from the elementary school to the college or university." It insisted that a four-year sequence should be considered minimum, and it addressed such details as the measurement of achievement in terms of proficiency rather than credits, as well as the need for an "agreement with regard to terminology used in the teaching of structure."[22] The symposium represents the grand summary of the concerns and hopes of the AATG since its inception. It was the most forceful formulation of professional and curricular goals in which the association had become involved up to that time. It anticipated in many ways the debates on proficiency and certification which have become so important in the 1980s.

The Philadelphia symposium must be considered a benchmark in the history of the AATG. What had begun as a humble organization of a few German teachers in New York City had grown into a major professional enterprise. To sketch the course of the new AATG will be a task for future historians.

The road from New York to Philadelphia was not an easy one. When we look back at the developments from 1926 to 1970, we find that the AATG was an accurate mirror of the profession as a whole. There were lofty ideals and there was confrontation with reality. There were courageous manifestos and timid cries for help. There was, above all, a great deal of honest hard work, without grants and supports and "released time." In reviewing those first forty years, one cannot help but gain respect for a generation of German teachers in colleges and high schools which took the teaching of German at all levels very seriously. The American Association of Teachers of German offered a modest, but important, forum for them.

Notes

1 Quoted in H. H. Fick, "Zur Geschichte des Nationalen Deutschamerikanischen Lehrerbundes," *Monatshefte* (1918): 217.
2 Robert Herndon Fife, "Some New Paths in Teaching German," *German Quarterly* 1 (1928): 7.

3 Sol Liptzin, "Early History of the A.A.T.G., (1926–1931)," *German Quarterly* 12 (1939): 20.

4 Camillo von Klenze, "The American Association of Teachers of German," *German Quarterly* 1 (1928): 4.

5 Fife, "Some New Paths in Teaching German" (1928): 17.

6 *Modern Language Journal* 11 (1927): 488.

7 Robert Herndon Fife, "To the Members of the Association," *The German Quarterly* 5 (1932): 51–52.

8 Fife, "Some New Paths in Teaching German" 12.

9 Ibid. 14.

10 For a detailed discussion see Liptzin 22–23.

11 "Foreword of the Editor," *German Quarterly* 1, (1928): 1.

12 This is a summary of the programs as published annually in *The German Quarterly*.

13 E. W. Bagster-Collins et al., "Minimum Standard Vocabulary for German," *German Quarterly* (1934): 87.

14 *German Quarterly* (1934): 124.

15 Ibid. 89.

16 "To the Members of the American Association of Teachers of German," *German Quarterly* 6 (1933): 105.

17 "Remarks of the President," *German Quarterly* 24 (1951): 73.

18 "After the War: A Blueprint for Action," *German Quarterly* 17 (1944): 241.

19 "A Report by the President of the AATG," *German Quarterly* 42 (1969): 313.

20 "Minutes of Annual Meeting," *German Quarterly,* 38 (1960): 170.

21 "Minutes of the Twenty-Ninth Annual Meeting, AATG," *German Quarterly* 35 (1962): 209.

22 "A National Symposium on the Advancement of the Teaching of German in the USA was held in Philadelphia," *German Quarterly* 41 (1968): 283.

German Teachers' Reaction to the Third Reich, 1933–1939

SUSAN L. PENTLIN
Central Missouri State University

In the aftermath of World War I, German had been virtually eliminated from the American school curriculum. The hate campaigns against Germany which occurred in America after her entry in the war had also targeted the study of the German language in American public schools. Educators had warned against "cultural vandalism" and "academic hysteria," as headlines announced "Taboo Hun Language." Thus, while in 1915 one of every four high school students had been studying German, not even one in a hundred was learning it by 1922.[1] As late as 1928 eleven states had not re-introduced German into their curriculum.[2] After 1924, however, German began showing a slow gain in enrollment and prestige and its position in the curriculum was again relatively stable by 1933.[3]

Hitler's rise to power alarmed German teachers in America. Recalling 1917, they knew that languages, particularly German, might once again be jeopardized and that the few German programs still in the schools would have to fight to keep their places in the curriculum. Even if Hitler's Reich were not ultimately to affect the course of German study in America in an adverse way, teachers understood that the next years might be filled with anxieties and conflicts for the profession and further impede the recovery of German study in American education.

In the 1930s, the German teaching profession had to overcome not only the barriers of rising hatred for Hitler and the Third Reich, but also isolationist attitudes opposing foreign language study in general. The final report of the Committee on Modern Foreign Languages in 1933 outlines the place German held in the schools. The report stresses the cultural and educational or practical value of modern languages. However, by culture the committee did not mean a closeness to German history or to the German people. Instead, languages are "the most exact and direct medium for acquiring a knowledge of the modern humanities" and foreign language study improves the student's learning skills for English. Although language study should contribute to the "spirit of international understanding and friendliness, leading toward world peace," there is no indication in the report of how this can be accomplished.[4]

The years prior to the outbreak of war in Europe were thus tense and demanding ones for the profession. German teachers met with disbelief initial news reports from National Socialist Germany and sought in the next years to postpone judgment. At the same time, the profession was eager to emphasize in America that German and Hitler were not the same. Teachers hoped to establish that the study of a language is not an endorsement of the politics of a country where that language is spoken, and that academics can admire and study the literature and culture of Germany without condoning its current policies and political system.

By concentrating their efforts on defending German study and keeping German in the school curriculum the profession failed, however, to take an active stand against Hitler and the Third Reich. It made no strong, public protest against the terror and oppression in Germany from 1933 to 1939. Arguing instead for the intrinsic value of language study, the profession tried to remain outside of politics. In their desire to be cautious and fair and to protect German studies from the excesses of World War I, German teachers did not use their knowledge of German culture and of the German people to sway opinions in America or in Germany. As a result they in fact supported actions which they wanted to refute, were misled and manipulated by political forces in Germany, and hid tendencies toward nationalism and racial prejudice within the profession itself.

There was also a note of personal conflict and tragedy underlying these concerns of the profession. German teachers, by virtue of their contacts with Germany and their knowledge of German language and culture, had a foot in two worlds. The native-born German instructor may have considered Germany his or her homeland and was naturally concerned for its future and the safety of relatives and friends there. Other foreign-born teachers were filled with self-doubt, perhaps even guilt for the rise of Hitler. In April 1933, Adolf Busse of New York questioned: "Die ganze Hitlerbewegung ist mir ein Buch mit sieben Siegeln. Sind wir Deutschen [sic] wirklich ein so *nüchternes* Volk, wie wir uns einbilden?"[5]

Painful reproaches came from both sides. Herman Almstedt in Missouri received the following poignant message from Arlesheym, Switzerland, in 1935: "Du hast mir im Jänner einen höchst vergnügten Brief geschrieben. Freilich sah ich daraus: nach Europa kommst du nimmer (wie die Schwaben sagen). . . . [du] magst dich um unser abgetrampeltes, zernagtes Vorgebirge von Asien nicht in Unkosten stürzen. Hast nicht so Unrecht. Was können euch Dinge bewegen wie die Saar?"[6]

Teachers not of German origin sensed the end of friendships and professional contacts made during journeys abroad and rebelled at being viewed with suspicion by friends and neighbors at home. W. F. Twaddell at Wisconsin outlined these suspicions by friends and neighbors. In 1938 he addressed their frustrations and pointed out convincingly that "It would be silly for the teacher of German to pretend that his anxiety on this account is not personal. Of course it is and to a personal extent . . . . We hear from our German friends, or we listen to shortwave broadcasts; and we rebel at the rosy picture of Utopia therein presented. Many of us, I dare say, are regarded as Nazis by our American friends and as a member of the Comintern by our German friends."[7]

Finally, most American Germanists who lived through the First World War were familiar with the hardships imposed on Germany by the Versailles Treaty and the American abandonment of Wilsonian ideals. A. B. Faust (1933) outlines an interview between an emeritus professor and a young instructor. The youth remarks: "I am a native American citizen and proud of it. . . . I am too young to have been in the 'war to end war,' too critical to believe my native country was not guilty in bringing about the present mess along with the other victors, too tolerant toward other people who have different ideologies derived from bitter historical experiences. Therefore, I feel no hostility toward other nations whatever."[8]

At first, the profession sought to affirm its confidence in the values of old Germany. The attitude toward the Third Reich was mainly one of disbelief or avoidance of discussion. Many agreed with Thomas Mann's sentiments in a 1933 interview with *B'nai B'rith Magazine:* "At the present time, the Nazis are too intoxicated with their newly acquired strength to realize what they are doing. But eventually it will dawn on them that they cannot hope to succeed with an entire world hostile to them. . . . when the Nazis learn that their attitude and behavior towards the Jew results only in arousing the disgust and the contempt of the rest of the world, they will probably realize how futile it is to attempt to bring the twentieth century back into the dark ages."[9] Others expressed a belief that Germany would overcome Nazism in due course. A. R. Hohlfeld, AATG President, counseled caution the same year because "our own Government have [sic] suggested that . . . continued agitation will not only fall short of its purpose, but even aggravate the situation and hamper those forces within the German government itself that do not approve of extreme measures and are just beginning to assert themselves with some success."[10] Finally, some argued that American involvement in German politics might even make the situation worse and have little positive effect on German policies.

The proper reponse to Nazi Germany was a sensitive issue charged with emotion. It is not surprising that it brought splits and open animosity even among German teachers. This rift became evident early in 1933 when the New York Chapter of the American Association of Teachers of German (AATG) decided to issue a political statement protesting the Nazi regime. By a narrow vote of approval, a committee was appointed in March to draw up a resolution. Some members of the chapter protested and sought support from Hohlfeld to block these actions. Frederich Heuser (Columbia) wrote, explaining the opposition's position: "[we] feel that our passing any kind of resolution would only make matters worse in Germany and do no good here. . . . I personally feel that *all* Germans . . . would look upon such a step as an unfriendly act in view of the violent anti-German press propaganda in New York during the last week . . . and simply mark the AATG for years to come as anti-German."[11] Hohlfeld as National President sided with this cautious view. He replied:

> . . . it must be considered at least doubtful whether a resolution of protest, no matter how carefully phrased, will prove helpful or detrimental to the cause we should wish to serve. . . . Even though a protest from our ranks would be based solely on humanitarian and cultural considerations, by entering the public arena it would of necessity assume a political aspect, and in the ultimate interests of our work as American teachers of German everything belonging to the sphere of politics and appearing to take sides should be avoided by our Association, as long as such course remains open to us.[12]

Regrettably, the quarrel also exposed latent feelings of anti-Semitism in the profession. Some chapter members felt that the resolution had been supported mainly by Jewish members. Heuser had remarked: ". . . our Jewish friends . . . tried to stampede the meeting into passing some sort of resolution . . . . it is really only the Jews who have strong convictions in this matter."[13] Busse wrote: "Die antisemitische Aufregung hat mir viel Sorge gebracht und kostbare Zeit geraubt. . . . Mit einigen jüdischen Kollegen wie Manckiewicz hatten wir einen schweren Stand; er wollte absolut eine Erklärung."[14]

When the New York Chapter did adopt a resolution, it was a statement confirming the chapter's belief in the value of German study and a plea for the profession and its mission. The resolution reflected the profession's cautious position:

> It seems, however, to those who are charged with the education of Young America and, more specifically, with their instruction in German, that in following our intellectual and emotional opposition to the present system of government in Germany, we disregard the fact that the study of a distinctly worthwhile modern language is by no means an indorsement [sic] of or even acquiescence in the policies of such government. . . . The teachers of German in our schools are in no sense of the word propagandists for the political system in Germany. They are teaching what is culturally valuable and eternally true in the writings of the great German authors and they are thus giving our students the same ethical, cultural and scientific values which have proven of benefit for generations. . . . We seriously appeal to all who have the intellectual welfare of our students at heart not to becloud the issue, but to permit the study of the German language to hold that place in our educational system to which its intrinsic value entitles it.[15]

Predictably, it contained no mention of Hitler or of the dictatorial and racial policies of the new Germany.

The program at the AATG meeting in December of 1933 carried words of admonition to the divided profession. It reminded members that: ". . . the object [of this organization] is to achieve solidarity of feeling and action on the part of all teachers of German as a national group."[16]

This statement had probably been necessitated by a second quarrel which had broken out in the New York Chapter in November. Most likely, this was in fact a continuation of the debates which had upset the chapter earlier. Chapter president J. B. E. Jonas wrote an "open letter" to Hohlfeld, protesting the lack of women, high school teachers, and Jews on the ballot for new officers of the organization:

> . . . Your Committee on Nominations has made about as wretched and dis-astrous a job of its work as it is humanly possible to do. I don't think they could even potentially have made a worse and more sorry mess of it if they had deliberately, studiously, and with malice aforethought [sic] set themselves the task of doing their worst. Viewed from any and every angle that I can conceive, the selections are wholly amiss. . . . I am writing simply and purely as a chapter president whose task is rendered infinitely more difficult, humil-iating, and crucial by this slate foisted upon us . . . the ballot is a tragedy. It is a travesty on justice and fairness, a rebuke and a slap in the face of the secondary school members, a direct breach of faith, a dishonest breaking of a solemn pledge.

This "open letter" was undeniably verbose, petty, and perhaps unbal-anced. But it initiated a correspondence full of bigotry and name-calling among AATG members.

Jonas also raised questions of a political nature when he pointed out to Hohlfeld:

> There is not, as far as I can see, one single member of the Jewish race or faith in nomination. In these days of acute racial antipathy, turmoil, strife, and hatred, I consider this an instance of shortsightedness, tactlessness, ineptitude amounting to nothing less than stupidity. This is not only inequitable; it is a crime on the own flesh; it is suicidal! It would have been not only an act of decency, courtesy, and graciousness, but a vital and essential step toward self-preservation to have acted not only fairly, but even generously in this hour of tribulation.[17]

Hohlfeld's "open answer to an open letter" was a calm attempt to answer Jonas' charges. In reference to the claim that the new slate did not have a Jewish member, he wrote: "first of all, I am not so sure as you seem to be that this is the case; and I too should be sorry if it proved to be so." He explained that "we wicked Westerners" were not responsible for the slate chosen, but that he had been willing to take time to reply to Jonas because of the importance of the issue in the AATG's ability to achieve unity among teachers of German. In conclusion, he added:

. . . I see in your attack the expression, perhaps not fully conscious, of a spirit of suspicion and resentment which clearly must be overcome before we can hope to develop into a genuinely unified and effective national organization; and only as a truly national body animated by a sense of solidarity and mutual responsibility, which can exist solely on the basis of mutual respect and confidence, can we look for any successful mastery of the many and trying difficulties that are now threatening our work perhaps even more than ever before. We need free discussion of conflicting points of view, frank criticism of evident errors and shortcomings, helpful suggestions for improvement in practice and procedure; but criticism, to be acceptable and effective, must be free from the spirit of rancor and the language of abuse.[18]

H. A. Buschek, Secretary-Treasurer of the New York AATG Chapter, replied to Hohlfeld's "open letter" in the same vein: "You speak of fences. It is true we speak of the West and the East, just as we still speak of the North and the South. That can't be helped, the country is big. But why should we waste hours of valuable time quarreling among ourselves, when so much vital work needs to be done, especially just now in these trying times."[19]

F. W. J. Heuser, AATG Secretary, wrote Hohlfeld that he had tried unsuccessfully to dissuade Jonas:

I have known Jonas for many years and feel that he is too naive and honest a soul to go off at a tangent like that. The only way I can explain it is that some sinister influences who have discreetly kept in the background have sicked [sic] him on. Of course you who live in the Middle West can scarcely realize the intensity of the anti-German feeling which exists in our large Jewish population, and the tremendous power which the latter wield in our press and in our city government. It may be that Jonas was threatened with dire consequences if he did not do something concrete. For this of course I have no evidence.[20]

In a letter a few days later, Heuser clarified whom he had meant by "sinister influences," writing to Hohlfeld: ". . . I suppose that other advisers counseled him [i.e., Jonas] to the contrary. I have no certain knowledge who they may be, but I suspect a few Jewish members whom you also know."[21]

However, the voices of moderation seem to have been in the minority. William A. Cooper in California wrote Hohlfeld with vehemence: "I received your open letter to the arch-ass of Gotham [i.e. the President of the New York Chapter]—I have never in all of my life felt so insulted. That such an ass should bray so loudly at the dean of American Germanists and spew out his vile Yiddish venom at decent Christian [sic] is *unaussprechlich ekelhaft* . . . after all it was the Yiddish *Drang* to the spotlight that inspired [his] letter."[22] Cooper later sent Hohlfeld a copy of his reply to Jonas. Cooper explained: "The suggested candidates were sent me by mail by Professor Handschin and I voiced my preferences, naming even first and second choice without having taken the trouble to inquire whether any one of the persons proposed was a Jew or a Gentile, a Lutheran or a Catholic or whether he believed in Christian Science." He closed his letter with a final note, requesting the cancellation of his AATG membership.[23] A. B. Faust wrote: "Your OPEN ANSWER to an OPEN LETTER squashes our opponent, who seemingly wanted to introduce the Jewish question where it does not belong. That is just what we do not like about the 'chosen people.' "[24]

These views may have served as excuses to the profession for their failure to express moral indignation at the Hitler takeover. They may also have been an expression of the German attitude that Jews were anti-German and not able to appreciate German culture. At any rate, they clearly represent the strength of the desire to remain outside of politics.

In 1934, a third quarrel erupted between some members of the New York Chapter and other AATG members. Heuser sent a letter of protest from the Western New York Chapter to B. Q. Morgan at Stanford. He wrote: "You have no doubt heard about the foolish spite-work of Mankiewicz and Jackson (alias Jacobowski or something like that) at the last meeting of the Metropolitan Chapter of the A.A.T.G." Apparently, Jonas and other members of the New York Chapter had written resolutions against the publishing of a word frequency list by Morgan. The justice of the New York Chapter's stand is difficult to assess, but the correspondence once again attests to the intensity of emotions among German teachers as they confronted Hitler's Reich.

Heuser comments: "What really actuated our two Jewish friends is hard to guess. There are probably a number of subconscious motives— spite, resentment, fear that their particular publishers and publications might be put at a disadvantage and God knows what. It is so easy nowadays to sway a heterogeneous meeting like that in New York by the bugaboo of regimentation, fascism and autocratic control."[25] These petty differences may also have served as excuses for not taking action or responding to the politics of Nazi Germany or only as an outlet for those in the profession who were anxious about the effect European politics were going to have on the study of German.

While many professionals continued to express disbelief, caution, or even unconcern, some teachers called on colleagues to prepare for the future. They feared another war and continued to feel that the profession should take a clearer stand against Nazi Germany. In 1934, Franz Schneider of California published an article entitled "Teachers to the Fore!" He showed an understanding of the role the profession could play in world events, counseling that "We teachers cannot control economics and politics, nor should we. But we can shape minds and can engender thought that in the course of time will produce in these two major fields of human activity conditions which are in keeping with the standards maintained by decent people in their private lives. We teachers by our great office in the structure of modern society can do a great, great deal if we but rise to a vision of our power and our opportunity—and try to live it serenely and unafraid."[26] German study could thus, indirectly, support individual freedom and American democracy.

Carl Baumann spoke at a meeting of the German Division of the Modern Language Association of Southern California in the winter of 1935, arguing that the value of language study for the individual "consists not so much in the intrinsic *better understanding* of the foreign country, as in that his eyes are opened as regards his own country." He argued that language learning could thus help to prevent the emotionalism and fanaticism prevailing in Europe. After all, he points out, "it could happen here."[27]

Other educators saw language study in the light of continued hopes for world peace. A Committee of the League of Nations under Professor Gilbert Murray was especially impressed by the possibilities for international understanding that can be achieved by the study of languages. An article on the Committee's work appeared in the *Christian Science Monitor* under the striking headline "Modern Language Study Helps Cause of Peace." The report concluded that "A knowledge of language necessarily promotes knowledge of the literature and mental processes of other countries. Understanding of each other should obviously have political consequences making for peace."[28] Many, however, felt such hopes to be strangely out of tune with the times, a vain refusal to deal with the political realities of the age. They sought to advance realistic, clear arguments for the study of German. B. Q. Morgan pointed out that a knowledge of foreign languages, especially German, could be vital for survival. Preparedness would come through knowledge of the German people. He cautioned: "By virtue of geographical situation, as well as its peculiar national character, Germany is bound to influence profoundly the future history of Western Europe. America's international destiny is involved, and it is essential that our youth should be given the opportunity to inform themselves at first hand of those developments in Germany which may affect our own future life."[29]

Theodore Huebener urged the profession to prepare its arguments for the defense of German study. He pointed out with alarm that ". . . ob man drüben einen Kaiser, einen Präsident oder einen Führer hat, dadurch wird nichts an dem eigentlichen Kulturwert der deutschen Sprache geändert. Die unsterblichen Schöpfungen eines Goethe, Schiller, Lessing, Wagner bleiben. Keine Regierung, kein Krieg, keine politische Partei kann sie zerstören."[30] Similarly, he noted in an address at the annual meeting of the AATG in 1936 that "it should be emphasized for the benefit of the general public that *Nazi* and *German* are not necessarily to be considered synonymous."[31]

While some German teachers favored the National Socialists, they were definitely in the minority. The excesses and divided loyalties of German teachers in World War I were not repeated. An interview was conducted with the staff of the German department at Hunter College in New York City in the early thirties. All but two of the faculty indicated their clear opposition to the Nazi regime.[32] On the whole, after 1933 the attitude of the general public and German teachers alike was negative regarding Germany. Friedrich Schönemann, in a monograph on America and National Socialism in 1934, had to admit: "Heute ist die freundlichere Volkstimmung Deutschland gegenüber vorbei. Seit der nationalsozialistischen Revolution haben wir in Amerika mit einer sehr schlechten, ja, offen gehässigen, jedenfalls immer ungünstigen Stellungnahme der gesamten öffentlichen Meinung zu rechnen, und zwar vom offiziellen Amerika her bis zu den Volksmassen."[33]

Many German teachers did make what seem in retrospect far too generous attempts to understand and give the new Germany a "fair" chance. Their work for over a decade to convince America to be open-minded about German and the German people may have made them slow to give up and to be objective about the realities of Hitler's Germany. This may also have had to do with personal fears for the safety of relatives, friends, and colleagues in Germany. E. Prokosch wrote to Hohlfeld in 1934, concerned that his own political opposition to the German government might endanger one of his graduate students were he to return to Germany. He commented: "Ich bin mir ganz klar darüber, daß die deutsche Regierung es weiß, daß ich bei verschiedenen Gelegenheiten . . . der Haltung des gegenwärtigen Regimes den Universitäten gegenüber offen entgegengetreten bin. Durch offizielle Dinge ist ihr zugleich Nordmeyers enge Beziehung zu mir bekannt."[34]

German teachers may have also been concerned that they could lose visa privileges and opportunities for visiting Germany or for receiving information and teaching aids from German organizations. In considering whether or not to endorse a 1939 resolution in the German Department at Wisconsin, one colleague admitted: "The implication that there be those who do not have such privileges [i.e., those enjoyed by Americans] can do these people no good, and may well do us harm either in Germany, by restricting our access to things we need or at home, by making us appear 'priggish.' "[35] Others in the profession may have been misled by the friendly appeals and recognition they received from officials of the new German state. Teachers may also simply have hesitated to express their concern publicly. Heuser wrote to Hohlfeld in the fall of 1933 after his return from four weeks in Germany: ". . . I naturally had an opportunity to talk to a large number of people about the political situation. The enclosed re-print from the New Yorker Staatszeitung is a sort of resume of my impressions, though of course there is also much to be said on the negative side of the situation. However, I feel that at the present juncture any outspoken criticism of the present regime in Germany is bound to be utilized by the anti-German forces, and no good will come of it."[36]

There are many examples of these efforts to be optimistic in print nonetheless. Joel Hatheway wrote:

> Those of us who in our youth knew and loved the old Germany have followed with interest and sympathy the endeavors of the new Germany to readjust herself to new conditions; to meet her obligations; to maintain herself as a self-respecting independent nation. We realize that a great revolution is being accomplished with its light and its shadows, its bad features and its good. We believe that the wrongs will be righted and that progress is being made. Let us have faith in the Germany that is to be.[37]

Werner Leopold of Northwestern University reported the impressions that Germany had made on a group of teachers traveling in 1935: "Die Urteile über das neue Deutschland waren nicht gleich. Aber jeder Teilnehmer fühlte besseres Verständnis für das Ringen des deutschen Volkes und lernte mindestens die eine oder andere aufbauende Bestrebung schätzen, die ihm vorher geblieben war."[38] H. Almstedt told a local Kiwanis Club about his sabbatical year in Europe from 1937 to 1938. According to a clipping from a local newspaper, he told the club that he had seen Mussolini and heard Hitler and Goebbels speak and "was impressed by them."[39] B. Q. Morgan spoke after a return from Germany over the NBC system on the "Stanford Hour." He affirmed his faith in the German people, telling the radio audience:

> It is therefore highly desirable that we should recognize the true face of the German people behind the official acts of the government now in power; for ultimately, it is that people which will determine its policy. . . . A great and admirable idealism animates the German people today, perhaps more consciously than at any previous period in their history. They believe that in defending their national rights and extending the scope of their national culture they are indirectly benefiting all mankind and advancing the standard of civilization for the entire western world. This conception is somewhat analogous to the imperialistic attitude which has been characterized as "carrying the white man's burden."[40]

The Nazi takeover of Austria in March of 1938 and the attacks on Jewish shops and synagogues the following November did, however, bring a change in the attitude of the German teaching profession in America. Clearly, the challenge of National Socialism could no longer be ignored.

Herbert Hoover spoke before the Modern Language Association of Central and Northern California in May 1938, emphasizing the need for national security. He told the group: "The Germans are developing a new ideology of government, economics, and society. . . . Whether we like it or not, these ideas are extending rapidly in the world and challenge our concepts of spiritual and intellectual liberty. If our people had that insight which teaching the language can afford, it would give greater national security to our national ideals."[41] An editorial in the *New York Times* urged high school students to continue their study of German. The editor questioned, in defense of German language programs: "What better challenge to Hitlerism can there be than to get to know Lessing, Schiller and Goethe?"[42]

On the same note, the AATG Committee on Resolutions presented a resolution to the Annual Meeting in 1938, stating: ". . . We pledge ourselves to maintain and defend the ideals of tolerance, humanity, and individual freedom as represented in the works of Lessing, Goethe, and Schiller. Our sympathy goes out to those teachers in Germany who have suffered or are suffering from intolerance and fanaticism. In this difficult time we believe it to be our patriotic duty to cultivate such common elements of our spiritual heritage as make for peace and understanding."[43] The defeat of this resolution in a vote of members indicated once again the profession's hesitancy to take an open stand against Hitler and its continuing efforts to stay free of politics.

In August of 1938, W. F. Twaddell had described the dilemma facing German teachers:

> The reintroduction of German into schools, the restoration of Germanist studies in colleges and universities since the War is ample evidence that their value cannot be denied. . . . Fortified by this faith in the usefulness of our work, we may with propriety take professionally legitimate steps to defend it. But what are those steps? Should we, as a group, through our professional organizations, issue statements or take group action? Whether we like it or not, we are by virtue of our subject-matter placed in an intermediate position between America and Germany, in our professional capacity. Should we therefore as a professional group attempt to "clarify" our position? Can we properly be expected to take a stand as to the present political government of Germany, irrelevant as that government may be to our real concerns? . . . if there were any prospect of success, we could draw up resolutions to that effect with the appropriate rhetorical grace and vigor. But such a demonstration can scarcely have any other effect than to indicate that our hearts were more or less in the right place.[44]

The defeat of the AATG resolution had come after a short, tense discussion which, President Ernst Feise concluded, "had not clarified but further confused the issues."[45] Twaddell reported later that "the somewhat weird press reports of the action on the resolutions leaves the present status of political affairs pretty uncertain and rather dangerous."[46]

The Executive Council of the AATG decided, therefore, to submit the four chief points of the resolution to a general referendum of the membership. Of the 501 ballots returned, there were 441 marked "yes," thirty abstentions, and thirty ballots which answered the individual questions. On these latter ballots, it should be noted that twenty-one persons abstained from answering and nine answered "no" to the part which read "we sympathize with the oppressed minorities in Germany." There were six abstentions and one "no" vote on the last resolution, which hinted of loyalty oaths teachers had signed in 1918, reading: "We believe in defending and promoting those principles of American democracy which make for peace and understanding."[47]

Twaddell returned his ballot marked "yes" on all four questions to Feise, but he struck out the word "Germany" in the third and amended it to read: ". . . with the oppressed minorities in all nations where an official ideology prescribes exclusion from political and social life on grounds of race, creed or political belief." In his comments to Feise, he argued against any political stand by the profession. He wrote:

> As an American citizen, I have no obligation to apologize for, am under no temptation to defend, assume—indeed—any interest in, the acts of a government whose area of political control happens at present to coincide with the geographical habitat and linguistic persistence of my teaching and research subject. This may seem over-finicky; but it is the only basis upon which we can straightforwardly do our job, as I see it. The moment we assume any responsibility, even the responsibility of explicit denunciation, for the acts of the German government, we invite the belief that our activities are not wholly cultural and non-political.

At the same time, Twaddell polled members of the German Department in Madison to see if its members wanted to define its position rather than wait for the AATG decision.

Twaddell suggested a statement which was essentially an affirmation of faith in American intellectual freedom and democracy.[48] The reply of one member of the department provides a clue to why some in the profession may have voted negatively on the AATG resolutions. In reference to a statement that candidates were accepted for teacher training without regard to their political, religious, or racial backgrounds, he wrote Twaddell: "Our acceptance of candidates for training etc. may bring you a flood of Hebrews, whom you can't accept and concerning whom you cannot make publicly the explanation that they are not good material, however true this may be. You can't turn a jew down without being accused of anti-semitism, no matter what the real reasons for rejecting him may be."[49]

Twaddell's resolution was adopted by the department unanimously in the spring of 1939, but not published. Some members of the department were apparently concerned that its publication would be "possibly prejudicial to relatives and friends."[50]

The religion or "race" of candidates was, undoubtedly, taken into consideration in decisions made during the 1930s in German departments at American schools as it undoubtedly was in other professional areas as well.[51] In 1933, Hohlfeld wrote Busse to inquire if an applicant's middle name "Rahel is an indication of her being a Jewess." He then added confidentially: "As you well know, we have no objection here to Jews, at least not in our department, but for this very reason we have gradually accumulated such a number, both among our younger teachers and students, that we should and probably ought to hesitate to attract any others through special arrangements of our own."[52] Cooper wrote with obvious prejudice about a colleague: "A few other exhibitions of the Jewish strain in him convince me that I would not want him back at Stanford at least during my term of office."[53]

Ernst Feise wrote from Middlebury about a student: "She is of Jewish extraction. . . . But she has all of the good and none of the bad qualities of her race and is in no way devoid of 'Gemüt.' "[54] George Danton at Union College ruled out a candidate in 1936, commenting: "At the moment a Jew would complicate the prestige problem here, and I am therefore not considering Mr. Valk."[55] Of course, other considerations may at times account for these reservations in the profession. Lawrence Price at Berkeley wrote in 1938 to the University of Wisconsin, looking for applications for an assistantship. He explained in the letter: "We are looking for someone with all the qualities of intellect and personality and some one if possible who is not a Jew but has a good American or German-American background." He then added sympathetically: "Some of our best students are Jews but when we have done all we could for them we cannot always place them in a good position."[56]

Caution and a reticence to get involved in the politics of the Third Reich were also evident in other decisions taken by the profession. Germanists were quite successful in isolating and disarming overt German propagandists and their efforts. As early as 1933, the program committee for the annual AATG meeting worried about inviting Reinhold Freytag, the German Consul in St. Louis, as a speaker. While he had been appointed by the republican Weimar government, the committee was nonetheless alert to the risks. Otto Heller at Washington University wrote to them: "Of course, there is no doubt that you will be taking a chance, for like all other German officials who do not want their heads chopped off by Hitler's axe, he has gone one hundred per cent Nazi."[57]

Eventually, the program committee agreed with this position. Richard Jente, the chair, wrote the AATG President:

I do not remember that at any group meeting of "Anglisten" in Germany, anyone ever thought of inviting the British or American consuls, and the idea never would have suggested itself to me. . . . Therefore, as far as I am concerned, the matter is settled: the German Consul or any other political representative of Germany shall not speak at any one of our group meetings. The German teachers in this country should have learned a lesson from what happened in this country during the war. Only damage can be done by introducing politics into our work, and during the present crisis we should have none of this.[58]

Upon his eventual return to Germany, Freytag worked as the Amerika-Referent in the Foreign Ministry, which would tend to support the committee's stance.[59]

The committee followed a similar suggestion and declined to invite Friedrich Schönemann, the head of the Amerika Institut of the University of Berlin, when he came to the United States for a lecture tour late in 1933, with apparent financial support from the German government. Although he had made many trips to America and had friendly contacts among German teachers, concern was expressed among Germanists that this tour was to be "an out-and-out Nazi propaganda tour."

Here the committee's foresight again proved to be accurate. Schönemann gave over forty lectures that fall and there were many protests that his speeches were strongly pro-Nazi. In Chicago, newspaper headlines announced: "Hecklers shout disapproval of Hitler defender."[60] In New York, he spoke before the Germanistic Society about "The Life of the New Germany" and at the Literarischer Verein on "Das kulturelle Gesicht des neuen Deutschlands." He laughed about a Midwest college which had requested he talk about literature strictly from a literary point of view, defended the book burnings of 1933, disparaged Remarque, and showered praise on Hans Grimm and *Mein Kampf*. After the lectures, Busse concluded: "Unter welcher Flagge Sch[önemann] auch segeln und sich ausgeben mag, er ist Propagandaredner des neuen Deutschlands."[61]

The years 1933 and 1934 marked the high point in overt attempts of the German government to reach America through direct propaganda activity. Heller remarked in 1933; "The present situation in Germany has produced a remarkable variety of propagandistic activity in this country."[62] These were likewise the years when the danger to American *Germanistik* was the most evident.

There were, of course, also teachers who openly expressed pro-Nazi sentiments and defended Germany. While they were the minority, they attracted public attention out of proportion to their strength in numbers. They thus intensified the aura of suspicion that surrounded the profession.

Anna Schafheitlin at Kent State can be cited as an example of a German-born teacher who returned to Germany for a visit in 1939 but remained after the invasion of Poland. Educated in Canada and the United

States, Schafheitlin went to Germany in the early 1930s and became convinced that Hitler was a great leader. A colleague recalls:

> Anna was a likeable person, enthusiastic over German Kultur and as Hitler
> came into power, doubly so over the great future in store for that country. In
> Kent she purchased an expensive short wave radio . . . to get wave lengths
> from Europe and she became a member of the German Bund in Cleveland. A
> time or two a small group of us were invited to her rooms and were introduced
> to Hitler's *Mein Kampf*. Once a brother-in-law on a flying trip from Germany
> to Chicago stopped in Kent to see her briefly. Afterwards she told me "He
> said Hitler would destroy Germany. What did he mean?"[63]

In 1934, a lecturer spoke on the Kent campus, revealing alarm at
German militarism and the lack of personal freedom in Nazi Germany.
Schafheitlin wrote a letter to the editor of the student newspaper and
defended the German labor camps for youth. She concluded that the
purpose of these camps was not military training but that "Rich and poor,
aristocrat and commoner, brain-worker and manual laborer are here to
learn to rub shoulders with each other, to understand each others point of
view, so that in future Germany may not be divided into warring classes,
ignorant and distrustful of each other, but may be one united nation of
brothers."[64] There was a general protest and reaction on campus at these
remarks.

During the war, Schafheitlin worked in Germany as an English teacher
and interpreter. Her connections with the Bund very likely prevented her
return to America after the war, and she died in Minden in 1967.[65]

The activities of two German teachers were reported by the U.S.
House of Representatives Special Committee to Investigate Un-American
Activities and Propaganda in the United States, which began hearings in
1938. In the proceedings, A. J. F. Zieglschmid of Northwestern University
was mentioned as a co-author with Peter Gissibl, Gauleiter of the Friends
of the New Germany and German-American Bund leader, of a book containing excerpts from various German and American propagandists. Werner Leopold, a colleague, recalls being questioned about Zieglschmid by
the FBI, but adds "I do not know why. It was a common occurrence in
those days."[66]

Frederic Auhagen, founder of the American Fellowship Forum, was
called to give testimony in 1940. The Fellowship Forum had been created
to spread Axis propaganda, to encourage appeasement and to oppose
American defense preparation. Auhagen was considered a paid Nazi agent
in New York and gained notoriety when he employed the well-known
propagandist George Sylvester Viereck as associate editor of the organization's publication *Today's Challenge*.[67]

At the hearings, Auhagen testified he had taught German and Spanish from 1927 to 1935. He also claimed to have been in charge of the German Department at the Lincoln School of Columbia Teacher's College and to having been head of a German department at Columbia University from 1930 to 1935, though these statements cannot be substantiated by available records today. It is clear, however, that Auhagen was a lecturer in German at the Seth Low Junior College in Brooklyn and also at the Lincoln School in the school year 1933–1934.[68] In 1941, Auhagen was arrested by federal authorities and served a prison term for failure to register as an agent of the German government.[69]

The most notorious case in the profession, however, is that of Max Oscar Otto Koischwitz, a native of Silesia, who was Chair of the German Department at the Lincoln School in 1927 and 1928 and an Associate at the New College of Columbia University in 1934. Koischwitz joined the Hunter College faculty in 1928 where he taught mainly classes in German philology and comparative literature. He soon became active as a scholar and published numerous articles on teaching methods, German drama, and world literature. In addition he served as the editor of the Lippincott German series and published six German language textbooks with F. S. Crofts.[70]

In 1935, his English-language publication *Germany: A German-American Interprets Germany* aroused attention in America and was rejected by some as out-and-out pro-Nazi material.[71] Koischwitz, who had supported leftist causes in the 1920s, had become an active supporter of the new Germany and was generally considered a Nazi sympathizer by friends and colleagues in New York.[72] Recently, S. Etta Schreiber recalled: "The story of the late Dr. Otto Koischwitz is really sad. He was definitely the most popular teacher in the department. He was also voted the most popular teacher in the college, he was a pleasant and cooperative colleague. Yet he was an ardent admirer of Nazi Germany . . . Dr. Koischwitz openly admitted his admiration for Hitler."[73] This became particularly evident after a year's leave of absence spent in Germany in 1935, while he worked on a book.[74] In 1937, Dr. and Mrs. Koischwitz attended the German Day celebrations in Madison Square Garden where the German-American Bund took an active part. The Koischwitzes reportedly sat in the press box next to the German ambassador.[75] The same year Koischwitz began to make contacts with the German Propaganda Ministry.[76] By August of 1939, the Non-Sectarian Anti-Nazi League began to report that Koischwitz was acting as a Nazi propaganda agent in New York.[77]

That same month Koischwitz began working in Berlin at the German Foreign Office.[78] A naturalized American citizen, he signed the register at the U.S. Embassy in Berlin on 1 September 1939[79] and his wife cabled

Hunter College to request a leave of absence for him. He continued working in the Foreign Office under his alias "Dr. Anders" until December, when he resigned his position at Hunter.[80]

Koischwitz soon embarked on his second career as a radio propagandist. In the spring of 1940 former colleagues, many of them prominent American Germanists, received letters with Argentinian stamps and postmarks that announced a series of lectures on literary and philosophical topics to be broadcast by Koischwitz beginning 27 June 1940.[81] To the embarrassment of American German teachers, he often spoke of his experiences at American schools and addressed old friends and students by name. His most famous broadcast program was the "College Hour," in which he argued in a professorial manner that America should keep out of the war.[82] Bluntly, he often ended his broadcasts with a question: "The world is divided into two camps: Bolshevism and the defenders of civilization. Why is America still in the wrong camp?"[83]

Koischwitz was probably "the most influential of the American commentators" in Berlin.[84] He is the only American whose name appears on the regular ministry staff and the only foreign commentator to have a civil service ranking.[85] In the Foreign Ministry, he often worked directly under Kurt Kiesinger,[86] and after 1942 he was also employed by the Ministry of Propaganda and Enlightenment where he continued to broadcast, write scripts for news programs, and write and direct dramas.[87] Small wonder, Koischwitz was among the eight Americans indicted for treason on 26 July 1943 at the U.S. District Court in Washington, D.C. He never came to trial, however. Evidence was found that he had died in Berlin of advanced tuberculosis in August 1944 and the case was dropped.[88]

Testimony was also gathered by the Special Committee to Investigate Un-American Propaganda Activities in its hearings from 1938 to 1941. It indicated that Nazi propaganda agencies had made attempts to influence American educational institutions through German officials in the United States. Testimony was given that a German Consul-General delegate had offered to give books and other forms of support to several universities provided the professors in their German departments were acceptable to the Nazi government.[89] It was also established that the German-American Bund had made attempts to attract German teachers and students to its cause, as it established German language schools of its own.[90] Two exchange students at the University of Missouri who were apparently active in the German Club were also accused of having disseminated German propaganda on the campus.[91]

Nazi efforts to reach the German teaching profession through cultural channels were initiated in about 1935, after the obvious failure of propagandists like Schönemann. While the profession had been able successfully to isolate and disarm most open propagandists, Germanists were probably less successful in resisting the more respectable, subtler forms of *Kultur-politik* adopted by the German Foreign Office.[92] The continued naiveté with which many viewed the tactics of "soft-sell" propaganda suggest that a knowledge of Goethe and Schiller had ill equipped teachers to deal with the Third Reich.

The profession's continued interest and faith in the German language and culture made teachers susceptible to this type of propaganda. Twaddell commented as a Germanist in 1938: "For us German literature is not Hitler . . . we must reflect that this Nazi business is not what we're fundamentally concerned with; that all the trouble caused in our attempt to deal with the present past is . . . . a distraction of attention from the significant past."[93] Such attitudes must have inadvertently given planners in the German Foreign Office hope for success with a *Kulturpolitik* approach.

Teachers habitually wrote the German Railway Information Office, the German Tourist Information Office, the Hamburg-Amerika lines and similar agencies in New York for free brochures and other teaching materials. They sought information and received free books from the German Library of Information.[94] Offices in Germany such as the Auslands-Institut, the Terramare Office,[95] and the anti-Semitic Fichte-Bund kept teachers on their mailing lists and their materials appear in many German language textbooks published in the 1930s.[96] American Germanists continued to plan and take student tours to Germany and to associate themselves with groups such as Heinrich Roenneburg's Educational Pilgrimage.[97] German professors continued their memberships in organizations such as the Deutsche Akademie and planned their trips to Germany through the Carl Schurz Vereinigung in Berlin, at times with their financial support.[98]

The materials and services from these German agencies appeared outwardly harmless. Few references were made to Hitler or to Nazi philosophy. Efforts were not made to propagandize openly, and favors and services were not requested in return for materials. Students and teachers were shown the positive features of the new Germany and given a pleasant, tourist view of the *Reich*. Beautiful landscapes, folk customs, and great moments in Germany's cultural past were emphasized.

Through such contacts German teachers were in fact touching at the heart of the Nazi propaganda machine. Archival sources reveal that these cultural agencies were supported covertly by organizations of the German government such as the Foreign Ministry, the Ministry for Propaganda, and direct branches of the Nazi Party.[99] The German teaching profession in America did eventually grow suspicious of these connections.

In the late 1930s, the profession began breaking off all relationships with Nazi Germany in fear of the ulterior motives of these agencies. Busse had mentioned in writing to a colleague his displeasure with advertisements of the Hamburg-Amerika line in the 1933 issues of *The Germanic Review* and *The German Quarterly*. He had also voiced early suspicions of Roenneburg's leadership of the Pilgrimage tours.[100] J. A. von Bradisch of the College of the City of New York wrote Hohlfeld in 1934: "Ubrigens trauen Sie, bitte, Roenneburg nicht."[101] Others followed these leaders and eventually withdrew their affiliation. Members of the Deutsche Akademie protested when an essay contest was announced. They made it clear that their institutions could lend no support if racial or political considerations were going to be made in the selection of a winner.[102] As a result, the Akademie changed the nature of the contest.[103]

In at least one instance, a German instructor refused a free trip to Germany sponsored by the Carl Schurz Vereinigung of Berlin. Otto Heller correctly surmised that the Vereinigung was a principal organ of Nazi propaganda and felt it would be against his principles as an American to participate.[104] The Carl Schurz Memorial Foundation in Philadelphia began to take a firm stand against Nazism after its honorary President, Jacob G. Schurmann, resigned in protest of its publication "A Fifth of a Nation," which used the term "American-Germans" in place of the usual hyphenated form "German-American." Prior to that, the Foundation had disavowed any connection with its Berlin counterpart, but there were unquestionably contacts through G. Kartzke, the Memorial Foundation's representative in Berlin.[105]

After 1938 German propaganda efforts in America came largely to a halt. Instead, the Nazis sought diligently to quiet any distrust between Germany and the United States. In their minds, the United States could be dealt with after Germany achieved hegemony in Europe.[106] Early propaganda efforts had failed because America had not been open to the type of policies advocated by the National Socialists. Later, more subtle types of propaganda had also failed because in the long run the German Foreign Office had found no means of making the revolutionary Nazi organizations "plausible."[107]

Of course, once war had broken out in Europe and Hitler had declared war on the United States, the situation was clearer, as was the duty of every teacher of German in America. Although this did not lessen the tension or the heartbreak for many in the profession, its members threw themselves into the war effort, both personally and in the classroom. All contacts with Germany were broken by necessity, and German teachers stood firmly behind America in the battle with European fascism. Teachers and students neither openly defended Hitler nor continued to voice strong pro-German sentiments nor to question American ideals. This may be explained by the intensity of the American war effort, the strength of public opinion, and, undoubtedly, by the presence of the FBI and the Special Committee in the U.S. House of Representatives to Investigate Propaganda Activities in the United States.

Once again, American German teachers were teaching the language of the enemy, but they were not questioned about their loyalty in the Second World War. Hatred for the Nazis was not associated with the study of language and literature as it had been in 1917. The Educational Policies Commission spoke out early in support of German study. Unequivocally, it stated: "Everything possible should be done to prevent cultural vandalism directed against the language, literature, music and art of the peoples with whom we are at war."[108] The American Association of School Administrators commented in 1944 concerning language: "Today we realize the necessity of knowing the language of our enemies as well as our friends."[109]

All in all, German study emerged from World War II somewhat weakened in numbers, but not in respect.[110] The profession's cautious stance and its deliberateness in standing behind the value of the study of German culture had paid off in one sense. The usefulness and ultimate value of German as well as the patriotism of the German teaching profession in America had not been questioned. American educators and the general public had learned that loyalty did not have to be demonstrated by removing German from the school program. German could in fact make a valuable contribution to the maintenance and defense of American democracy.

On the other hand, it must be acknowledged that no clear record has been found of leaders who took an open, public stand against the oppression and atrocities of the Nazis. None of the professional organizations decried the rise of Hitler or the reports of Jewish persecution. In an effort to remain outside of politics, the profession bent over backward in the 1930s to avoid confronting the rise of Hitler and the Nazi state. By far the majority of German teachers were anti-Nazi and were concerned about the policies of the new Germany. Yet their attachment to German culture and anxiety for their own subject in American education made them hesitate, initially, to confront the Third Reich and made them try to remain optimistic about Germany's future.

This is not to say that the profession reacted to the policies of the Third Reich less responsibly than did other professional groups or the American public in general. There is some question, however, as to whether German teachers do not have a special responsibility in assessing the policies of the German-speaking countries and in using their knowledge of German culture to inform students and others in America about these policies. The profession must also learn from the experiences of World War II to disassociate itself from Germany and not to be tempted by praise and favors to hold back criticism, to remain silent, or to support policies which are in opposition to American democracy.

The profession waited too long to take a stand against the Third Reich. By the 1940s teachers of German had thrown themselves into the war effort, both in terms of their personal lives and in their language class-rooms. The voices of optimism had grown quiet. The minority in the profession who had supported the Nazis either returned to Germany, were drafted, or kept silent.

It is, of course, mere speculation to wonder if earlier efforts on the part of the profession to use its knowledge of German language and culture to oppose the rise of Hitler could have made any significant difference—or to wonder if having taken a public stand might have helped strengthen and reestablish German programs in America. An understanding of the experiences of the profession in the 1930s can perhaps help assess its responsibilities and its position in American education. In any case, one may hope that the profession will now seek a *Germanistik* which is inde-pendent, critical, and uniquely American in political judgement.

Notes

1 Carl A. Jessen, "Registrations in Languages," *School Life* 23 (September 1937): 23.
2 Sister M. Clarissa Riebenthaler, "Trends in the Teaching of German in the Secondary Schools of the United States," Master's Thesis, University of Cincinnati, 1941, p. 32. The author has written permission to quote from this work.
3 Emory M. Foster, *Statistical Summary of Education 1890–1934*, Bulletin No. 2, (Washington: U.S. Office of Education, 1937) 39.
4 *Final Report of the Committee on Modern Foreign Languages* (Milton, Mass.: Secondary Education Board, 1933); rpt. in *Twentieth Century Modern Language Teaching*, ed. Maxim Neward (New York: Philosophical Library, 1948) 104–5.
5 Adolf Busse, Letter to A. R. Hohlfeld, 19 April 1933, General Correspondence Files 7/14/2, College of Letters and Science (German), Box 2, University of Wisconsin, Division of Archives, Madison, Wisconsin.
6 Postcard to Hermann B. Almstedt, 3 March 1935, Collection #2408, folder 56, Western Historical Manuscripts Collection, University of Missouri, Columbia, MO.
7 "The German Teacher: Professor on the Spot," August 1938, folder W. F. Twaddell, German, Box 15, Wisconsin Archives.
8 A. B. Faust, "Teaching German Today," *American-German Review* 5 (April 1939): 2.
9 David Ewen, "Thomas Mann Discusses Hitlerism," *B'nai B'rith Magazine* 47 (September 1933): 341.
10 Hohlfeld, Letter to F. W. J. Heuser, 5 April 1933, folder AATG, German, Box 1, Wisconsin Archives. Only page one of this letter exists in the file.
11 Heuser, Letter to Hohlfeld, 2 April 1933, folder AATG, German, Box 1, Wisconsin Archives.
12 Hohlfeld, Letter to Heuser, 5 April 1933.
13 Heuser, Letter to Hohlfeld, 2 April 1933.
14 Busse, Letter to Hohlfeld, 19 April 1933, German, Box 2, Wisconsin Archives.
15 Back cover page of a program invitation to a Grand Concert of the Inter-High School

German Glee Club of New York to be held 16 May 1936 at the College of the City of New York, F. Mankiewicz, sponsor, Record Group 131, German-American Bund, Box 134, File 1, National Archives. Suitland, Maryland.

16 Folded program of 1933 AATG meeting, folder AATG, German, Box 1, Wisconsin Archives.

17 J. B. E. Jonas, Letter to Hohlfeld, 24 November 1933, folder AATG, German, Box 1, Wisconsin Archives.

18 Hohlfeld, Letter to Jonas, 19 December 1933, folder Hohlfeld, German, Box 1, 7/14/6, Wisconsin Archives.

19 H. A. Buschek, Letter to Hohlfeld, 26 December 1933, folder AATG, 7/14/2, Wisconsin Archives.

20 Heuser, Letter to Hohlfeld, 18 December 1933, folder AATG, German, Box 1, Wisconsin Archives.

21 Heuser, Letter to Hohlfeld, 22 December 1933, folder AATG, German, Box 1, Wisconsin Archives.

22 William A. Cooper, Letter to Hohlfeld, 21 December 1933, German, Box 3, Wisconsin Archives.

23 Cooper, Letter to Jonas, carbon to Hohlfeld, 6 January 1934, folder AATG, German, Box 1, Wisconsin Archives.

24 A. B. Faust, Letter to Hohlfeld, 27 January 1934, German, Box 5, Wisconsin Archives.

25 Heuser, Letter to B. Q. Morgan, carbon to Hohlfeld, 14 March 1933, folder AATG, German, Box 1, Wisconsin Archives.

26 Franz Schneider, "Teachers to the Fore!" *Modern Language Forum* 21 (1936): 38.

27 Carl Baumann, "Why Study Foreign Languages?" *Modern Language Forum* 21 (1936): 33–34.

28 Quoted in Mary Elizabeth Davis, "Aims and Obstacles," *Modern Language Forum* 21 (1936): 138.

29 B. Q. Morgan, "The Case for German in the American High School," *Monatshefte* 27 (1935): 293.

30 Theodore Huebener, "Lernt Deutsch!" *Monatshefte* 27 (1935): 293–94.

31 Secretary's Report of the Annual Meeting of the American Association of Teachers of German," *Monatshefte* 29 (1937): 79.

32 Letter received from S. Etta Schreiber, 25 July 1976.

33 Friedrich Schönemann, *Amerika und der Nationalsozialismus*, Heft 4, *Schriften der Deutschen Hochschule für Politik*, ed. Paul Meier-Benneckenstein (Berlin: Junker & Dünnhaupt, 1934): 11.

34 E. Prokosch, Letter to Hohlfeld, 13 December 1934, German, Box 8, Wisconsin Archives.

35 R.M.S.H. Memo to W. F. T., n. d., folder 1939 WFT., 1956 RMH, AATG, Box 1, German, Wisconsin Archives.

36 Heuser, Letter to Hohlfeld, 20 September 1933, folder AATG, German, Box 1, Wisconsin Archives.

37 Joel Hatheway, "German in Our Public Schools," *German Quarterly* 7 (1934): 30.

38 W. F. Leopold, "Reise durch Deutschland 1935," *Monatshefte* 27 (1935): 300.

39 Clipping from *Monitor-Index and Democrat*, Moberly, Missouri, 11 May 1939: 12, in Almstedt papers, Collection #2408, Western Historical Manuscripts.

40 Transcript of "Germany on the Inside," 17 May 1939, attached to B. Q. Morgan, Letter to Hohlfeld, 30 June 1939, German, Box 14, Wisconsin Archives.

41 "Herbert Hoover on Languages," *Modern Language Journal* 22 (1938): 645–46.

42 "Editorial," *New York Times,* 11 April 1938: 22.

43 Ernst Feise, "Report on Referendum," *German Quarterly* 12 (1939): 221–22.

44 "The German Teacher: Professor on the Spot" (Note 7).

45 Feise 221.

46 Twaddell, Letter to "Dear Colleague," 7 January 1939, folder 1934 WFT 1956 RMSH, AATG, German, Box 1, Wisconsin Archives.

47 Feise 221–22.

48 Twaddell, Letter to Feise, 23 January 1939, folder 1939 WFT, 1956 RMSH AATG, German, Box 1, Wisconsin Archives.

49 R.M.S.H. Memo to W.F.T., n.d., folder 1939 WFT 1956 RMSH, AATG, German, Wisconsin Archives.

50 Twaddell, Letter to C. A. Dykstra, 8 September 1939, German, Box 3, Wisconsin Archives.

51 See David S. Wyman, *The Abandonment of the Jews: America and the Holocaust, 1941–1945* (New York: Pantheon, 1984) 14–15.

52 Hohlfeld, Letter to Busse, 23 November 1933, carbon copy, German, Box 2, Wisconsin Archives.

53 Cooper, Letter to Hohlfeld, 27 October 1933, German, Box 3, Wisconsin Archives.

54 Feise, Letter to Hohlfeld, 4 December 1937, German, Box 14, Wisconsin Archives.

55 George Danton, Letter to Hohlfeld, 6 January 1939, German, Box 3, Wisconsin Archives.

56 Lawrence M. Price, Letter to Hohlfeld, 26 May 1938, German, Box 9, Wisconsin Archives.

57 Otto Heller, Letter to Hohlfeld, 26 June 1933, folder AATG, German, Box 1, Wisconsin Archives.

58 Richard Jente, Letter to Hohlfeld, 27 September 1933, folder AATG, German, Box 1, Wisconsin Archives.

59 Gernot Graessner, "Deutschland und Die Nationalsozialisten in den Vereinigten Staaten von Amerika," diss., U Bonn, 1973, 234.

60 Unidentified clipping from Chicago newspaper, 15 November 1933, German, Box 11, Wisconsin Archives. A letter in file, 1 October 1929, is on letterhead of the Amerika-Abteilung des Englischen Universitätsseminars and indicates Schönemann, Leiter of the Amerika Institut.

61 Busse, Letter to Hohlfeld, 23 October 1933, German, Box 2, Wisconsin Archives.

62 Heller, 26 June 1933, German, Box 1, Wisconsin Archives.

63 Letter received from Florence G. Beall, 6 March 1981.

64 Anna Schafheitlin, "Letter [to the Editor]," *Kent Stater,* 11 October 1934, n.p.

65 Interview with Adolf E. Schroeder, Spring 1976; Schafheitlin, Letter to Beall, 9 April 1946, Florence Gray Beall papers, Kent State University Archives, Kent, Ohio; Letter received from Beall; "Obituary," *Kent Courier Tribune,* August 1967 clipping; date of death 12 July 1967.

66 Letter received from Werner Leopold, 12 July 1976.

67 U.S. House Special Committee to Investigate Un-American Activities and Propaganda in the United States, *Hearings,* 76th Cong., 1940, Appendix, 2, 1063–66.

68 Letter received from Paul R. Palmer, archivist, Columbiana Collection, Columbia University, 16 August 1985. Mr. Palmer writes: "Auhagen was never a Columbia professor, nor was he ever the chairman of any German department at Columbia University or any of its affiliated schools."

69 Michael Sayers and Albert E. Kahn, *Sabotage! The Secret War Against America* (New York: Harper, 1942) 161.

70 Otto Koischwitz, Staff Personnel Record, Board of Higher Education, Archives, Hunter College, City University of New York.

71 File 61-9477, section 2, Otto Koischwitz, FBI., U.S. Department of Justice, FOIA 8202797.

72 File 61-9477, sec. 1.
73 Letter from S. Etta Schreiber (note 32).
74 File 61-9477, sec. 2.
75 File 61-9477, sec. 1.
76 Otto Koischwitz Confidential File, 362.113, U.S. Department of State, National Archives, Rundfunkabteilung Personalreferat, 25 October 1941; declassified.
77 G. Egerton Harriman, Letter to James Marshall, 10 August 1939, Archives, Hunter College.
78 Koischwitz Confidential File, memo LR Dr. Schirmer, Abt. Rundfunk, 31 December 1941.
79 Report to the Secretary of State from Consular Section, Berlin, 26 October 1940, U.S. Department of State Files, FOIA request.
80 Board of Education, Letter to Koischwitz, 29 January 1940, carbon copy, Archives, Hunter College.
81 File 61-9477, sec. 1.
82 Referat IX: USA, Rundfunkpropaganda nach den USA, Bd. 2, Gründung und Mitschrift der Sonderreihe "College Hour" von Mai 1940 bis Dezember 1941, Bd. 106, Rundfunkpolitische Abteilung, 1939–1945, Politisches Archiv des Auswärtigen Amtes, Bonn.
83 Tape of Koischwitz broadcast, 9 April 1943, 262-39193, Record Group 262, Foreign Broadcast Intelligence Service, Motion Picture and Sound Recording Branch, National Archives, Washington, D.C.
84 Willi A. Boelcke, *Die Macht des Radios, Weltpolitik und Auslandsrundfunk, 1924–1976* (Frankfurt/Main: Ullstein, 1977) 387.
85 Referat IX: USA, Rundfunkpolitische Abteilung, Personalbestand, Bd. 2, Haushalt, Personal, 1941–1943, pp. 18–19, Politisches Archiv.
86 Auswärtiges Amt, Vol. 77, Bl. 183, Personalbestand der Rundfunkpolitischen Abteilung, 14 August 1943, Zentral Staatsarchiv, Potsdam.
87 File 61-9477, sec. 4.
88 "Charges Dropped," *New York Times*, 28 October 1947: 25.
89 U.S. House Special Committee (1939) 6: 3961–665.
90 U.S. House Special Committee, 75th Cong. (1938) 1: 84–85.
91 U.S. House Special Committee (1938) 1: 1133.
92 Graessner 231–59.
93 "The German Teacher: Professor on the Spot," (Note 7).
94 Suggestions to write these offices appear in professional articles on *Kulturkunde*, in handbooks on teaching, and in the German Service Center Bulletin published in the *Monatshefte*.
95 The Terramare Office was a cultural exchange agency of the German government.
96 The Fichte-Bund published a news information leaflet on topics such as "The Truth about the Jews in Germany," RG131, National Archives; the Fichte-Bund was dedicated to "World Veracity" and headquartered in Hamburg.
97 Pamphlets on Roenneburg tours, German, Box 12, Wisconsin Archives.
98 Almstedt papers, General Correspondence Files, German, Western Historical Manuscripts.
99 Evidence can be found in: *Documents on German Foreign Policy, 1918–1945,* series C (U.S. GPO, 1962) and Captured War Records at Alexandria, Virginia, in series Kul Pol g, 857/285328-612; 637/25335-498, Kul Pol 2wVI; K1808/456206-K456235, Pol u. Kul; and others.
100 Busse, Letter to Hohlfeld, 28 February 1933, German, Box 2, Wisconsin Archives; Letter to Hohlfeld, 9 October 1933, Wisconsin Archives.
101 J. A. von Brandisch, Letter to Hohlfeld, 9 January 1934, German, Box 12, Wisconsin Archives.

102 Twaddell, Letter to Dr. Fochler-Hauke, 1 August 1938, German, Box 3, Wisconsin Archives.
103 Twaddell, Letter to G. C. Sellery, 17 November 1938, German, Box 12, Wisconsin Archives.
104 Heller, Letter to Hohlfeld, 26 June 1934, German, Box 6, Wisconsin Archives.
105 " 'American-German' Angers Schurmann," *New York Times,* 22 May 1940: 15.
106 Graessner 231–59.
107 Graessner 120.
108 Educational Policies Commission, *A War Policy for American Schools* (Washington, D.C.: National Education Association and American Association of School Administrators, 1942) 3, 18.
109 American Association of School Administrators, *Morale for a Free World, America and Not America Only* (Washington, D.C.: Commission of Education for Morale, 1944) 22: 217.
110 *Historical Statistics of the United States from Colonial Times to 1970,* 2 vols., Bicentennial ed. (Washington, D.C.: U.S. Department of Commerce Bureau of the Census, 1975) 1: 363, 377.

Traces of Fascist Ideology in American Professional Journals, 1933–1945

ERIKA SALLOCH
Washington College

The Hitler years were a difficult period for German teachers in the United States. It was less than two decades since the anti-German reaction of World War I had led to a drastic reduction of the teaching of German at American institutions, and now the changed political situation in Germany challenged professionals to take a stand. Many professors of German were either native Germans or had studied in Germany under the leaders of *Geistesgeschichte,* such as Julius Petersen, Josef Nadler, Gerhard Fricke, etc. George L. Mosse convincingly demonstrates "the intimate relationship between völkish thought and German educational institutions," which dates back to the nineteenth century.[1] The methodology of the *Geistesgeschichtliche Periode* is summarized by Eberhard Lämmert: "Der Impuls . . . , einzelnen großen Gestalten der Geschichte die Bewahrung und Erneuerung des Volksgeistes als höchste Leistung zuzumessen, verfestigt sich zu einem methodischen Axiom: Allenthalben begegnet . . . [man der] Hervorkehrung großer Einzelpersönlichkeiten, in denen sich . . . der Seelengrund eines Stammes, der Adel deutschen Menschentums oder deutscher Geist schlechthin inkarnieren."[2] According to Sol Liptzin, German studies at American universities were only a copy of the German system, lacking in originality.[3] Background, training, and job insecurity, as attested by frequent statistics on German enrollment in *The German Quarterly,* hindered the emancipation of American Germanists from the German model.[4]

This paper examines four major journals of the profession, *The German Quarterly, The Germanic Review,* the *Journal of English and Germanic Philology,* and *Monatshefte für deutschen Unterricht* for symptoms of a fascist ideology similar to the one professed inside Germany from 1933 to 1945. The intent of this paper is to look for both explicit and implicit political content in supposedly apolitical professional journals. Due to the long history of strong nationalistic tendencies in *Germanistik* as described by Lämmert, some of the writers who will be quoted might not have been aware of their fascist ideology. It is as difficult, of course, to define fascist literature as it is to define fascist interpretation, but J. M. Ritchie's criteria seem to be commonly accepted: a positive emphasis on the peasant and his "old" values as against the decadent city dweller and his nihilism, on woman as child-bearer and keeper of the hearth—the term *Blut und Boden* is often applicable particularly to these first two characteristics—approval of German nationalist, expansionist, and racist tendencies, a pro-war attitude coupled with hero glorification, and a "message of the pure Krist (a Germanic version of Christianity of an anti-Semitic kind)."[5]

A conservative, reactionary attitude in literary scholarship had existed in Germany long before the advent of the Third Reich. What is surprising, however, is that even under the impact of the news of the book burnings, the crystal night, the start of the war, some Americans did not feel the need to distance themselves from the National Socialist (NS)-approved writers and to study instead the writings of the many talented men and women who had emigrated. In fact, some of the most blatantly pro-fascist essays were published as late as 1944 while relatively little was published on the refugees. The "white list" of writers approved by the NS-regime, the members of the Deutsche Akademie der Dichtung, was published by *Monatshefte* in October 1933 (181). After that, American Germanists should have been aware of the political views of Rudolf G. Binding, Hans Grimm, Hanns Johst, Erwin Guido Kolbenheyer, Agnes Miegel, Wilhelm Schäfer, Ina Seidel, Hermann Stehr, etc.

Four areas to be investigated for indications of fascist ideological content suggest themselves: (1) critical articles on literature and, especially, the tone of the writer which can show him to be a mindless fellow-traveler or someone who consciously espouses specifically nationalistic or racist doctrines; (2) articles and book reviews on philology, *Volkskunde*, and related topics; (3) pedagogy, specifically how the profession viewed the problem of dealing with National Socialism in the classroom; and (4) editorial policies and politics of the journals.

An article on Hans Grimm's best seller, *Volk ohne Raum*, seems a suitable beginning. This book, with its emphasis on the superiority of the Nordic races over "inferior" ones, particularly Africans and Jews, and its militant nationalism and expansionism, epitomizes many aspects of fascist literature. In 1935, George Danton recommended it as a text for German literature classes.[6] Though reluctant to give a definitive evaluation of the book, Danton is clearly impressed by its success and the rave reviews which praise it as Germany's *Schicksalsformel* (33). By that time, "Volk ohne Raum" had already been adopted as a slogan by the German regime and was later used to justify the invasion of Poland. Danton clearly underestimates the political content and impact of the book and overestimates its literary value when, somewhat apologetically, he states: "Most criticism

. . . is based on the book's social and political nexus, rather than on its merit as literature" (34). In an appended index on the book's subject matter Danton lists "anti-Semitism" twenty-one times, an anti-Semitism which he calls "not rabid" (34). This seems a questionable distinction since Grimm's Jews embody all the stereotypes.[7]

One finds much closer adherence to the official German dogma in Godfrey Ehrlich's article about the popular novelist Wilhelm Schäfer.[8] Ehrlich not only attacks the arrogance of the nineteenth century's belief in progress and its cult of freedom—these were ideas dating back to the Romantic period—but he specifically praises *völkisch* ideas: "Nicht völkischen Nationaldünkel, sondern völkisches Gewissen . . . will er [Wilhelm Schäfer] beleben. Dieses Ziel ist ebenso unvereinbar mit den zersetzenden . . . Tendenzen des Naturalismus und materialistischem Zynismus einerseits, wie mit weltfremdem Aesthetentum . . . andererseits" (138–39). Ehrlich's article is studded with biological metaphors and the epithets then current in contemporary German criticism, such as "urwüchsig," "aufbauende Kräfte im deutschen Geistesleben," and "Hüter der deutschen Volksseele." While Ehrlich never mentions the word "Jew," anti-Semitism is clearly implied when he supports Schäfer's belief: "Die deutsche Jugend [wendet sich] gegen ein Dasein, in dem es auf Gewinnsucht, Schläue . . . auf Verstellung ankommt" (140), all attributes which had, by then, long been associated with Jews.

That ideological blinders can deprive a critic of meaningful insights is proven in two essays on Edwin Kolbenheyer and Agnes Miegel by E. P. Appelt.[9] The articles are almost interchangeable in their hymnic praise of the nobility of the authors, of the novels' themes and characters, and, what is more pertinent here, their relegation of woman to a fertility symbol. Appelt summarizes Kolbenheyer's view of woman as "ein Wesen, dem die Natur einen fruchtbaren Schoß, nährende Brüste und Instinkt für Familie [gegeben hat]" (212). In an article with the somewhat misleading title "The Attitude towards Woman in the Modern German Novel," Mimi Jehle only discusses writers on the "white list" approved by the NS-regime: Ernst Wiechert, Karl Benno von Mechow, Friedrich Schnack, Friedrich Griese, and Edwin Kolbenheyer.[10] In the novels by these men— Jehle's article does not deal with women writers—she finds that women are "first of all 'Trägerinnen des Geschlechts' " (112). Here, a professional woman expresses no dismay that in these works one sees "a decided turning away from the emancipation of woman"; to the contrary, she extols the fact that "the specific womanly activity of the care of house, garden, and soil has been given a new dignity and significance, and especially woman as mother has received a new idealization" (114). A general spiritual reform seems to Jehle to be the result of this change: "Regeneration and salvation through woman has been greatly emphasized. . . . She has achieved a new dignity'' (114). The fact that these "ideals" also follow the party line seems not to bother her.[11]

Rootedness and defense of the soil are the main themes of Selina Meyer's "The Plow and the Soil in Ernst Wiechert's Works" and Lambert Shears's "The Treatment of Landscape in Some Recent Writers."[12] The repetitiousness of the *Blut und Boden* style in these articles divulges the fact that they are hortatory, not analytical. Meyer uses many of the standard combinations, such as "deeply rooted" (314, 318, 319) and its opposite "violently uprooted" (316, 317), and she commends valor: "The soldiers fight and fight bravely . . . [in] the firm belief that the soil for which they are sacrificing themselves is eternal" (315–16). Meyer apparently agrees that these soldiers "find salvation only in rooting themselves again firmly in their native soil" (316) even if this means the grave. Shears contrasts the rootedness in the works of Josef Ponten, Lothar Schreyer, and Ewald Banse with the American inability to "cherish for long intimate ties with the soil" (7), and he documents his chosen authors' mystical beliefs with rapturous quotations, such as: "Die Seele des deutschen Menschen schafft die Landschaft. Landschaft entsteht aus dem Zusammenleben von Menschenseele und Heimat" (6, quoted from Lothar Schreyer).

The educational value of war is praised in John R. Frey's "The Function of the Writer: A Study in the Literary Theory of Carossa, Grimm, and Kolbenheyer."[13] World War II had already begun, yet Frey still agrees with Kolbenheyer that "as a destroyer of false values the war had turned out to be a good teacher" (268). This is reminiscent of the way NS-propaganda turned the material loss of World War I into a spiritual victory. In summarizing Hans Grimm's literary theories, Frey absolves him from writing propaganda. Grimm "gives his own interpretation of 'political' . . . [namely] to have German literature portray the German character in its national significance" (275). What is most important according to Frey is that the writer "must be aware of the *völkische Verbundenheit*" (273). Frey's amazing conclusion implies that no attempt to control free expression exists in Germany: "The most significant aspect . . . is that striking unanimity of views which is not the outgrowth of . . . programmatic efforts, but the result of rigid self-examination" (278). Rudolf G. Binding, who had supported the book burnings by the German authorities in his "A German's Answer to the World," is extolled in two articles by V. Bezdek, "Der Kampf um neuen Menschenwert bei Rudolf G. Binding" and "Rudolf Bindings Kunstauffassung."[14] According to the back cover of the volume of *Monatshefte* that contained the latter article, Bezdek was serving on active duty in the U. S. Navy at the time of publication, a fact which did not inhibit him from expressing overt right-wing propaganda. Both articles espouse the ideas of war as a purifier and of the new Germanic religion. After quoting Binding's "Ich zieh in einen heiligen Krieg; / Frag nicht nach Lohn, frag nicht nach Sieg" (63), Bezdek concludes: "Der Dichter sah im Kriege ein ewig brauchbares . . . Erlebnis" (65). Binding's philosophy is defined as *Wehrhaftigkeit:* "Bindings ethischer Zug ist nur eine dichterische Fassung des deutschen 'wehrlos-ehrlos' " (71). Not even women escape Bezdek's appreciation of Binding's martial ethos: they are "Ritter in Frauenkörpern. Sie verlangen vom Manne dasselbe, was der Autor selbst: Mut, Geradlinigkeit, Ehrlichkeit—kurz: *Männlichkeit* in dem ursprünglichen Sinne vir-tus" (69). Bezdek's hymnic conclusion praises the new Germanic religion of the German Reich: "Die Empfindung . . . der Volkszugehörigkeit wurde zum Zunder, aus dem später der berauschende Zauber einer neuen germanischen Religion emporsteigen und den deutschen Raum umspannen sollte" (71). It does not come as a surprise that, as a consequence, Bezdek elevates Binding to the role of a high priest: "Der soldatische Künstler [vermacht uns] seine heidnische Religion des Erdenmenschen" (72).

The only glaringly ideological article published in *The Germanic Review* during the entire period is Henriette von Klenze's "Three Post-War German Poets in Their Relation to Paul Ernst's Philosophy."[15] Perhaps because of the war, the journal experienced difficulties in obtaining articles, as did *The German Quarterly,* or a slackening of the selection process had taken place.[16] Von Klenze claims that Binding's poems, especially his collection of war poems, *Stolz und Trauer,* are "perhaps the most original contribution to German lyric poetry since Goethe" (116). At a time in World War II when there were high technology attacks, von Klenze manages to admire the courage of Binding's cavalry horse in "Der Heilige Reiter": "Greif aus mein Pferd, greif aus mein Rapp, / Greif aus und hilf uns weiter!" (115). As an adherent of Nadler's *Stamm* theories and their related racism, von Klenze believes that the Russian element in Wiechert's background is negative and that it must be overcome by the healthy German one: "If there are still remnants of the umbilical cord of the Russian elements in Wiechert's art, if the notorious Rasputin haunts the pages . . . they give way to the healthy elements, to the hero's nearness to nature and God" (121).

Even marginal areas of literature sponsored by the NS-regime were given their due by the American Germanists. Walter J. Mueller admonishes his colleagues that no "study of modern German literature can overlook the growing significance of *auslandsdeutsche Dichtung*" (198). In his article on "Heinrich Zillich," Mueller holds his protagonist to be the most important representative of the *auslandsdeutsche* writers, an opinion which he substantiates with Zillich's definition of the Sudeten Germans' mission: "Dieses Menschentum in seiner Wesenhaftigkeit . . . zu verkünden."[17] According to Ritchie (97), Zillich was one of the most virulent National Socialist writers and one who was highly subsidized by the regime.

A number of survey articles tread a thin line between outright espousal of *völkisch* literature and guarded reserve. Detlev Schumann's "Expressionism and Post-Expressionism in the German Lyric" is ambivalent in its evaluation of the "formless ecstasy (too often pseudo-ecstasy) of expressionism" (55) and the new trend towards *radikale Sachlichkeit,* a term coined by Heinz Kindermann and taken over by Schumann (55).[18] Schumann appreciates Franz Werfel but criticizes most expressionists for their lack of "a numinous feeling for nature. This applies to most . . . of the *Menschheitsdämmerung* group, more especially, it would seem, to the Jews" (115). He quotes Johannes R. Becher, " 'Ja-; brüderlich verschmelzen! Nicht einsam, sondern jeder sein! . . . ' " as proof of the "stupendous *Unsachlichkeit* that expressionism can attain at its worst" (64). While he claims that Becher's "communistic activism destroys the poet in him" (120), he does not believe that a similar destruction has taken place in Johst. Most of the other poets whom Schumann discusses are on the "white list." In *PMLA,* Schumann supported a racist interpretation of literature: "The near future will produce literary criticism from an anthropological, racial point of view. As a matter of fact, it is already under way, cf. Nadler's 'Rassenkunde—Volkskunde—Stammeskunde' in *Dichtung und Volkstum.* . . . I see no reason why such an approach should be regarded as illegitimate as long as the principle is not ridden to death."[19]

Rudolf A. Syring's review of "Contemporary Authors in the New Germany" answers his rhetorical question whether "there can be literature in the real sense of the word under the new regime" with "decidedly yes!" (311).[20] Ignoring the fact that many German histories of literature had been written by nationalistic professors prior to 1933, men who had no problem with *Gleichschaltung,* Syring uses the circular argument that if the writers approved by the current regime were discussed in such books, they deserved the American Germanist's attention (312). A similarly conservative approach to methodology is expressed in Ernst Jocker's "Philosophie und Literaturwissenschaft."[21] "Rassenmäßig gebundenes Pathos" leads Jockers to deny credibility to Adolf Bartels and Walther Linden but he acknowledges Ludwig Klages, Hans Leisegang, Hermann August Korff, and Hermann Pongs (79). Klages' pro-Nazi views must have been known, though Korff's "Forderung des Tages" and Pongs' "Krieg als Volksschicksal im deutschen Schrifttum" were perhaps inaccessible.[22] Jockers ends his article with a virulent attack against a psychoanalytic interpretation of literature, that "Freud selbst, wie seine Anhänger . . . Ausfälle auf das geisteswissenschaftliche Gebiet unternehmen, ist . . . eine jener Ironien, die ohne Annahme einer Zwangsneurose ein

Rätsel bleiben'' (284). Marjorie Lawson's "Trends in Recent German Literature" discusses "the division between emigrant authors and those remaining in Germany" (49).[23] According to Lawson, the United States makes life easy for the emigrants but is prejudiced against the literature of the new Germany: "The work of the emigrant figures most prominently in the foreign language collections of American bookstores, monopolizes criticism in the American literary columns, and even penetrates to the New York stage. But if Americans are the ones to condemn discrimination . . . they must themselves transcend it" (49). Lawson correctly reports the switch in approved German literature from "the horror of war" to its "glorification" which she documents admiringly with Hanns Johst's exclamatory verses: "Das Volk ist eins! Unser Volk ist groß / Heiß, heilig fordert es das Blut" (56). Aside from a sarcastic allusion to Thomas Mann, stating that "the blond, lucky children that Tonio envied now have their day" (54), the literature of the emigrants is not mentioned. The literature of the approved writers Lawson considers "important and supernationally human" (59).

Lydia Roesch is more forthright in her title "Der völkische Dichter und seine nationale Sendung."[24] She quotes profusely from Johst and Linden to explain National Socialist literary theories to the American reader and concludes in her models' jargon: "Die neue Forderung ist demnach eine klare Herausstellung der deutschen Art, des deutschen Volkstums, nämlich: tiefe, lebendige Naturverwurzelung" (158). Roesch's article enraged Ernst Feise. After the clichés of so many preceding quotations his *Verriß* deserves more space than the original:

> Was bedeutet "Seher und Deuter seines Volkes" sein?—Bedeutet es durch Herrn Roman Hoppenheit im Dichterschulungslager . . . zu einer anonymen Gemeinschaftskunst herangezüchtet zu werden? . . . Ist *der* Dichter die Stimme des "Sehers und Deuters," der sein Volk den Zielen zuzuführen sucht, die ihm selbst als die ewigen Sterne am Himmel leuchten, oder ist es der, welcher "der neuen Bewegung . . . blutbewußt" ihre Ziele . . . verwirklichen hilft?"[25]

Clearly, the largest number of ideologically colored articles appeared in *Monatshefte* where, between 1933 and 1945, twenty articles on writers on the "white list" were published: Rudolf G. Binding (2), Waldemar Bonsels (1), Hans Carossa (1), Paul Ernst (2), Erwin Guido Kolbenheyer (1), Agnes Miegel (1), Josef Ponten (1), Hermann Stehr (7), Karl Heinrich Waggerl (1), Ernst Wiechert (2), Heinrich Zillich (1). It is perhaps noteworthy that the reactionary critics did not write on those writers on the approved list who do not lend themselves to a simplistic interpretation, such as Gottfried Benn and Ernst Jünger. Nine articles appeared on writers on the "black list": Franz Kafka (1), Thomas Mann (5), Ernst Toller (2),

Jacob Wassermann (1), Franz Werfel (1). Not included in this tally are articles on Gerhart Hauptmann and Stefan George whose own unclear political stance could lead some critics to a more right-wing interpretation than their works might warrant.[26] Contributors on both sides appear to have refrained from attacking writers on the opposite political side.

The German Quarterly, in those years a predominantly pedagogical journal, gave approximately equal space to both groups. *The Germanic Review* side-stepped the political issue by publishing mostly studies on writers and genres of preceding periods. When articles on contemporary literature did appear they avoided any reference to current events. Thus Adolf D. Klarmann's comparison of Werfel's *Das Opfer* and *Jacobowsky and the Colonel* mentions only that "two conflagrations separate the two works" (200) but not that *Jacobowsky* depicts the fate of the refugees, including Werfel himself.[27] Similarly F. K. Richter's article on Stehr's *Heiligenhof* contains biographical information but fails to mention the fact that Stehr was on the approved NS-writers' list.[28]

The *Journal of English and Germanic Philology* was edited by Albert Arons, who did not print any *Blut und Boden* articles. Several rebuttals of a nationalistic revaluation of older German writers appeared in this journal.[29] Lydia Baer's thorough and illuminating article, "The Literary Criticism of Ludwig Klages and the Klages School," is the only critical survey of NS-literary theory that was published in the four journals. Unbelievable as it might seem, Baer's essay also contains the only mention of a National Socialist attack on the emigrants: " 'Zeitgenossen wie Thomas Mann . . . geschwollene kleine Journalisten wie Ludwig Marcuse wetteiferten . . . durch giftige Einstellungen . . . und Ghetto-Gegeifer,' um Klages herabzusetzen" (136).[30]

In Germany, the division between literary history and philology has long been blurred. After 1933 all Germanists who held positions at German universities were servants of the regime and of the *völkische Deutschwissenschaft* postulated by the leading Germanists, such as Heinz Kindermann, Hans Naumann, Wolfgang Kayser, Herbert Cysarz, and many others.[31] This *Deutschwissenschaft* included the entire range from literary criticism to philology, *Volkskunde,* and *Rassenkunde.* In the United States, philology and linguistics remained separate fields of scientific research and the articles published in the journals under discussion are free from any National Socialist influence. The equation *germanisch = urgermanisch = arisch* never occurs; the very word *indogermanisch* is referred to in English as "Indo-European."

Articles on contemporary spoken German are divided into those by nationalistic language purifiers on the one hand, and internationally minded scholars on the other. Actually, there were two opposing trends inside

Germany: *Propaganda*minister Goebbels did not see a parallel between linguistic and racial purism and, despite criticism of the foreign word "Propaganda," persisted in using this title. In the meantime, others tried to purge all *Fremdwörter* from the German language.[32] Some Americans belonged to the latter category. A prime example is Theodor Schreiber, in whose article "Vom Fremdwort im deutschen Unterricht" content and style abound with the marks of a repressed fellow traveler.[33] He complains about his colleagues "die dem stammesdeutschen Ausdruck eine un-deutsche Bezeichnung [vorziehen]" (160), thus showing their lack of feeling for the pure German word. His essay teems with the prevalent German vocabulary, such as "unvölkisch," "urdeutsch," "wahrhaft deutsches Wortbild," "Sinnendingwörter," etc. Two witty articles by Meno Spann, "Fremdwort und Fremdphrase" and "Veil? Flied? Violett? Veilchenblau?" protest this nonsense.[34] Spann points out that the battle against the *Fremdwort* historically belongs in the same category as the battle for preservation of German script, of *völkisch* customs: "In diesen Scharmützeln . . . bereitet sich die Entscheidungsschlacht für die Zukunft unserer Kultur vor" (49). This affinity between advocates of language purification and German script is proven in a review by Max Griebsch in which he calls *Fraktur* "wertvolles Kulturgut" and quotes approvingly from Adolf Richter's *Deutsche Schrift und höhere Schule:* "Untersuchungen der Ärzte und Physiologen haben die Überlegenheit der deutschen Schrift erwiesen."[35]

Harry Pfund, a Ph.D. from Harvard, one of the founders of the *American German Review,* and Secretary of the Carl Schurz-Gesellschaft, gave the readers of *Monatshefte* an introduction to NS-vocabulary: "Kleine Sprachwanderung—Neue Wörter in neuer Zeit."[36] Pfund's formulations indicate that he not only wishes to give his readers an objective translation of unfamiliar vocabulary, but that he also is favorably impressed by the effect of language on the "Neugestaltung des Lebens" (41). Pfund seems to admire the fact that concrete new terms were created through "intensiveres soziales Pflichtbewußtsein, die moderne Wehrbereitschaft, die Ertüchtigung der Jugend" (42). Terms like "Pimpf" and "Sturmbann" show the "Werdegang des jungen deutschen Menschen im Rahmen der Volksgemeinschaft" (44). One cannot but agree with Pfund's conclusion that familiarity with NS-vocabulary gives one insight into the mentality of that regime: "Vertrautheit mit dem neuen Wortschatz führt schnell zu einem klareren Verständnis des deutschen Umbruchs und Aufbaus" (45). These last words, *Umbruch* and *Aufbau,* however, which are taken right out of the rhetoric of the Nazi leaders, give the ultimate clue to Pfund's political position.

Books on philology occasionally were reviewed by both sides. Alfred Senn praises *Deutsches Volk und deutsche Sprache* by Johann Leo Weisgerber: "[Der] weitbekannte Sprachphilosoph . . . umreißt die Gedanken, die die reichsdeutschen Forscher heute im Hinblick auf ihre Muttersprache bewegen." Leo Spitzer, a more justly renowned philologist than Weisgerber, who already in 1918 had warned against language chauvinism in his book *Fremdwörterhatz und Fremdwörterhaß*, mocks Weisgerber's theories and Senn's review of them: "Dem unvoreingenommenen Forscher, dem es keine Sonderbefriedigung gewährt, wenn er einen deutschen Ausdruck auf 'echt germanisches' Empfinden zurückführen kann . . . wird eine Abweisung der Weisgerberschen Theorie keine Erschütterung eines lebensnotwendigen Glaubens verursachen."[37]

The new German publications on *Volkskunde* and *Rassenkunde* frequently found American reviewers who were themselves interested in this peculiar German science. Werner Neuse first praises the high standard of new German books on this subject and then recommends Paul Gauß's *Das Buch vom deutschen Volkstum: Wesen—Lebensraum—Schicksal:* "Auch das Volkstum der Auslandsdeutschen [ist] eng in den Bereich der Untersuchung . . . gezogen worden."[38] Approvingly he adds: "Der rassenkundlichen Betrachtung werden nur wenige Seiten und Bilder gewidmet." Johannes Bühler's *Deutsche Geschichte Erster Band: Urzeit, Bauerntum und Aristokratie* gets a high recommendation from C. M. Purin, who is convinced that Bühler's theory of the origin of the Nordic race is scientifically irrefutable.[39] R. O. Röseler, in an admiring review of *Langenscheidts Deutsche Lesehefte,* expresses surprise and pleasure at the continuity of German thought: that "der Nationalsozialismus sich auf Herders Gedankengänge über Volkstum beruft, daß er auf rassische Erkenntnisse in Goethes Denken hinweist, wie von Walther von der Vogelweide . . . [bis] Nietzsche der Kampf der deutschen Seele gegen Überfremdung . . . geführt worden ist."[40]

E. P. Appelt adapted his reviews to the changing political situation. In a first review of Adolf Helbock's *Was ist deutsche Volksgeschichte?* he commends German scholarship for its racial investigations: "Das Grundproblem . . . ist die Rassenfrage . . . , [um] der Staatspolitik Unterlagen für die nationale Schutzarbeit zu liefern." Appelt then calls upon the Americans to follow Germany's lead. Two years later, writing on Arno Mulot's *Das Bauerntum in der deutschen Dichtung unserer Zeit,* Appelt acknowledges a split between pro- and antiracist readers, though he still expresses approval of the German viewpoint: "Der Kampf gegen Überfremdung [wird] dargestellt. . . . Neue Gesichtspunkte kommen zur Anwendung, die, mag man ihnen zustimmen oder nicht, Beachtung . . . heischen" (230). By 1942 Appelt has, of course, reversed his opinion on how the United States can best protect its national interest. He now recommends that Americans study National Socialist theories for a better understanding of the enemy. In a third review, again of a book by Mulot, *Der Soldat in der deutschen Dichtung,* written in 1942, Appelt denies this book's scientific value.[41] Now, however, he considers it to be in the interest of those who are fighting a war against the Germans and who are, therefore, studying the National Socialist attitude toward war, to read this book "zur Vervollständigung des Bildes" (151). Such an attempt to praise the great new insights of *NS-Volkskunde* and, simultaneously, to feign neutrality on this subject, is bound to fail. In similarly evasive fashion J. A. von Bradish prevaricates in a review of Karl Saller's *Weg der deutschen Rasse:*[42] "Man mag der neudeutschen Bewegung gegenüberstehen, wie man will, jedenfalls wird man . . . ihr Folgerichtigkeit nicht absprechen können. In ihrem Mittelpunkt steht, zum religiösen Axiom erhoben, die Rassenfrage" (161). At first von Bradish claims not to be in total agreement with all of Saller's views, but he then concludes everyone "wird seine Anschauungen zu ergänzen haben" (162). Von Bradish's curious neutrality, expressed in his "wie man will" attitude to *Rassenkunde,* perverts a moral question to one of simple taste. Furthermore, *Rassenkunde,* for von Bradish, apparently means only an acceptable addition to the existing body of knowledge.

Otto Koischwitz was a prolific writer of textbooks and probably the most outspoken National Socialist among the American Germanists. Since readers are probably not familiar with his *A German American Interprets Germany,* a few quotations are needed for an appreciation of its review:[43] "This Jewish age came to a rapid end in the national-socialist movement,— as the Latin age . . . ended in the revolutionary movement of the Storm and Stress. In both cases, a powerful emotional nationalism revolted against 'foreign' elements. In both cases, German mysticism, irrationalism, and romanticism waged war against rationalism and intellectualism, heart against brain, blood against ink" (47). Werner Neuse seems impressed: "Der Nachweis ist . . . gelungen, daß das dritte Reich . . . organisch mit den früheren Reichen zusammenhängt und daß gewisse . . . Züge deutscher Geisteshaltung erst jetzt . . . zu reiner . . . Gestaltung gekommen sind." Nevertheless, Neuse refrains from unrestrained approval, smoothly equivocating between praise of Koischwitz' method and regret that the results would leave many people dissatisfied. He concludes that Americans must try to understand the new Germany, for "aus dem Verstehen wird, wenn nicht Liebe, so doch Achtung erwachsen. Dazu ist das Buch ein guter Führer."[44]

The book reviews in the *Journal of English and Germanic Philology* never treated *Volkskunde* publications from Nazi Germany as scientific material: they sometimes severely criticized them and occasionally derided them.[45]

Strained attempts at neutrality in articles on pedagogy and reviews of textbooks for classroom use testify to the tension in the profession. C. M. Handschin, in two reviews of textbooks on German civilization, accuses the American press of hysteria in reporting the news from Germany.[46] He advocates that teachers "choose a text which stands well above the controversial" (68). Werner Leopold counsels abstention from classroom discussion of National Socialism, though he thinks it would be "overscrupulous" not to mention the fact that Hitler became Chancellor in 1933. Instead of factual information, according to Leopold, students should be given a glimpse into the Germans' "own special way of thinking," for which he recommends Erich Kästner's *Das fliegende Klassenzimmer.*[47] Blandness was advocated as late as 1941 when Richard Lemke favored adoption of E. P. Appelt's and A. M. Hanhardt's *Deutsches Leben* because the book dealt mainly with the peasant traditions "which are least affected by the hullabaloo of the moment."[48] Not only were evasion of political issues and repression of facts advocated but, far from counseling neutrality, Camillo von Klenze obviously thinks that a junior year abroad would convert the American students to the new German ideals: "Rheinpoesie und Rheinromantik würden dann . . . seelische und geistige Erlebnisse sein. . . . Hier erscheinen den Juniors . . . die Musikdramen Wagners als der Ausdruck der Volksseele und bestärken das Streben, die Schöpfung einer völkisch-amerikanischen Musik nach Kräften zu unterstützen."[49] Dieter Cunz decried such exaggerated praise by German-Americans of German culture: "[Sie überhöhen die Verdienste] in einem solch haltlosen und marktschreierischen Ton . . . [daß einem] die Schamröte ins Gesicht steigen muß."[50]

Classroom texts of contemporary literature published during the Hitler years run the gamut from blandness to outright fascism. On the innocuous side, *Emil und die Detektive* was the favorite, as shown by many advertisements, recommending it "for zest in the classroom." After 1942, the advertisement for *Emil* was flanked by one for *Kriegsdeutsch.* The *Emil* flood led Meno Spann to write "Emil und die Professoren" in which he deplores the fact that the profession does not face the problem of teaching German culture:[51] "Ein Schritt zur Lösung wird es sein, wenn wir den Emil-Ausweg vermeiden" (169). The fascist side was supported by R. O. Röseler, who recommended for classroom use *Sonnige Heimat* by Tremel-Eggert, a book published by the official Nazi publishing house. "In allen Geschichten . . . lebt der starke Odem erdnaher Wahrheit."[52] Fellow travelers edited texts by Nazi writers for American students, and they wrote original textbooks with a strong ideological slant. Both types of books were promptly and favorably reviewed by their sympathetic colleagues. The insipid titles often point to their lack of content.[53] Holt and Lippincott were the publishers who brought out most of these *völkisch* textbooks. In the reviews of such textbooks anti-Semitism and criticism of refugee writers crop up. Thus Friedrich Bruns comments on *Aus reinem Quell,* a poetry anthology: "Wie es einer völkisch bewegten Zeit entspricht

. . . [fehlen] alle jüdischen Dichter . . . so natürlich Heine" who, according to Bruns, had been "überschätzt."

A. J. Prahl, reviewing Toller's *I Was a German (Eine Jugend in Deutschland)* asserts that its only purpose is "propaganda." In a survey of new books, Edmund K. Heller belittles *Im Westen nichts Neues* and recommends the books by Koischwitz and Paulus instead of those by Erich Maria Remarque and Stefan Zweig. August Mahr, a former soldier in the German Army during World War I, warns the readers not to believe Zweig's depiction of justice in *Erziehung vor Verdun:* "Zweig [ist] von der künstlerischen Höhe seines *Grischa* herabgestiegen, um sich für deutsche Unbill gegen seine jüdischen Volksgenossen . . . zu rächen."[54]

There was considerably more protest from the democratic part of the profession against this spread of propaganda in the classroom than one finds against the *Blut und Boden* articles on literature. John Hess voices his outrage that American journals and publishers were printing right-wing propaganda: "In an article on the new German poets . . . a German teacher in one of our state universities [praises] the new *völkische Dichter* who spend their energy as the interpreters of *Volkstum* and *Gemeinschaft.*" William R. Gaede wrote a devastating review of Jane Goodloe's *In Dichters Lande.* How careful one had to be about praise of the possibly unpopular Thomas Mann is illuminated by Edwin Zeydel's review of *Thomas Mann's Novel "Der Zauberberg"* by Hermann Weigand: "Weigand's is a brave defense of a book which, 'von der Parteien Gunst und Haß verwirrt' will long remain a bone of contention, not among lovers of poetry but in the camp of the intelligentsia. Some may be proud that the honor of serving as the leading attorney for Mann . . . falls to the lot of this champion."[55]

Despite the fact that journals are professional publications for literary and pedagogical purposes, a few columns and special reports are of purely political import. At the 1939 AATG meeting, the Association's Committee on Resolutions put the following to a vote: "Be it resolved: That the American Association of Teachers of German assembled in its Annual Meeting declares anew its faith in the continuing value of the many elements in German culture which have enriched the spiritual life of this country. We pledge ourselves to maintain and defend the ideals of tolerance, humanity, and individual freedom as represented in the works of Lessing, Goethe, and Schiller. Our sympathy goes out to those teachers in Germany who have suffered or are suffering from intolerance and fanaticism. In this difficult time we believe it to be our patriotic duty to cultivate such common elements of our spiritual heritage as make for peace and understanding."[56] After its defeat at the meeting, the Executive Council, under President Feise's direction, decided to mail a questionnaire with the following questions to all AATG members:

I. We believe that there are traditional and enduring values in German culture which we, as teachers of German, should help to preserve.

II. We pledge ourselves to maintain and defend the ideals of tolerance, humanity, and individual freedom.

III. We sympathize with the oppressed minorities in Germany.

IV. We believe in defending and promoting those principles of American democracy which make for peace and understanding.[57]

A sizable majority adopted the resolution, though it is noteworthy that the largest number of negative votes was cast on the question regarding "sympathy with minorities." Job insecurity may have influenced the vote. To assuage the profession's fear of the refugees, *Monatshefte* (1934): 47 reported that among 1100 immigrant applicants, 36 professors had found positions of whom 18 were members "der jüdischen Rasse." The journal does not mention whether any of these immigrants were Germanists, but it assures its readers: "Die Anstellungen sind nicht permanent, nach Ablauf der Periode [one year, E. S.] können . . . die Emigranten keine weiteren Ansprüche stellen."[58]

One of Werner Neuse's regular reports on "German Club Activities" in *The German Quarterly* (1934): 43–44 reads *in toto:* "Current political events, as can easily be understood, are a prominent part in many programs, and one Club (Kent State College) has enclosed [sic] the *Horst Wessel Lied* among its German songs 'um ganz auf der Höhe zu sein.' "[59] *Monatshefte* solicited its readers to join the Verein für das Deutschtum im Ausland: "Beitrittserklärungen werden erbeten und zwar möglichst bald."[60] In 1933 and 1934 Max Griebsch edited a column in *Monatshefte,* "Umschau der Schriftleitung," which was followed, from 1935–37, by J. P. von Grueningen's "At Random from Current Periodicals," periodicals which were official NS-publications, such as the *Zeitschrift des NS-Lehrerbundes* or the *Zeitschrift für die Kunde vom Auslandsdeutschtum.* Von Grueningen usually introduced these excerpts with a brief laudatory remark. One excerpt will suffice: "[Die] folgenden Auszüge dürften auch für uns etwas Beachtenswertes enthalten: 'Wir erheben Anspruch auf unseren Platz in der Welt, weil das deutsche Volk mit seinen schöpferischen Kräften . . . berufen ist, am Aufbau der Welt . . . aktiveren Anteil . . . zu nehmen.' "[61] When yet another column in *Monatshefte,* "Berichte und Mitteilungen," gave space to the Nazi literary propagandist Heinz Kindermann for a eulogy to Bartels, "Adolf Bartels zum 75. Geburtstag," Ernst Feise reacted with anger: "Schulden wir in Amerika einem Adolf Bartels Ehrfurcht? . . . Sollen wir hier in Amerika auch zu den 'neuen Wertmaßstäben' bekehrt werden?"[62] Feise's protest resulted in some changes. In 1938, he joined the Editorial Board of *Monatshefte,* followed in 1939 by Albert Aron. One immediate result was the disappearance of the column "At Random from Current Periodicals," which had been a mouthpiece for contemporary publications within Germany. Another result was that, although *Blut und Boden* articles continued to appear in the journal, more articles on blacklisted writers were published.

This summary of ideologically colored quotations from the professional journals is a distillate and as such is more concentrated than the originals. What it does indicate is that the profession was politically divided and that each journal's editorial policy is reflected in its content. Not only the members of the Wisconsin group, Röseler, Purin, and Koischwitz, published *völkisch* material. Judging by their names, native Americans were also impressed by this movement. The opposite of the Wisconsin group seems to have been at The Johns Hopkins University, which was founded on the model of the German university. No by-line by any member of this institution betrays a fascist frame of mind. Three of its members, Dieter Cunz, Leo Spitzer, and Ernst Feise, were among those who were most outspoken in their rebuttal of *völkisch* publications. *The German Quarterly* tried to stay uncommitted by publishing essays and reviews by both sides, a stance publicly affirmed in 1943: "Your Managing Editor would like also to add a personal word: This is primarily a pedagogical, and secondarily a literature-critical journal. It is not, and never has been, a political organ. It is our duty to be loyal *followers* of our government," signed: "The Editorial Board."[63] This statement (Curtis D. Vail was the editor) contains, of course, a two-fold contradiction: Acceptance of an article is, among other considerations, a political act and to be an apolitical "loyal follower" is impossible.

After Harold von Hofe had sent Thomas Mann a recent issue of *The German Quarterly* containing von Hofe's article on "German Literature in Exile: Thomas Mann," Mann sent the following reply: "Daß die germanistischen Studien in diesem Land so ungestört weitergehen, ist ein schönes Zeichen für die Unberührtheit des amerikanischen wissenschaftlichen Geistes vom Kriegsgeiste. Ich wollte, diese Blätter gelangten nach Deutschland."[64] It would seem doubtful that Mann had read many prior issues. *The Germanic Review,* with few exceptions, ignored the political dilemma by publishing mostly articles and reviews on by-gone periods. Only the *Journal of English and Germanic Philology* had a firmly democratic leadership which kept out *völkisch* ideology. *Monatshefte,* on the other hand, at least from 1933 to 1937, was dominated by fascist ideology, although some articles on black-listed writers and rebuttals were accepted. R. O. Röseler remained its editor until 1948, but the outbreak of the war brought a conversion which is symbolized by the house advertisements in the journal. Instead of an invitation to "Visit the New Germany During Olympiad Year" the readers, immediately following Pearl Harbor, were asked to "Buy United States Savings Bonds and Stamps."[65]

Notes

1 George L. Mosse, *The Crisis of German Ideology* (New York: Grosset & Dunlap, 1968) 152.

2 Eberhard Lämmert, "Germanistik—Eine deutsche Wissenschaft," in *Nationalismus in Germanistik und Dichtung,* ed. Benno von Wiese and Rudolf Heuss (Berlin: Erich Schmidt, 1967) 20.

3 *Monatshefte* 32 (1940): 296.

4 *German Quarterly* 7 (1934): 129–44.

5 J. M. Ritchie, *German Literature under National Socialism* (London & Canberra: Helm, 1983) 10 & 15–20.

6 *Monatshefte* 26 (1935): 33–34.

7 To characterize the book's anti-Semitism as "not rabid" is a dubious distinction. Grimm's Jews are described in terms of the standard clichés: "Vor der Hauptverhandlung erschien ein kleiner jüdischer, hämischer Mann mit einem schwarzen Zwickelbarte. . . . Fritz Wessel sagt, der Fremde heiße Rechtsanwalt Dr. Levi. . . . Der Fremde fragte vielerlei im unangenehmen Tone einer hohen überschrieenen Stimme . . . und er wirtschaftete mit den Händen und trampelte mit den Füßen und befahl und bestimmte von oben her" Hans Grimm, *Volk ohne Raum* (Munich: Langen, 1932) 336.

8 *Monatshefte* 27 (1935): 130–39.

9 *Monatshefte* 28 (1936): 67–70 and 209–12.

10 *Monatshefte* 29 (1937): 109–14.

11 For an attack on this article and on "collectivistic" literature, see Erika Meyer, "Revaluation of the Individual in the Modern German Novel," *Germanic Review* (henceforth *GR*) 13 (1938): 208–36. Meyer warns that the nationalistic tendency will "lead to extremes . . . and its militant nature causes the rest of the world to tremble" (218).

12 *Monatshefte* 30 (1938): 314–28; *GR* 16 (1943): 1–7.

13 *Monatshefte* 32 (1940): 266–78.

14 Ritchie 65; *Monatshefte* 35 (1943): 62–72 & 36 (1944): 224–32.

15 *GR* 18 (1943): 113–22.

16 "The war has caused a reduction in the number of literary papers submitted," *GQ* 17 (1944): 40.

17 *Monatshefte* 32 (1940): 198–204; quotations from 198 and 199.

18 *GR* 9 (1934): 54–72; 115–29.

19 *PMLA* 51 (1936): 1180.

20 *Monatshefte* 27 (1935): 311–16.

21 *GR* 10 (1935): 73–97; 166–86.

22 Korff professed the new credo: "Die Zeit der reinen Wissenschaft ist vorbei. . . . So verstanden aber ist Deutschkunde das Gegenteil von Historismus, sie ist *Politik.* . . . Mit Recht wirft Hitler den Deutschen vor, daß sie so schlecht verstanden haben, aus ihrer Geschichte zu lernen (*Zeitschrift für Deutschkunde* 47 [1933]; quoted from *Materialien zur Ideologiegeschichte der deutschen Literaturwissenschaft,* ed. Gunter Reiss [Tübingen: Niemeyer, 1973] 2: 84–85). Pongs asks: "Wieweit sind es große völkische Inhalte, die die Volksdichtung tragen müssen? . . . Sind Führergestalten unserer Zeit wie Schlageter und Wessel, wie Hindenburg und der deutsche Volkskanzler selbst nicht viel mehr Volkssymbol als das, was Dichter erdichten können?" (*Materialien* 101).

23 *Monatshefte* 28 (1936): 49–55.

24 *Monatshefte* 29 (1937): 158–60.

25 *Monatshefte* 29 (1937): 223–24. The political division of the profession is visualized on page 224. Feise's protest is followed by a nationalistic eulogy of the liberal Ludwig Uhland by R. O. Röseler, "Zum 150. Geburtsjahre und 75. Todesjahre." Röseler quotes

Heinrich von Treitschke on "Der Gute Kamerad": "Einfacher ist nie gesagt worden, wie den streitbaren Germanen seit der Zimbernschlacht bis zu den Franzosenkriegen im Schlachtgetümmel zumute war." It is hard to say whether this clashing juxtaposition occurred due to careless editorial layout or whether Röseler intended it as a reply to Feise.

26 One example is a report by Albert Scholz on an open air stadium performance, in *Thing* style, of Hauptmann's *Florian Geyer* (*Monatshefte* 25 [1944]: 16–22) in which he quotes the enthusiastic reviews by NS newspapers and reports with admiration that the huge audience joined the actors in chanting an epilogue.

27 *GR* 20 (1945): 195–217.

28 *GR* 18 (1943): 107–12.

29 Arthur Davis, "Theodor Fontane and German Conservatism," refutes the theory of strong Prussian nationalistic tendencies in Fontane (35 [1936]: 259–70); Walter Silz protests Friedrich Bruns' interpretation of Kleist's *Prinz von Homburg* as a primarily patriotic drama (*JEGP* 36 [1937]: 500–16); and William R. Gaede objects to *Minna von Barnhelm* as a *laudatio* to the great king (37 [1938]: 546–65).

30 *JEGP* 40 (1941): 91–138. Quotation from Hans Prinzhorn's "Der Kampf um Ludwig Klages," *Deutsche Rundschau* 235 (1933): 103–11.

31 Carl Otto Conrady, "Deutsche Literaturwissenschaft und Drittes Reich," *Nationalismus in Germanistik und Dichtung* (Berlin: Schmidt, 1967) 37–60.

32 Peter von Polenz, "Sprachpurismus und Nationalsozialismus," *Nationalismus in Germanistik und Dichtung* 83.

33 *GQ* 8 (1935): 160–68.

34 *GQ* 9 (1936): 49–54 and *GQ* 10 (1937): 169–72.

35 *Monatshefte* 25 (1933): 50.

36 *Monatshefte* 31 (1939): 41–45.

37 Senn, *Monatshefte* 28 (1936): 232; Spitzer, *Monatshefte* 36 (1944): 113.

38 *Monatshefte* 28 (1936): 185.

39 *Monatshefte* 29 (1937): 41–42.

40 *Monatshefte* 29 (1937): 93.

41 "Volksgeschichte," *Monatshefte* 27 (1936): 89; "Bauerntum," *GR* 13 (1938): 229–30; "Soldat," *GR* 17 (1942): 150–51.

42 *Monatshefte* 26 (1934): 161–62. By 1944 von Bradish saw the situation very differently: "One of the most difficult problems that the allies face in their rehabilitation program of Post-War Germany will be the reeducation of the German youth. . . . We should send from here broad-minded, experienced educators who . . . are acquainted with the German mentality" (*GQ* 17 [1944]: 161).

43 Milwaukee: Gutenberg, 1935.

44 *Monatshefte* 27 (1935): 343–44.

45 Ernst A. Philippson attacked such books several times: "Es wäre wissenschaftlich, die Rassenseelen auf sich beruhen zu lassen" (*GR* 14 [1939]: 138). For another attack by him, see *GR* 15 (1940): 231. C. A. Williams ridicules the echolalia in one writer's style: "*Schau* and compounds are everywhere: not merely *Überschau*, but *Völkerschau*, and *Kuriositätenschau*, yes even *Blickschau* while *Wesensschau* is the most beloved word" (*JEGP* 36 [1937]: 427).

46 *GQ* 8 (1935): 169; *GQ* 11 (1938): 68.

47 *Monatshefte* 29 (1937): 24.

48 *Monatshefte* 33 (1941): 48.

49 *Monatshefte* 29 (1937): 166–67.

50 *Monatshefte* 33 (1941): 343.

51 *GQ* 17 (1944): iii; *GQ* 14 (1941): 165–69.

52 *Monatshefte* 27 (1935): 209; Tremel-Eggert (Munich: NSDAP-Verlag, 1934).

53 The following are a random selection: Otto Koischwitz, *Reise in die Literatur* (Philadelphia: Lippincott, 1937); Werner Neuse, *Wege zur deutschen Kultur,* ed. Otto Koischwitz (Philadelphia: Lippincott, 1937); Helmut Paulus, *Der Auserwählte und Der Bamberger Reiter,* ed. Paul McCarthy (New York: Crofts, 1938); Friedrich Schnack, *Klick aus dem Spielzeugkasten,* ed. Werner Neuse (New York: Holt, 1937); Will Vesper, *Sam in Schnabelweide,* ed. Jane Goodloe (New York: Holt, 1935).

54 Bruns, *Monatshefte* 29 (1937): 189; Prahl, *Monatshefte* 26 (1934): 279; Heller, *GQ* 12 (1939): 53; Mahr, *Monatshefte* 29 (1937): 184.

55 Hess, *GQ* 11 (1938): 7; Gaede, *GQ* 13 (1940): 111–13; Zeydel, *JEGP* 39 (1937): 299.

56 *GQ* 12 (1939): 221.

57 Ibid.

58 *Monatshefte* 26 (1934): 47.

59 *GQ* 7 (1934): 43–44.

60 25 (1933): 50. The Verein für das Deutschtum im Ausland was a Pan-Germanic organization which disseminated völkisch propaganda long before Hitler came to power. After 1933 the VDA became a political arm of the NSDAP.

61 *Monatshefte* 28 (1936): 379.

62 Kindermann, *Monatshefte* 29 (1937): 298–99; Feise 417. Feise actively fought the German American right-wing adherents in the "German-American League for Culture" to which he invited refugees as guest speakers. In *The Maryland Germans* (Princeton: Princeton University Press, 1948), Dieter Cunz reports Feise's attempts "to convince the German American organizations to take a stand against the politics of the Hitler government . . . but the organizations . . . remained cool" (416).

63 *GQ* 17 (1942): 160.

64 von Hofe on *GQ* 12 (1944): 145–54; Mann 277.

65 *Monatshefte* 28 (March 1936): third cover and 34 (Jan. 1942): back cover.

"The British are coming! The British are coming!": Notes for a Comparative Study of Institutions

JEFFREY M. PECK
University of Washington

Amid the sparse scholarship on the institution of *Germanistik* in the United States Germanists speak in the vocabulary of crisis.[1] We return repeatedly to the *goldenes Zeitalter* from the 1870s to the early decades of the 1900s when American students flocked to Halle, Göttingen, and Berlin; when millions of Germans immigrated to the United States; when there were 800 German daily and weekly newspapers and nine million German-speaking Americans; and, most important of all from our contemporary standpoint, when German was the most popular foreign language in the American schools.[2] Weakened by the prejudices and hostilities of two world wars with Germany as America's enemy, *Germanistik* in America was expelled from this paradise.

The late 1960s, twenty years after the end of the Nazi regime, marked the beginning of an attempt to write a new history of *Germanistik,* as well as of Germany itself, two historiographic efforts not at all unrelated. At this time, university revolts compelled the German university and especially *Germanistik* to reflect seriously on its function in society and its part in the entire educational enterprise. While in the United States this critical scrutiny of the origins and ideologies of our discipline has come late, it can give, if shaped properly, this American brand of *Wissenschaftsgeschichte* a very specific and productive orientation. To quote Richard Spuler, who has written the first comprehensive study on the topic, "[a] full appreciation of American *Germanistik* would have to account for its situation within an expansive socio-historical context; it would need to consider, for example, its position within the American academic system, the relationship between American and German methods and schools."[3] That Victor Lange specifically sees the urgent need to address in the same vein as Spuler "the difference between the function of *Germanistik* in the German academic context, and that of German studies in an American pedagogical framework" raises a *rezeptionstheoretisch* and comparative perspective which has been neglected.[4] That German studies may play a minor role in the American university should not merely be pointed to and bemoaned, but analyzed in order to understand more clearly the social, political, and institutional problems of the relationship between English and German departments.

While the field of Anglo-American/German literary relations has been a legitimate field of study for quite a long time, often focusing (not surprisingly) on the nineteenth century in general and in particular on the idealist philosophical and Romantic literary traditions, a comparative analysis of the institutions, the disciplines, and the departments, which I propose here, is a new area of inquiry. It is a realm of analysis prompted by a special need for Germanists in America today, plagued by government assaults on the humanities, falling enrollments, and fewer jobs, to find a rationale for their existence and for their continued education of graduate students. For American English departments, on the other hand, finding themselves looking back at the history of their own discipline without the awareness of history and historicity which has always had an intrinsic role in German *Methodengeschichte,* a new and stronger link to the German tradition may in fact provide a critical apparatus for such projects.

Thus any study of *Germanistik* in America will have to take into account the nature, conduct, and function of other literature departments, especially those of the indigenous English. My goal here approaches Lange's suggestion to "look, in analogy, at German studies of English literature or French studies in American letters, [since] their grounding in the American or French literary experience is unmistakable." What Lange calls a "less controversial topic: [that] the historian of our discipline should consider the readiness (or the capacity) of the professors of German to look seriously at what their neighboring English or French departments offer as literary criticism" is anything but unproblematic since it raises questions of power and authority which are translated into jobs, students, and money.[5] In the English departments themselves, the growth of particular trends in literary criticism and theory as a topic of study has provoked schisms which have led critics there to reflect on the history of their discipline. An article by the renowned Harvard English scholar Walter Jackson Bate, "The Crisis in English Studies," set off a fiery polemic on the pages of *Critical Inquiry* by the likes of Stanley Fish and Edward Said.[6] A timely series of articles in the *Times Literary Supplement* collected under the title "Professing Literature: A Symposium on the Study of English" brought together major American critics such as Paul de Man, E. D. Hirsch, René Wellek, and Fish.[7]

At this point in the comparison of the two fields, I would suggest a most basic and essential question. How is it that certain departments, especially English, manage to dominate the discipline of literary studies so that not only alternative approaches to literary criticism but literary texts themselves do not get a fair hearing? These texts are presented, especially when one looks at the introduction to the "canonized" *Norton Anthology of English Literature,* in the context of the a-historical Anglo-American New Critical tradition which furthers a solipsistic and narrow linguistic ethnocentrism.[8] Both Lange and Jeffrey Sammons call for an American domestication of *Germanistik,* which is especially praiseworthy seen against the Germanification of departments conceived in the negatively Romantic aura of "oom-pah-pah," *Lederhosen,* and *Gemütlichkeit.*[9] Still, one has to recognize that the urge to conceive American *Germanistik* more in the image of the indigenous culture is challenged by the enormous strength of the English department, which has already established its credentials and privileges as home of the mother tongue.

Those Germanists aware of the relationship of German to English departments cannot help but notice, on the one hand, the exclusion or mere passing reference to German writers such as Schlegel, Novalis, and Kleist in English courses on Romanticism and, on the other hand, the inclusion of the "greats" of German literature, such as Goethe, Mann, or Kafka, in world literature courses taught by English departments.[10] "Success" in the area of recognition is often measured against the role of French literature and, in the last ten years, the impact of French criticism on American criticism as well as on "intellectual" culture in general. Why Goethe, Kafka, and Mann and not the Romantic writers I mention above? Why were Staiger, Kayser, and Stanzel ignored in the fifties and sixties? Why Barthes, Derrida, and Foucault in the seventies rather than Gadamer, Jauß, and Iser? My analysis will attempt to answer in part some of the series of questions I initiated here.

In defense of what can be perceived as a more open dialogue between the two traditions, one must first acknowledge that these German theorists—ironically, now that they have lost much of their authority in Germany—are finally making a mark in American critical circles dominated by English departments. In part this change is due to the general reorientation of all literary study, not always smoothly, toward theoretical concerns. In addition, the influx into German departments of younger comparatists and Americans trained in Germany *and* America is superseding the irreplaceable immigrant generation which dominated German studies for so long and is making the departments broader, more international, and, most of all, more critical in scope. The enormous public popularity of German filmmakers of the so-called New German Cinema, such as Wenders, Herzog, and Faßbinder, and the impact of film on literary studies cannot be ignored. Also American journals have contributed a great deal to the change: *New German Critique* has contributed a long-neglected look at the "political" nature of German culture, promoting critical scrutiny of topics from feminism to film; *New Literary History* has been devoted, as its title suggests, to the promotion of historiographic inquiry and an obvious commitment to articles by German critics such as Jauß, Iser, and Weimann. That Iser is perhaps the most well-known of German theorists has certainly to do with his being a professor of *Anglistik,* his writings on English texts, and his increasingly pragmatic and less historical orientation.[11] He is, in fact, one of the few, if not the only German participant in the well-known and institutionalized School of Criticism and Theory.

It is therefore not surprising that it took an East German critic like Weimann to present in his *"New Criticism" und die Entwicklung bürgerlicher Literaturwissenschaft* (1962) a view of the most influential critical movement in the history of American criticism from an historical and ideological perspective; fifteen years elapsed before an equivalent study appeared in English (from England).[12] The recognition of Weimann, it seems, came only after his work was translated into English and published in a prestigious journal in American critical studies, *New Literary History.* That German popularity comes with translation and the German tradition's relation to history is not at all coincidental.

With the largest faculty, student enrollments, course offerings, funding, and prestige (the superlatives can go on and on), the English department dominates literary study in America not only by sheer size. Its own brand of cultural hegemony is built primarily on an *English* tradition of literature and an ever increasing *American* critical orientation which started in the fifties and sixties to control publication (which it no longer does) and pedagogy (which still continues): the infamous and now sorely maligned New Criticism, which although officially dead, has, to quote a colleague in English, the longest running obituary notice in history. While said to be deceased, its ghost continues to be exorcized and still rides rather like Paul Revere through English departments, warning against the attack of a philosophical tradition which promotes history. Geoffrey Hartmann's words on the state of affairs are not surprising: "The New Critics fused a peculiarly 'American' with a markedly 'English' prejudice against mixing art with anything, especially with philosophy. Only the empirical tradition of Locke contributes to English studies. Hegel has never been received; and despite Coleridge and Carlyle, German Idealism penetrated mainly into theological circles [i.e., hermeneutics, as his footnote indicates]."[13]

In the seventies and eighties American interpreters of French criticism such as Robert Scholes, Fredric Jameson, and especially the guru of "Frenchified" American criticism, Jonathan Culler, expanded their own authority as well as that of the critical movement they represented. In what I read as a highly ironic political metaphor Frank Lentricchia claims Culler "made Structuralism safe for us" (read Americans!);[14] his *Structuralist Poetics* (1975), which emphasized the linguistic foundations of structuralism, affirmed the connection to a verbally oriented New Criticism and the maintenance of a particularly pedagogical reading technology. New Criticism continues to assert its authority even in the poststructuralist phase of a movement which in its early structuralist period was blatantly ahistorical: "The traces of the New Criticism are found . . . in the repeated and often extremely subtle denial of history by a variety of contemporary theorists. The exploration and critique of this evasive antihistorical maneuver is one of my fundamental concerns."[15] In his study *After the New Criticism,* Lentricchia is one of the few Americans, using Murray Krieger's classic *New Apologists for Poetry* as the watershed, to explain politically the opening of the critical void which was only to be deepened later into the poststructuralist abyss.

What the Americans seem to fear is a speculative, metaphysical, and historistic German tradition which goes back ironically to Romanticism, the field which should inspire the most exchange. While this thought has culminated in the philosophical hermeneutics of Gadamer which, unfortunately for Culler, "gives rise to no method, or indeed to any sort of activity"[16] and therefore is unattractive to American audiences who are seeking practical answers, it has been reshaped for "real" literary interpretation through Jauß, Weimann, and Iser. It seems, however, that only after being translated both literally and figuratively into more American pragmatic terms through American reader-response theorists such as Norman Holland and especially Stanley Fish could hermeneutics receive its hearing here, through the back door so to speak.[17] When the translation of *Wahrheit und Methode* finally came out in the seventies, sixteen years after the original, some American critics bemoaned the triumph of the French over the Germans:

> [H]ad Gadamer's book been available, it . . . might very well have become overnight a bench mark for American critical thought . . . . The new avant-garde is, of course, composed of those who are converting criticism into a department of semiotics: under the tutelage of various European theorists (Saussure, Lévi-Strauss, Michel Foucault, Roland Barthes, Jacques Derrida, among others). . . .[18]

The *European* theorists Scott enumerates are all French. In his review Culler acknowledges that "critical discussion becomes easier when the arguments one must deal with are no longer contained in 500 pages of difficult German."[19] It is unfortunate that German looks to a sophisticated scholar, especially *the* mediator of French criticism in America, so much more difficult than French and a "grumpy mystification" at that.[20] This situation is summed up by another critic with the word "puzzlement": "While 'hermeneutics' has been a relatively familiar word in the German philosophical tradition for some time, and recently even *à la mode,* its interjection into Anglo-Saxon philosophical discussion in the past few years has tended to provoke puzzlement."[21] Americans outside of "certain Anglo-Saxon theological circles" may indeed be uncomfortable with "the unfamiliarity and density of the word [hermeneutics which] tends to strike our analytically attuned ears as just another bit of Teutonic obscurantism."[22] Another American critic's complaint is even more to the point: "I have seen most of it before, and in English too, and even much of it in plain English."[23] It seems that advanced literary critics and philosophers are using Mark Twain's humorous diatribe "The Awful German Language" as a critical prolegomenon. Another nineteenth-century reviewer of German ideas took a similar pose as a response to Mme de Staël's recently published *De l'Allemagne:* "A scoffer might with some truth tell us that German philosophy is founded in a repugnance to every system which has experience for its basis, or happiness for its end."[24]

While the allusion to a more congenial empirical tradition may implicitly be a criticism of the English then and the Americans more recently in the 1960s and 1970s to favor the French over the Germans, one might rather attribute the preference to cultural factors. It certainly did not help in furthering a German-American alliance that America's philosophical and political postwar ally could export Sartre and existentialism for the growing American bohemian subculture whereas the mostly negative fascination with Germany's past focused on the war and the Third Reich. The stereotypes seemed to confirm the national clichés of German warriors and French bohemians until the warriors were replaced by businessmen, when Germany became not only a strong political and economic power but also a full-fledged member in the international cultural and ideological community. These events alone cannot explain the turn to structuralism rather than hermeneutics. They can point, however, to both an American attraction to the French and the Anglo-American aversion to an obvious nationalism based in history and ideology with which Germany was identified and which English departments rejected through their New Critical heritage.

These attitudes towards language and an idealist/Romantic epistemological tradition not only reflect this rejection but also provide reasons for such hostility. In contrast to the empirical tradition of Locke, which Hartmann mentions above in comparison to Herder and Humboldt, Romantic theory postulated by Schlegel and Novalis conceives of language as having transcendental power to create, almost magically, new worlds. Translation of a language itself implies interpretation and the recognition of one's own historical and linguistic mediation of the world: in Humboldt's own words, "Sprachansicht" as "Weltansicht."[25] This linguistic and philosophical orientation is built on a consciousness of history and historicity and thus provides the underpinnings for a contemporary *Ideologiekritik* of our own disciplines, emphasizing the Anglo-American's own ignorance of the ideological nature of the rejection. Weimann, a critic himself of English literature, points out:

> In the present state of English and American literary criticism, any new approach to literary history is bound to raise basic problems of theory and method for the study of literature at large. Perhaps it is not going too far to say that without a new and more profound understanding of the historical nature and the social function of literature, the most pressing problems of criticism cannot be coherently and systematically redefined; without a new awareness of history, the study of literature is unlikely to move beyond the confines of the intrinsic school of criticism.[26]

Releasing the text from history, especially through what seems to be an unreflective philosophy of translation based on Lockean pragmatism and a "conventional" model of language, has contributed to the hegemony English departments wield. Once texts are translated into English, they assume a kind of transparency which bestows upon the critic, especially the New Critic, the genial and visionary power "to interpret the hell out of it" and to look through the verbal artifact, bypassing the contextual and linguistic bonds to culture, nation, or history. The text seems almost to float to a neutral and deceptively free region where it is no longer anchored to the author or public. This critical strategy neutralizes and flattens out all texts into equally innocuous "verbal icons," to make light of Wimsatt's well-worn phrase, which may indeed provide the critic with metaphoric mobility, but also whitewashes historical interests informing the writing and reading.

This "arrogance of power," a phrase coined by J. William Fulbright, founder of grants for international study and understanding, in order to describe a particularly American attitude, informs an ideology which promotes itself as strangely free from any kind of nationalist ideology. New Criticism was indeed ideological and intimately tied to the Cold War. Its dominance is rooted in appropriation, consensus, and conviction: English departments teach in the language of this country, they instruct basic compositional skills highly esteemed and necessary for success in all other disciplines and professions;[27] they are the progenitors of the liberal education, the haven for the generalist seeking a truly liberal education; they do not send their students routinely to England to acquaint them with an "alien" culture which might throw their own American culture into critical relief; and they take on texts in courses which, once translated, miraculously become their domain.

Theory is the most striking example. A few years ago in my own university in an interdepartmental colloquium on criticism and theory, the English Department participants chose for what were supposed to be representative critics of their tradition Derrida, Bakhtin, and Foucault.

The French participant who chose René Girard, not a cult figure, was surprised and critical of the acceptance of these critics into the American tradition. Not surprisingly, the Germanists selected Gadamer and Jauß.

The appropriation of texts both linguistically and critically broadens the bounds of critical inquiry and falls into Burton Bledstein's distinctly American theory of institutional structure, which he specifically compares to the German system: "Departments grew by accretion, by means of the simple addition of members who both individually represented specific areas of knowledge and individually expanded the range of a department's specialized offerings. . . . A new methodology or new sphere of discovery usually dictated the hiring of a new man [sic]"[28] In an article entitled "Where Do English Departments Come From?" written by an English professor who sees this "imperialistic" policy in the history of English departments as having obviously deleterious effects, comes the following description:

> Early chairmen and early professors of English *literature* were willing if not eager to increase the prestige of their subject and the numbers of their students and course offerings by embracing, not only *linguistics* . . . but also *rhetoric,* which normally included, of course, oratory, elocution, and all forms of written composition. . . . let us remind ourselves of the full scope of the aggressiveness (some would say acquisitiveness) exhibited by departments of "English." They were later to embrace, just as greedily, journalism, business writing, creative writing, writing for engineers, play-writing, drama and thea-ter, and American literature, and were eventually to be offering courses in contemporary literature, comparative literature, the Bible and world classics in translation, American civilization, the humanities, and "English for for-eigners." In sum, English departments became the catchall for the work of teachers of extremely diverse interests and training, united theoretically but not actually by their common use of the mother tongue.[29]

The quality of transparency in the mother tongue allows the critic to view his/her new expanse of literary and critical terrain from the ideological standpoint which Phyllis Franklin depicted in her account of English stud-ies, as if somehow "the discipline gave birth to itself."[30] These repeated references to origins in the childlike tone of discovery reflect not only the beginnings of a delayed self-consciousness but also the ignorance of one's own ontological impermanence. This autogenic narcissism promotes the dangerous illusion that neither text nor discipline had to be constituted. To continue the metaphor and the English-German comparison, the trans-lucency of *Germanistik* in America through the foreign language and in Germany because of historical frictions compels the Germanist to reflect on the shaping power of language and history to inform understanding as much as what is understood. The evidence of this constituted quality of the discipline is particularly visible in the methodological history of *Ger-*

manistik, since it cannot be separated from the history of German ideologies and the understanding of those ideologies: in other words, the history of our own historical interests. That David Bathrick in extrapolating from Michael Pehlke can see "the history of American *Germanistik* [as] . . . an ideological history of intellectual alienation" is one version of the highly historical and ideological quality of this tradition.[31] One can at least say that, since literary texts cannot be separated from the philosophical tradition of German idealism and Romanticism which influence contemporary critical theories of hermeneutics, *Rezeptionsaesthetik,* and *Ideologiekritik,* the Germans are inclined to be aware of the historical, if not always the ideological, dynamics in their interpretation of texts.

If one were to measure the number of critical studies on a discipline's own history by the degree of alienation, it is no wonder that English studies has been "only mildly interested in the story of its own past" and therefore has not produced more than a handful of substantial works.[32] Much of the theoretical concern with English studies has been phrased less in the vocabulary of specific disciplinary crises than in the general and theoretical analysis of "politics," "economy," "social," "authority," and "power."[33] To Robert von Hallberg, from whose introduction to a volume of *Critical Inquiry* devoted to "Canon Formation" I have just quoted, the issue may seem "timely" since "art seems less private than social."[34] This recent collection of articles, as well as a previous volume on "The Politics of Literature" (Sept. 1982), indicates a shift in English departments and its tone reflects the surprising newness of these questions to American English-speaking audiences.[35]

Like his predecessor in the previous volume, von Hallberg introduces these concerns as if he had just discovered that politics and society had an effect on art. He states: "Interest in canons is surely part of a larger inquiry into the institutions of literary study and artistic production. . . . More particularly, the formation of canons is a measure of the strength of institutions devoted to the study of art."[36] It is significant that an initial impetus in the reevaluation and reconstitution of canons comes from traditionally marginalized groups such as women, Blacks, Indians, and gays. By rewriting anthologies and reading lists that reflect in their editing only "those who occupy positions of some cultural power," these groups are performing a function in English studies which was fought in the now more established legitimacy struggle of *Trivialliteratur* in Germany years before.[37]

The post New Critical rediscovery of history by the English may indeed attract them to German models of study, especially when the history of disciplines is at stake, especially if one were to agree with a leading literary critic in English studies, Hazard Adams, that "the study of history of one's subject is the best antidote to slavery to fashion."[38] But for Germanists it would be a naive and futile endeavor to think we could perform the same function. The nineteenth-century Germanophilia, which one critic referring to the 1820s has described "as the most fruitful period of intellectual interchange between England and Germany," will more than likely never be recreated in today's American English departments.[39] It would be heartening, however, to think that the Romantic tradition which inspired de Quincey to call "German literature . . . at this time beyond all question, for science and philosophy properly so-called the wealthiest in the world" might now give the English departments, albeit transmitted through the French poststructuralists, the necessary perspective to historicize their understanding of their own discipline.[40]

Although we might look nostalgically to late nineteenth-century America as well and note that at the prestigious Johns Hopkins University "English and German were combined into a single department . . . in 1882–83 with a future professor of German as head," today in America German departments will need to maximize our alien and even marginalized status.[41] The identity crisis of American *Germanistik* draws the discipline schizophrenically toward the German "fatherland" on the one hand and, on the other, to the English/American "mother" country. (Could this be an attraction to the maternal as a source of life?)[42] Like the adolescent with divorced parents, *Germanistik* struggles to find a home, to create a place for itself, to draw the methodological, intellectual, and even psychological parameters of a field of inquiry which is continually being intruded upon by the English department, especially as long as literary texts remain the exclusive focus of Germanistic study. Thus to recognize, as Valters Nollendorfs has said, that we are "mediators of cultures and not simply . . . transmitters of a foreign culture"[43] can emphasize the very different task we as Germanists perform from our colleagues in English.[44]

Both Russell Berman and David Bathrick, two contributors to the *Monatshefte* project, have developed this line of thinking in relationship to a "concept of culture" for German studies programs. Bathrick would like to see *Germanistik* "as an attempt to understand and mediate a foreign culture from one's own perspective." He contends that "the results of this study as manifested in scholarly publications and traditional course offerings often do not reflect such interchange and mediation."[45] "Our roles as transmitters of [culture]"[46] imply that by reflecting on "the investigation of the organisation of meaning in society or the production of ideologies," German studies "would take on a decidedly interpretive character."[47] In essence, by taking advantage of our own philosophical and critical German tradition reaching back to the Romantic hermeneutics of Schleiermacher and Schlegel, we could provide an interpretive framework for a concept of culture enabling us to reflect critically on the understanding of our understanding of *Germanistik* in an alien environment or, phrased in German which uncovers the self-reflective quality of the language itself, "die eigene Fragestellung in Frage stellen zu können!"

The urge to domesticate *Germanistik* should be built on an understanding of the institutionalizing and therefore shaping power of the American university rather than merely on a rejection of a German *Germanistik* which is seen by many to be connected to the radical reorientation of the German university and literary study, the politicization and theorization of German studies. To naturalize German *Germanistik* does not necessarily have to be a negation of its dual status which should be maintained and cultivated here as well as in Germany. For Richard Brinkmann, introducing a Tübingen symposium on "Germanistik im Ausland,"

> ... die deutsche Germanistik braucht das. Sie braucht die andere, die Außenperspektive, Sie braucht auch den Versuch, von außen her ihre, die deutsche Perspektive auf ihre eigene, die deutsche Literatur kritisch zu verstehen. Das kann sie selbst und allein nicht zureichend leisten. . . . Und nicht zuletzt die deutsche Germanistik selbst sollte daran interessiert sein, das dieser Unterschied nicht verwischt wird.[48]

American *Germanistik* needs it as well. Since we are "not what *Germanistik* is to the Germans and English to Americans," we should reside in both traditions, like the citizen with two passports and two nationalities.[49] Like Hermes, the namesake himself for the "rejected" hermeneutics, whose image often stood at the crossroads of two cultures, *Germanistik* in America can take on this interpretive function, especially in the context of developing German culture studies. Through this kind of mediation the means by which we constitute and create our subject becomes as important as the subject of inquiry itself. *Germanistik* in the United States then can reclaim for itself some of the territory and recognition it has lost.

Notes

1 I am indebted in the writing of this essay to colleagues in the Department of English at the University of Washington, especially Nick Visser and Evan Watkins, and to the discussion which followed the presentation of an earlier version of this paper in a session at the 1983 MLA: "How has Departmentalization influenced National Traditions of Literary Theory?" sponsored by the Society for Critical Exchange and the GRIP Project (Group for Research on the Institutionalization and Professionalization of Literary Studies).

2 Jeffrey L. Sammons, "Die amerikanische Germanistik: Historische Betrachtung zur gegenwärtigen Situation," *Germanistik international. Vorträge und Diskussionen auf*

dem internationalen Symposium, "Germanistik im Ausland" von 23. bis 25. Mai 1977 in Tübingen, ed. Richard Brinkmann, Kennosuke Ezawa, and Fritz Hachert. (Tübingen: Niemeyer, 1978) 106.

3 Richard Spuler, *"Germanistik" in America: The Reception of German Classicism, 1870–1905* (Stuttgart: Heinz, 1982), 7–8.

4 Victor Lange, "The History of German Studies in America: Ends and Means," *Monatshefte* 75 (1983): 251. See also 3–14 in this volume.

5 Lange 252–53.

6 W. Jackson Bate, "The Crisis in English Studies," *Harvard Magazine* 85.1 (1982): 46–53; Stanley Fish, "Profession Despise Thyself: Fear and Loathing in Literary Studies," *Critical Inquiry* 10 (1983): 349–64; W. Jackson Bate, "To the Editor of *Critical Inquiry*" 365–70; Edward Said, "Response to Stanley Fish" 371–73.

7 *Times Literary Supplement,* 10 Dec. 1982: 1355–63. See Paul de Man, "The Return to Philology"; René Wellek, "Respect for Tradition"; Anthony Burgess, "The Writer among Professors"; Iain McGilchrist, "A Pessimist's Solution"; E. D. Hirsch, Jr., "The Contents of English Literature"; Ian Donaldson, "A Foreign Field"; George Watson, "The Charm of Being Useless"; Raymond Williams, "Beyond Specialization"; Stanley Fish, "Professional Anti-professionalism."

8 "Preface to the Revised Edition," *The Norton Anthology of English Literature,* ed. M. H. Abrams et al. (New York: Norton, 1968) 2: xxxi–xxxiv. Statements such as the following indicate that this textbook, the most widely used for introducing students in English to the task of reading English literature, still reaffirms New Critical tenets. It furthers "precise and sensitive reading, and enhances an intelligent delight in literature as literature." Predigested biographical and historical "background" information is provided rather than any critical apparatus.

9 I refer here to Sammon's article, "Some Considerations on Our Invisibility," and Victor Lange's "Thoughts in Season," *German Studies in the United States: Assessment and Outlook,* ed. Walter F. W. Lohnes & Valters Nollendorfs (Madison: University of Wisconsin Press, 1976) 17–23 & 5–16 respectively.

10 At my own university the two professors of English who most often deal with German texts in their classes are both Romanticists who received their degrees at the same university in a department of "Literature" rather than English. One of these more "comparatively" oriented English professors received in 1983 the following negative review from an Englishman on a book manuscript dealing with the relationship of Coleridge to German Idealist philosophy: "My only disappointment with the book is that concluding with *Naturphilosophie* it takes its leave of the reader in the less attractive territories of nineteenth-century thought. One might prefer more attention to the scientific speculation of the 1790s which was in many ways a good deal more exciting and intellectually stimulating. She is less inclined to attend to work of this early period particularly that by English scholars which though sometimes less professional, is often fascinating."

11 It is therefore not surprising that Iser's important study *Der implizite Leser* is available in English but not in German at my own university's library.

12 See Robert Weimann, *"New Criticism" und die Entwicklung bürgerlicher Literaturwissenschaft: Geschichte und Kritik neuer Interpretationsmethoden* (Halle/Saale: Niemeyer, 1962) and John Fekete, *The Critical Twilight: Explorations in the Ideology of Anglo-American Literary Theory from Eliot to McLuhan* (London: Routledge & Kegan Paul, 1977).

13 Geoffrey Hartmann, "Literary Criticism and Its Discontents," *Critical Inquiry* 3 (1976): 213.

14 Frank Lentricchia, *After the New Criticism* (Chicago: University of Chicago Press, 1980). It is also significant to note Lentricchia's comment on the outrage that accompanied Culler's winning the MLA's Lowell Prize for 1975.

15 Lentricchia xiii.

16 Jonathan Culler, rev. of *Truth and Method,* by Hans Georg Gadamer, *PTL* 2. 1 (1977): 190.

17 See Norman Holland's *The Dynamics of Literary Response* (New York: Oxford University Press, 1968), and especially Stanley Fish's *Self-Consuming Artifacts. The Experience of Seventeenth-Century Literature* (Berkeley: University of California Press, 1972), and *Is There a Text in This Class?: The Authority of Interpretive Communities* (Cambridge: Harvard University Press, 1980).

18 Nathan Scott, rev. of *Truth and Method,* by Hans Georg Gadamer, *Boundary 2* 5. 2 (1977): 634.

19 Culler 189.

20 Culler 190.

21 Theodore Kisiel, rev. of *Hermeneutics: Interpretation Theory in Schleiermacher, Dilthey, Heidegger and Gadamer,* by Richard Palmer, *Zeitschrift für allgemeine Wissenschaftstheorie* 2 (1971): 130.

22 Kisiel 130.

23 Arthur Child, "Hermeneutics Again" (review of Palmer), *Genre* 3. 1 (1970): 107.

24 *The Edinburgh Review* cited in John Mander's *Our German Cousins: Anglo-German Relations in the 19th and 20th Centuries.* (London: Butler & Tanner, 1974) 47.

25 See my study *Hermes Disguised: Literary Hermeneutics and the Interpretation of Literature. Kleist, Grillparzer, Fontane* (Berne: Lang, 1983).

26 Robert Weimann, *Structure and Society in Literary History: Studies in the History and Theory of Historical Criticism* (Charlottesville: University of Virginia Press, 1976) 1.

27 For discussion of the role of rhetoric and its influence on the teaching of composition in American English departments see William Riley Parker's "Where Do English Departments Come From?" *College English* 28 (1967): 339–51. For the most well-known work on English studies in America see Richard Ohmann's *English in America: A Radical View of the Profession* (New York: Oxford University Press, 1976). Since this essay was written, more studies have appeared, including most recently Gerald Graff's *Professing Literature: An Institutional History* (Chicago & London: University of Chicago Press, 1987).

28 Burton J. Bledstein, *The Culture of Professionalism: The Middle Class and the Development of Higher Education in America* (New York: Norton, 1976) 300–301.

29 Parker 348.

30 Phyllis Franklin, "English Studies in America: Reflections on the Development of a Discipline," *American Quarterly* (Spring 1978): 21.

31 David Bathrick, "On Leaving Exile: American *Germanistik* in Its Social Context," *German Studies in the United States* 254 (Note 9).

32 Franklin 21.

33 Robert von Hallberg, "Editor's Introduction," *Critical Inquiry* 10 (1983): iii.

34 von Hallberg iii.

35 Most of the historical, i.e., materialist critiques in English have in fact come from British Marxists, such as Raymond Williams at the Center for Contemporary Cultural Studies in Birmingham or Oxford's Terry Eagleton, whose studies *Criticism and Ideology: Marxism and Literary Criticism* and the more recent *Literary Theory: An Introduction* are taken up quickly by critics here searching for more historical and ideological approaches in English.

36 von Hallberg iii.

37 Barbara Herrnstein Smith, "Contingencies of Value," *Critical Inquiry* 10 (1983): 25.

38 Hazard Adams, "How Departments Commit Suicide," *Profession 83* (New York: MLA, 1983) 34.

39 Mander 64.

40 de Quincey as cited in Mander 71.

41 Parker 346.

42 For a very interesting and detailed analysis of the relation between the institutionalization of literary study and the return to material origins see Lionel Gossman's "Literature and Education," *New Literary History* 13 (1982): 341–71.

43 Valters Nollendorfs, "German Studies: A Pragmatic Look Ahead," *German Studies in the United States* 37 (Note 9).

44 It should be noted here that this view of American *Germanistik* as a mediator of culture has a historical foundation in Alexander Hohlfeld, Professor of *Germanistik* at the University of Wisconsin from 1901 to 1936, chairman during the tumultuous years of the World War I era, president of the AATG (1933), and president of the MLA (1913). Perhaps because of the broader perspective evidenced by his leadership of this association, which represented all languages and literatures, Hohlfeld saw "German Departments hav[ing] a unique mission" in the context of "their potential as centers of cross-cultural literary studies." Hohlfeld led the "Wisconsin Project of Anglo-German Literary Relations" (I quote here from Cora Lee Nollendorf's article in this volume 176–195). In an article of his own from a 1932 *Monatshefte*, Hohlfeld uses the term "Vermittler" repeatedly to describe the task he sees for himself, as well as for other Germanists in the United States. One must add here that Hohlfeld's understanding of the mediation of culture is more grounded in positivism and influence studies than one would expect today in an age of *Rezeptionsaesthetik* and *Ideologiekritik*. I am also grateful to an article reprinted in this volume (pp. 165–175): Henry Schmidt's "The Rhetoric of Survival: The Germanist in America from 1900–1925" *America and the Germans: An Assessment of a Three-Hundred-Year History,* eds. Frank Trommler and Joseph McVeigh (Philadelphia: University of Pennsylvania Press, 1985) 2: 204–16.

45 Bathrick 253.

46 Bathrick 254.

47 Russell Berman, "The Concept of Culture in Culture Studies Programs," *Monatshefte* 74 (1982): 245.

48 Richard Brinkmann, "Zur Eröffnung des internationalen Symposiums 'Germanistik' in Ausland," *Germanistik international* 2 (Note 2).

49 Nollendorfs 34.

Interview with Hermann J. Weigand (1892–1985)

HENRY J. SCHMIDT
Ohio State University

Hermann J. Weigand, Sterling Professor Emeritus of Germanic Literature at Yale University, was indisputably one of the towering figures of American *Germanistik*. He achieved several of the profession's highest honors, including the presidency of the Modern Language Association in 1966, and created a body of scholarship of extraordinary versatility that spanned more than sixty years. Between his first published article on Heine in 1919 and his last on Rilke, written in 1980–81 and published in 1982, lies a wealth of scholarly analysis ranging from medieval and Scandinavian literature to Goethe, Hauptmann, Rilke, Kafka, and Thomas Mann. His first book, *The Modern Ibsen: A Reconsideration,* appeared in 1925; subsequent books dealt with Mann's *Der Zauberberg* (1933) and courtly love (1956). After his retirement in 1961, three collections of his essays were published: *Surveys and Soundings in European Literature* (1966), *Fährten und Funde: Aufsätze zur deutschen Literatur* (1967), and *Critical Probings: Essays in European Literature From Wolfram von Eschenbach to Thomas Mann* (1982). Such productivity is all the more remarkable since he was handicapped by failing eyesight for many decades.

Professor Weigand was kind enough to agree to be interviewed immediately after I called him on 7 July 1980. I had planned in a general way to focus on his recollections about the state of the profession from World War I to the present. He spoke at length about former teachers and students, weaving anecdotes into a roughly chronological description of his life. What he clearly wished to discuss above all, however, was the "literary detective work" he had produced over the years. To this end, he asked me to read aloud titles from a list of his published works, which prompted him to describe their origins and their contributions to scholarship. He spoke of his interest in medieval German and French literature and in modern authors from Rilke to Broch. Two examples of his elucidations of his own work (on Hauptmann's *Florian Geyer* and Thomas Mann's *Der Erwählte*) are included here. Much of the interview has been condensed and restructured for greater readability, but as a reflection of Professor Weigand's innate bilingual facility, I preserve verbatim his shift from English to German during his discussion of *Florian Geyer*. Toward the end of the interview, we switched back to English.

SCHMIDT: How did you begin?

WEIGAND: I was born in Philadelphia in 1892, and I was chiefly educated at home until I was of high school age. My father was a great educator. He was a Lutheran minister, and he thought he would make another minister of me. The Bible and Greek mythology were my main reading as a child. I spoke and read German long before English. When I was about seven, my father gave me a big notebook and German poetry to copy, and I somehow automatically memorized most of it: practically all of Schiller's *Balladen,* Freiligrath's "Der Löwenritt," and some other things that I'm still very fond of. I went to a country school across from the parsonage until I was ready for high school. Then I got a scholarship for Stratford, Ontario, because my father was a country minister in Canada, even though I was born in Philadelphia. After a year I went to Rochester, New York, where they had a six-year course on the basis of the German *Gymnasium.* Most of the teaching was done in German, with great emphasis on religion, German history, Latin, and Greek. I was the only one of the group who did not go on to the seminary to become a Lutheran minister because I was quite sure, long before those five years of my adolescence were over, that I would never go into the Church—to the great disappointment of my father.

Then I went to the University of Michigan. They gave me enough advanced credit so that I completed my A.B. in two years. I got a half-time instructorship immediately and went on to graduate work. From the second year on—1914 to 1918—I was a full-time instructor, and I got my Ph.D. in 1916.

SCHMIDT: Who were your teachers there?

WEIGAND: There were good people in Philosophy and English. In Philosophy there was my very best friend, DeWitt Parker, who died some years ago. There was Alfred Lloyd, a great head and a very tolerant man. He had a fivefold theory of phenomenology—I wrote a paper to refute him and he gave me an "A" on it.

SCHMIDT: And your German teachers?

WEIGAND: The one who really counted was Ewald Boucke, a real scholar from Freiburg who had written on Goethe and Heine. He was almost totally bald, with huge bushy eyebrows and a reddish-blond mustache. Then World War I broke out, and the university split into two camps. Boucke had retained his German citizenship, and they put him on indefinite leave without salary. He never forgave them. Eventually he got a position in Heidelberg as the successor to Gundolf. He died there during World War II.

Another teacher, Edgar Eggert, got into trouble with the trustees because he made some remarks about England that they didn't like and they sacked him. He was an assistant professor and already advanced in age. He went to Chicago and got a position in high school. Chicago was very pro-German, because of the *Chicago Tribune.*

During the war the teaching of German was largely stopped, and we younger people weren't dismissed, but we were let out, as they said, when America entered the war in 1917. Having already a family and very poor eyesight, I was classified in such a way that I never had any taste of the army. For ten days I worked in the Bath Ironworks making destroyers. I had a Russian vocabulary in my pocket, and when there wasn't anything to do, I memorized a lot of Russian. But the good people there thought I must be a spy.

When they told me they didn't want me anymore, I got a job in Philadelphia with the Curtis Publishing Company. For sixteen months, from July 1918 to October 1919, I answered mail there. I had gone to Daniel Shumway, the chairman of the German department at the University of Pennsylvania, and he had told me there would be no chance for any position in the immediate future. I didn't know whether I'd ever get back into the profession. This had been my main interest, my first interest. My dissertation had been on Heine: "Spiritualismus und Sensualismus in Heines Dichten und Denken." I still have a copy of it but I never published it. Very shortly afterward I wrote another essay on the philosophical background of Heine's *Buch le Grand.* I sent it to the *Journal of English and Germanic Philology* at the University of Illinois, where Julius Goebel was the great chief. He wrote me he would very much like to publish it, but it would have to be translated, because they could not afford to publish anything in the German language while the war was going on. So I translated it, and it came out in January 1919. That was my first publication, and I followed it up with other Heine publications for quite a few years. They're all in my file and in my bibliography.

After November 1918 the occupation didn't last as long as expected, and the GIs came flocking back much more rapidly than expected. So one day, Daniel Shumway asked me: "We need another man, will you come in?" "Well, of course," I said. So I was hired overnight, and that started me for the second time on the road upward. I graduated from the youngest instructor to a full professor by 1928.

Shumway saw that I was really interested in literature, so he gave me a chance to teach an advanced course immediately. During the second year he said, "We have college courses for teachers who enroll for late afternoon and evening hours, and they pay extra. We have a course on the books of Scandinavian literature in translation. Would you like to teach that?" I said, "Why, certainly, I should be delighted to teach that, and I'll make it my business immediately to learn the Scandinavian languages, to get a fluent reading knowledge." Having had Old Norse at Michigan, I found it very easy to learn Norwegian and Danish. Within months I was reading Ibsen fluently. Before the year was over, I had read all of Ibsen, not only all of his plays, but all his letters and materials from his workshop, and I'd started on a book that developed into *The Modern Ibsen*.

Very soon after that, Shumway asked me, "Would you like to teach a course on the Christianization of the Germans and the Age of Charlemagne in the Graduate School?" Of course I said yes—I was just eager to take up everything, whether I was prepared or not. I was largely self-educated anyway, having read so much outside of courses. I think that was regarded very favorably at Penn. I never heard any discussion of tenure during the whole time I was there, but riding to Philadelphia one day in the local electric train—I'd been living on the Main Line—I read I'd been promoted to a full professorship.

SCHMIDT: You *read* this?

WEIGAND: I didn't know I had been up for consideration, so this was very nice. And then the year after that came the call from Yale. Yale had never made very much of graduate study in Germanics, but just a year or two before I came Eduard Prokosch, a nationally known philologist and a great enthusiast, had come to Yale and between us we had the chance to set up a whole graduate program. I don't know whether anybody in America had so ideal an opportunity to work on matters that interested him with regard to Germanics. I taught two graduate seminars every term. The first years I found very difficult, because we had few students, and Yale is a place where an outsider finds it difficult to work his way in.

SCHMIDT: Was there still anti-German sentiment in Yale at that time?

WEIGAND: There was anti-German sentiment everywhere in America, I would say, and it's not gone yet. The younger generation grew up knowing no German and knowing Germany only as the enemy. So we built up things slowly. Prokosch's term was short because he died in an auto crash at the age of 63 in 1938. Then I took charge of the Directorship of Graduate Studies in Germanics, and I held that post until my retirement in 1961.

SCHMIDT: What can you say about anti-Semitism among German professors?

WEIGAND: I didn't meet with any anti-Semitism in Michigan, but Yale was very anti-Semitic in the 1930s. Somebody in the department here would say of somebody else: "He's a Yid." Or: "Der hat einen kleinen Webfehler," meaning a Jewish grandmother, or so. During World War II many Jews were seeking asylum in America, and there were a lot of anti-Semitic people who tried everything to slow up the influx especially of educated people, professional people. They often felt "it's our bread and butter." That was unfortunate. I had quite a few Jewish friends in Europe, mostly acquired on my visits to Germany. When they became immigrants, you had to sign a guarantee to keep the person from becoming a burden to the U. S. government. You took that pledge more or less literally, so you had to be careful. If you had more than half a dozen like that on your hands . . . I was very poor, and I couldn't count on supporting them myself.

SCHMIDT: Was there a similar cutback in language teaching programs during World War II as there had been during World War I?

WEIGAND: We didn't have many regular students for a time, and I had to teach elementary German to army trainees for a while. I know how difficult it was to give them any sense of pronunciation. I ruined my lungs at the time.

SCHMIDT: How were the years right after World War II? Were they an uphill struggle again?

WEIGAND: Those were good years, because so many students came back.

SCHMIDT: Did you teach many undergraduate courses, or were they mainly on the graduate level?

WEIGAND: During the whole period I was at Yale, I taught a three-hour college course in addition to two graduate seminars of two hours each. After I retired, everything apparently changed: nobody teaches more than two courses, and they get a term sabbatical every three years. I got my first sabbatical in 1933.

SCHMIDT: As you look back on your career, do you have any regrets about things not accomplished, or were there conditions within the university that were less than favorable?

WEIGAND: I had a feeling all the time that I should have been on the college faculty as well as the faculty of the graduate school, because the college was the one body of influence in regard to questions of university policy. So you were somewhat on the sidelines in the graduate school. But I felt happy here so far as my profession was concerned.

SCHMIDT: Was financial compensation adequate over the years?

WEIGAND: The raises we received during my first twenty-five years at Yale were certainly not equal to the rise in the cost of living. Full professorships started at $6,000. All that changed radically just about the time I was retired in 1961.

SCHMIDT: During the time you were teaching, what were your goals and motivations? Why did you become a teacher and a publishing scholar rather than choosing another kind of work?

WEIGAND: I had a very good foundation in German, of course, and I found teaching to my taste. But in literature I was stimulated very early by problems. I never worked in such a way that I read all the bibliography first and then deliberated on what I could add. I always got my problem first, and when I had worked it out to my satisfaction, I looked up some of the bibliography, to see what other people had done. People who write to me say, "this is a great piece of detective work, you're a detective"—partly because of the close reading and analyzing that I do.

SCHMIDT: Were there any particular literary critics who influenced your approach to literature?

WEIGAND: To an extent, the New Critics, who emphasized the structure of the individual poem. I've never written a biography. The poem had to come on its own. In the case of a poet like Rilke, each poem adds something to the group as a whole; it gets its elucidation, its manner, from the whole. One of the things that helped me very much was getting introduced to Freud, psychology, and psychoanalysis when I was still a graduate student.

SCHMIDT: Did you know Kuno Francke?

WEIGAND: No. That is to say, on my first trip to Germany, Kuno Francke was on board the same ship, and he walked the decks. I was simply too shy to start talking with him. So my friend, the philosopher DeWitt Parker, and I walked with him, and we would occasionally use a phrase like "die Psychopathologie des Alltagslebens," thinking it might attract Kuno Francke's attention. But we never did talk.

SCHMIDT: You seem to have worked quite independently of *Germanistik* in Germany. Do you think that's characteristic of American *Germanistik?*

WEIGAND: No. You see, I've never studied in Germany. I came to Germany the first time in 1922, when I was already thirty years old. So I never attended a German university. I got to know some of the professors, particularly in Berlin. There was Julius Petersen, who was very charming, very learned. But he wrote a book, *Die Sehnsucht nach dem dritten Reich,* which I reviewed—I would say it's the only political review I ever wrote, and it allows itself some slight sarcasm about the Third Reich because Petersen, with a lot of historical scholarship, went to great lengths to show that the Third Reich corresponded to this religious longing for the Third Empire. But I keep away from politics in all my writing.

SCHMIDT: Did you feel more comfortable writing in German or in English over the years?

WEIGAND: German came much more easily at first, because I was not at my ease in English until I had been at the University of Michigan for some years. It depends on the subject matter. When I write on poetry, I much prefer to write in German.

SCHMIDT: Have you ever had the urge to translate literature, since you have such facility in both languages?

WEIGAND: I have never believed in translating poetry, because it usually distorts it, makes something entirely different out of it.

SCHMIDT: Can you still dictate essays into a tape recorder?

WEIGAND: I've done that for nearly twenty years, but I don't have the instant recall, and I'm inhibited terribly by machines because I'm likely to press a wrong button. When I did write that way, I always had two machines. I had a first draft on one machine and then I set up another, on which I made a new, improved version. You could carry that on *ad infinitum*. Now an excellent reader comes in two hours a week to read to me. But you can't even handle a chapter in two hours, because we discuss things.

. . . .

WEIGAND: I once found something in a book by Thomas Zweifel, the city secretary of Rothenburg, that showed me there was a passage in Hauptmann's *Florian Geyer* that nobody had understood and nobody could understand. It was simply due to egregious misreading. When Florian Geyer is about to be trapped on the hunt in the last act, he has fled for refuge to his brother-in-law, Wilhelm von Grumbach, who had himself been implicated in the beginnings of the movement on the peasant side. And he begs him, "hide me because they're on my trail." And he says: "Wilhelm, wenn mich der Henker itzt an der Bank streckt, so kann ich für mein Urgesicht nit einstehn." That goes through all the editions of the play. No one ever asked any questions. But in Thomas Zweifel's book there came chapter after chapter: "Urgicht von soundso." "Urgicht"— das ist dasselbe Wort wie das deutsche Wort "Beichte." "Bejechen"— "jechen" ist sagen, sprechen, und "bejechen" heißt beichten, bezeugen. Also die Urgicht vor Gericht: ein Angeklagter sagt unter Eid aus, was er von der Sache weiß. Urgicht—das ist das Wort hier: "Wenn mich der Henker itzt an der Bank streckt, so kann ich für mein['] *Urgicht* nit einstehn." Also wenn ich unter Tortur leide, dann könnte ich dich implizieren. Das war kurz vor Hauptmanns Tod, aber er hat das noch gesehen und hat den Kopf geschüttelt, wie mir einer seiner Getreuen gesagt hat. Ich glaube aber, in der Ausgabe letzter Hand ist es korrigiert.

SCHMIDT: Haben Sie sich für die Literatur der Nachkriegszeit interessiert?

WEIGAND: Sehr wenig. Böll und Grass habe ich zum Teil vorlesen lassen. *Gruppenbild mit Dame* habe ich mir wiederholt angehört. Ich hatte sogar ganze Kassetten mit Bemerkungen dazu aber habe nie etwas darüber veröffentlicht. Auch nie über Grass.

SCHMIDT: Und andere modernere Autoren?

WEIGAND: Was steht da noch [auf der Publikationsliste]?

SCHMIDT: Thomas Manns *Gregorius* . . .

WEIGAND: O ja, das war etwas ganz faszinierendes für mich. Das war wieder Detektivarbeit. Als Gregorius nach Rom gebracht und als Papst installiert wurde, beschreibt Thomas Mann den ganzen Zug: den Weg, die

Gebäude, Installationen. Dafür hatte er eine große Quelle: Ferdinand Gregorovius, *Geschichte der Stadt Rom im Mittelalter,* sieben dicke Bände. Ich hatte einen Wink von meinem lieben Freund, Curt von Faber du Faur, der mir sagte, ich sollte doch einmal einen Blick in den Gregorovius werfen, wo es sich um Baulichkeiten Roms handelt. Ich habe dann vier Bände Gregorovius durchgelesen und Stellen gefunden, wo ein halber Satz, sagen wir auf Seite 50 zu finden war, und die andere Hälfte des Satzes hundert Seiten später. Also eine Art von Montage. Das hat so riesigen Spaß gemacht, eins nach dem anderen zu finden, wie in *Florian Geyer.* Es klang alles ganz authentisch. Thomas Mann hat mir ganz reizende Briefe darüber geschrieben. Was mir eigentlich am meisten leid tut in Bezug auf Thomas Manns Tod, ist, daß er meinen letzten Aufsatz nicht gesehen hat, "Spiritual Therapy in Wolfram's *Parzifal.*"

SCHMIDT: Have you ever had an interest in Brecht's works?

WEIGAND: Very little, I must say. I have never liked Brecht; I thought he was in some ways like Grass, the author of *The Tin Drum.* I think his talent was overrated. And the arrogance of the man, trying to instruct the public. I know that many people of your generation adore Brecht. Some of my students did. But I never taught Brecht. He came into vogue in America just about the time I stopped teaching.

But as for Günter Grass, I once had a graduate student who was quite nervous. Grass came and gave a lecture. She came up to him beaming after his lecture and said, "Herr Blech, Ihre Grasstrommel ist doch was Großartiges." You can imagine what kind of a laugh she got. He came again a year later, I was told, and he remembered her face and greeted her, saying: "Sie sind ja die Dame mit der Grasstrommel."

Index